Multistate Practice Exams

How To Use This Book

Final Review Outlines
   Civil Procedure
   Constitutional Law
   Contracts
   Criminal Law
   Criminal Procedure
   Evidence
   Real Property
   Torts

Milestone Exam One
Milestone Exam Two

Simulated Multistate Bar Exam

Additional Practice Questions

All other trademarks are the property of their respective companies.

The material herein is intended to be used in conjunction with the myThemis Portal™ in order to provide basic review of legal subjects and is in no way meant to be a source of or replacement for professional legal advice.

ISBN 978-1-943808-06-9
1-943808-06-6

How To Use The MBE Practice Exams Book

This MBE Practice Exams Book is designed to work in tandem with the Themis Bar Review course. Included are Final Review outlines, two Milestone Exams, and the 200-question Simulated MBE assigned within your Directed Study schedule. To get the most out of these exams, ***do not attempt—or even view—these exams until you are told to do so in your myTo-Do List***. If you wish, after you complete all of the assigned practice question sets in the course, you are welcome to practice using the additional practice questions included in the back of this book.

There are two modes of learning with Themis Bar Review: Directed Study and Flex Study. In Directed Study mode, you will study according to a structured, sequential daily task schedule called *myTo-Do List*™. In Flex Study mode, you may choose to complete tasks in any order, at your own pace.

STEP 1: REVIEW FULL-LENGTH OUTLINES

- Full-length substantive outlines are located in your Multistate book and also in the course under the Outlines section of your home page.
- If you have never been exposed to a subject, read the outline before proceeding. Otherwise, review the outline to refresh your memory of the subject and refer back to the outline when you need clarification or further discussion of a topic.

STEP 2: WATCH LECTURES

- Lectures are divided into 20-minute chapters. Checkmarks next to chapters will change from white to green as you complete each chapter.
- Select the chapter to begin the video and to download the corresponding handout (via the myHandout link).
- After each chapter, thoughtfully complete the series of post-lecture assessment questions (via the Assessments link), which will reinforce the key concepts and assess whether you mastered the particular chapter.
- Refer back to the substantive outline and the lecture handout as you review the assessment questions you did not get correct.

STEP 3: PRACTICE QUESTIONS

- Your myTo-Do List will present you first with single-subject practice question sets, and later with mixed-subject sets. You can complete each practice question task in either Interactive Mode or Test Mode. Interactive Mode allows you to immediately grade each question and view the explanation. Test Mode allows you to complete the entire session before issuing a score report and showing the answer explanations.
- Once the practice question task has been completed, access the task to see the questions you have completed and to thoroughly review each answer explanation. Make sure you understand why each incorrect answer choice is incorrect, and why the correct one is correct. Refer back to the outline, lecture handout, and your notes to understand the substantive law that you missed.

STEP 4: MILESTONE EXAMS

Milestone Exam 1 is a 45-question test covering three MBE subjects; Milestone Exam 2 is 55 questions covering the remaining four subjects. They are scheduled in your myTo-Do List after you have watched the lectures and completed the practice question sets for the corresponding subjects, but will not be available online until their assigned dates.

- The day before the exam, review the Themis Final Review Outlines in this book and your notes and lecture handouts for the tested subjects. Set aside the time indicated in the instructions for each exam, allowing 1.8 minutes per question, just like on the MBE.
- Access the Milestone Exams by clicking on the Milestone Exams link of your course home page. Or, use the enclosed paper version and scantron sheet to better mimic exam conditions.
- If you choose to take these exams on paper using the enclosed paper versions and scantron sheets, you will need to log in to the course to enter your answers and view the answer explanations. This also allows you to compare your performance on the exam with other students taking Themis nationwide. This is an important check on where you stand so that you can make sure you are on track (or ahead of the curve)!
- After completing each Milestone Exam, carefully review each answer explanation.

STEP 5: SIMULATED MBE

The 200-question Simulated MBE is the third Milestone Exam you will be assigned, and appears in your schedule toward the end of the course.

- A few days before the exam, you should begin reviewing your notes for all seven MBE subjects so that the substantive law is fresh in your mind. You have six hours to complete the 200-question Simulated MBE, and you should take the entire exam in one day. Take three hours to complete the AM session in the morning, and after a one-hour break, take three hours to complete the PM session in the afternoon. Make sure you take the exam in a quiet place where you can concentrate and will not be distracted.
- Access this exam via the Milestone Exams link. This simulated exam can be taken in the portal, or offline using the enclosed paper version and scantron sheet. As with the first two Milestone Exams, log your answers in the online version to view the explanations and comparison data.
- After you take the Simulated MBE, you will be assigned two full days of review. Take this time to carefully review the explanatory answers as presented in the MBE Analysis lecture series, which reviews and analyzes each of the 200 questions in depth. For your convenience, the explanations to these questions are also included in the handout associated with the MBE Analysis lectures.
- As always, contact your state director with any concerns or questions.

STEP 6: ADDITIONAL PRACTICE

- Continue to take mix-subject practice question sets as assigned in your Directed Study schedule, now armed with the information you have from your careful review of the previous practice sessions and exams. If you need further clarification or guidance, contact your state director for last-minute advice. Otherwise, be sure to continue to practice every day, making sure you continue to review each answer carefully.
- Use the additional practice questions contained in the back of this book if you wish to do more paper-based practice, but only after you have followed the steps above.
- Good luck on the MBE!

Final Review Outlines

HOW TO USE THE FINAL REVIEW OUTLINES

Following are the Final Review Outlines for each MBE subject. These will appear in your Directed Study schedule as a "Review" task, after you have completed your in-depth review of the corresponding outline, lecture series, assessment questions, and practice questions. These outlines are not meant to replace the full-length outlines, but rather are designed to be used only as final review. We urge you to refrain from using these outlines until after you have completed your thorough review of the main course components for each topic.

FINAL REVIEW OUTLINE: CIVIL PROCEDURE

I. Subject Matter Jurisdiction (SMJ)

A. In general—a court's competence to hear and determine cases of general class and subject to which proceedings in question belong

B. Federal question (FQ)

1. District courts have original jurisdiction (JX) of all civil actions arising under the Constitution, laws, or treaties of the U.S.

2. **Concurrent/exclusive JX**—state courts and federal courts have concurrent JX of FQ claims, except when Congress expressly provides that JX of the federal courts is exclusive

3. **Scope**

   - **Express**—FQ exists if cause of action (c/a) in question is expressly created by federal law and federal law provides the underlying right

   - **Implied**—FQ likely to be found if right is created by federal law, and a c/a can be fairly implied and was intended by Congress

   - **Not express/implied**—complaint must involve real and substantial issue of federal law and its determination must necessarily depend on resolution of federal issue

4. **Well-pleaded complaint**—FQ exists only when federal issue is presented on the face of the complaint (P's c/a—not defenses, answers or counterclaims)

5. **No amount-in-controversy requirement**

C. Diversity jurisdiction (DJ)

1. Federal courts have JX when parties are citizens of different states or citizens of a state and citizens of a foreign state, and amount in controversy exceeds $75,000

2. **Complete diversity**—no diversity if any P is a citizen of the same state or citizen of the same foreign country as any D in the case

3. **Citizenship of parties**

   - **Individuals**—domicile is state in which person is present and intends to reside for an indefinite period; person can only have one domicile at a time; and domicile determined when action is commenced

   - **Corporations**—citizenship is state of incorporation and state where it has its principal place of business ("nerve center" from which the high-level officers direct, control, and coordinate the activities of the corporation)

4. **Creating/destroying diversity**—assignment of claims, failure to name indispensable parties, voluntary change of state citizenship, and replacement of parties

5. **Amount in controversy**

   - **Standard of proof**—P's good-faith assertion in complaint is sufficient unless there is legal certainty that P cannot recover alleged amount

   - **Aggregation of claims**—permitted for multiple Ps with common/undivided interest (counterclaims generally not counted in determining whether P has met amount)

   - Permissive counterclaim must meet jurisdictional amount requirement; compulsory counterclaim need not

D. Supplemental jurisdiction (SJ)

1. Federal court with JX may exercise SJ over additional claims which court would not independently have SMJ (usually state law claims against a nondiverse D), but that arise out of a "common nucleus of operative fact" such that all claims should be tried in a single judicial proceeding

2. **FQ**—additional claims against same party can be heard through SJ if common nucleus of operative fact test is met (same requirements for pendent JX over claims involving joinder or intervention of additional parties)

3. **DJ**

   • **Permissive joinder**—addition of a plaintiff asserting additional claim cannot violate complete diversity rule (and not required to satisfy jurisdictional amount)

   • **Counterclaims**—compulsory counterclaims need not satisfy jurisdictional amount, but permissive counterclaims must satisfy both DJ requirements

   • **Cross-claims**—okay if they arise out of same transaction/occurrence as long as court has SMJ (and do not need to satisfy either DJ requirement)

E. Removal jurisdiction

1. D may generally remove case from state court to federal district court having SMJ

2. **Determination**

   • **Generally**—right to remove determined by pleadings filed when petition to remove is filed

   • **DJ**—diversity must exist at time of filing of original action as well as at time notice of removal is filed

3. **DJ**—if removal based solely on DJ, claim may be removed only if no D is a citizen of the state in which the action was filed

4. **FQ**—if FQ claims are joined with claims that aren't independently removable, entire case may be removed

5. **Notice**

   • D must file notice within 30 days after receipt by or service on the D of the initial pleading

   • **FQ**—only Ds against whom federal claim is filed must consent/join in removal

   • **Removal based on DJ**—cannot occur more than one year after action is commenced (unless P acted in bad faith)

6. **Remand**

   • **Lack of SMJ**—any time before final judgment is rendered

   • **Other reasons**—motion to remand for any defect other than SMJ must be within 30 days after filing of notice of removal

II. Personal Jurisdiction (PJ)

A. In general

1. **Three types**—in personam, in rem, and quasi-in-rem JX

2. A federal court will look to state long-arm statutes to determine if it has PJ over the parties

3. **Due process**—federal court may not exercise PJ over a D unless the D has "minimum contacts" with the forum state and the exercise of JX would be fair and reasonable

4. **Consent**—a party may expressly, impliedly, or voluntarily consent to PJ

5. **Defenses**—lack of JX, insufficiency of process or service of process must be asserted in responsive pleading (or motion before it is submitted), and failure to object waives the objection

B. In personam

1. Generally required whenever judgment is sought that would impose a personal obligation on a D

2. **Bases for in personam JX**

- **Voluntary**—state has PJ if D is voluntarily present in the forum state and served with process while there

- **Domicile**—if authorized by statute, a state has JX over person domiciled in state (person with capacity intends to make that state his home)

- **Consent**—D can expressly consent to JX by K or once an action is brought, impliedly through conduct, or voluntarily through appearance in court (unless to object to JX)

- **Long-arm statute**—authorizes PJ over nonresidents who engage in some activity in state or cause some action to occur within state to extent permissible under Due Process Clause

- **Attachment of property**—if claim is not related to ownership of attached property, there must be minimum contacts between D and forum state to establish JX

3. **Due-process requirements**—satisfied if nonresident D has certain minimum contacts with the forum state such that the maintenance of the action does not offend traditional notions of fair play and substantial justice

- **Minimum contacts** (MC)

  o **Purposeful availment**—D's contacts with forum state must be purposeful and substantial, such that D should reasonably anticipate (foresee) being taken to court there

  o **Specific and general JX**

    ▪ **Specific**—when c/a arises out of or closely relates to a D's contact with forum state even if it's the only contact

    ▪ **General**—when c/a doesn't arise out of or relate to D's contacts with forum state, JX warranted only when D is "at home" in the forum state (it is incorporated there or has its principal place of business there)

  o **Imputed contacts**

    ▪ **Partnerships**—each partner is generally an agent of partnership

    ▪ **Corporations**—out-of-state corporation's contacts with forum state doesn't automatically establish JX over wholly-owned subsidiary unless it is parent's alter ego or acting as agent

    ▪ **Employees/agents**—contacts by nonresident employer's agents/employees imputed to employer if acting within the scope of agency/employment (not usually applicable to independent contractors)

- **Fair play and substantial justice**—once minimum contacts are established, a court must still examine the facts to determine if maintenance of the action would "offend traditional notions of fair play and substantial justice." Factors include:

    o Interest of forum state in adjudicating matter

    o Burden on D of appearing in case

    o Interest of judicial system in efficient resolution of controversies, and

    o Shared interests of the states in promoting common social policies

4. **In personam JX over corporations**—corporation is a resident for PJ purposes only if it is incorporated in the forum state (otherwise must apply MC analysis)

5. **Internet website**—JX over a nonresident's website is based on the degree of interactivity between the website and the forum, ranging from passive sites to those that are integral to D's business

6. **Suits based on K**—K can be a significant factor in determining whether MC exist, and choice-of-law provisions are a significant factor as they establish that the nonresident purposefully availed herself to benefits of forum state's laws

C. **Jurisdiction over things**

1. **In rem**

    - **Definition**—gives court authority to determine issues concerning rights to real/personal property

    - **Due process**—proceedings against property must still satisfy due-process requirements for PJ and property must generally be present within the forum state

2. **Quasi in rem**

    - **Definition**—determines only the interests of the parties to the action regarding property located in forum state (e.g., lien foreclosure or quiet title action), and not personally binding against D

    - **Due process**—if disputes are unrelated to ownership of property and no close relationship is formed, in addition to having property located in forum state, MC must be shown between D and forum state

D. **Notice and opportunity to be heard**

1. **Notice**

    - **Rule**—must be reasonably calculated, under all the circumstances, to apprise interested parties of pending action and afford them the opportunity to object

    - **Form**—via in-person delivery, registered mail, etc. if identity/address known or obtainable through reasonable efforts

2. **Opportunity to be heard**—for D whenever there is state-sponsored interference with a D's property interest

E. **Defenses to jurisdictional claims**—special appearance to challenge PJ (abolished under FRCP) and collateral attacks

III. **Venue**

    A. **Venue in federal court**

        1. **General rule**—venue proper in judicial district where any D resides in state where all Ds reside; or where substantial part of the events/omissions occurred; or where property that is subject of the action is located (otherwise where any D is subject to PJ)

        2. **Residence**—judicial district where D is domiciled for individual; where D subject to PJ for an entity; or, when entity is P, where principal place of business is located

    B. **Change of venue in federal court**

        1. **Original venue proper**

- **General rule**—transfer permitted to any district where case might have been brought or to which all parties consent

- **DJ**—new district court must apply law from previous court

- **FQ**—new district court in another appellate circuit will apply federal law as interpreted by its court of appeals (not the appellate circuit of the transferring district court)

        2. **Original venue improper**

- **General rule**—dismiss case or transfer case to proper district if it's in the interest of justice

- **DJ**—district court to which the case is transferred applies the choice-of-law rules of the state in which it is located (not the state law of the court transferring the case)

- **FQ**—new court will apply its own court of appeals' interpretation of law (not the appellate circuit of the transferring district court)

- **No PJ**—a court lacking PJ over the D may transfer the case to a different venue

    C. **Forum non conveniens**

        1. **Federal**—only used when forum that is deemed most appropriate for the action is a foreign court

IV. **Choice of Law: The *Erie* Doctrine**

    A. **In General**

        1. **FQ**—federal substantive and procedural law controls, as well as federal common law

        2. **DJ**—state substantive law and applicable federal procedural law

    B. **Substance or procedure**—determination is unclear

        1. **Valid federal statute on point when state and federal laws conflict**

- Apply federal law

- Before applying a Federal Rule (rather than a federal statute), court must determine the Rule is valid under the Rules Enabling Act: does the Federal Rule abridge, enlarge, or modify any substantive right?

      o If **no**, then apply the Federal Rule

      o If **yes**, then apply the Federal Rule if it only incidentally affects a litigant's substantive rights

        2. **No federal rule on point**—apply state law if failure to do so would lead to different outcomes in state and federal court

3. **Substantive law**—elements of claim or defense, statute of limitations (S/L) and tolling provisions, and burden of proof

4. **Procedural law**—judge/jury allocation, assessment of attorney's fees, equitable/legal determination

C. Federal common law

1. In general

- Created when there is no applicable federal statute or constitutional provision

- There is no **general** federal common law; general areas that federal common law is applicable to will be limited

2. FQ—apply federal common law in the following instances:

- Admiralty cases

- When the U.S. is a party to the case

- Interstate disputes

- Cases implicating relations with foreign countries

- Cases in which the government acts in a proprietary role (e.g. enters into contracts, issues commercial paper, and oversees regulatory programs), and

- When Congress has left a gap in a statutory scheme

3. DJ—when a "uniquely federal interest" is at stake and a significant conflict exists between that interest and the operation of state law

4. State court cases—if state JX is concurrent with FQ JX and federal common law would have applied in federal court, then it will also apply in state court

D. State conflict-of-law rules—federal court must apply state's conflict-of-law rules

1. DJ—district court bound by conflict-of-laws rules of state in which the district court is located, but only to extent that state's rules are valid under Full Faith and Credit and Due Process Clause

2. Procedural or substantive law—states apply their own procedural laws and sometimes apply the substantive law of a foreign JX

V. Pleadings

A. Service of process

1. Timing—within 120 days after filing of complaint (must be within 90 days as of December 1, 2015)

2. Methods of service for individual

- Personally

- At D's usual place of abode with a person of suitable age/discretion who resides there, or

- Delivering to D's agent

3. Service on corporations/associations—to officer or agent, or by following state law

4. **Waiver of service**
   - Request for waiver must be in writing and addressed to individual D, or officer/agent of corporation, and must give D reasonable time of at least 30 days after request sent to return waiver
   - **Effect**—extends time to serve answer from 21 (after service of process) to 60 days (after waiver request sent)

B. Injunctions

1. **Temporary restraining order** (TRO)
   - Preserves the status quo until an opportunity for a full hearing
   - Effective for a limited time (no longer than 14 days unless good cause exists or adversary consents)
   - May be issued without notice to adverse party if immediate and irreparable injury will result and movant's attorney certifies efforts made to give notice and the reason why notice should not be required

2. **Preliminary injunction (PI)**
   - Issued prior to a full hearing on the merits, upon notice to the defendant
   - May be issued to a P if:
     - P is likely to succeed on the merits
     - P is likely to suffer irreparable harm in the absence of relief
     - Balance of equities is in P's favor, and
     - Injunction is in the public interest

3. **Permanent injunction**
   - Once issued, it continues until dissolved by the court, but any affected person may move for modification or dissolution
   - Same standard as for PI but P must show actual success on the merits

C. Complaint

1. **Federal rule**—short/plain statement of court's SMJ, P's entitlement to relief, and demand for judgment (notice pleading)
2. **Timing**—filing generally occurs before service; service generally within 120 days of filing

D. Motions against the complaint (within 21 days of service)

1. **Rule 12(b) motion to dismiss**
   - Lack of SMJ (can be raised at any time)
   - Lack of PJ, improper venue, insufficient process or service (can be raised in preanswer motion or answer, otherwise waived)
   - Failure to state a claim upon which relief can be granted and failure to join necessary/indispensable party (can be raised in any pleading, motion for judgment on pleadings, or at trial)

2. **Rule 12(b)(6) motion to dismiss**
   - Claim will be dismissed if it fails to assert legal theory of recovery cognizable at law or allege facts sufficient to support cognizable claim; and court treats well-pleaded facts

as true, resolves doubts/inferences in P's favor, and views pleading in light most favorable to P

- **Strength of facts**—must raise right to relief above speculation, assuming that allegations in complaint are true; and raise reasonable expectation that discovery will reveal evidence of necessary element
- **Court can consider**—only allegations and attached exhibits in the complaint
- **Court's two-step analysis**
    - o Identify and reject legal conclusions unsupported by factual allegations
    - o Assume truth/veracity of well-pleaded facts and include context specific analysis that draws on court's judicial experience and common sense to determine if allegations plausibly give rise to relief

3. **Motion for judgment on the pleadings [Rule 12(c)]**—after answer filed, allows court to dispose of a case when material facts are not in dispute and judgment on merits can be achieved based on content of pleadings

4. **Motion for more definite statement**—responding party may move for more definite statement if claim for relief is so vague or ambiguous that party cannot reasonably draft responsive pleading

5. **Motion to strike**
    - **Federal rule**—when pleading contains insufficient defense, or redundant, immaterial, impertinent, or scandalous material – court may order such defense or material stricken

E. **Answer**

1. **Admission/denial**—answer must admit/deny P's allegations, or plead lack of sufficient knowledge (with reasonable investigation)

2. **Affirmative defenses**—D must state them or they are deemed waived

3. **Timing**
    - **No motion to dismiss**—21 days after being served with summons and complaint (or 60 days if D timely waived service)
    - **Motion to dismiss**—no filing while motion is pending, and within 14 days after notice of court's action

F. **Reply**

1. **Response**—by P to D's answer within 21 days after being served with order to reply

G. **Amendments**

1. **Rule**
    - Party may amend a pleading once as of right within 21 days if no responsive pleading is required, or after being served with an answer or 12(b) motion; otherwise during/after trial if it conforms to evidence and opposing party has opportunity to prepare
    - Court should freely give leave to amend a pleading when justice so requires and will not result in undue prejudice to opposing party

2. **Relation back**

- **New claim**—relates back to date of original pleading if amendment asserts claim/defense that arose out of same conduct, transaction, or occurrence as original pleading

- **New party**

  o Relates back to date of original pleading if amendment asserts claim/defense that arose out of same conduct, transaction or occurrence as original pleading

  o New party receives notice of action within 120 days after original complaint filed

  o D knew or should have known about action but for mistake concerning proper party's identity

3. **Time to respond**—within 14 days after service of amended pleading or time left on original pleading, whichever is later

H. **Supplemental pleadings**—to describe events occurring after filing of earlier pleading

I. **Rule 11 sanctions**

1. Court may impose sanctions limited to what suffices to deter repetition of conduct by others similarly situated

2. **Types**—nonmonetary directives, penalties to court or payments to movant for attorney's fees and other expenses directly resulting from violation

VI. Multiple Parties and Claims

A. Joinder of parties

1. **Permissive joinder**

- Ps and Ds may join/be joined in one action if any right to relief is asserted jointly, severally, or with respect to or arising out of same transaction, occurrence or series of them and question of law or fact common to all Ps or Ds will arise

- **SMJ**—need SMJ:

  o **Ds**—SJ doesn't apply so there must be complete diversity between Ps and Ds and each claim must exceed $75,000

  o **Ps**—SJ is permitted for JX amount less than or equal to $75,000 but there must still be complete diversity

- **In personam JX**—court needs in personam PJ over D for proper joinder

- **Venue**—joinder subject to applicable venue requirements

2. **Compulsory joinder**

- **Necessary parties**—necessary for just adjudication:

  o Complete relief cannot be provided to existing parties in absence of that person, or

  o Disposition in absence of that person may impair person's ability to protect his interest, or

  o Absence of that person would leave existing parties subject to substantial risk of multiple or inconsistent obligations

- **SMJ**—need SMJ, so if exclusive basis for JX is DJ, party can't be added if it would destroy diversity

- **In personam JX**—court needs in personam PJ over D for proper joinder
- **Venue**—joinder subject to applicable venue requirements
- **Indispensable parties**—if parties cannot be joined because of JX or venue, court may dismiss case and will consider following factors:
  - Extent to which judgment without party would prejudice them or existing parties
  - Extent to which protective measures could prevent prejudice
  - Whether judgment rendered in necessary party's absence would be adequate, and
  - Whether P would have adequate remedy if action were dismissed

B. Intervention

1. **Intervention as of right** (if not through federal statute)
   - Nonparty has interest in property or transaction that is subject matter or action
   - Disposition of action may impair nonparty's interest
   - Nonparty's interest not adequately represented by existing parties

2. **Permissive intervention**—court must consider undue delay/prejudice to rights of original parties
   - Movant has conditional right to intervene under federal statute, or
   - Movant's claim/defense and original action share common question of law or fact

3. **Timeliness**—court will consider following factors:
   - Length of time movant knew or reasonably should have known that its interest was threatened before moving to intervene
   - Prejudice to existing parties if intervention is permitted, and
   - Prejudice to movant if intervention is denied

4. **SMJ**—cannot be joined in a case based exclusively on DJ if the exercise of JX inconsistent with requirements of DJ

C. Interpleader—allows person holding property (stakeholder) to force all potential claimants into single lawsuit

1. **Federal interpleader rule**
   - **Rule:**
     - **Ps**—persons with claims that may expose P to multiple liability may be joined as Ds and required to interplead claims though they lack common origin or are adverse and independent rather than identical or P denies liability
     - **Ds**—exposed to similar liability may seek interpleader through a cross-claim or counterclaim
   - **SMJ**—court must already have JX over all parties, and for DJ, only stakeholder needs to be diverse from claimants (claimants need not be diverse among themselves)
   - **In personam JX**—court needs in personam PJ over claimants in order to join them
   - **Venue**—interpleader subject to venue requirements

2. **Federal statutory interpleader**
   - **SMJ**—DJ met if any two claimants are citizens of different states, and property at issue must merely exceed $500
   - **In personam JX**—nationwide PJ and service of process permitted
   - **Venue**—proper in any district where a claimant resides

D. **Joinder of claims**

   1. **Permissive joinder**
      - A party may join independent or alternative claims of whatever nature against opposing party
      - **SMJ:**
        - **DJ**—P may aggregate all claims to satisfy amount-in-controversy requirement
        - **FQ**—nonfederal claims can be joined only if DJ exists or if claims are part of same case/controversy as federal claim so SJ applies
      - **Venue**—joinder subject to venue requirements

   2. **Counterclaims** (must be answered within 21 days of service)
      - **Compulsory:**
        - At time of service, counterclaim is compulsory if it arises out of same transaction/occurrence that is subject matter of opposing party's claim and doesn't require adding another party over whom court has no JX
        - **SMJ**—by definition court will have SJ so don't need independent SMJ from original claim
      - **Permissive:**
        - Party has discretion if counterclaim isn't compulsory
        - **SMJ**—need DJ or FQ
      - **Third parties**—can assert counterclaims against original P or D, and governed by requirements for counterclaims and joinder

   3. **Cross-claims** (must be answered within 21 days of service)
      - A claim against coparty may be asserted if they arise out of same transaction or occurrence that is subject matter of original action or counterclaim and new parties subject to joinder rules
      - **SMJ**—by definition court will have SJ so don't need independent SMJ from original claim
      - **In personam JX and venue**—PJ satisfied because parties are already before the court; proper venue over original claim, party cannot object to venue over cross-claim

   4. **Third-party claims (impleader)**
      - **Definition**—defending party (third-party P) can implead nonparty (third-party D) for liability on original claim
      - **Timing**—can be asserted any time after complaint is filed, but third-party P must get court permission if filed more than 14 days after service of original answer

- **SMJ**— by definition court will have SJ so don't need independent SMJ from original claim, but if original claim is based only on DJ, claims by P against third-party D must meet DJ or FQ JX requirements on its own
- **In personam JX**—court needs in personam PJ over third parties

E. Class actions

1. Basic requirements

- Class is so numerous that joinder of all members is impracticable
- Must be questions of law or fact common to class
- Claims/defenses of representatives must by typical of class, and
- Representatives must fairly and adequately protect the interests of class

2. Three situations when class can be certified:

- **Risk of prejudice**—separate actions would create risk that the class opponent would be subject to inconsistent adjudications or if separate actions would impair the interests of class members
- **Final equitable relief**—equitable relief based upon a shared general claim must be the primary relief sought
- **Common legal/factual questions**—must predominate over questions affecting individual members and class action is superior method for bringing about fair and efficient adjudication of controversy

3. SMJ—FQ, DJ (class representatives must be diverse from class opponents and at least one P must meet $75,000 jurisdictional amount), or Class Action Fairness Act of 2005

4. Venue—venue requirements must be met and residence of class representatives (not class members) is what matters

VII. Pretrial Procedure and Discovery

A. Mandatory disclosures

1. Initial disclosures

- **Generally**—subject to certain exceptions, must disclose information regarding individuals having discoverable information, documents supporting claims/defenses, computation and backup of damages, or relevant insurance agreement for satisfying judgment
- **Standard**—information reasonably available to it, and party not excused for not fully investigating case, challenges to insufficiency of another party's disclosures, or because another party failed to disclose
- **Timing**—within 14 days after the parties' discovery conference

2. Expert testimony

- **Generally**—identify expert witnesses and produce expert report subject to certain requirements
- **Timing**—at least 90 days before trial or 30 days after disclosure of opposing party's expert evidence on same subject matter

3. Pretrial (evidence to be presented at trial other than for impeachment)

- **Generally**—witness list by testimony or deposition, and documents and exhibits

- **Timing**—at least 30 days before trial
- **Objections**—within 14 days after disclosures are made or else waived unless excused by court for good cause or pursuant to relevance rules of the FRE

B. Discovery scope and limits

1. Scope

- Generally permitted with regard to any non-privileged matter relevant to any party's claim or defense in action
- As of December 1, 2015—limited also to matters that are proportional to the needs of the case
- **Relevance**—information need not be admissible in evidence to be discoverable
- **Privileged information** (not discoverable)—determined under federal common law for FQ cases, and state law for DJ or SJ

2. Limitations (balance discovery and privacy interests)

- Discovery sought is unreasonably cumulative or can be obtained from a more convenient or less expensive source
- The party seeking discovery had ample opportunity to obtain information by discovery
- The proposed discovery is not relevant and proportional

3. Trial preparation materials

- Party may not discover documents and tangible things prepared in anticipation of litigation or for trial, unless other party shows that it has substantial need for the materials to prepare its case and cannot, without undue hardship, obtain their substantial equivalent by other means
- Mental impressions, conclusions, opinions, or legal theories of party's attorney or other representative are protected

4. Experts

- Expert witnesses may be deposed, but expert report drafts and disclosure are protected, as well as any communications between the party's attorney and expert witness unless they relate to compensation, facts/data used or assumptions relied upon by expert in forming his opinion

C. Discovery conference—Parties must confer at least 21 days before scheduling conference to consider nature and basis of their claims/defenses and possibility of settlement, automatic disclosures, preserving discoverable information, and developing discovery plan

D. Discovery devices

1. Oral depositions—can take place anytime after mandatory initial disclosure and limited to 10 per party (unless showing of good cause to court)

2. Interrogatories

- 25 written interrogatories per party relating to non-privileged matters relevant to any party's claim/defense and proportional to the needs of the case
- Must be fully and separately answered under oath unless timely objected to with specificity

3. **Requests to produce documents**—a party has 30 days from being served with request or 30 days from the parties' first rule 26(f) conference, if the request was served prior to that conference to respond

4. **Physical/mental exams**—the court may order person to submit to physical/mental exam if physical/mental condition is in controversy

5. **Requests for admission**—a party can serve written request for admission of any relevant, non-privileged matters relating to statements or opinions of fact or to application of law to fact, which once admitted is conclusively established

E. **Enforcement**

1. **Motion to compel**—party can move to compel disclosure or discovery against a party failing to make automatic disclosures, or to respond to discovery requests (including evasive or incomplete disclosure)

2. **Sanctions**—if a party fails to obey a court order regarding discovery, the court may impose sanctions subject to the abuse of discretion standard

3. **Electronically stored information**—if information that should have been preserved is lost because a party failed to take reasonable steps to preserve it, the court may order measures to cure the prejudice or, if the party acted with the intent to deprive the another party of the information, instruct the jury that it may or must presume that the information was unfavorable to the party or dismiss the action or enter a default judgment

F. **Pretrial conferences**—the court may direct counsel and unrepresented parties to appear for pretrial conferences for purposes such as expediting disposition of the action, effective case management, and facilitating settlement

G. **Adjudication without trial**

1. **Dismissal**—of complaint, counterclaim, cross-claim, or third-party claim

   • **Voluntary**—can be filed without prejudice (unless same claim dismissed by P in prior action) any time before opposing party serves answer, motion for summary judgment, or dismissal

   • **Involuntary**—when P fails to prosecute or comply with the Rules or court order, D can move to dismiss, which if granted is with prejudice and operates as an adjudication on the merits

2. **Default judgment**—when a party fails to defend an action, P may seek default judgment, which can be set aside for good cause by the court, depending upon whether movant's failure to act was willful, setting aside default would prejudice nonmoving party, and the movant presented a meritorious claim

3. **Summary judgment**

   • **Standard**—no genuine dispute as to any material fact and the movant is entitled to judgment as a matter of law; court will construe all evidence in the light most favorable to the nonmoving party and resolve all doubts in favor of nonmoving party

   • **Burden of proof**—the movant has burden of persuasion to show prima facie case before the burden shifts to the opposing party to set forth specific evidence showing the existence of a genuine issue of fact

   • **Timing**—may be filed anytime until 30 days after close of all discovery

4. **Declaratory judgment**—the court tells the parties their rights and responsibilities without awarding damages or ordering parties to do (or refrain from doing) anything

VIII. Trial Procedure

A. Jury trial

1. **Right to jury trial**—action at law tried on demand to a jury, but for state-law claims in diversity actions, federal law will determine whether there is a right to a jury trial

2. **Jury demand**—must be served within 14 days after service of the last pleading directed to the issue that is to be tried by jury

   - A party may specify the issues for which a jury trial is demanded (otherwise, the demand is treated as requesting a jury trial for all issues triable by a jury)

   - A party may withdraw a jury trial demand with the consent of the other parties

   - **Case removed from state court**—a party who has made a jury trial demand in accord with state law need not renew the demand; if state law does not require a party to make a jury trial demand, a party need not make one after removal (unless the court orders the parties to do so)

3. **Jury size**

   - At least six and no more than 12

   - Once selected, a juror must participate in the verdict unless dismissed for good cause

   - No provisions for alternate jurors

4. **Jury selection**—peremptory challenges may not be made for racial or gender-based reasons; court will allow three for each party in civil cases but an unlimited number of challenges are permitted for cause (e.g., bias or personal relationship to a litigant)

5. **Jury instructions**

   - A party may request the court to give specific instructions at the close of evidence (or earlier if ordered by the court)

   - Prior to final arguments, the court must inform the parties of any instructions it proposes to give to the jury; the parties may object to the court's proposed instructions on the record and out of the jury's hearing

   - Unless a party objects on the record to an erroneous instruction given or proposed to be given by the court or to the court's failure to give an instruction requested by a party, the party generally cannot raise the matter on appeal

6. **Jury verdicts**

   - Unless the parties stipulate otherwise:

     o The verdict must be unanimous

     o The verdict must be returned by a jury of at least six jurors

   - **Form of verdict**

     o **Special**—written finding made by the jury on each issue of ultimate fact; judge determines the legal consequences of those findings

     o **General**—typically a decision by the jury as to the prevailing party and, if the plaintiff is the prevailing party, the amount of damages

     o **General with special interrogatories**—couples a general verdict with a special verdict; used to ensure that the jury independently considered the material facts of the case in arriving at its verdict

7. Juror misconduct

- Concealing facts relating to his qualifications or giving false testimony during voir dire
  - Party must show that the juror failed to answer honestly a material question and that a proper response would have provided a valid basis for a challenge for cause
- **Other forms of juror misconduct**—violating the confidentiality of deliberations, being improperly influenced by non-jurors, or investigating facts outside of those presented at trial
  - Court may dismiss juror or order a new trial
  - A juror may testify about whether extraneous prejudicial information was improperly brought to the jury's attention or whether any outside influence was improperly brought to bear on a juror

B. Trial by the court

1. The court must make findings of fact and conclusions of law on the record at the close of evidence or in an opinion or memorandum of decision filed by the court

2. On appeal, a court's findings of fact can be set aside only if clearly erroneous

C. Judgment as a matter of law (directed verdict)

1. The court must view evidence in light most favorable to the opposing party and draw all reasonable inferences from evidence in favor of opposing party

2. **Timing**—any time before the case is submitted to the jury

D. Renewed motion for judgment as a matter of law (JNOV)—if the court doesn't grant a directed verdict, movant can file a JNOV no later than 28 days after entry of trial judgment

E. Motion for new trial—for actions that have been tried to a jury, a new trial may be granted for any of the reasons for which new trials have traditionally been granted

IX. Post-Trial Procedure

A. Alteration of or relief from judgment—a court can relieve party of final judgment no later than one year following judgment entry for mistake, inadvertence, surprise, excusable neglect, newly discovered evidence (not previously discovered through reasonable diligence), fraud, misrepresentation, or misconduct by opposing party

B. Appeals—if more than one claim is presented in case, or there are multiple parties, a district court may direct entry of a final judgment as to one or more issues/parties, but only if the court expressly determines that there is no just reason for delay

C. Full faith and credit—if valid judgment is rendered by a court that has JX over the parties, and parties receive proper notice of the action and a reasonable opportunity to be heard, judgment will receive the same effect in other states as state where it was rendered

D. Claim preclusion (res judicata)

1. **Valid final judgment on the merits**—court must have PJ and SMJ, D must have had proper notice and opportunity to be heard, court must have nothing further to do but order entry of judgment, and decision must be made on merits of claim/defense (rather than technical grounds)

2. **Sufficiently identical causes of action**—original and later-filed c/a must be sufficiently identical to be barred under claim preclusion (federal "transactional" approach)

3. **Sufficiently identical parties**—P and D must be the same, and in the same roles, in both the original action and subsequently filed action

E. **Issue preclusion** (collateral estoppel)

1. **Same issue**—facts relevant to particular issue and applicable law must be identical

2. **Final, valid judgment**—first determination of issue was within authority of court that decided it and the determination was made in final decision on the merits

3. **Essential to judgment**—issue that constitutes a necessary component of the decision reached will be considered essential

FINAL REVIEW OUTLINE: CONSTITUTIONAL LAW

I. **Judicial Power**

   A. **Source and scope**

      1. **Source—Article III**

      2. **Scope**

- Limited to cases and controversies, and
- Has the power to review
  - Another branch's act and declare it unconstitutional
  - The constitutionality of a decision by a state's highest court, and
  - State actions under the Supremacy Clause to ensure conformity with the Constitution

      3. **Eleventh Amendment Limitation**

- Jurisdictional bar prohibiting citizens of one state from suing another state (not local government) in federal court; immunizes states from suits for money damages or equitable relief
- Bars suits against state officials for violating state law
- Exceptions to application of 11th Amend.
  - Consent
  - Injunctive or declaratory relief
  - Damages paid by state officer
  - Congressional enforcement of 14th Amend. rights

   B. **Supreme Court jurisdiction**

      1. **Original jurisdiction over**

- All cases affecting ambassadors
- Other public ministers/consuls
- When state is a party

      2. **Appellate jurisdiction over other cases through certiorari and direct appeal**

- Final state-court judgment resting upon adequate/independent state grounds not reviewable by Supreme Court

   C. **Judicial review**

      1. **Standing**

- General rule – Plaintiff (P) must establish
  - Injury-in-fact—Concrete and particularized; injury need not be physical/economic and future injury must be actual and imminent
  - Causation—Injury caused by D's conduct
  - Redressability—Relief requested is likely to prevent/redress the injury

- o Prudential standing—Established by federal judiciary, requires that P is proper party to invoke judicial resolution of dispute
- Taxpayer status – Generally no standing to challenge government allocation of funds – However, taxpayer has standing to
  - o Litigate how much owed on tax bill, and
  - o Challenge government expenditures as violating the Establishment Clause
- 3rd party standing – Generally no standing to bring lawsuit based on 3rd party claims – However, exceptions include
  - o When 3rd party unable to assert his own rights
  - o If there is a special relationship between P and 3rd party, or
  - o P's injury adversely affects the P's relationship with 3rd party
- Organizational standing—Organization can sue on its own behalf or on behalf of its members if
  - o Member has standing to sue in his own right, and
  - o Interests at stake germane to organization's purpose

2. Timeliness

- Ripeness—P must have experienced a real injury (action brought too soon is "unripe")
- Mootness—Must be a live controversy at each stage of review (action brought too late is "moot") – But case not moot if:
  - o Controversy is capable of repetition but is "evading review," i.e., will not last long enough to work through judicial system
  - o Defendant voluntarily ceases its illegal/wrongful action upon commencement of litigation until court is assured wrong will not be repeated
  - o Named P's claim in class action suit is resolved

3. Justiciability

- Advisory opinions – No advisory opinion unless an actual case or controversy exists
- Declaratory judgments – Challenged action must pose "real and immediate danger" to party's interests
- Political question matters (to be resolved by another branch of government) not subject to judicial review

4. Abstention

- Federal court may abstain from ruling on unsettled issues of state law

II. Powers of Congress

A. Commerce

1. Interstate commerce - Power to regulate

- Channels and
- Instrumentalities of interstate commerce, and
- Any activity that substantially affects it

2. **Substantial economic effect - Power to regulate any activity or combination thereof that has substantial economic effect on interstate commerce**

   - Aggregation—Even if an intrastate activity has no direct economic impact, Congress can regulate as long as there is

     o A **rational basis** for concluding

     o That the **"total incidence"** of activity in the aggregate

     o **Substantially affects** interstate commerce

3. **Non-economic activity**

   - If regulation involves a non-economic activity of traditional state concern, Congress must establish connection between the activity and substantial economic effect in order to regulate it

B. **Taxation and Spending**

   1. **Taxing**

      - Tax upheld if it has reasonable relationship to revenue production

        o Congress has plenary power to impose taxes to raise revenue (or for any public purpose) through General Welfare Clause

   2. **Spending**

      - Power to spend for the general welfare (any public purpose), including conditional federal funding

C. **War and defense powers**

   1. Power to declare war

   2. Raise and support armies/navy

   3. Govern land/naval forces, and

   4. Organize militia

   5. Whatever action necessary to provide for national defense

D. **Property power**

   1. No express limit on power to dispose of US property

   2. However, Congress may only take private property for public use with just compensation and to effectuate an enumerated power

E. **Power over aliens and citizenship**

   1. Plenary power over aliens

      - Subject to due process clause

   2. Exclusive authority over naturalization

F. **Necessary and Proper Clause**

   - Power to enact any legislation necessary/proper to execute federal government authority

     o But clause not independent source of power so must carry into effect other enumerated powers

G. Enabling Clause of 14th Amendment

- Enables Congress to enforce equal protection and due process rights
  - As defined by Supreme Court
  - Enforcement must have **"congruence and proportionality"** between injury to be prevented and means adopted to achieve that end

III. Powers of the President

A. Domestic power

1. Power to pardon federal offenses
2. Veto power
3. Appoint officers of US with advice/consent of the Senate, and remove executive appointees without cause or Senate approval
   - Presidential authority—varies with degree of congressional authorization

B. Foreign affairs

1. Commander in Chief - President can take military action against actual hostilities against US
   - But only Congress can declare war
2. Exclusive power to negotiate treaties
   - Ratified by Senate (two-thirds)
3. Power to enter into executive agreements with foreign nations
   - Without Senate approval

IV. Federal Interbranch Relationships

A. Congressional limits on the executive

1. Impeachment
2. If Congress explicitly mandates expenditure of funds, President cannot impound funds
3. Unconstitutional for Congress to attempt legislative veto of executive action

B. Delegation of legislative power

- Delegation to executive branch constitutional if Congress specifies "intelligible principle" to guide delegate

C. Judicial limitation of congressional power

- Congress cannot reinstate right to bring legal action after rejected by Supreme Court

D. Immunities and privileges

1. **Judicial**
   - Absolute immunity from civil liability for damages from judicial acts
2. **Legislative**
   - No civil/criminal liability for statements and conduct made in regular course of legislative process

3. **Executive**

- No civil liability for performance of official responsibilities

- Executive privilege regarding non-disclosure of confidential information

V. **State Regulation and Taxation of Commerce**

A. **Dormant Commerce Clause**

1. **General rule—If Congress has not, States can regulate interstate commerce so long as regulation does not**

- Discriminate against out-of-state commerce

- Unduly burden interstate commerce, or

- Regulate wholly out-of-state activity

2. **Discrimination against out-of-state commerce (protecting local economic interests at the expense of out-of-state competitors)**

- State or local discriminatory regulation may be upheld if

  o Important government interest—Not allowed unless important local interest being served and no other nondiscriminatory means available to achieve that purpose

  o Market participant—State can favor local commerce or discriminate against nonresident commerce like a private business

  o Traditional government function—Regulation can favor state/local government entities if entities are performing traditional government function

  o Congressionally permitted discrimination—Must be unmistakably clear that Congress allows impermissible state regulation

3. **Undue burden on interstate commerce**

- Balancing test - purpose of state law against burden on interstate commerce and evaluate whether there are less restrictive alternatives

  o If benefits are grossly outweighed, even nondiscriminatory regulation may be struck down

B. **State Taxation of Commerce**

1. **Interstate commerce**

- General rule—Permitted only if Congress has not already regulated a particular activity and tax does not discriminate against or unduly burden interstate commerce

- Four-part test

  o Substantial nexus between activity being taxed and taxing state

  o Fair tax apportionment such that interstate commerce doesn't pay total taxes greater than local commerce

  o No local direct commercial advantage over interstate competitors (even if neutral on its face), and

  o Tax must be fairly related to services provided by taxing state

2. **Foreign commerce—States must have congressional consent to impose import/export taxes**

VI. Preemption

A. Express preemption

- When Constitution makes federal power exclusive or Congress enacted legislation explicitly prohibiting state regulation in same area
  - Must be narrowly construed

B. Implied preemption

1. Congress intended for federal law to occupy the field
2. State law directly conflicts with federal law, or
3. State law indirectly conflicts with federal law by creating obstacle to law's purpose

C. Absence of preemption

- State law can set more stringent standards or recognize greater individual rights than federal law if no preemption

VII. Relations Among States

A. Full Faith and Credit

- Out-of-state judgments must be given in-state effect if
  - Court rendering judgment had jurisdiction over the parties/subject matter
  - Judgment was on the merits, and
  - Final judgment

VIII. State Action (Prerequisite to triggering constitutional protections)

A. Traditional governmental function

- Private person carries on activities traditionally performed exclusively by the state

B. Significant state involvement

- Sufficient mutual contacts between conduct of a private party and government, and
- State must act affirmatively to facilitate, encourage, or authorize the activity (licensing or regulation of private party not enough)

C. Insignificant state involvement

- Business that government substantially regulates to which it grants a monopoly (e.g., utility company)
- Nursing homes that accept Medicaid
- Schools receiving government funds but operated by private corporation

IX. Procedural Due Process—Fifth Amendment (federal government) and Fourteenth (states)

A. Due Process Generally

- Necessary procedures before depriving individuals and other "persons," e.g., corporations, of "life, liberty, or property"
- 14th Amend. - Most provisions of the Bill of Rights applicable against states
- Both Due Process Clauses – "Substantive" component guarantees fundamental rights to all persons – "catchall"

B. **Procedural Due Process Applied**

1. **Fundamental Fairness – Includes right to be notified of charges/proceedings and opportunity to be heard**
   - Is threatened interest a protected one?
   - If so, what process is due?
     - o Neutral decision maker
     - o Intentional governmental act

2. **Protected Interests**
   - Liberty
     - o Significant governmental restraint on one's physical freedom, fundamental rights, or freedom of choice or action
   - Property
     - o Legitimate claim of entitlement

3. **Notice and hearing—amount of process due determined by three factors**
   - Private interest affected
   - Value of additional safeguards, and
   - Burden (cost) of additional process

4. **Court access**
   - Court fees waived for indigent person if fees will deny fundamental right

X. **Substantive Due Process**

A. **Standard of review in substantive due process cases**

1. **Strict scrutiny (burden of proof on government) if government action infringes fundamental right**
   - Law must be least restrictive means to achieve compelling government interest
     - o Least restrictive—Cannot be a less restrictive way to achieve interest and law should not be over/under-inclusive
     - o Compelling interest—necessary or crucial

2. **Rational basis (burden of proof on challenger) in cases when strict or intermediate scrutiny not applicable**
   - Law must be rationally related to legitimate state interest (minimal scrutiny)
   - In practice, applied to laws related to lifestyle, taxation, zoning, and punitive damages

B. **Fundamental Rights**

1. **Travel**
   - From state-to-state or become permanent resident

2. **Voting and Ballot Access**
   - More significant the government restriction, the greater the degree of scrutiny

3. **Privacy**

  - Marriage, contraception, intimate sexual behavior, abortion (undue burden test), parental rights, family relations, obscene material, right to refuse medical treatment, and right to avoid disclosure of personal medical information

4. **Second Amendment**

  - Right to possess a firearm

XI. Equal Protection

A. General considerations

1. **Constitutional basis**—14th Amend. Equal Protection Clause for states and 5th Amend. Due Process Clause for federal government

2. **Standards of review** (depends on classification of persons or type of right)

  - Strict scrutiny (least restrictive means to achieve a compelling governmental interest)—applies if fundamental rights or suspect classification involved

  - Intermediate scrutiny (substantially related to important governmental interest)—applies if gender or legitimacy involved

    o Gender cases require "exceedingly persuasive justification" for the classification

  - Rational basis (rationally related to legitimate governmental interest)—applies when higher standards do not apply

    o Applies to laws distinguishing people based on age, wealth, weight, and distinctions drawn for business reasons

3. **Proving discrimination—Discriminatory intent** on government's part necessary to trigger strict or intermediate scrutiny

  - Discriminatory on its face—law that creates distinctions between classes of persons by its very language

  - Discriminatory application—neutral on its face, but applied in discriminatory fashion

  - Discriminatory motive—disparate impact coupled with proof of discriminatory motive/intent

B. Suspect classifications (strict scrutiny – law must be least restrictive means to achieve a compelling governmental interest)

1. **Race, ethnicity, national origin**

  - School integration—De jure (intentional) segregation violates Equal Protection clause

  - Programs favoring racial or ethnic minorities (affirmative action) subject to strict scrutiny

2. **Alienage (in some cases – depends on level of government and nature of classification)**

  - Federal classifications valid unless arbitrary and unreasonable

  - Strict scrutiny applied to state laws that discriminate against aliens

    o Exception for state restrictions on resident alien's participation in government functions – rational basis standard applied

C. **Quasi-suspect classifications (intermediate scrutiny – substantially related to important governmental interest)**

   1. **Gender**

      • Need discriminatory intent by government (not just disparate impact)

      • Government must show "exceedingly persuasive justification" exists for gender distinction, and separate facilities must be substantially equivalent

      • Benign discrimination (affirmative action) permissible under intermediate scrutiny as remedy for past gender-based discrimination

   2. **Legitimacy**

      • Legislation designed to punish nonmarital children will not be upheld

D. **Non-suspect classifications (rational basis - rationally related to legitimate governmental interest)**

   1. **Age**

   2. **Poverty**

   3. **Sexual orientation**—Supreme Court has not resolved the issue of whether discrimination based on sexual orientation is subject to heightened scrutiny

E. **Fundamental rights unique to equal protection (i.e., no overlap with substantive due process)**

      • "One person, one vote"

      • Gerrymandering (based on racial or political discrimination) is unconstitutional

XII. Privileges & Immunities Clauses

A. **Comity Clause**

   1. Applies only to citizens (not corporations or aliens)

   2. Prohibits one state from discriminating against citizens of another state with respect to fundamental rights or essential activities

      • Examples include pursuit of employment, transfer of property, access to state courts, and engaging in the political process

   3. Substantial justification exception

      • Applies if nonresidents are cause or part of problem state trying to solve, and

      • No less-restrictive means to solve problem

B. **14th Amend. – National Citizenship**

   1. Applies only to citizens (not corporations or aliens)

   2. Protects against infringement on privileges and immunities of **national** citizenship

      • Right to travel interstate, vote for national offices, enter public lands, and peaceably assemble

      • Provision is seldom successfully invoked, rights are redundant to rights protected elsewhere in constitution, and in practice applies only to right to travel

XIII. Takings Clause (a check on the power of eminent domain)

   A. Challenger to a taking must have property interest

   - Includes real property and tangible/intangible personal property
   - Interests include fee simple, easement, leasehold, lien, and rights of property owner

   B. Types of takings

   1. Seizure of, destruction of, or damage to property

   2. Re-characterization of private property as public

   3. Regulatory taking, and

   4. Exaction of promises from developer

   - Does not violate the Takings Clause if there is
       - Essential nexus between legitimate state interests and conditions imposed on the property owner, and
       - Rough proportionality between burden imposed on property owner and impact of proposed development

   C. Just compensation

   - Fair market value at time of taking measured in terms of loss to the owner (not benefit to government)

XIV. Prohibited legislation

   A. Bills of attainder—legislative act declares person(s) guilty of crime and punishes without trial

   B. Ex post facto laws—criminalizes act that was not a crime when committed, authorizes more severe penalty after act committed, deprives D of defense available when act committed, or decreases prosecution's burden of proof below that required when act committed

   C. Impairment of contracts

   - Applies only to state legislation
   - That retroactively impairs contractual rights

XV. Freedom of Religion

   A. Establishment

   1. Standard of review (Lemon test) – Governmental action benefitting religion may be valid if

   - Secular purpose
   - Primary effect neither advances nor prohibits religion, and
   - Does not result in excessive government entanglement with religion

   2. Financial aid to religiously affiliated institutions (Lemon test)

   - Indirect aid to parochial schools—valid if widely available to class of persons (not defined by religion)
   - Direct aid to colleges/hospitals—upheld if aid used only for nonreligious purposes
   - Tax exemptions—valid if equivalent to exemptions to other charitable institutions not advancing/inhibiting religion (i.e., can't be available only to religious organizations)

3. Held invalid as clearly promoting religion at school

- Prayer/Bible reading
- Period of silence for meditation/voluntary prayer
- Nondenominational prayer by cleric at graduation
- Posting of Ten Commandments
- Prohibiting teaching of Darwinism

4. Religious displays

- Ten Commandments on public property not allowed if it has predominantly religious purpose
- Government holiday displays permissible unless reasonable observer's conclusion is that they endorse religion

B. Free Exercise

1. Religious belief

- Absolutely protected and cannot be restricted by law
- Government cannot deny benefits or impose burdens based on religious belief
  - o Court may determine sincerity of person asserting belief, but may not determine reasonableness of belief

2. Religious conduct

- Not absolutely protected
- State laws that intentionally target religious conduct subject to strict scrutiny
- Neutral state laws of general applicability that have an impact on religious conduct only subject to rational basis test

XVI. Freedom of Expression/Association

A. Regulation of Speech

1. Expressive conduct (symbolic speech)—Regulation upheld if

- It is within the government's power to enact
- It furthers an important governmental interest
- Interest is unrelated to suppression of ideas, and
- Burden on speech no greater than necessary

2. Overbreadth

- Void if burdens substantially more speech than necessary to protect a compelling governmental interest
- A few possible impermissible applications of statute not sufficient to make it overbroad
- Overbroad statutes may be challenged as "facially invalid" to prevent chilling effect on protected speech

3. Vagueness

- Statute void for vagueness if it fails to provide a person of ordinary intelligence with fair notice of what is prohibited

4. **Prior restraints (regulation of speech in advance of its expression)**

- Invalid unless there is a **particular harm** to be avoided and certain **procedural safeguards** are provided to the speaker, for example
  - o Narrowly drawn/reasonable/definite standards
  - o Promptly sought injunction
  - o Prompt/final decision on validity of restraint
- Burden on government to prove censored material not protected speech

5. **Unfettered discretion**

- Statute giving officials unfettered discretion is void on its face; speakers need not apply for permit and may not be punished for violation
- Statute must provide definite standards to officials on how to apply the law to restrict speech
- Statute must be related to important governmental interest and contain aforementioned procedural safeguards

6. **Freedom not to speak**

- Cannot be forced to speak
- Cannot be forced to fund political speech by a group one is compelled to join with respect to one's employment

7. **Government speech**

- Need not be viewpoint-neutral, but is subject to the Establishment Clause

8. **Campaign related speech**

- Statutes limiting campaign contributions subject to intermediate scrutiny
- Restrictions on campaign expenditures on communications during election campaign regarding a candidate subject to strict scrutiny

B. **Time/place/manner of expression**

1. **Public forum**

- Traditional—historically associated with expression (e.g., sidewalks, streets or parks)
- Designated (limited)—not historically used for speech-related activities but which government has opened for such use (e.g., civic auditoriums, publicly owned theaters, or school classroom off-hours)
- Restrictions must be
  - o Content-neutral as to both subject matter and viewpoint
  - o Narrowly tailored to serve a significant governmental interest, and
  - o Leave open ample alternative channels for communication
- Subject to strict scrutiny if not content-neutral
- Injunction in public forum
  - o Content-neutral—Must not burden more speech than is necessary to achieve an important governmental interest

- o Content-based—Must be necessary for the government to achieve a compelling governmental interest

2. **Nonpublic forum**

- Definition—All public property that is not a traditional or designated forum

- Regulation—Must be viewpoint-neutral and reasonably related to a legitimate governmental interest

  - o Viewpoint-neutral—Government may prohibit speech on certain issues altogether but can't allow only one side of issue to be presented

  - o Reasonable—Restriction only needs to satisfy rational basis test

- Speech on one's own private property—regulations rarely upheld

C. **Regulation of Content (generally subject to strict scrutiny), except**

1. **Obscenity and child pornography not protected by 1st Amend.**

- Obscenity test—Average person, applying contemporary community standards, must find that material taken as a whole

  - o Appeals to the prurient interest

  - o Depicts sexual conduct in a patently offensive way, and

  - o Lacks serious literary, artistic, political, or scientific value (national standards)

2. **Incitement to violence—State may forbid speech advocating use of force or unlawful action if:**

- Speech is directed to inciting or producing imminent lawless action, and

- It is likely to incite or produce such action (a clear and present danger)

3. **Fighting words—Words that by their very nature are likely to incite an immediate breach of the peace**

- Annoying/offensive words not enough

- Must be genuine likelihood of imminent violence by hostile audience

4. **Defamation**

- If P is public figure, or statement involves matter of public concern, P must prove **fault** and **falsity** in addition to prima facie case

  - o Public figure—if P known to general public or voluntarily injects herself into public eye, must prove D acted with actual malice

  - o Public concern—if P is private figure but statement is matter of public concern, need only prove negligence with respect to falsity

5. **Commercial speech—Restrictions subject to four-part test**

- Commercial speech must concern lawful activity and be neither false nor misleading

- Asserted governmental interest must be substantial

- Regulation must directly advance asserted interest

- Regulation must be narrowly tailored to serve interest (meaning a "reasonable fit" between government's ends and means chosen to accomplish them)

D. Regulation of Media

1. General considerations

- Regulation of right to publish matters of public concern subject to strict scrutiny

  o Gag orders—Subject to prior restraint analysis and rarely upheld

  o Attending trials—Right to attend may be outweighed by overriding interest that can't be accommodated by less restrictive means

  o Illegally obtained private info—Permitted to publish if 3rd party (unknown to publisher) obtained info and involves matter of public concern

  o No constitutional right to protect source

2. Broadcast

- Greater responsibility to public, thus more closely regulated than print and other media

3. Cable television

- Content-based regulations subject to strict scrutiny

4. Internet

- Any regulation of content subject to strict scrutiny

E. Regulation of Association

1. Freedom of association protects right to form or participate in any group, gathering, club, or organization virtually without restriction, but right not absolute

- Infringement may be justified by compelling state interest

- Deprivation of public employment based on political association is allowed if

  o Person is active member of subversive organization

  o Has knowledge of organization's illegal activity, and

  o Has specific intent to further those illegal objectives

FINAL REVIEW OUTLINE: CONTRACTS & SALES

I. **Formation of Contracts** (Ks)—binding K requires mutual assent, consideration, & lack of valid defenses

   A. **Offer**—objective manifestation of a willingness by offeror to enter into agreement that creates power of acceptance in offeree

   1. **Intent**—statement is an offer only if:

   - Person to whom it's communicated could reasonably interpret it as an offer

   - Expresses present intent of a person to be legally bound by a K

   2. **Knowledge**—offeree must know of offer in order to have the power to accept

   3. **Terms**—must be certain and definite or the K fails for indefiniteness

   - **Under common law** (CL)

     o Essential terms (parties, subject matter, price, quantity) must be covered in K

     o If the parties intended to create a K, the court may supply missing terms

   - **Under UCC**

     o Only essential term is quantity

       ▪ **Exception**—requirements or output Ks (UCC implies "good faith")
       ▪ UCC "fills the gap" if other terms are missing

     o K formed if both parties intend to K and reasonably certain basis for giving remedy

   4. **Language**—offer must contain words of promise, undertaking, or commitment, and be targeted to a number of people who could actually accept

   - If a return promise is requested—bilateral K

   - If an act is requested—unilateral K

   5. **Invitation to deal**—advertisements are only an invitation to receive offers (but may qualify as an offer if sufficiently specific and limit who can accept or if associated with a stated reward)

   B. **Termination of offers**

   - **Lapse of time**—specified termination date or reasonable period of time if none stated

   - **Death/mental incapacity of offeror**—offer terminates unless offer for option K

   - **Destruction/illegality**—offer terminated

   - **Revocation**

     o Offer can be revoked any time prior to acceptance (even if it states it will be open for specific amount of time)

     o Not effective until communicated

     o Revocation sent by mail not effective until received

   - **Limitations on revocation**

     o **Option K**—offeree must generally give consideration for option to be enforceable

     o **UCC firm offer rule**

- Offer irrevocable (for reasonable time but no more than 90 days) if offeror is a merchant (or any business person), and assurances (in authenticated writing) are made that offer will remain open
- No consideration needed to keep offer open
  - o **Promissory estoppel**—if offeree reasonably and detrimentally relies on offer it may become irrevocable
  - o **Partial performance**—for all Ks, offeree must have knowledge of offer when performance begins
    - **Unilateral K**—offeror cannot revoke once offeree has begun performance
    - **Bilateral K**—commencement of performance operates as promise to render complete performance
- **Revocation of general offers** (to large number of people)—revocable only by notice given at least same level of publicity as offer (effective even if potential offeree acts in reliance on offer)
- **Rejection by offeree**
  - o Offeree clearly conveys to offeror that he no longer intends to accept the offer
  - o Rejection usually effective upon receipt
  - o *Counteroffer*—acts as rejection of original offer and creates new offer

C. **Acceptance**—objective manifestation by the offeree to be bound by the terms of the offer

1. **Bilateral v. unilateral**
   - **Bilateral K**
     - o Exchange of promises that render both enforceable
     - o Commencement of performance operates as promise to render complete performance
   - **Unilateral K**
     - o Promise to do something by one party in return for an act of the other party
     - o Starting to perform is not enough, but it will make offer irrevocable for a reasonable period of time to complete performance
     - o Offeree must be aware of offer before acting

2. **Means of acceptance**—unless offeror specifies, offeree can accept in any reasonable manner/means
   - **Silence**—is not acceptance unless offeree has reason to believe offer could be accepted by silence or previous dealings make it reasonable to believe that offeree must notify offeror if he does not intend to accept
   - **Shipment of goods**
     - o Buyer's request that goods be shipped is inviting acceptance either by seller's promise to ship or by prompt shipment of goods
     - o **Nonconforming goods shipped**—both an acceptance and a breach, unless seller seasonably notifies buyer that goods are an accommodation (counteroffer); buyer may then accept or reject the nonconforming goods

3. **Mailbox rule** (applies only to acceptance - bilateral Ks)

- **Acceptance**—effective when sent (not upon receipt), unless offer provides otherwise

- **Rejection following acceptance**—acceptance will control even if offeror receives rejection first (but if offeror detrimentally relies on rejection then offeree estopped from enforcing K)

- **Acceptance following rejection**—mailbox rule does not apply; first one received will prevail (offeror need not actually read communication)

- **Revocation**—effective upon receipt

- **Irrevocable offer**—mailbox rule does not apply; acceptance must be received by offeror before offer expires

4. **Notice**

- **Unilateral K**

  o Offeree not required to give notice after completing performance, unless:

    ▪ Offeror wouldn't learn of performance with reasonable certainty and promptness, or

    ▪ Offer requires notice

  o **Notice required but not provided**—offeror's duty is discharged, unless:

    ▪ Offeree exercises reasonable diligence to give notice,

    ▪ Offeror learns of performance within reasonable time, or

    ▪ Offer indicates notice of acceptance is not required

- **Bilateral K**—offeree must give notice of acceptance

  o **Mailbox rule**—acceptance valid when sent (even though offeror hasn't received it)

  o **UCC**—if acceptance is made by beginning performance, notice is required within a reasonable time; failure to give notice results in offer's lapse

D. **Additional or different terms (**mirror-image rule v. battle of the forms)

1. **CL mirror-image rule**—acceptance must mirror the terms of the offer, so any change or addition to the terms acts as a rejection and a new counteroffer

- Conditional acceptance terminates the offer and acts as new offer from original offeree

2. **UCC** (no mirror-image rule)—acceptance containing additional or different terms generally treated as acceptance

- **Both parties not merchants**—definite and seasonable expression of acceptance or written confirmation that is sent within a reasonable time is acceptance, except when acceptance is expressly conditioned on assent to new/different terms (then it's treated as proposed additions to the K that must be separately accepted by offeror)

- **Both parties are merchants** (battle of the forms)

  o **Additional terms**—automatically included in the K, unless:

    ▪ Term materially alters original K

    ▪ Offer expressly limits acceptance to terms of the offer, or

    ▪ Offeror objects to new terms within a reasonable time after notice of new terms is received

    If one of these exceptions is met, original terms of offer control

- o **Different terms** ("knock-out" rule)—different terms in offer/acceptance nullify each other, and court uses Article 2's gap-filling provisions to patch holes in K
- **Acceptance based on conduct**—if offer and purported acceptance differ too much to create a contract but the parties begin to perform anyway, then UCC allows for a contract to be recognized with the following terms:
    - o Any terms actually agreed upon in the parties' writings, and
    - o Any supplementary terms filled in by the UCC

E. Consideration

1. **Bargain and exchange**—must be a bargained-for legal detriment to the promisee

    - **Legal detriment and bargained-for exchange**

        - o To constitute sufficient consideration, must be bargained-for in exchange for the promise, promise must induce the detriment, and detriment must induce the promise

        - o Consideration can be return promise to do or refrain from doing something, or performance of or refraining from doing some act

    - **Gift**

        - o Test to distinguish gift from valid consideration is whether offeree could reasonably believe intent of offeror was to induce the action. If yes, then there is consideration and promise is enforceable.

        - o **Promissory estoppel**—if promisor/donor knows that promise to make a gift will induce substantial reliance by promisee and failure to enforce it would cause substantial injustice, promise is enforceable

2. **Adequacy of consideration**

    - **Subjective value**—benefit to promisor need not have economic value; if promisor wants it, giving of it will constitute adequate consideration

    - **Preexisting duty rule**

        - o **CL**—does not qualify as consideration unless promisor gives something in addition to what is owed, or varies preexisting duty in some way

        - o **Exception for third party**—third party promise contingent upon performance of another party's contractual obligation is sufficient consideration

    - **Past consideration**—modern trend towards enforcing past promises when necessary to prevent injustice, unless promisee intended act to be a gift

    - **Modification**

        - o **CL**—must be supported by consideration, and agreements to modify K are enforceable if:
            - ▪ Rescission of existing K and entering into of new K
            - ▪ Unforeseen difficulties arise and one party agrees to compensate other party for them, or
            - ▪ New obligations arise on both sides

        - o **UCC**
            - ▪ Requires only good faith

- No consideration is necessary
- **Accord and satisfaction**
  - Generally, consideration is required for accord to be valid
  - Satisfaction is performance of the accord agreement, and will discharge both the original and accord K
  - Original K not discharged until satisfaction is complete
- **Illusory promise**—not legally binding because it is vague or promisor can choose whether or not to honor it
- **Voidable/unenforceable promises**—can still constitute consideration
- **Requirements** (buyer agrees to buy all that he requires) **and output** (seller agrees to sell all that she manufactures) **Ks**
  - There is consideration because promisor suffers legal detriment
  - Quantities may not be unreasonably disproportionate to estimates
- **Legal claim settlement**—promise not to bring legal action or assert a claim/defense serves as consideration because the promisor is foregoing a legal right

F. **Promises binding without consideration**

1. **Pay a debt barred by statute of limitations** (SoL)—new promise to pay debt after SoL has run is enforceable without new consideration
2. **Perform voidable duty**—new promise to perform voidable duty is enforceable if it doesn't suffer from an infirmity rendering it voidable
3. **Material benefit rule**—when a party performs an unrequested service for another party, the modern trend permits the performing party to enforce the promise of payment for material benefits received to extent necessary to prevent injustice (unless donative intent)
4. **Promissory estoppel** (consideration "substitute")—a promise is binding if:
   - Promisor should reasonably expect it to induce action on the part of the promisee or a third person
   - Promise does induce such action, and
   - Injustice only avoided by enforcement of promise

G. **Enforceability**—a defense to formation or a defense to enforcement may render K void, voidable, or unenforceable

1. **Void Ks**—entire transaction is null, as if no K existed
2. **Voidable Ks**—operates as valid K until/unless one party takes steps to avoid it
3. **Unenforceable Ks**—valid K that cannot be enforced if one party refuses to carry out its terms

H. **Defenses to formation**—no "meeting of minds" due to mistake or misunderstanding, misrepresentation or fraud, undue influence or duress, or lack of capacity

1. **Mistake**
   - **Unilateral**
     - One party is mistaken as to essential element of K, but either party can enforce K on its terms

- o Mistaken party can void K if he didn't bear risk of mistake and either:
  - ▪ Mistake would make enforcement of K unconscionable, or
  - ▪ Non-mistaken party caused the mistake, had duty to disclose or failed to disclose mistake, and knew or should have known the other party was mistaken
- o Must be absence of serious prejudice to other party to rescind K
- **Mutual**
  - o Both parties mistaken as to essential element
  - o K generally voidable by party adversely affected if:
    - ▪ Mistake existed when K was formed
    - ▪ Mistake relates to basic assumption of K
    - ▪ Mistake has material impact on transaction, and
    - ▪ Adversely affected party did not assume the risk of mistake
  - o Neither party can avoid K if reformation available to cure mistake
- **Reformation** (mutual mistake)
  - o Court can reform writing except to extent that rights of third parties who relied on K would be unfairly affected

2. **Misunderstanding**—both parties believe they are agreeing to same material terms, but they in fact agree to different terms
   - **Neither party knows**—no K if material term involved
   - **One party knows**—K formed based upon meaning of material term as understood by unknowing party
   - **Both parties know terms ambiguous at time of K formation**—no K unless both parties intended same meaning
   - **Waiver**—one party can choose to enforce K according to other party's understanding

3. **Misrepresentation**—an untrue assertion of fact that can make K void or voidable
   - *Fraudulent misrepresentation*—requires proof that:
     - o The misrepresentation is **fraudulent**:
       - ▪ Knowing or reckless false assertion of fact
       - ▪ With intent to mislead
     - o The misrepresentation **induced assent** to the K, and
     - o **Justifiable reliance** on the misrepresentation by the adversely affected party
   - **Nondisclosure**—conduct to conceal a fact or nondisclosure of known fact tantamount to an assertion that fact does not exist
   - **Effect**
     - o **Fraud in the factum (execution)**—fraudulent misrepresentation prevents party from knowing character/essential term of transaction, so no K is formed and apparent K is **void** unless reasonable diligence would have revealed K's true terms

- o **Fraud in the inducement**—fraudulent misrepresentation is used to induce another to enter into a K; K **voidable** by adversely affected party if she justifiably relied on the misrepresentation
- **Nonfraudulent misrepresentation** (innocent/negligent)—renders K voidable by adversely affected party who justifiably relied on **material** misrepresentation and was induced to assent to K because of it
- **Cure of misrepresentation**—K not voidable if facts cured before deceived party has avoided the K
- **Avoidance/reformation for misrepresentation**—when content/legal effect of K is misrepresented, deceived party can avoid K or reform it to express what was represented

4. **Undue influence**—unfair persuasion of a party to assent to a K

- **Unfair persuasion**
  - o Relationship between dominant party and dependent party due to lack of expertise or experience, or diminished mental capacity
  - o Persuasion of one party seriously impairs the free and competent judgment of other party
- **Confidential relationship**—dominant party has burden of proving K was fair (may be held to higher standard of disclosure)
- **Third party undue influence**—victim may void K unless nonvictim party to K gave value or materially relied on K in good faith and without knowledge of undue influence
- **Damages**—restitution available

5. **Duress**—improper threat that deprives party of meaningful choice

- **Improper threat**
  - o Threats of criminal or civil action (made in bad faith), or
  - o Threats to breach K in violation of good faith and fair dealing
- **Deprivation of meaningful choice**—person has no reasonable alternative such that threat induced his assent
- **Effect on K**—K is **void** when duress is through physical compulsion and **voidable** in other instances

6. **Capacity to K**

- **Infancy** (under 18)—**voidable by infant** but not by adult (except for reasonable value of necessaries)
- **Mental illness**—K is **void** for one who is adjudicated mentally incompetent, but only **voidable** if there has been no adjudication
- **Guardianship**—K is **void** for individuals under guardianship (except for reasonable value of necessaries)
- **Intoxication**—K is **voidable** by intoxicated party if she was unable to understand nature/consequences of K and other party knew of intoxication

I. **Defenses to enforcement**

1. **Illegality**

    - K is **unenforceable** if consideration/performance under K is illegal

    - K is **void** if it contemplates illegal conduct

    - Duty to perform is **discharged** if K becomes illegal after formation

    - If one party is justifiably ignorant of facts making K illegal or lacks illegal purpose he can recover (assuming guilt of other party)

    - **Exceptions**

        o **Ignorance of illegality**—a party may recover if the party is justifiably ignorant of the facts making K illegal and the other party had knowledge of the illegality

        o **Lack of illegal purpose**—a party who has substantially performed may recover if:

            ▪ **K does not involve illegal consideration/performance**—the party is unaware of the other party's illegal purpose

            ▪ **The party knows of the other party's illegal use**—unless the party furthered the illegal use or the use involves grave social harm

        o **Divisible Ks**—if K can easily be divided into legal and illegal parts, a party may recover on the legal part(s)

        o **Restitution**

            ▪ **Not *in pari delicto*—**when parties are not equally at fault, the less guilty party may recover under restitution

            ▪ **Withdrawal**—a party who withdraws from an illegal K before the improper purpose has been achieved may recover under restitution when the party has not engaged in serious misconduct

2. **Unconscionability—K is unconscionable when it is so unfair to one party that no reasonable person in the position of the parties would agree to it** (e.g., hidden, complex boilerplate language, adhesion Ks)

3. **Public policy**—K may be unenforceable if it violates significant public policy

J. **Implied-in-fact Ks and quasi-Ks**

1. **Implied-in-fact**—conduct, not words, indicates assent or agreement

2. **Quasi-Ks**—a plaintiff confers benefit on a defendant and the plaintiff has reasonable expectation of compensation and court implies K to prevent unjust enrichment

    - **Requirements:**

        o Plaintiff conferred measurable benefit on defendant,

        o Plaintiff acted without gratuitous intent, and

        o Unfair to let defendant retain benefit

K. **Warranties in sale-of-goods Ks**

1. **Express warranty**

    - Any promise, affirmation, description, or sample that is part of the basis of the bargain, **unless it is merely the seller's opinion**

- **Disclaimers**—disclaimers that unreasonably negate or limit express warranties are inoperative

    2. **Implied warranty of merchantability**
       - Implied whenever seller is a merchant
       - Goods must be fit for their ordinary purpose
       - Warranty can be disclaimed by use of "as is," "with all faults," or similar language
       - Disclaimer may be oral, but must use the term "merchantability" and be conspicuous if in writing

    3. **Implied warranty of fitness for a particular purpose**
       - Implied whenever seller has reason to know (from any source) buyer has particular use for goods and buyer is relying on seller's skill to select the goods
       - Warranty can be disclaimed by conspicuous writing

II. **Discharge**

   A. **Impracticability**

      1. **Defense available if:**
         - Performance becomes illegal after K is made,
         - Specific subject matter of K is destroyed,
         - Performing party to the K dies or becomes incapacitated (personal services K), or
         - Performance becomes impracticable

      2. **Elements**
         - Unforeseeable event has occurred,
         - Nonoccurrence of event was basic assumption on which K was made, and
         - Party seeking discharge is not at fault

      3. **Assumption of risk**—impracticability defense not available to a party who assumes the risk of an event happening

      4. **Partial impracticability**
         - If seller is able to deliver some of the goods, they must be apportioned among all of the buyers with whom the seller has contracted
         - Buyer may refuse to accept and may cancel K

      5. **Failure of a particular source**—if K specifically identifies a source, and source of supply fails, performance is discharged even if other sources are available

   B. **Frustration of purpose**

      1. Applies when unexpected events arise that destroy one party's purpose in entering into K, even if performance of K not rendered impossible

      2. Frustrated party entitled to rescind K without paying damages

      3. Unexpected event need not be completely unforeseeable, but must be so severe it's not within assumed risks inherent under K

C. Rescission—cancelling of K so as to restore parties to their positions before K was made

    1. Parties may seek to rescind for a variety of reasons but grounds for rescission must have existed at the time the K was made

    2. Rescission also possible by mutual agreement of the parties—surrender of rights under the original K is consideration for the rescission

        • Third party beneficiaries—K **not** discharged by mutual rescission if third party rights have already vested

D. Release

    1. Writing that manifests intent to discharge another party from an existing duty

        • **CL**—release must be supported by **consideration**

        • **UCC**—written waiver or renunciation signed/delivered by aggrieved party is enough (**no consideration** necessary)

E. Destruction/damage to identified goods

    1. **Destruction**—goods identified when K made are destroyed by no fault of either party before risk of loss passes to buyer; K is avoided, both parties are discharged, and neither party is in breach

    2. **Goods damaged but not destroyed**—K avoided or buyer can choose to take goods at reduced price without any other claim against seller

    3. **Risk of loss**—if risk of loss has passed to buyer, K is not avoided and seller may demand performance by buyer

III. Third-Party Beneficiary Contracts—when two parties contract with the understanding and intent that performance by one of the parties is to be rendered to a third person

  A. Intended and incidental beneficiaries—third party can recover if she is an intended beneficiary

        • **Intended beneficiary**—one to whom the promisee wishes to make a gift of the promised performance or to satisfy an obligation to pay money owed by promisee to beneficiary; has the right to bring an action on the K

        • **Incidental beneficiary**—one who benefits from a K even though there is no contractual intent to benefit that person; no right to enforce K

  B. Vesting of beneficiary's rights—rights of intended beneficiary vest when beneficiary:

        • Detrimentally relies on rights created,

        • Manifests assent to K at one of the party's request, or

        • Files lawsuit to enforce K

  C. Defenses—promisor can raise any defense against third party that he had against original promisee

IV. Assignment of Rights & Delegation of Duties

  A. Assignment of rights

    1. Not allowed when it materially increases duty or risk of obligor or materially reduces obligor's chance of obtaining performance

    2. Need present intent to transfer the right immediately

    3. If assignment is for consideration, it is irrevocable

4. Assignee takes all of the rights of assignor as the K stands at time of the assignment, but she takes subject to any defenses that could be raised against the assignor

B. Delegation of duties

1. Generally allowed, except when other party to K has substantial interest in a specific individual's performance (for example, personal services K involving special skill)

2. When obligations are delegated, delegator is not released from liability, so he is still liable if delegate doesn't perform (unless there is a novation)

3. Delegate's acceptance of a delegation constitutes a promise to perform the delegated duties; promise is enforceable is there is consideration or a consideration substitute

4. Delegation in contracts for the sale of goods may be treated by the other party as creating reasonable grounds for insecurity; the other party may demand assurances from delegate

C. Assignment of contract—assignments not limited to contractual rights (e.g., "this contract is assigned to") are generally treated as both an assignment of rights and a delegation of duties

V. Statute of Frauds (SoF)

A. Writing required—memorandum must:

1. Be in **writing**

2. Be **signed** by the party to be charged

3. Contain the **essential elements** of the deal

B. Types of Ks within the SoF

1. **M**arriage—any agreement in consideration of marriage

2. **S**uretyship—K to answer for debt/duty of another

3. **O**ne year—K that cannot be performed within one year after K is made

4. **U**CC—when K for the sale of goods is at least $500, memo must indicate that K has been made, identify **parties**, contain a **quantity** term, and be **signed** by the party to be charged

   - **Exceptions**—writing not required under UCC for:

     o Specially manufactured goods,

     o Part payment,

     o Receipt and acceptance,

     o Judicial admission, or

     o Failure to object to memo within 10 days (when both parties are **merchants**)

5. **R**eal property K—applies to Ks providing for subsequent conveyances of an interest in property (subsequent acts showing existence of K may also make oral Ks for transfers of interest enforceable)

VI. Parol Evidence (P/E)—prevents introduction of prior extrinsic evidence that contradicts terms of written K

A. Integration—parties intended writing to be their final agreement (P/E rule applies)

1. **Total integration** (complete expression of all terms of parties' agreement)—parties cannot introduce extrinsic evidence of prior/contemporaneous understandings or negotiations

- **Partial**—if writing sets forth only some terms, then parties are permitted to introduce supplementary extrinsic evidence of other terms that are **consistent** with writing (not contradictory)

2. **Intent of the parties**—determines if there is total, partial, or no integration

- **CL** ("four corners" rule)—can only look to writing itself for intent

- **Second Restatement**—if an extrinsic term of agreement would naturally be omitted from a writing, then term can be introduced so long as it isn't contradictory

- **UCC**—assumes written K is only a partial integration and allows almost any outside terms

B. **When P/E is inapplicable**—does **not** apply to communications occurring **after** the execution of the written K and when parties are (partial list):

1. Raising a defense to formation

2. Raising a defense to enforcement

3. Proving condition precedent to existence of the K

4. Interpreting/clarifying ambiguity in K

5. UCC—supplementing even apparently unambiguous terms by evidence of trade usage or course of dealing (priority, highest to lowest: express terms, course of performance, course of dealing, trade usage)

VII. Conditions and Performance

A. **Condition**—future event that must take place before rights or obligations are created, destroyed, or enlarged

1. Failure of a condition relieves a party of the obligation to perform

2. **Express**—K includes words like "on the condition that" or "provided that"

- Condition must be complied with fully unless excused; substantial performance will not suffice

3. **Implied**—those deemed to be part of K because agreement suggests that parties truly intended the condition but failed to expressly include it, or because fairness requires its inclusion

- Only substantial performance required to satisfy condition

- UCC—implies duty of cooperation when performance of one party depends on the cooperation of the other party

B. **Timing of conditions**

1. **Condition precedent**—condition precedes the obligation to perform

2. **Condition subsequent**—condition excuses the duty to perform after a particular event occurs

3. **Concurrent conditions**—each party's duty to perform is conditioned on the other party's duty to perform (each party must perform simultaneously)

C. **Satisfaction of conditions**—examined against objective, **reasonable person standard** unless aesthetic taste is involved (then **subjective standard**; the party must use **good faith** when assessing satisfaction)

D. Performance

1. **Order of performance**—unless the language or circumstances indicate otherwise, performance is due:

   - **When one party's performance requires a period of time**—that party must complete his performance before the other party is required to perform

   - **When both parties' performance can be rendered at the same time**—both parties must perform at the same time; one party's failure to perform excuses the other party's performance

2. **Substantial performance** (does not generally apply to Ks for sale of goods)

   - **Express condition precedent**—parties are generally held strictly to the condition; full compliance is required before other party's performance is due

   - **Implied or constructive condition precedent**—a party who substantially complies with the condition can trigger the other party's obligation to perform

   - **Damages**—K price minus any amount it will cost other party to obtain complete performance as promised

     o Even if no substantial performance, potential recovery through restitution

     o Failure to substantially perform is a material breach

   - **Willful breach**—more likely to be treated as a material breach (i.e., substantial performance is less likely to be found when the breach is willful)

3. **Perfect tender under the UCC**

   - **Seller** must **transfer ownership** and **tender goods** conforming to warranty obligations

   - **Buyer** may **inspect goods** and, upon acceptance, has an **obligation to pay** for them

   - **Perfect tender rule**—substantial performance insufficient (except for installment Ks and when parties agree)

   - **Transferring ownership**

     o Automatic warranty of good title, rightful transfer, and goods free of security interest of which buyer is unaware

     o Actual knowledge of security interest nullifies warranty of title

   - **Seller's obligation to tender goods**—must be in accordance with K provisions or with UCC if K is silent on tender

   - **Method of tender**

     o **Seller's place of business**—seller must place goods at the disposition of the buyer and give the buyer notice, if necessary

     o **Shipment contract** (e.g., "F.O.B. seller's place of business")—seller must deliver goods to a carrier and make a contract for their shipment; when the K is silent, a shipment K is presumed when the K requires shipment by third-party carrier

     o **Destination contract** (e.g., "F.O.B. buyer's place of business")—seller must deliver goods to the place specified in contract and tender them there by holding them at the buyer's disposition

- **Buyer's obligations**—once conforming tender is made, buyer obligated to accept and pay K price; rejection amounts to breach of K

- **Buyer's right to inspect before payment**—generally, a right to inspect goods that are tendered, delivered, or identified to the K for sale, unless K provides otherwise

4. **Divisible or installment Ks**

- **CL**—various units of performance divisible into distinct parts

  o Recovery limited to amount promised for the segment of K performed

  o Damages recoverable for breach of other segments

- **UCC**—goods delivered in multiple shipments, each to be separately accepted

  o Perfect tender rule doesn't apply

  o Right to reject determined by "substantial conformity" standard—buyer can only reject if nonconformity **substantially impairs value** to buyer and cannot be **cured**

  o Buyer may cancel K only if nonconforming tender **substantially impairs the value** of the entire K

E. **Suspension or excuse of conditions**

1. **Waiver**—party whose duty is subject to a condition can waive a **nonmaterial** condition by words or conduct; the condition may be reinstated if:

   - The waiving party communicates the retraction of the waiver before the condition is due, and

   - The other party has not suffered detrimental reliance

2. **Wrongful interference**—if party whose duty is subject to a condition wrongfully prevents or interferes with occurrence of that condition, then the condition is excused and interfering party has absolute duty to perform – per implied duty of **good faith and fair dealing**

3. **Election**—a party who chooses to continue with a K after a condition is broken effectively waives that condition

4. **Estoppel**—once a party waives condition, he can be estopped from using that condition as a defense if other party **reasonably relied** on waiver

VIII. Breach of Contract and Remedies

A. **Breach of K**—once duty to perform exists, nonperformance is a breach unless duty is discharged

1. **CL**

   - **Material breach** (nonbreaching party does not receive substantial benefit of bargain)—allows nonbreaching party to withhold any promised performance and to pursue remedies for breach, including damages

   - **Minor breach** (breaching party has substantially performed)—nonbreaching party entitled to pursue remedies for nonmaterial breach (damages) but must perform under the K

2. **UCC**

   - In general, seller must strictly perform all obligations under K or be in breach

- Material breach only applies to installment Ks or when parties stipulate it in K

B. **Anticipatory Repudiation**

1. **CL**

    - **Promisor repudiates before time of performance is due**—repudiation must be clear and unequivocal through words or acts

    - **Nonbreaching party's options:**

        o Treat repudiation as a breach, or

        o Ignore repudiation and demand performance of promisor, but suspend any performance by promisee if it would increase promisor's damages

        o If date of performance has not passed and the only performance left is payment, must wait for actual breach before filing suit

    - **Retraction of repudiation**—can be retracted until promisee acts in reliance on repudiation, accepts repudiation, or commences action for breach of K

    - **Unilateral Ks**—anticipatory repudiation does **not** apply

2. **UCC**

    - Anticipatory repudiation occurs when there has been an **unequivocal refusal** of buyer/seller to perform or when reasonable grounds for insecurity arise and the other party fails to provide adequate assurances within reasonable time (not to exceed 30 days)

    - **Retraction of repudiation**—permitted if other party has not canceled the K or materially changed position

3. **Prospective inability to perform**—party's expectations of performance may be diminished by an event occurring after K formation

    - **UCC**

        o Either party can demand assurances if reasonable grounds for insecurity about other party's ability to perform (and may suspend performance until provided)

        o Failure to provide adequate assurances within reasonable time (not to exceed 30 days) treated as repudiation

C. **Remedies: damages for breach of K**

1. **Expectation damages**

    - **In general**

        o Intended to put injured party in same position as if K had been performed

        o Must be calculated with reasonable certainty

        o Expectation damages = loss in value + other loss − cost avoided − loss avoided

    - **Partial performance**—partially performing party recovers work performed + expectation damages for work not yet performed

    - **Defective performance**

        o **Construction Ks**—damages equal to the difference between K price and cost of construction by another builder

- **Sale of goods**—damages equal to the difference between the value of the goods as warranted and the actual value of the tendered nonconforming goods
  - **Diminution in value (economic waste)**—occurs when the amount of damages owed is disproportional to any economic benefit/utility gained as a result of the award

2. **Consequential damages and foreseeability**
   - **Consequential damages—reasonably foreseeable losses** to nonbreaching party that go beyond expectation damages (e.g., loss of profits)
   - **Foreseeability**—damages are recoverable if they are natural and probable consequences of breach, or if they were contemplated by the parties at K formation, or if they were otherwise foreseeable
   - **Causation**—D's defense that P's losses would have occurred regardless of D's breach
   - **Reasonable certainty**
     - Dollar amount of damages must be proven with reasonable certainty
     - If lost profits are too speculative, courts may limit recovery to reliance damages (reasonable expenditures made in connection with the K)
   - **UCC breach of warranty**
     - Limitation of consequential damages for personal injury in the case of consumer goods is prima facie unconscionable
     - Limitation of damages when the loss is commercial is **not** prima facie unconscionable

3. **Liquidated damages and penalties**—damages stipulated by the parties to the K as a reasonable estimation of actual damages to be recovered in the event of a breach
   - **Enforceable if:**
     - Parties intended to agree in advance to damages that might arise from breach
     - Stipulated amount was reasonable at time of K, bearing some relation to damages that might be sustained, and
     - Actual damages would be uncertain in amount and difficult to prove

4. **Incidental damages**—compensation for commercially reasonable expenses incurred as a result of other party's breach

5. **Punitive damages**—rarely available in K actions but may be available if conduct constituting breach is also recoverable under tort theory

6. **Nominal damages**—when no damages are alleged/proven

7. **Mitigating damages**
   - Party to K must avoid or mitigate damages to the extent possible by taking such steps as to not involve undue risk, expense, or inconvenience
   - Nonbreaching party held to standard of **reasonable conduct** in preventing loss
   - Failure to mitigate reduces damages that may be recovered by nonbreaching party

D. Restitution and reliance recoveries

    1. Restitutionary damages (restores to a party the benefit conferred on the other party)

- Measured by either the reasonable value of the D obtaining that benefit from another source, or increase in the D's wealth from having received that benefit

- If P has not substantially performed and is in breach, P not permitted to recover

- **Recovery by nonbreaching party**

      o Nonbreaching party may recover for any benefit conferred on breaching party by way of part performance or reliance

      o Nonbreaching party may not recover restitution if he has fully performed and the only remaining performance by the other party is the payment of a definite sum of money

- **Recovery by breaching party**

      o If D has benefitted from P's performance, P can recover for benefit conferred less the D's damages for the breach

      o P generally cannot recover if P's breach was willful or if K provides that nonbreaching party may retain the value of the breaching party's performance as liquidated damages

    2. Reliance damages (reasonable out-of-pocket expenses incurred by nonbreaching party)

- Recoverable if nonbreaching party incurs expenses in reasonable reliance upon the promise that other party would perform

- Party **cannot recover both reliance and expectation damages**

E. Specific performance—an equitable remedy possible when damages are an inadequate remedy

    1. Factors considered in determining whether damages are adequate

- Difficulty of proving damages with reasonable certainty

- Hardship to D

- Balance of the equities

- Practicality of enforcement

- Mutuality of agreement

    2. Real property—specific performance granted because **real property is considered unique**

    3. UCC—specific performance may be granted to the buyer when goods are rare or unique

    4. Equitable defenses—laches (prejudicial delay in bringing the action) or **unclean hands** (nonbreaching party guilty of some wrongdoing in the transaction) may be raised by breaching party

F. UCC remedies

    1. Buyer's remedies when seller fails to perform or makes a nonconforming tender

- **Failure to tender goods**

      o **Damages**—market price minus K price plus incidental and consequential damages

- o **Cover**—buyer may purchase similar goods elsewhere and recover replacement price minus the K price
- o **Specific performance**—for **unique** goods
- o **Replevin**—buyer can obtain undelivered goods from seller if at least partial payment is made or the buyer is unable to effect cover
- **Nonconforming tender**—buyer has right to accept or reject all or part of the goods (and the right to inspect before making that decision)
  - o **Rejection**—buyer can reject goods if he gives notice to seller within a reasonable time and before acceptance, and is then entitled to a return of any payments made or to seek same remedies as if no tender was made
  - o **Acceptance**—buyer accepts goods by expressly stating acceptance, using the goods, or failing to reject the goods
  - o **Right to cure**—seller has right to cure defective tender if time of performance under K has not yet elapsed or seller had reasonable grounds to believe that buyer would accept despite the nonconformity

2. **Seller's remedies**

- **Right to price upon acceptance**—price is due after goods are physically delivered to the buyer and buyer has had opportunity to inspect
- **Right to reclaim goods**—from insolvent buyer if he makes a demand within 10 days after buyer receives goods
- **Stoppage of goods in transit**—permitted if buyer breaches or is insolvent
- **Wrongful rejection by buyer**—seller can collect damages, resell the goods, or recover the price, and also collect incidental damages and, if the seller is a "lost volume" seller, lost profits

3. **Risk of loss**

- **Unidentified goods**—if goods are damaged/destroyed and there is no breach, risk of loss is on seller until he satisfies delivery obligations (and then risk shifts to buyer)
  - o **Shipment K**—risk of loss passes to buyer when the seller gives possession of the goods to the carrier and makes proper contract for their shipment
  - o **Destination K**—risk of loss passes to buyer when the seller tenders the goods at the place specified in the K
- **Identified goods**—seller is excused if goods are totally destroyed through no fault of the seller prior to the risk of loss being shifted to the buyer
- **Effect of a breach of K**
  - o **Seller's breach**—if seller delivers nonconforming goods, risk of loss remains on the seller until buyer accepts or there is cure
  - o **Buyer's breach**—if buyer breaches/repudiates after goods have been identified but before risk of loss shifts, then risk immediately shifts to buyer (to extent of lack of insurance coverage by seller)

4. **SoL on a breach of a sales K**

- **Four years** after cause of action accrues

- o Generally, cause of action accrues when breach occurs, regardless of whether aggrieved party knows
- Parties may reduce four-year limitations period to not less than one year, but they may not extend it

FINAL REVIEW OUTLINE: CRIMINAL LAW

I. **General Principles**

    A. ***Actus reus***—voluntary/affirmative act or omission/failure to act causing criminally proscribed result

        1. **Voluntary act**

- Physical and voluntary

- Unconscious/asleep/under hypnosis—not voluntary

        2. **Failure to act when a duty exists**

- Imposed by statute

- Contract

- Special relationship

- Detrimental undertaking

- Causation

    B. ***Mens rea***—guilty mind or legally proscribed mental state (none for strict liability crimes)

        1. **Specific intent (SI) crimes**—subjective desire, specific objective, or knowledge to accomplish prohibited result (FIAT):

- **F**irst-degree murder

- **I**nchoate offenses

- **A**ssault with intent to commit battery

- **T**heft offenses

        2. **Malice crimes** (CL murder, arson)

- Reckless disregard of a high risk of harm

- Requires only a criminal act without excuse, justification, or mitigation

- Intent is inferred from the accomplishment of the act

        3. **General intent crimes** (e.g., battery, rape, kidnapping, and false imprisonment)

- Require the intent to perform an unlawful act

- **Intent**—knowingly, recklessly, or negligently

- **Transferred intent** (unintended victim rule)—usually confined to homicide, battery, and arson

        4. **Model Penal Code**

- **Purposely**—D's conscious objective is to engage in the conduct or to cause a certain result

- **Knowingly/willfully**—D is aware or knows that the result is practically certain to occur based on his conduct

- **Recklessly**—D acts with conscious disregard of a substantial and unjustifiable risk

- **Negligently**—D should be aware of a substantial and unjustifiable risk that a material element of a crime exists or will result from his conduct (gross deviation from standard of care)

5. **Strict-liability crimes** (e.g., statutory rape, bigamy, regulation of food and drugs)

   - No *mens rea*; proof of the *actus reus* is sufficient for conviction

   - Generally disfavored; there must be clear legislative intent to dispense with the *mens rea*

6. **Vicarious liability**

   - No *actus reus*; proof of the *mens rea* is sufficient for conviction

   - Generally limited to regulatory crimes; punishment generally limited to fines

   - **Corporations**—may be vicariously liable when the act is performed by a high-ranking corporate agent who likely represents corporate policy

7. **Causation**—D's act must cause the particular result made unlawful by statute

8. **Mistake as a defense**

   - **Mistake of fact**

     o Negates criminal intent (if honest)

     o Defense to specific-intent crime even if unreasonable mistake

     o Defense to general-intent/malice crime only if reasonable

   - **Mistake of law**—only valid if:

     o D relied on court decision/administrative order or official interpretation

     o Statutory definition of *malum prohibitum* crime not available before conduct, or

     o Honestly held mistake of law negates required intent

C. Parties to crime

1. **Principal**—the person whose acts or omissions are the *actus reus* of the crime; must be actually or constructively present at the scene of the crime

2. **Accomplice liability**

   - Aids/abets principal prior to/during crime with the intent that crime be committed

   - **Accessory before the fact**—neither physically nor constructively present during the commission of the crime, but possesses the requisite intent

   - **Principal in the second degree**—physically or constructively present during the commission of the crime

   - Responsible for crime and all natural and probable consequences

   - To withdraw, an accomplice must:

     o Repudiate prior aid

     o Do all that is possible to countermand prior assistance, and

     o Do so before chain of events set in motion and unstoppable

3. **Accessory after the fact**

   - Aids or assists felon to avoid apprehension or conviction after felony committed

- Must know felony was committed
- Only liable for separate crime (e.g., "obstruction of justice" or "harboring a fugitive")

D. Responsibility

1. Insanity

- ***M'Naghten***—D didn't know nature/quality of act or wrongfulness of act because of defect due to mental disease ("right from wrong" test)
- **Irresistible impulse**—D lacked capacity for self-control and free choice due to mental disease or defect—inability to conform conduct to the law
- ***Durham***—unlawful act was product of D's mental disease/defect ("but for" test)
- **MPC** (combines *M'Naghten* and irresistible impulse)—at time of conduct, D lacked substantial capacity to appreciate wrongfulness of act or conform conduct to law as a result of mental disease or defect

2. Intoxication

- **Voluntary**
  - ○ Intentional taking of known intoxicating substance
  - ○ Need not intend actual intoxication
  - ○ Defense to SI crimes if it prevents required intent
- **Involuntary**
  - ○ Taken without knowledge of the intoxicating nature or under duress
  - ○ Negates element of general intent, specific intent, or malice crime

II. Homicide

A. Murder—unlawful killing of another human being committed with malice aforethought

1. Malice—can be shown by any one of the following:

- **Intent to kill**—conduct that is the legal cause of death + intent to kill
- **Intent to do serious bodily injury**—serious bodily injury + unintentional killing
- **Reckless indifference to human life**—results from reckless indifference to an unjustifiably high risk to human life + unintentional killing
- **Intent to commit a felony**—proximately caused by and during the commission or attempted commission of an inherently dangerous felony + unintentional killing (felony murder)

2. Felony murder rule (FMR)

- Unintended and foreseeable killing proximately caused by/during commission or attempted commission of inherently dangerous felony (BARRK—**b**urglary, **a**rson, **r**obbery, **r**ape, and **k**idnapping)
- D must be guilty of underlying felony
- Bystander death falls under FMR under proximate cause theory if direct consequence of felony
- D not liable for co-felon's death by victim/police

- Does not encompass death occurring after flight from scene of crime

B. Statutory murder

1. **First-degree** (specific intent crime)—deliberate/premeditated (after forming intent to kill D had time for reflection) or FMR

2. **Second-degree** (malice crime)—necessary malicious intent (common-law murder) or default category if not first-degree murder

C. Voluntary manslaughter

1. **"Heat of passion"**

- Murder committed in response to a situation that would inflame a reasonable person (serious battery, threat of deadly force, but usually not words)

- NOT a defense but can reduce murder to voluntary manslaughter

- If there was sufficient time between provocation and killing for a reasonable person to cool down, murder is not mitigated to manslaughter

D. Involuntary manslaughter—unintentional homicide committed with criminal negligence or during an unlawful act

1. **Criminal negligence**—grossly negligent action (or inaction when there is a duty to act) putting another person at significant risk of serious injury/death

2. **Unlawful act**

- *Malum in se* misdemeanor (e.g., assault, battery)

- Killing during felony that isn't first-degree felony murder or second-degree murder

III. Other Crimes

A. Crimes against property

1. **Larceny**

- Trespassory

- Taking

- Carrying away

- Of personal property

- Of another

- With the specific intent to permanently deprive owner of property

2. **Larceny by trick**—obtaining possession of, but not title to, property owned by another through fraud or deceit with the intent to convert the property

3. **Forgery**

- Fraudulent

- Making

- Of a false writing

- With apparent legal significance

- With the intent to defraud

4. **Embezzlement**
   - Fraudulent
   - Conversion
   - Of property
   - Of another
   - By person in lawful possession of property

5. **False pretenses**
   - Obtaining title to property
   - Of another person
   - Thru reliance of that person
   - On known false representation of material past/present fact
   - Representation made with intent to defraud

6. **Robbery**
   - Larceny
   - From the person or presence of the victim
   - By force or intimidation

7. **Extortion**
   - Taking of money/property from another by threat
   - Threat need not be of physical or of immediate harm
   - Property need not be on person or in presence of victim
   - Threat is the essence of the crime (majority view)

8. **Burglary** (common law)
   - Breaking and
   - Entering
   - Of the dwelling
   - Of another
   - At nighttime
   - With the specific intent to commit a felony therein

9. **Arson**
   - Malicious
   - Burning
   - Of the dwelling
   - Of another
   - Definition not strictly applied on MBE

10. **Possession offenses**
    - Defendant exercises dominion and control over a prohibited object or substance

- Defendant not required to be aware that possession is illegal
- **Duration of possession**—must be for a period long enough to have provided the defendant with an opportunity to cease such dominion and control

11. **Receipt of stolen goods**
- Receiving control
- Of stolen property
- With knowledge that it is stolen, and
- Intent to permanently deprive the owner of the property

B. **Crimes against the person**

1. **Battery**
- Unlawful
- Application of force
- To another person
- That causes bodily harm to that person or
- Constitutes an offensive touching

2. **Assault**
- An attempt to commit a battery or
- Intentionally placing another in apprehension of imminent bodily harm

3. **Mayhem**—common-law felony battery that causes dismemberment or permanent disfigurement of a person

4. **Kidnapping**
- Unlawful
- Confinement of a person
- Against that person's will
- Coupled with either:
  o Movement, or
  o Hiding of that person

5. **False imprisonment**
- Unlawful
- Confinement of a person
- Without consent

6. **Rape**
- Unlawful
- Sexual intercourse
- With a female

- Against her will by force or threat of immediate force
  - o No force requirement under most modern statutes
  - o Required intent negated if reasonable belief that lack of resistance was consent

IV. Inchoate crimes (specific-intent crimes)

A. Merger—defendant may be tried, but not punished, for solicitation and the completed crime or for attempt and the completed crime (conspiracy does not merge with the completed crime)

1. Solicitation

- Enticing, encouraging, or commanding another person
- To commit a crime
- With the intent that the other person commits the crime
- **Renunciation**—voluntary renunciation may be a defense if D thwarts commission of the solicited crime

2. Conspiracy

- An agreement
- Between two or more persons
- To accomplish an unlawful purpose
- With the intent to accomplish that purpose
- **Unilateral conspiracy**—may be formed when only one party actually agrees (modern trend and MPC; not recognized under common law)
- **Overt act**
  - o **Common law**—no overt act required
  - o **Majority/federal law/MPC**—require legal/illegal overt act in furtherance of the conspiracy
- **Scope**—conspirator liable for conspiracy and co-conspirators' substantive crimes in furtherance of conspiracy (*Pinkerton* Rule)
- **Withdrawal**
  - o **Federal/majority rule**—withdrawal possible between date of agreement and commission of overt act but must give notice to co-conspirators or give timely notice to police
  - o **MPC/minority rule**—subsequent withdrawal OK only if timely notification allows police to thwart success of conspiracy

3. Attempt

- Substantial step toward commission of crime (beyond mere preparation)
- Coupled with specific intent to commit the crime
- **Factual impossibility**—not a defense (legal impossibility OK)
- **Abandonment**—not a defense after substantial steps are taken (CL)
- If the crime is completed, the attempt merges into the completed crime

V. Defenses

A. Generally

1. Mistake of fact

- Viable defense if mistake is a reasonable one
  - Consider D's physical characteristics, experiences, and knowledge
- Unreasonable mistake only a defense to specific-intent crimes

B. Specific defenses

1. **Self-defense**—one who is not the aggressor is justified in using reasonable force against another person to prevent immediate unlawful harm to himself

- **Reasonable force**—may be used to prevent immediate unlawful harm
- **Deadly force**—may be used in self-defense only if reasonably necessary to:
  - Prevent death/serious injury
  - Prevent serious felony
- **Nondeadly force**—may be used to repel nondeadly force
- **Retreat**
  - No self-defense duty to retreat before using nondeadly force, deadly force in home, or (majority view) deadly force elsewhere
  - Retreat required if it can be safely accomplished (minority view)
- **Imperfect self-defense** (killing in self-defense not justified)—reduces murder to voluntary manslaughter
- **Aggressor's right to use self-defense**—an initial aggressor may gain the right to act in self-defense if:
  - The aggressor's nondeadly force was met with deadly force, or
  - When aggressor in good faith withdrew from the altercation and communicated it to victim

2. **Defense of others**—right to defend others exists under the same circumstances in which self-defense would be acceptable

3. Defense of property

- Reasonable steps, including nondeadly force, may be used to protect property
- D must reasonably believe real property is in immediate danger of unlawful trespass or that personal property in immediate danger of being carried away
- Force cannot be unreasonably disproportionate to perceived harm
- Generally, deadly force not OK in defending property—only OK to prevent forcible felony in dwelling
- Deadly mechanical devices cannot be used to protect property

4. Arrest

- Police can use reasonable force to make lawful arrest
- Deadly force only if suspect is a threat to the officer or third parties

- **Resisting unlawful arrest**
  - D may use nondeadly force in resisting unlawful arrest
  - Deadly force never permitted

5. **Duress**
   - D violated law because third party's unlawful threat caused D to reasonably believe death/harm to himself or another could only be avoided by violating the law
   - Not a defense to intentional murder

6. **Necessity**
   - Natural forces of nature (not human actions) caused D to commit what otherwise would be a crime
   - Not a defense if D set the natural forces in motion or if there was a noncriminal alternative

7. **Consent**
   - Not a defense unless:
     - Consent negates required element of crime, or
     - Precludes harm sought to be avoided by crime
   - Consent must be:
     - Voluntary
     - Involve no fraud
     - Be given by one who is competent to consent

8. **Entrapment**
   - Criminal offense planned and induced by police/government agent
   - D was not predisposed to commit crime

FINAL REVIEW OUTLINE: CRIMINAL PROCEDURE

I. **Fourth Amendment: Application to Arrest, Search and Seizure**

   A. **General principles**

     1. **Standing**—D must have standing to assert claim

     2. **Exclusionary rule**

       • Prevents introduction at a subsequent criminal trial of evidence unlawfully seized

       • **Does not apply** to federal habeas corpus review, grand jury proceedings, preliminary/bail/sentencing hearings, proceedings to revoke parole, evidence used as impeachment evidence against the defendant, or civil proceedings

     3. **Government conduct**—publicly paid police, private person directed by police, or deputized private police

     4. **Reasonable expectation of privacy (REP)**—as to place searched or item seized

   B. **Arrest**—unreasonable seizure of persons

     1. **Seizure**—when police, by means of physical force/show of authority, terminate/restrain freedom of movement and D actually submits

       • Totality of circumstances

         o If police intent to restrain is ambiguous, or

         o If D's submission is only passive acquiescence,

         o Then a seizure occurs if totality of circumstances would lead reasonable person to believe he is not free to leave

     2. **Stop and frisk**—temporary detention that constitutes seizure if the officer, by means of physical force/show of authority, has in some way restrained (physical restraint or an order to stop) the liberty of a citizen

     3. **Warrant**

       • **Arrest**—must be issued by detached/neutral magistrate upon finding of probable cause (PC) and describe with particularity the D and crime; deficient warrant does not invalidate arrest as long as there was PC (no warrant required for proper arrest based on PC)

       • **Search**—issued by detached/neutral magistrate upon finding of PC, supported by oath or affidavit, & must describe with particularity places to be searched and items to be seized (reasonable belief that contraband will be found)

       • **Facts supporting PC**

         o Officer's personal observations

         o Information from reliable, known informant or verified unknown informant

         o Evidence seized during stop and based on reasonable suspicion, discovered in plain view, or during consensual search

       • **Particularity**

         o Must specify place to be searched and objects to be seized

- o Can also refer to contraband as "other fruits, instrumentalities, or evidence of crime at this time unknown" and still be valid

- **Knock & announce rule**

  - o Police must generally announce purpose when executing a warrant (unless state allows exception for exigent circumstances)

  - o Violation does not trigger exclusionary rule

4. **Warrantless arrests**—arrest warrant not needed in public place or for felony/misdemeanor in arresting party's presence, but invalid arrest alone not a defense to crime charged (but will affect any seizure of evidence)

C. Search and seizure

1. **Government conduct**—search must be by government employee or agent

2. **Reasonable expectation of privacy (REP)**

   - **Home, private room, or office**—home and curtilage, motel rooms, and business premises are protected; use of drug-sniffing dog is a search if physically intrudes onto constitutionally protected property

   - **Luggage**—REP for invasive searches but not for canine sniff

   - **Automobiles**—need reasonable suspicion of law violation to effectuate a stop, and PC for pre-textual stops when traffic law violated to investigate whether another law has been violated

   - **Open areas**—outside curtilage – no reasonable (objective) expectation of privacy

   - **Odor from car**—no REP

   - **Technological device**

     - o Attaching a tracking device to a person without consent is a search

     - o Physically intruding on a suspect's property to install a technological device may be a search

     - o Use of sense-enhancing devices not used by general public is a search

3. **Exceptions to search warrant requirement**

   - **Search incident to lawful arrest**—must be reasonable in scope and incident to a lawful arrest

     - o **Wingspan**—includes contemporaneous search of person/immediate surrounding area including pockets/containers large enough to conceal a weapon or evidence of a crime (**does not** include a cell phone unless exigent circumstances exist)

     - o **Home**—includes closets/other spaces immediately adjoining place of arrest in home from which an attack could be launched

     - o **Vehicle**—justified if:

       - Arrestee is within reaching distance of passenger compartment (weapons/evidence) during search, or

       - It is reasonable that evidence of the offense of arrest might be in vehicle

- **Exigent circumstances**
  - **Totality of circumstances test**
    - Must have PC and exigent circumstances
    - Police may not create the exigency by threats or conduct that violates the Fourth Amendment
  - **Hot pursuit**—police in pursuit of a suspect can seize "mere" evidence (not fruits/instrumentalities of crime) from a private building if they have PC to believe the suspect committed a felony
  - **Emergency**—reasonable apprehension that delay in getting warrant would result in immediate danger of evidence destruction, police/public safety or fleeing felon (judged by police officer's objective reasonable belief)
- **Stop and frisk**
  - **Stop**—reasonable suspicion (totality of circumstances), based on articulable facts that detainees involved in criminal activity, and is a limited/temporary intrusion on D's freedom of movement
  - **Frisk**
    - An officer without probable cause may pat down a person's outer clothing if the officer has reasonable suspicion that the suspect was/is involved in criminal activity and that the frisk is necessary for safety
    - Under "plain feel" exception, if officer conducting a valid frisk feels an object whose identity is immediately obvious (i.e., PC of contraband) it can be seized
  - **Passenger compartment**—permitted if police have reasonable belief suspect is dangerous and may get immediate control of weapons, and the search is limited to places where a weapon could be hidden
  - **Limitations**—least intrusive means reasonably available to frisk for weapons only, but if suspicion becomes PC, then officer can make arrest and conduct a full search
- **Automobile exception**—can search any part of car (compartments, containers, trunk, etc.) if PC that it contains contraband/evidence of crime
- **"Plain-view" doctrine**
  - **In public view**—no REP
  - **In private view**—officer on premises for lawful purpose and incriminating nature of item immediately apparent
- **Consent**
  - **Voluntary**—no threats of harm, compulsion, or false assertion of lawful authority (totality of circumstances)
  - **Third party**—can consent to own property search, but D's property only if agency relationship to D or D assumes the risk of search when giving right to third party to consent to search
- **Warrant authorizing wiretapping**
  - Limited period of time
  - PC that a specific crime has been or is about to be committed
  - Identify persons and describe particular conversations to be tapped

- o When to terminate tapping
- o Reveal intercepted conversation to court

4. **Standing to object**—D must show a legitimate expectation of privacy with regard to the search

5. **Exclusionary rule**

- **Fruit of the poisonous tree**—applies not only to evidence initially seized as a result of government illegality but also to secondary derivative evidence resulting from primary taint

- **Exceptions**

  - o **Inevitable discovery**—through lawful means

  - o **Independent source**—unrelated to tainted evidence

  - o **Attenuation**—passage of time and/or intervening events may purge primary taint

  - o **Good faith**

    - ▪ Applies to police relying in objective GF on either facially valid warrant later found invalid or existing law later held unconstitutional

    - ▪ **Does not apply** if no reasonable officer would rely on affidavit underlying warrant, warrant defective on its face, warrant obtained by fraud, magistrate wholly abandons judicial role, or warrant improperly executed

  - o **Isolated police negligence**—not enough to trigger the exclusionary rule; must be sufficiently deliberate that exclusion can meaningfully deter it

  - o **Knock and announce**—exclusionary rule doesn't apply when police fail to knock and announce their presence

  - o **In-court ID**—not fruit of an unlawful detention

- **Harmless error**—court can refuse to order new trial if error harmless beyond reasonable doubt, i.e., illegal evidence did not contribute to result

II. Fifth Amendment Rights and Privileges

A. The privilege against compulsory self-incrimination

1. **Rule**—no person shall be compelled in criminal case to testify against himself; applies to states through the Fourteenth Amendment

2. **Testimonial evidence only**—nontestimonial physical evidence (blood, urine, breathalyzer, etc.) not protected

3. **Proceedings**—applies to civil/criminal, formal/informal proceedings if answers provide reasonable possibility of incriminating D in future criminal proceeding

4. **Waiving privilege**—D waives by taking the stand and answering prosecution's questions; witness waives it by disclosing self-incriminating information in response to a specific question

B. The Fifth Amendment in a police interrogation context—any incriminating statement obtained as result of custodial interrogation may not be used against suspect at subsequent trial unless police inform subject of *Miranda* rights

1. **Custodial interrogation**

   - **Custodial**—substantial seizure where D reasonably believes he is not free to leave or is otherwise deprived of his freedom in significant way

   - **Interrogation**

     o Questioning and also words/actions likely to elicit incriminating response

     o Voluntary statements not protected

     o Confessions involuntary only if coerced by police (totality of circumstances)

2. **Compliance**

   - **Content/timing**—warning must be given before interrogation begins (or given again if stopped for long time), need not be verbatim, but must inform D of right to remain silent, any statement can be used in court, right to an attorney (or one will be appointed)

   - **Right to counsel**—D must make a specific, unambiguous statement asserting his desire to have counsel present, and once invoked, all interrogation must stop until counsel is present, unless D voluntarily initiates communication with police (including spontaneous statements) or 14-day break in custody and fresh *Miranda* warnings given

   - **Right to silence**—D must make a specific, unambiguous statement asserting his desire to remain silent (mere silence is not enough); interrogator must scrupulously honor right if invoked, but if D indicates desire to speak, subsequent interrogation lawful if D not coerced, and *Miranda* warnings must be given again

   - **Exceptions**

     o Public safety

     o Routine booking questions

     o Undercover police

   - **Waiver**—D must knowingly, voluntarily, and intelligently waive right (silence insufficient)

C. **Fruits of a tainted confession**

   1. Giving *Miranda* warning removes taint of prior *Miranda* violation

   2. Second confession inadmissible if circumstances make it clear police approach was intentional attempt to circumvent *Miranda*

D. **Fifth Amendment in the trial context**—D can refuse to testify at criminal trial or other proceedings that might incriminate him in future criminal proceedings

III. **Sixth Amendment**—right to public trial, confront witnesses against him, cross-examine witnesses, be present at his own trial, and assistance of counsel for his defense

A. **Applicability: right to counsel**

   1. **Types of proceedings**—any case in which actual/suspended incarceration is imposed

   2. **Applicability**—automatically applies at all critical stages of prosecution after formal proceedings begin, and right automatically attaches when the State initiates prosecution with indictment/formal charge, and ends at sentencing stage

   3. **Waiver**—D has right to refuse counsel and proceed pro se unless request is untimely or D unable/unwilling to follow rules of procedure

B. Offense-specific

1. ***Blockburger* test**—two different crimes in one criminal transaction deemed to be same offense unless each offense requires proof of an element that the other does not

2. ***Miranda* comparison**—Unlike *Miranda*, presence of counsel only applies to interrogations about offense charged; like *Miranda*, D may make knowing/voluntary waiver of right

C. Remedies for denial of counsel

1. **Effect on conviction**—D's conviction is automatically reversed even without specific showing of unfairness

2. **Effect on guilty plea**—D has right to withdraw it and it can't be used against him as an admission

3. **Nontrial proceeding**—harmless error analysis

4. **Defendant's statements to informants**—post-indictment statement to informant where situation is likely to induce D to incriminate himself without counsel is inadmissible (but police may place an informant in D's cell to listen without questioning D)

5. **Exclusionary rule**

    *   **Fruit of the poisonous tree**—the doctrine applies to statements and physical evidence obtained as result of violation; such evidence will be inadmissible

    *   **Impeachment**—incriminating evidence obtained in violation of Sixth Amendment may be used for impeachment

D. Ineffective assistance of counsel

1. **Reasonable competence presumed**—to prove ineffective, claimant must show:

    *   Counsel's representation fell below objective standard of reasonableness; and

    *   Counsel's deficient performance prejudiced D, resulting in unfair/unreliable outcome

        o   Mere inexperience, strategy, or failure to produce mitigating evidence insufficient

2. **Conflict of interest**—representation of Ds with conflicting interests may amount to ineffective assistance of counsel; must show actual conflict and an adverse effect on counsel's performance

    *   **Actual conflict**—occurs when a court determines that the defense attorney is subject to an obligation/unique personal interest that, if followed, would lead her to adopt a strategy other than that most favorable to the D

    *   **Adverse impact**—occurs when a plausible alternative strategy/tactic might have been pursued but was inherently in conflict with, or not undertaken, due to the attorney's other loyalties or interests

IV. Pre-Trial Procedures

A. Eyewitness ID procedures

1. **Types**

    *   **Corporeal**—"in-person" (e.g., lineups)

    *   **Non-corporeal**—not in-person (e.g., photo arrays)

2. **Sixth Amendment right to counsel at lineups**

    *   Sixth Amendment right to counsel at post-indictment lineup

- Inadmissible if violated but witness can ID the D at trial if ID has independent reliability

3. **Admissibility of pre- and post-indictment IDs**
    - **Two-prong test**
        - D must prove ID was impermissibly suggestive; and
        - Court must determine if it was nonetheless reliable (opportunity to view, degree of attention, accuracy of witness's description, level of certainty, length of time)
    - **Remedy**—suppression hearing (usually outside jury's presence) to determine admissibility; finding of impermissibly suggestive procedures will result in suppression

4. **Non-corporeal IDs**
    - No right to counsel during pre- or post-indictment photo spread (not a critical stage of prosecution)
    - Two-prong test for admissibility (above) applies

B. **Preliminary proceedings**
    1. **Probable cause to detain**
        - Must be held within 48 hours of arrest to determine PC
        - Fourth Amendment guarantees D right to be released if no PC
        - No remedy if detention is unlawful (other than exclusion of evidence)
    2. **Initial appearance**—judge advises D of the charges and his rights and appoints counsel if the defendant is indigent; judge may also decide conditions of bail and accept a plea

C. **Right to bail**—no constitutional right to bail, but denial of or excessive bail must comply with Due Process Clause

D. **Competency**—D must comprehend nature of proceedings against him and have ability to consult with lawyer with reasonable degree of rational understanding to be competent to stand trial

E. **Grand juries**—D has no right to present/confront witnesses or introduce evidence, and no dismissal due to procedural defect unless substantial impact on decision to indict

F. **State's duty to disclose**
    1. Affirmative duty to disclose any material evidence favorable to D and relevant to prosecution's case-in-chief that would negate guilt or diminish culpability/punishment
    2. Failure is grounds for reversal if D shows:
        - The evidence is favorable to the defendant, and
        - The failure to disclose caused prejudice against the defendant

V. **Trial**

A. **Jury trial**
    1. **Federal**—Sixth Amendment right to jury trial
    2. **State**—Under Fourteenth Amendment, D has a right to jury trial in criminal cases for serious offenses
    3. **Length**—right attaches for serious offenses (authorized sentence of more than six months imprisonment) regardless of actual penalty imposed

4. **Waiver**—D can waive right to jury trial and opt for trial by judge by obtaining court's approval, and freely/intelligently entering a voluntary waiver

5. **Jury**

- FRCP requires 12 members unless waived in writing and approved by court, but a verdict by 11 permitted if 12th juror excused for good cause after deliberations begin

- **Cross-section**—jury must be selected from a representative cross-section of the community, but actual jury selected need not be

- **Standing**—D can challenge selection process without showing of actual bias

- **Prima facie case**—for absence of representative cross-section:

  o Distinctive group excluded

  o Group not fairly represented in jury pool, and

  o Underrepresentation resulted from systematic exclusion of group

- **Neutral principles**—in response to claim of intentional racial discrimination in jury selection, state can use neutral/nonracial principles and must prove absence of discriminatory intent

- **Peremptory challenge**

  o **Discriminatory use**—Fourteenth Amendment prohibits challenges solely based on race/gender

    ▪ Moving party must establish prima facie case of discrimination

    ▪ Party who exercised the peremptory challenge must provide race-neutral explanation

    ▪ Moving party carries burden of proving other party's reason was pretextual

  o **Loss of challenge**—doesn't violate right to impartial jury

  o **Harmless error**—state can choose between harmless-error review or automatic reversal when judge in good faith erroneously denies D's peremptory challenge

- **Impartiality**

  o Accused entitled to trial by impartial jury, and claims of juror bias/misconduct subject to harmless-error rule

  o **Race**—D may question a potential jury member's views on race only when racial prejudice involved in case or when race is inextricably bound up in the case

  o **Capital punishment**—jurors opposed to death penalty can be removed for cause if opposition substantially impairs duties during sentencing

- **Sentencing enhancement**—enhancement of sentence by judge absent jury determination of existence of additional facts violates D's right to a jury trial

B. **Guilty pleas**

1. **Knowing and voluntary**

- Must be intelligent and voluntary, and made in presence of judge

- Judge must advise D and determine that plea not due to force or promises other than in plea agreement

2. **Right to counsel**—D has a right to counsel when entering a plea

3. **Plea bargain**

- D has no constitutional right to a plea bargain

- Plea made in response to prosecutor's threat to bring more serious charges does not violate Due Process Clause

- Prosecutor not required to disclose impeachment information or information related to affirmative defense

- **Enforcement**

  o Plea bargain is enforceable against prosecutor and D, but not the judge (judge can reject plea)

  o If prosecutor violates bargain, judge can decide whether to order specific performance of bargain or whether D can withdraw plea

  o If D violates bargain, prosecutor can have sentence vacated and reinstate original charges

4. **Effect on D's rights**—D can attack plea for ineffective assistance of counsel, lack of jurisdiction, or violation of due process

C. Speedy trial

1. **Due Process Clause**—protects pre-accusation delay and SoL is primary safeguard

2. **Sixth Amendment**—protects post-accusation delay and time period starts at time of arrest/formal charge

3. **Balancing test**—length and reason for delay, D's assertion of right, and prejudice to D

4. **Remedy**—dismissal of charges with prejudice

D. Fair trial

1. **Impartial judge**—no actual/apparent bias permitted

2. **Prosecutor**—cannot misstate law/fact, talk to D without counsel present, express opinions about D's guilt/innocence, make improper remarks about D, or comment on D's failure to testify

E. Right to confrontation

1. **Trial**—accused has right to encounter and cross-examine adverse witnesses and be present at any stage of trial

2. **Face-to-face**—not absolute right and may be prevented for public policy reasons

3. **Confrontation Clause and the hearsay rule**

- Out-of-court statements by witnesses that are "testimonial" are barred under the Confrontation Clause, unless the witnesses are unavailable and the defendant had a prior opportunity to cross-examine those witnesses

- Out-of-court testimonial statements are not barred by the Confrontation Clause when they are used for a purpose other than establishing the truth of the matter asserted

- **Testimonial statements**—the declarant would reasonably expect it to be used in a prosecution

- **Non-testimonial statements**—statements made for the primary purpose of assisting the police in the investigation of an ongoing emergency are not testimonial

4. **Admission of confession** (*Bruton* rule)—by non-testifying co-D at joint trial against D violates Sixth Amendment

F. Due process

1. **Permissive presumption**—regarding an element of an offense is not a due-process violation unless it is irrational

2. **Mandatory presumption**—per se violation

3. **Reasonable doubt**—prosecution must prove all elements beyond a reasonable doubt; state may place burden of proving an affirmative defense (e.g., insanity, self-defense, entrapment, or duress) on D

G. Sentencing

1. Applicable rights include right to counsel, confrontation, and cross-examination

2. Any fact (other than prior conviction) that can be used to increase statutorily prescribed maximum must be charged in indictment, submitted to jury, and established beyond a reasonable doubt

H. Cruel and unusual punishment (Eighth Amendment)

1. **Non-death penalty**—prisoner must show prison officials had actual knowledge of substantial risk to prisoners or serious injury, or sentence grossly disproportionate to crime

2. **Capital punishment**—can only be imposed under statute that provides clear/objective standards, specific/detailed guidance, and opportunity for rational review of process

VI. Post-Trial Considerations

A. Double jeopardy (Fifth Amendment)—protects against second prosecution for same offense after acquittal/conviction and against multiple punishments for the same offense

1. **Same offense**—*Blockburger* test applied if D's conduct can be prosecuted as two or more crimes so it generally bars successive prosecutions for greater/lesser included offenses unless jeopardy attaches to lesser-included offense before event necessary for greater offense

2. **Attachment**—when jury is impaneled/sworn in or when first witness is sworn in for bench trial

3. **Different jurisdictions**—D can be charged/convicted in federal and state court

4. **Civil actions**—not precluded by criminal punishment for same conduct

5. **Guilty plea**—not automatically waived

6. **Collateral estoppel**—applies when earlier decision must have necessarily determined issue on which collateral estoppel is sought by D

B. Convictions—D can attack conviction after unsuccessful appeal under writ of habeas corpus (civil action, so standard is preponderance of the evidence)

FINAL REVIEW OUTLINE: EVIDENCE

I. **Presentation of Evidence**

A. **Applicability of FRE**—FRE do not apply to:

1. Court's determination of a preliminary question of fact governing admissibility;

2. Grand jury proceedings; and

3. Criminal proceedings for issuance of a search or arrest warrant or a criminal summons; preliminary examination in a criminal case; extradition or rendition; consideration of bail or other release; sentencing; and granting or revoking probation or supervised release.

B. **Introduction of evidence**

1. **Role of judge/jury**

   - Judge—decides preliminary questions of competency of evidence

   - Jury—determines weight and credibility of the evidence

2. **Challenge to evidence ruling**

   - Ruling must affect **substantial right** of a party and the party must **notify** judge of error

     o Through an **objection** if evidence is admitted

     o Through an **offer of proof** if the evidence is excluded

   - Need not renew challenge after definitive ruling to preserve for appeal

   - **Plain error** (error that is obvious to the court)—if it affects a substantial right, grounds for reversal even without challenge

   - **Completeness rule**—for partial introduction of evidence, adverse party may compel introduction of omitted portion to help explain admitted evidence

   - **Limited Admissibility**—evidence may be admissible for one purpose but not for another; court must restrict evidence to its proper scope and instruct jury accordingly

3. **Judicial notice**—court's acceptance of a fact as true without requiring formal proof

   - Adjudicative facts (facts of the case at hand typically decided by jury)—subject to judicial notice if fact is not subject to reasonable dispute because:

     o Generally known within the community, or

     o Can be accurately and readily determined from reliable sources

   - Jury must be instructed that it **may or may not** accept any judicially noticed fact as conclusive in criminal cases; conclusive in civil cases

C. **Mode and order of presentation of evidence**

1. **Trial process**

   - Judiciary has control over order of witnesses/presentation of case to effectively determine truth and avoid wasted time or witness harassment; may also question or call witness

   - Court must exclude witnesses from the courtroom so that they do not hear the testimony of other witnesses except for (i) natural person parties to the case, (ii) individual designated as a representative of non-natural person parties,

(iii) persons essential to a party's presentation of the case, and (iv) persons whose presence is permitted by statute (i.e., victim)

2. Examination of witnesses

- Scope of cross generally limited to subject matter of direct and witness credibility; redirect and recross may be permitted, with scope w/in discretion of court

- **Motions to strike**—if witness's answer makes testimony improper, move to strike; only examining counsel may move to strike unresponsive answers

3. Form of questions

- Leading questions suggest answer within question

  o Direct—not permitted unless hostile witness, needed to develop witness's testimony, or witness struggles with communication

  o Cross-examination—no restrictions on using leading questions

- Improper questions

  o Compound—requires answers to multiple questions

  o Assumes facts not in evidence—assumes as true certain facts that have not been established yet

  o Argumentative—intended to provoke rather than elicit a factual response

  o Calls for conclusion/opinion—requires witness to draw conclusion or state opinion not qualified to make

  o Repetitive—already asked and answered

  o Lack of foundation—failure to establish necessary predicate, such as authentication of tangible evidence

D. Burdens and presumptions

1. Burden of proof

- Production—must produce legally sufficient evidence for each element of claim such that reasonable trier of fact could infer alleged fact has been proven (prima facie case)

- Persuasion

  o Civil—preponderance of the evidence (or clear and convincing for certain cases)

  o Criminal—beyond a reasonable doubt

2. Presumptions

- Rebuttable—shifts burden of production (not persuasion) to opposing party

- Conclusive—cannot be challenged by contrary evidence

- Destruction of evidence—generally raises rebuttable presumption that evidence would be unfavorable to destroying party if other party establishes (i) destruction intentional, (ii) evidence relevant, and (iii) other party acted with due diligence as to destroyed evidence.

II. Relevance

A. General considerations

1. **Generally, all relevant evidence is admissible** unless excluded by a specific rule, law, or constitutional provision. Evidence is relevant if **probative** and **material**

   - Probative—fact has a tendency to make a fact more or less probable than it would be without the evidence

   - Material—fact is of consequence in determining the action

2. **Direct and circumstantial evidence**

   - Direct—identical to factual proposition it is offered to prove

   - Circumstantial—indirect proof of factual proposition through inference from collateral facts

3. **Exclusion of relevant evidence** (Rule 403 exclusion)—if probative value is substantially outweighed by the danger of unfair prejudice (confusing issues, misleading jury, undue delay, wasting time, needless presentation of cumulative evidence)

4. **Relevance dependent on existence of fact**—proof must be sufficient to support finding that the fact does exist; may be admitted on condition that proof is later introduced

5. **Curative admission of irrelevant evidence**—admitted when necessary to rebut previously admitted irrelevant evidence to remove unfair prejudice

B. Character evidence (generalized information about a person's behavior)—typically inadmissible

1. **Civil cases**

   - Inadmissible to prove person acted in accordance with that character (or trait) on a particular occasion

   - Admissible when character is essential element of claim/defense instead of proving a person's conduct (usually defamation, negligent hiring/entrustment, & child custody)

2. **Criminal cases**

   - D's character

     o By prosecution—not permitted to introduce evidence of D's bad character to prove D has propensity to commit crimes so likely to have committed crime in question

     o By defense—D permitted to introduce evidence of good character as being inconsistent with type of crime charged, but must be pertinent to crime charged, and must be reputation/opinion testimony

     o D "opens the door"—once D offers evidence of his good character (or victim's bad character), prosecution can rebut D's claims by attacking D's character

   - Victim's character

     o By defense—D may introduce reputation/opinion evidence of victim's character when relevant to defense asserted (evidence of victim's sexual conduct very limited)

     o By prosecution—prosecution can offer rebuttal evidence of victim's good character when D has introduced evidence of victim's bad character (and trait for peacefulness in homicide case to rebut evidence homicide victim was first aggressor)

3. **Methods of proving character**—when character evidence is admissible, may be proven by testimony about person's reputation or witness opinion

4. **Impeachment**—character evidence of witness's untruthfulness is admissible/relevant to impeach witness

C. **Prior bad acts**—not admissible to show D's criminal propensity to prove he committed crime in question

1. **MIMIC evidence** (**M**otive, **I**ntent, absence of **M**istake, **I**dentity or **C**ommon plan)

   - Admissible

   - Subject to admissibility restrictions, may be introduced for any other purpose except to prove D committed the charged crime because D had propensity to commit crimes

   - When criminal D requests, prosecution must provide reasonable notice of the general nature of MIMIC evidence prosecution intends to offer at trial; must give notice before trial unless court excuses lack or pretrial notice for good cause

2. **Specific acts as character evidence**

   - Civil—when character evidence is an essential element of claim/defense, can be proven by specific acts or opinion/reputation testimony

   - Criminal—specific acts not admissible to show D's criminal propensity; when character is essential element of charged crime, D may offer specific prior acts inconsistent w/ element of crime

   - Cross-examination—character witness can be asked about specific acts committed by person witness is testifying about

D. **Habit evidence**

1. **Definition**—a person's particular routine reaction to a specific set of circumstances

2. Evidence of person's habit (or organization's routine) admissible to prove person acted in accordance with habit on a particular occasion

3. **May be admitted without corroboration** and without an eyewitness

III. **Witnesses**

A. **Competence**

1. **Personal knowledge**—non-expert witness must have personal knowledge of matter in order to testify

2. **Oath**—witness must give an oath or affirmation to testify truthfully

3. **Judge**—cannot testify at trial

4. **Juror**—can testify at trial in limited circumstances, but generally may only testify after trial about (i) extraneous prejudicial information brought to jury's attention (ii) improper outside influence, or (iii) mistakes on verdict form

5. **Child**—can testify if able to differentiate truth from falsehood

6. **Dead Man's statutes**—protects decedent's estate from parties with financial interest in estate; predecessors in interest or those directly affected financially may be disqualified

   - Waiver—protected party can waive by failing to object to disqualified witness or introducing protected evidence

   - Not applicable in criminal cases

B. Impeachment—challenge to witness's testimony can be based on character for truthfulness, bias, ability to perceive/testify accurately, contradictory prior statement, or another witness

1. **Witness's character for truthfulness**

   - Cannot bolster witness credibility, and evidence of truthful character only admissible after witness's truthful character directly attacked

   - Opinion/reputation testimony—admissible to attack witness's character for untruthfulness

   - Specific instances of conduct—generally not admissible as indication of character for truthfulness

     o On cross-examination OK if probative of witness' truthfulness or truthfulness of another witness about whose character the witness has testified

     o When witness denies specific act, extrinsic evidence not admissible to prove specific act (exception exists for criminal convictions)

2. **Criminal conviction** (but not arrest)—can be used to impeach witness's character for truthfulness

   - Crimes involving dishonesty/false statement can be used to impeach any witness for any conviction

   - Conviction NOT involving dishonesty/false statement—admissible to impeach witness only if crime is punishable by death or imprisonment > 1 year

     o If witness is criminal D—admissible only if its probative value outweighs the prejudicial effect to that D (stricter than usual balancing test)

     o Other witnesses—generally admissible; discretion to exclude if probative value is substantially outweighed by its prejudicial effect

   - Conviction or release > 10 years ago—admissible if probative value substantially outweighs prejudicial effect and reasonable written notice of intent to use evidence

   - Pardon—conviction not admissible if subject of a pardon, annulment, or other action based on a finding of innocence; pending appeal does not prevent impeachment

   - Juvenile adjudication—not admissible to impeach D; may impeach other witness's character for truthfulness in criminal case if an adult conviction for that offense would be admissible and admitting it is necessary to determine guilt or innocence

3. **Prior inconsistent statements**—can be used to impeach if inconsistent with material part of the witness's testimony

   - Extrinsic evidence of prior inconsistent statement admissible only if witness has chance to explain/deny statement and opposing party can examine witness about it (this opportunity not required for hearsay declarants or opposing party statements)

4. **Bias or interest**—can be used to impeach witness because relevant to credibility

5. **Sensory competence**—can be impeached for deficiency in capacities to perceive, recall, or relate information

6. **Impeachment of a hearsay declarant**—credibility of declarant can be attacked by any evidence admissible if declarant had testified as witness; if declarant called as a witness, he can be examined as if under cross-examination

7. **Rehabilitation of a witness**

   - Explain/clarify on redirect examination

- Offer opinion/reputation evidence of witness's character for truthfulness (only if character was attacked on that ground)

- Offer prior consistent statement to rebut express/implied charge that witness lied due to improper motive/influence

8. **Religious opinions and beliefs**—cannot be used to impeach credibility, but admissible to show bias/interest

9. **Contradictory evidence**—can be used to impeach if it contradicts witness's testimony, including contradictory material extrinsic evidence

10. **Collateral issues**—generally, cannot impeach credibility of witness by introducing extrinsic evidence of a collateral matter

C. **Recollection refreshed**

1. **Present recollection refreshed**—witness may examine any item to refresh witness's present recollection; testimony must be based on refreshed recollection, not item

- Adverse party may inspect item and enter relevant portions as evidence

- Item may be redacted by court, and admissible for substantive purposes only if satisfies other restrictions on admissibility

2. **Past recollection recorded**—memo/record about matter witness once had knowledge of but now has insufficient recollection of to testify about may be admissible under recorded recollection hearsay exception; may be read into evidence, but received as an exhibit only if offered by an adverse party

D. **Opinion testimony**

1. **Subject matter of testimony**

- Lay witness opinion—admissible if based upon the perception of witness and helpful to clear understanding of witness's testimony or determination of a fact in issue

   Expert witness testimony—subject matter must be scientific, technical or some other specialized knowledge (testimony is **reliability**) that helps trier of fact understand evidence or determine fact at issue (testimony is **relevant**)

2. **Qualified expert**

- **Requirements:**
  o Qualified as an expert by knowledge, skill, experience, training, or education
  o Testimony based on sufficient facts/data
  o Testimony product of reliable principles and methods
  o Witness applied principles/methods reliably to facts of case, and
  o Reasonable degree of certainty (i.e., "probably")

- **Ultimate issue**—expert may not state an opinion about whether criminal D had the requisite mental state

- **Basis of opinion**—opinion based on inadmissible facts admissible if experts in the particular field would reasonably rely on those kinds of facts and data in forming an opinion on the subject; may disclose underlying facts to the jury if probative value substantially outweighs prejudicial effect; need not ask in form of hypothetical

IV. Tangible Evidence

A. **Authentication**—all tangible evidence must be authenticated with sufficient evidence to support a finding that the thing is what its proponent claims it is

1. **Physical objects**—generally authenticated through **personal knowledge, distinctive characteristics, or c**hain of custody (when applicable)

   - Reproductions (photos, diagrams, maps)—authenticated by testimony of witness with personal knowledge that object accurately depicts what its proponent claims it does

   - X-rays, EKGs—process used was accurate, machine works, and operator qualified

2. **Documentary evidence**—usually authenticated by stipulation, eyewitness testimony, or handwriting verification

   - Ancient documents—at least 20 years old, in condition unlikely to create suspicion, and found in a likely place if it were authentic

   - Public records—recorded/filed in public office

   - Reply letter—written in response to communication

   - Handwriting verification—comparison or non-expert with personal knowledge

   - Self-authenticating—doesn't require extrinsic evidence (e.g., gov't authorized documents, certified public records, or newspapers)

3. **Oral statements**

   - **Voice ID**—can be identified by any person who has heard voice at any time

   - **Telephone**—party to telephone conversation may authenticate statements made during that conversation if caller recognized the speaker's voice; speaker knew facts that only a particular person would know; caller dialed number believed to be speaker's, and speaker identified himself upon answering; or caller dialed a business and spoke about business regularly conducted over the phone

B. **Best Evidence Rule (BER)**

1. **Original document (or reliable duplicate)**—must be produced to prove contents of writing when contents are at issue or witness is relying on contents when testifying

   - Duplicate reliable unless there is a genuine question as to the authenticity of the original; or the circumstances make it unfair to admit the duplicate

     o Handwritten copies of original are not duplicates

   - Original not required when originals are lost or destroyed in good faith, party against whom original would be offered failed to produce it, or document not closely related to controlling issue

   - Contents of a public record are generally proved by a certified copy

   - **Voluminous documents**—contents of voluminous documents may be presented as summary if such contents cannot be conveniently examined in court; proponent must make originals or duplicates available for examination and copying by other parties at a reasonable time and place; court may order proponent to produce the originals or duplicates in court

   - May prove contents of original by admission by party against whom it is offered without accounting for original

C. **Parol Evidence Rule (PER)**—operates to exclude evidence that, if introduced, would change the terms of a written agreement

    1. **Complete integration**—contains all terms to which the parties agreed; PER in effect and no extrinsic evidence is admissible

    2. **Partial integration**—contains some but not all agreed upon terms

       • Extrinsic evidence that adds to writing admissible

       • Evidence that contradicts not admissible

    3. **Exceptions—Extrinsic evidence always admissible to clarify ambiguity, prove course of dealings, show fraud/duress/mistake, or s**how presence/absence of consideration

    4. **Only evidence of prior or contemporaneous negotiations is subject to the rule**; negotiations after contract executed not prohibited by the rule

V. Privileges and Other Policy Exclusions

A. Privileges:

    1. **Confidential communications**—necessary for a privilege to apply

       • If overheard, privilege destroyed unless (i) no knowledge of third party's presence; or (ii) third party is necessary to assist in communication (e.g., a translator)

       • Privilege waived if privilege holder (i) fails to timely assert it, (ii) voluntarily discloses communication, or (iii) contractually waives it in advance

    2. **Spousal privilege**

       • Spousal immunity

           ○ Married person cannot be compelled to testify against his spouse in any criminal proceeding regardless of who D is

           ○ Witness spouse holds privilege in federal court and majority of states; party spouse holds privilege in minority of states

           ○ Applies to testimony about events before/during marriage; privilege expires upon divorce or annulment

       • Confidential marital communications

           ○ Spousal communication during marriage is privileged when made in reliance on sanctity of marriage

           ○ Majority—Both spouses hold privilege in civil and criminal cases

           ○ Privilege begins with marriage and continues indefinitely

       • Neither spousal privilege applies when one spouse sues another or spouse is charged with a crime against the other or the children of either

    3. **Attorney-client privilege**

       • Confidential communication between client (who holds privilege) & attorney for the purpose of seeking legal advice or representation (attorney doesn't need to give advice or agree to representation)

           ○ Privilege exists until waived—can survive client's death

- o Federal law extends privilege to communications by a non-control-group employee (i) about matters within the employee's corporate duties (ii) made for the purpose of securing legal advice for corporation client

- **Exceptions** for communications:
  - o Made to enable or aid commission of what client knew or should have known was crime/fraud
  - o Relevant to dispute between attorney and client (e.g., a malpractice allegation)
  - o Relevant to dispute between parties who claim through the same deceased client
  - o Between former co-clients who are now adverse to each other

- **Work product**—not "communication," but protected unless party seeking disclosure (i) demonstrates **substantial need**, and (ii) cannot obtain the information by any other means without **undue hardship**

4. **Physician-patient privilege**
   - Statement privileged so long as made for the purpose of obtaining medical treatment
   - Patient holds privilege
   - Privilege doesn't exist if
     - o Info acquired for reasons other than treatment
     - o Patient's physical condition is at issue
     - o Statement is part of crime
     - o Dispute exists between patient and physician
     - o Patient contractually waives privilege
     - o Federal question case

5. **Psychotherapist-patient privilege**—patient holds privilege, but doesn't exist if patient's mental condition is at issue, statement was result of state ordered exam or case is commitment proceeding against patient

6. **Self-incrimination**—Fifth Amendment protection allowing witness to refuse to give testimony that may tend to incriminate him
   - Covers only current statements
   - Does not apply to physical characteristics or mannerisms
   - Does not apply to corporations or other organizations

7. **Other privileges**
   - Clergy-penitent
   - Accountant-client
   - Professional journalist—no federal privilege regarding source
   - Government privilege—government privileged against disclosing informant's identity in a criminal case and communication of official information by or to public officials

B. **Public policy exclusions**

1. **Subsequent remedial measures**
   - Not admissible to prove negligence, culpable conduct, defective product/design, or need for warning/instruction
   - Admissible for other purposes such as impeachment, ownership/control, or feasibility of precautionary measures

2. **Compromise offers and negotiations**
   - Not admissible by either party to prove/disprove validity or amount of disputed claim, or for impeachment by prior inconsistent statement or contradiction
   - Admissible to prove bias or prejudice of witness, negate claim of undue delay, or prove obstruction of criminal investigation/prosecution
   - Admissible in a subsequent criminal case if made during compromise negotiations w/ governmental agency during its regulatory, investigative, or enforcement authority

3. **Evidence of payment, offers, or promise to pay medical expenses**—not admissible to prove liability for the injury, but statements that accompany the payment, offer, or promise to pay are admissible

4. **Plea negotiation**—withdrawn guilty pleas, pleas of no contest, and statements made while negotiating plea bargain or during plea proceeding are not admissible
   - **Exceptions**—another statement made during the same plea or negotiation has already been admitted and fairness requires that the statement in question also be admitted; also admissible in subsequent perjury prosecution if they were false statements made under oath, on the record, and with counsel present

5. **Liability insurance**
   - Not admissible to prove whether person acted negligently or wrongfully
   - Admissible to prove agency, ownership/control, or witness's bias/prejudice

6. **Sexual conduct**
   - Victim's conduct
     - **Rape shield**—evidence of sexual behavior/predisposition generally not admissible in any proceeding involving sexual misconduct
     - Specific acts admissible to prove D not source of physical evidence in criminal case
     - Sexual behavior/predisposition of victim admissible in civil case if probative value substantially outweighs unfair prejudice
     - Reputation admissible only if placed in controversy by victim
   - Defendant's conduct—evidence of sexual assault in criminal/civil case admissible to prove any relevant matter (not limited to convictions)

VI. **Hearsay**

A. **Definition**—out-of-court statement offered to prove the truth of matter asserted

1. **Declarant**—must be a person

2. **Statement**—oral, written, or assertive nonverbal conduct

3. **Offered to prove the truth of the matter asserted**—if offered to prove something other than the truth of the matter asserted (legally operative facts, effect on recipient, state of mind, and impeachment), not hearsay

4. **Multiple hearsay**—hearsay within hearsay may be admissible as long as each part of combined statement conforms to hearsay exception

B. **Non-hearsay**

1. **Prior statements**—declarant must testify at present trial to be admissible; cannot apply if witness is dead or otherwise unavailable to testify

   - Prior inconsistent statements made under penalty of perjury admissible to impeach declarant's credibility and as substantive evidence

   - Prior consistent statements admissible to rebut express/implied charge that declarant recently fabricated it or acted with improper motive, but must be made before declarant had reason to fabricate

   - Prior statement of identification of a person after perceiving that person is admissible as non-hearsay substantive evidence even if witness has no memory of identification

2. **Opposing party's statement**—made by party to current litigation; admissible without personal knowledge and can be in form of an opinion; need not have been against the party's interest at the time that it was made

   - **Judicial admission**—an admission made during pleading, discovery process or proceeding is conclusive evidence

     o Withdrawn guilty plea generally not admissible in subsequent proceedings

   - **Adoptive admission**—statement of another person that party expressly/impliedly adopts as his own

     o Silence in response to a statement is considered an adoptive admission if:

       ▪ The person was present and heard and understood the statement;

       ▪ The person had the ability and opportunity to deny the statement; and

       ▪ A reasonable person similarly situated would have denied the statement.

   - **Vicarious statements**—statement made by one person imputed to another based upon relationship between them (employee/agent, authorized speaker, co-conspirators)

VII. **Hearsay exceptions**

A. **Declarant unavailable as witness**

1. **Unavailable declarant** unless unavailable due to procurement/wrongdoing of proponent in order to prevent the declarant from testifying at or attending the trial

2. **Former testimony** given as witness is not hearsay if party against whom testimony is offered had an opportunity and similar motive to develop testimony

3. **Dying declaration**

   - Declarant believes her death is imminent and statement pertains to cause/circumstances of her death (need not actually die)

   - Applies only in homicide prosecutions and civil cases

4. **Statement against interest**—was against declarant's proprietary/pecuniary interest at time made and reasonable person would not have made statement unless it was true

5. **Statement of personal/family history**—birth, adoption, marriage, divorce or other similar fact of personal or family history

6. **Statement against party that caused declarant's unavailability**—statement offered against party that wrongfully caused declarant's unavailability is not excluded

B. **Declarant's availability as a witness immaterial**

1. **Present sense impression**—statement explaining or describing event/condition made while or immediately after declarant perceived it

2. **Excited utterance**—statement about startling event/condition while declarant is under stress of excitement that it caused

3. **Statement of mental, emotional or physical condition**: Statement of then-existing state of mind (present intent, motive or plan) or emotional, sensory or physical condition

4. **Statement made for medical diagnosis/treatment**—describing medical history or past/present symptoms is not hearsay if it is made for purpose of medical diagnosis or treatment; can be made to physicians, other medical personnel or even family members; need not necessarily be made by the patient

5. **Recorded recollection** (witness no longer able to testify)—record not excluded if on a matter that witness once knew, made when matter was fresh in witness's memory, accurately reflects witness's knowledge, and witness states that he cannot recall even after consulting record on the stand

6. **Business records** (extends to any organization, including nonprofit)—record must be kept in course of regularly conducted business activity, making of record was regular practice, and record was made at or near the time by someone with knowledge

7. **Public records**—statement of public office/agency that sets out activities of office, observation of person under duty to report (but not police in a criminal case), or factual findings of a legal investigation

8. **Learned treatises**—statement in treatise, periodical or pamphlet not excluded if expert witness relied on statement during direct/cross, and publication is reliable authority

9. **Judgment of previous conviction**

   • Final judgment must be entered after trial or guilty plea

   • Conviction was for crime punishable by death or imprisonment for > 1 year

   • Evidence offered to prove any fact essential to sustain judgment

C. **Residual exception**—"catch-all" exception for a statement that is not otherwise covered by the FRE

VIII. Constitutional Limitations

A. **Hearsay Evidence Restrictions**—two grounds

1. **Sixth Amendment—Confrontation Clause and Hearsay Evidence**

   • Requires declarant to be unavailable and D had prior opportunity to cross-examine declarant

   • Testimonial statements—Objective analysis—if primary purpose is emergency assistance, not testimonial

   • Unavailability of the declarant—D must have purpose of making declarant unavailable, and fact that D made declarant unavailable does not mean he had purpose if he is on trial for the act that made witness unavailable

2. **Fourteenth Amendment—Due Process Clause**—may prevent application of hearsay rule when rule unduly restricts D's ability to mount defense

B. **Face-to-Face Confrontation**—Confrontation clause prefers face-to-face confrontation, but can be denied if important public interest at stake

FINAL REVIEW OUTLINE: REAL PROPERTY

I. **Ownership**

   A. **Present estates**—an estate is a freehold if immobile and for indeterminate duration

   1. **Fee simple absolute (FSA)**—absolute ownership of potentially infinite duration

      - "To A" or "to A and his heirs"
      - Freely alienable and no accompanying future interest

   2. **Defeasible fee**—potentially infinite duration, subject to termination by the occurrence of an event

      - **FS determinable (FSD)**
        - Limited by specific durational language (e.g., "so long as," "while," "during," "until")
        - Automatically terminates upon happening of a stated event and reverts to grantor
        - Alienable, devisable, and descendible, but always subject to a stated condition
        - Grantor retains possibility of reverter

      - **FS subject to condition subsequent (FSSCS)**
        - A present fee simple that is limited by specific conditional language (e.g., "upon condition that," "provided that," "but if," or "if it happens that")
        - Alienable, devisable, and descendible
        - Grantor reserves right to terminate estate upon happening of a stated event (will terminate only if the grantor affirmatively demonstrates intent to terminate)
        - Grantor must specifically retain right to reenter (devisable/descendible)

      - **FS subject to executory interest (FSSEI)**
        - A present fee simple that is limited by specific durational or conditional language
          - Automatically terminates upon happening of stated event, and
          - Title passes to third party (i.e., someone other than the grantor)
        - "To A, but if X event occurs, then to B"
        - The future interest held by the third party is an executory interest

   3. **Life estate (LE)**—present possessory estate fully transferable during measuring life

      - If third party: "to A for life," "to B after the life of A," or "to B for the life of C" (*pur autre vie*); "to A for life, but if he drinks, then to B" (*defeasible*)
      - If measured by the grantee's life, not devisable/descendible
      - Life tenant's (LT) rights/duties:
        - Right to possess
        - Right to collect rents/profits, lease/sell/mortgage (must pay taxes on income or rental value of land)
        - Duty not to commit waste

B. **Waste**—may limit the rights of a holder of any estate except a fee simple

   1. **Affirmative**—occurs when overt conduct causes a decrease in property value; can't consume/exploit natural resources unless prior use; must make reasonable repairs

   2. **Permissive**—occurs when tenant permits the premises to deteriorate through neglect, failure to preserve, or a failure to reasonably protect the property; tenant must make reasonable repairs (up to amount of income produced by property) and pay all property taxes and mortgage interest

   3. **Ameliorative**—occurs when a change in use of the property increases its value; life tenant may alter structures on the property when a substantial and permanent change in the neighborhood makes it necessary in order to continue reasonable use of the property, so long as the property value is not diminished

C. **Concurrent estates (co-tenancies)**

   1. **Tenancy in common (TC)** (default co-tenancy)

      - Two or more grantees with unity of possession

      - No right of survivorship (ROS)

      - Each co-tenant holds undivided interest with unrestricted rights to possess whole

      - Interest freely devisable/transferable

   2. **Joint tenancy (JT)**

      - Requires express language creating JT

      - Two or more tenants own the property with ROS

      - Interest is alienable (but not devisable/descendible)

      - **Four unities (PITT)**

         o Equal rights to **p**ossess the whole

         o With identical equal **i**nterests

         o Created at the same **t**ime

         o By the same **t**itle

      - **Severance**—converts a JT into a TC (but only with respect to the severed share)

         o **Sale**—don't need consent; severs JT as to seller but JT of non-transferors remains intact

         o **Mortgage**—severs JT under title theory, but not under lien theory

         o **Judicial lien**—the lien typically will not sever the JT; severance occurs when the property is levied and sold

   3. **Tenancy by entirety (TE)**

      - JT between married persons with ROS

      - Neither party can alienate or encumber the property without the consent of the other

      - Not recognized in community-property states

   4. **Rights/obligations**

      - Each co-T has the right to possess the entire property and is generally not required to pay rent when other co-Ts do not use the property (unless co-T has been ousted)

- A co-T is liable to other co-Ts for third-party rents

- A co-T can collect contribution from other co-Ts for operating expenses (e.g., taxes) but not for repairs or improvements (unless in an accounting or partition action)

- **Partition**—a TC or JT (but not a TE) generally has the right to unilaterally partition property; a partition in kind, preferred by courts, is a physical division of the property

D. **Future interests (FI)**—an interest in presently existing property or in a gift or trust, which may commence in use, possession, or enjoyment sometime in the future

1. **Reversion**—held by grantor who transfers a LE or estate for years without conveying the remaining FI to a third party; not subject to RAP

2. **Possibility of reverter**—automatically reverts to grantor upon occurrence of stated event when FSD conveyed

3. **Right of reentry**—held by grantor after FSSCS granted

4. **Remainder**—FI that becomes possessory upon the expiration of a prior estate of known fixed duration created in same conveyance in which the remainder is created

   - **Vested**—not subject to any conditions precedent; ascertainable grantee

     o **Vested subject to open (class gifts)**

       ▪ **Class gift**—group of unspecified persons whose number, identity, and share of the interest is determined in the future

       ▪ If at least one class member is qualified to take possession at the time of the conveyance, then each class member's share is subject to partial diminution because additional takers not yet ascertained can still vest

       ▪ Once a class closes, any person who might otherwise have become a class member cannot claim an interest in the property as a class member

       ▪ **Rule of convenience**—closes the class when any class member is entitled to immediate possession

     o **Vested subject to complete**—the occurrence of a condition subsequent will completely divest the remainder

   - **Contingent**—created in an unascertainable grantee or is subject to an express condition precedent to grantee's taking (because of unknown beneficiary or known beneficiary subject to condition precedent that has not yet occurred)

5. **Executory interests**—FI in third party (not a remainder) that cuts the prior estate short upon the occurrence of a specified condition; transferable and subject to RAP

   - **Shifting**—cuts short a prior estate created in same conveyance, so the estate shifts from one grantee to another grantee upon the happening of a condition

   - **Springing**—divests the grantor's interest or fills a gap in possession in which the estate reverts to grantor

6. **Transferability**—remainders/executory interests are transferable inter vivos and devisable/descendible

7. **Rule Against Perpetuities (RAP)**

   - Specific FIs are valid only if they must vest or fail by the end of a life in being plus 21 years

   - **Affected FIs**—RAP applies to contingent remainders, vested remainders subject to open, executory interests, powers of appointment, rights of first refusal, and options;

RAP does **not** apply to FIs that revert to the grantor (reversion, possibility of reverter, right of reentry)

- **Measuring lives**—must be human; there can be more than one; if not specified, then the measuring life is the life directly related to the FI that is subject to RAP

- **Creation events**—RAP tests the FI as of the time that it is created

- **"Vest or fail" requirement**—if there is **any possibility** that it will not be known whether the interest will vest or fail within the applicable period, then RAP has not been satisfied

- **Effect of violation**—except in rare cases when voiding the FI undermines the grantor's intent, only the offending interest fails

- **Special rule for class gifts** ("bad as to one, bad as to all")—if RAP voids a transfer to any class member, then the transfer is void as to all class members, even those whose interests have already vested

  - **Rule of convenience**—can operate to prevent application of RAP to a class transfer, but the application of the rule of convenience to a class transfer does not automatically forestall the application of RAP

  - **Exceptions**—transfers of a specific dollar amount to each class member; transfers to a subclass that vests at a specific time

- **Common violations:**

  - **"Survival beyond age 21" condition**

  - **Fertile octogenarian**

  - **Unborn spouse**

  - **Defeasible fee followed by executory interest**

  - **Conditional passage of interest**

II. Landlord (L) and Tenant (T)

A. Types of tenancies

1. Tenancy for years

- Any fixed period of time

- Created by express agreement

- Term longer than one year must be in writing to satisfy Statute of Frauds (SoF)

- Automatically terminates at end of term (no notice needed)

- May be terminated before the end of the term (e.g., breach of lease covenant gives rise to right to terminate)

2. Periodic tenancy

- Repetitive, ongoing estate by set periods of time with no predetermined termination date

- Automatically renews at end of each period unless valid termination notice

- SoF does not apply

- Created by express agreement, implication (no mention of duration), or operation of law (holdover tenant)

- **Termination notice**—must be given before last period begins; late notice is effective for the next period; generally effective as of the last day of the period

3. **Tenancy at will**

   - Does not have a specific term; continues until terminated by L or T

   - Created by express agreement or by implication

   - May be terminated by either party at any time, but reasonable demand to vacate usually required; may also be terminated by operation of law

4. **Tenancy at sufferance (holdover tenancy)**

   - T wrongfully remains in possession after the expiration of a lease

   - T is bound by terms of the lease the existed before expiration, including payment of rent

   - Tenancy lasts until T vacates, L evicts T, or L elects to hold T to periodic tenancy

B. **Duties of the tenant**

1. **Pay rent**—duty to pay unless premises destroyed (lease terminated and tenant excused), or material breach by landlord

2. **Avoid waste**

   - **Affirmative waste**—T is prohibited from committing voluntary waste

   - **Ameliorative waste**—T may make changes to physical condition of property that increase the property value if reasonably necessary for T to use property in reasonable manner, unless L and T agree otherwise

   - **Permissive waste**—unless relieved by lease, statute, or ordinance, T has a duty to repair the premises to keep it in its pre-rental condition; no duty to repair normal wear and tear (unless L and T agree)

3. **Repair**—non-residential leases, T may be contractually liable for all damage to property (unless caused by L)

4. **L's remedies for T's breach**

   - **Failure to pay rent**—L can sue for damages **and** evict

   - **Abandonment**—L can retake premises if T abandons but duty L must mitigate damages by re-renting premises; T will be liable for any deficiency

   - **Holdover T**—L can accept holdover tenant as periodic tenant or tenant at sufferance or sue after notice to vacate

C. **Duties of L**

1. **Possession**—L must deliver actual physical possession or no obligation for T to pay rent

2. **Repair**—except for T damages, L must repair for residential but not for commercial leases

3. **Warranty of habitability (residential)**—premises must be fit for basic human habitation (health/safety), and if breached:

   - T must notify L of defect and give reasonable time to repair, **and**

   - Then T can refuse to pay rent, make reasonable repairs and deduct cost from future rent, or remain in possession, pay rent, and seek damages

4. **Covenant of quiet enjoyment (commercial and residential)**

- T has a right to quiet use and enjoyment of the premises without interference from L
- L has duty to control other tenants' nuisance in common areas
- **Eviction**
  - **Actual**—if L excludes T from premises, then lease is terminated and T's obligation to pay rent ends
  - **Partial**—T excused from paying rent for L's partial eviction, but must pay reasonable rental value if partial eviction by third party with superior claim; T not excused from paying rent for partial eviction by adverse possessor/trespasser
  - **Constructive**—substantial interference caused by L's actions or failure to act, T must give notice of problem, L fails to respond, and T **must vacate** premises within reasonable time after L fails to fix problem
  - **Retaliatory**—L may not evict residential T for reporting housing code violations

D. Tort liabilities

1. **Tenant**—duty of care to invitees/licensees/foreseeable trespassers and may be liable for dangerous conditions/activities

2. **Landlord**
   - **CL**—liable for injuries in common/public areas, non-common areas under L's control, or from hidden defect/faulty repair by L or L's agent
   - **Modern trend**—general duty of reasonable care; liability for defects existing prior to T's occupancy, failure to make required repairs, and criminal activities of third parties who injure Ts

E. Assignment/sublease

1. **Assignment**—complete transfer of T's remaining lease term

2. **Sublease**—any transfer for less than the entire duration of lease

3. **Parties**
   - **Assignee tenant**
     - Assignee-T liable to L for rent/covenants running with lease because assignee-T is in privity of estate (P/E) with L
     - If assignee-T reassigns lease, his P/E with L ends and the subsequent T is now in P/E with L
   - **Sublease tenant** (sub-T)
     - Not liable for rent/covenants in lease to L because not in P/E or privity of contract (P/C) with L (still liable to original lessee)
     - If sub-T expressly assumes covenants, then personally liable to L
     - Sub-T can enforce all covenants made by original lessee in sublease, but not any made by L
   - **Original tenant**
     - Liable for lease covenants unless **novation** by L because still in P/C with L
     - P/E with L ends upon assignment but not sublease

- **Landlord assignments**
  - Generally, L may assign lease rights to a third party (e.g., as part of a transfer of ownership) but L remains liable to T for all covenants in the lease
  - T must pay rent to assignee-L and obey lease covenants; assignee-L must perform any burden imposed by lease covenant
  - **Attornment** (T's acknowledgement of a new L)—usually arises automatically upon payment of rent to assignee-L or notice to T but formal acknowledgement of an assignee-L's ownership may be required in commercial leases

4. **Limitations**
   - T can still assign/sublet if lease prohibits, but L can terminate for breach and recover damages
   - L can only withhold permission to grant assignment or sublease on **commercially reasonable grounds**

III. **Disputes About Ownership in Land**

   A. **Adverse possession (AP)**

   1. **Continuous/uninterrupted**
      - Through statutory period (20 years at CL)
      - Seasonal use okay if consistent with type of property
      - Tacking permitted, but no gaps and via non-hostile connections only (e.g., descent, devise, contract, or deed)

   2. **Actual**—actual entry giving exclusive possession that is open/notorious, but if only actually possess portion of property, constructive AP gives title to whole

   3. **Hostile**—must possess the land without owner's permission and with intent to claim land against claims of others

   4. **Exclusive**—possession cannot be shared with true owner, but two or more people can adversely possess as tenants in common

   B. **Land sales contract**

   1. **Statute of Frauds (SoF)**
      - **Formalities**—land sales K must be in writing, signed by the party to be charged, and contain all of the essential terms (parties, property description, terms of price/payment)
      - **Part performance** (SoF exception)—buyer takes possession of land, buyer remits all or part of purchase price, and/or buyer makes substantial improvements (most jurisdictions require at least two acts)
      - **Detrimental reliance**—specific performance (SP) permitted when party seeking enforcement has reasonably relied on K and would suffer hardship

   2. **Performance**
      - **Marketable title**
        - Title free from defects or unreasonable risk of litigation
        - Seller generally not required to deliver marketable title until closing

- Buyer can rescind/recover out-of-pocket and earnest money payments, sue for breach, or sue for SP with an abatement of purchase price
- **Time of the essence**—not enforced unless part of K (express/implied), but party failing to perform on closing date is in breach
- **Implied warranty of fitness**—only for new homes, and disclosure duty of known material physical defects not readily observable/known to buyer for all homes
- **Tender of performance**—concurrent conditions, so if one party repudiates then non-repudiating party excused, but B must give S sufficient time to cure title defect
- **Merger**—land sales K obligations merge into deed upon delivery unless obligations collateral to/independent of conveyance

3. **Remedies for breach**
- **Damages**—difference between K price and market value (some jurisdictions: limited to B's out-of-pocket expenses if seller (S) is unable to deliver marketable title but acted in good faith)
  - **Buyer's deposit as liquidated damages**—generally, deposits of no more than 10 percent of the purchase price have been found to be reasonable liquidated damages, but courts may consider factors relating to the transaction or refuse to enforce liquidated damages clauses when the S suffers no actual loss
- **Specific performance** (mutuality of remedies)

4. Equitable conversion—S's interest converted by K into interest in proceeds of sale not in RP, once K is signed, B is owner of land subject to the condition he pay the purchase price at closing, but in interim between K and closing, B bears risk of loss if land is destroyed

5. **Security interests in real property**
- Mortgages must be in writing
- Debtor/mortgagor has title and right to possession until foreclosure and creditor/mortgagee has lien and right to land if there is default
- Lien stays on land if mortgage instrument properly recorded
- Creditor can foreclose by judicial proceedings which terminate junior interests (subordinate interests must be joined or remain on land and B takes subject to senior interests)

C. **Delivery and recording of deeds**

1. **Delivery**
- At time of transfer, grantor must **intend to make present transfer** of property interest to grantee
  - Rebuttable presumption of delivery/intent
    - Physical transfer of deed (not required but creates presumption of grantor's intent)
    - Recording of deed
  - Intent can be implied from words/conduct of grantor
  - Parol evidence admissible to establish intent when grantor keeps deed
- Transfer to grantor's agent is not delivery but transfer to grantee's agent is

- Transfer to third party with a condition is not delivery if grantor keeps absolute right to recover deed, but if not, treated like future property interest
- If conditioned upon death, grantor must intend to make a present gift
- Acceptance presumed for beneficial transfers

2. **Valid deed requirements**
   - Identified parties
   - Grantor's signature
   - Words of transfer
   - Reasonably definite property description (extrinsic evidence admissible)

3. **Recording acts**
   - **Types**
     - **Notice**
       - BFP (purchaser for value without notice) of **prior interest prevails** over prior grantee who failed to record
       - Must record against subsequent purchaser (e.g., "no conveyance/mortgage of RP good against subsequent BFP unless same be recorded according to law")
     - **Race**
       - **First to record prevails**, regardless of knowledge of prior conflicting interests (e.g., "no conveyance/mortgage of RP good against subsequent purchaser of value unless first recorded by law")
     - **Race-notice**
       - Subsequent BFP protected only if he takes **without notice** *and* **is first to record** (e.g., "no conveyance/mortgage of RP good against subsequent BFP unless first recorded by law")
   - **Notice**
     - **Actual**—actual, personal knowledge of prior interest cannot prevail under notice or race-notice statute
     - **Inquiry**—if reasonable investigation would disclose prior claims, grantee cannot prevail against them (e.g., someone other than grantor has possession or documents referenced in chain of title)
     - **Constructive**—properly recorded and appears in chain of title

4. **Types of deeds**
   - **General warranty**
     - **Present covenants**
       - **Seisin**—grantor owns land as described in deed
       - **Right to convey**—grantor has right to transfer title
       - **Against encumbrances**—no undeclared encumbrances against land
     - **Future covenants**
       - **Quiet enjoyment**—grantee not disturbed in possession by third party's claim

- **Warranty**—grantor will defend grantee against third party's claim
- **Further assurances**—grantor will do whatever future acts reasonably necessary to pass title if later determined title is imperfect

- **Special warranty**—same covenants of title but only warrants against defects arising during the time grantor has title

- **Quitclaim deed**—no covenants of title

D. **Fixtures**—structures built on RP and items incorporated into structure become part of realty, but can be removed if:

- Seller reserves right to remove fixture upon sale K

- Leased property can be restored to former condition without damage in reasonable time

IV. Land Use Disputes

A. Easements

1. **Types**

- **Express**—affirmatively created by parties in writing that satisfies SoF

- **Implied**

  o **Necessity**—created when property is virtually useless without benefit of easement across adjacent property, dominant/servient estates must be under common ownership and necessity must arise when estate severed

  o **Implication**—if easement previously used on servient estate by earlier owner, court implies intent for easement to continue if prior use was continuous, apparent, and reasonably necessary to dominant estate's use/enjoyment, the estates were once under common ownership, and a quasi-easement existed at severance

- **Prescription**—continuous, actual, open and hostile for statutory period (20 years at CL)

- **Estoppel**—good faith, reasonable, detrimental reliance on permission by servient estate holder, issued to prevent unjust enrichment

- **Negative**—prevents owner from using land in specific ways, must be expressly created by writing signed by grantor, and usually only recognized for light/air/support/stream water from artificial flow

2. **Transfer**

- **Easement appurtenant**—benefit transferred automatically with servient estate

- **Easement in gross**—benefits individual/legal entity, not RP, and usually commercial easements freely transferable to third party

3. **Scope**—court looks to reasonableness of use and intent of original parties and ambiguities resolved in favor of grantee

4. **Termination**

- **Release**—by writing that satisfies SoF

- **Merger**—merges into title when owner of easement acquires underlying estate

- **Severance**—severed by attempt to convey appurtenant easement separate from land it benefits

- **Abandonment**—owner affirmatively acts to show clear intent to abandon right (statements of intent without conduct and mere non-use insufficient to extinguish easement right)
- **Destruction/condemnation**, prescription, estoppel and written easement—not recorded against servient estate against BFP

5. **Duty to maintain**—easement owner has right and duty to maintain the easement; may seek contribution from co-owners of the easement after notice and opportunity to participate in repair decisions

6. **Profits**—entitles holder to enter servient land and take from it the soil or some substance of the soil such as mineral, timber, and oil

7. **Licenses**
   - Privilege to enter another's land
   - Freely revocable unless estoppel
   - Does not need to satisfy SoF
   - Invalid oral easements create revocable license

B. **Covenants running with the land**

1. **Covenants**
   - **Writing**—must comply with SoF unless implied reciprocal servitude
   - **Intent**—rights/duties to run with land through explicit language or implied from totality of circumstances
   - **Touch/concern**—benefit or burden must affect promisee/promisor as owners of land
     o **Negative covenants**—run with the land if they restrict the owner's use or enjoyment of the land
     o **Affirmative covenants**—run with the land if they require the owner to do something related to the use and enjoyment of the land
   - **Notice (burden only)**—must be constructive or actual
   - **Privity**
     o **Horizontal privity**—(burden only) when estate and covenant in same instrument
     o **Vertical privity**—(covenant based on mutual/successive interest in land burdened/benefited by covenant)
     o **Modern trend**—no privity required; affirmative covenants run to successors of an estate of the same duration as the estate of the original party; negative covenants are analyzed similarly to easements

2. **Equitable servitudes**
   - Intent for restriction to be enforceable by and against successors
   - Touch/concern (no privity required)
   - Notice (actual, record, or inquiry)

3. **Implied reciprocal servitude**
   - Intent to create servitude on all plots (common scheme)
   - Negative servitude (promise to refrain from doing something)

- Notice (actual, record, or inquiry) by party against whom enforcement is sought

C. **Water rights**

1. **Theories**

- **Riparian rights**—water belongs to those who own land bordering the watercourse; owners may make any reasonable use of the water; water rights cannot be transferred separate and apart from the adjoining land

- **Prior appropriation**—water rights are determined by priority of beneficial use; subsequent users must not infringe upon the rights of prior users; water rights may be transferred separately from the adjoining land

2. **Support rights**—the right to have the land supported in its natural state

- **Lateral support**

   o **Undeveloped** (i.e., no improvements)—landowner who excavates on his land is strictly liable for damage to undeveloped adjoining land

   o **Improvements**—landowner who excavates on his land is strictly liable only if adjoining land would have collapsed in its undeveloped state

   o **Improvements contribute to collapse**—landowner who excavates on his land is only liable if he is negligent

- **Subjacent support**—owner of the mineral rights is strictly liable for any failure to support the land and any buildings on the land **at the time the rights were conveyed**

3. **Air rights**—landowner has limited right to reasonable use and enjoyment of the airspace above his land as long as it does not interfere with another's reasonable use and enjoyment of land

FINAL REVIEW OUTLINE: TORTS

I. **Intentional Torts Involving Personal Injury**

   A. **In General**

      1. **Act**—voluntary

      2. **Intent**—purposeful; D knows consequence is substantially certain

   B. **Battery**

      1. **Harmful or offensive contact** (objective standard; no actual harm required)

      2. **To person of another** (or anything connected to it)

      3. **Causation** (direct or indirect)

      4. **D's intent** (transferred intent applies)

   C. **Assault**—act or threat by D intended to cause apprehension of imminent harm or offensive contact

      1. **Conduct or other circumstances** (mere words not enough)

      2. **P must have reasonable apprehension and awareness of D's act**

      3. **Imminent threat of harm**

      4. **Intent** (includes transferred intent)

   D. **IIED**

      1. **Intent** (not transferred) **or recklessness**

      2. **Extreme and outrageous conduct by D** (beyond human decency, outrageous)

      3. **Third party liability** (distresses member of victim's immediate family—with or without resulting bodily injury—or other bystander resulting in bodily injury)

      4. **Causation** (substantial-factor test)

      5. **Damages**—severe emotional distress (beyond reasonable person's endurance or D knows of plaintiff's heightened sensitivity)

   E. **False Imprisonment**

      1. Intent to **confine or restrain** another w/in boundaries (no reasonable means of safe escape); **confinement**; victim is **conscious** of confinement or **harmed** by it

      2. **Methods of confinement** (physical barriers or force, threats, invalid use of legal authority, duress, failure to provide means of escape)

      3. **Time**—immaterial except as to amount of damages

      4. **Intent**—purposeful act or knowing confinement is substantially certain to result

      5. **Damages**—actual damages necessary only if P was unaware of confinement

      6. **Shopkeeper's privilege**—reasonable detention of suspected shoplifter

II. **Defenses to Intentional Torts Involving Personal Injury**

   A. **Consent**

      1. **Express**—invalidated by duress, fraud as to essential matter, and mistakes caused or knowingly utilized by D

2. **Implied**—implied by custom/usage, emergency situations, consensual combat/athletics

3. **Invalid due to incapacity**

B. **Self-Defense**

1. **Reasonable force**—force proportionate to anticipated harm; reasonable mistake does not invalidate defense

2. **Deadly force**—ok only if reasonable belief of serious bodily injury/death

3. **No duty to retreat (majority)**—past trend towards retreating unless in home; most now extend "no retreat" to any place D might legally be ("stand your ground" statutes)

4. **Initial aggressors**—generally not entitled to claim self-defense

5. **Not liable for injuries to bystanders**—so long as injuries were accidental and actor was not negligent

C. **Defense of Others**

1. **Reasonable belief** that defended party entitled to use force to defend self; reasonable mistake ok

2. **Reasonable force**—force proportionate to anticipated harm

D. **Defense of Property**

1. **Reasonable force allowed**—if reasonable to prevent tortious harm to property

2. **No deadly force allowed**—including deadly traps

3. **Reasonable force to prevent intrusion on one's land**—ok unless visitor acting under necessity; generally not permitted to repossess land/realty

4. **Reasonable force to reclaim personal property wrongfully taken**—ok

E. **Parental Discipline**

1. **Reasonable force/confinement ok**—considering age of child and gravity of behavior

2. **Educator has same privilege**—unless parent restricts privilege

F. **Privilege of Arrest**

1. **Felony**

- **Private**—ok if crime was actually committed and reasonable to suspect the person arrested committed it (reasonable mistake only defense as to identity of felon)

- **Police**—ok for felonies if reasonable to believe it was committed and to suspect the person arrested (no tort liability for mistake as to commission of felony)

2. **Misdemeanor**—only if committed in presence of arresting party; private only if breach of peace

III. **Harms to Property Interests**

A. **Trespass to Chattels** (tangible personal property)

1. Intentional **interference with P's right of possession** by either—

- Dispossessing or

- Using or intermeddling with P's chattel

2. **Only intent to do the act is necessary**—transferred intent applies

3. **Mistake about legality is not a defense**

4. **Damages** (actual and loss of use; no loss of use damages without dispossession)

5. **Remedy** (compensation for diminished value or cost of repair)

B. **Conversion**

1. **Intentional act** (must only intend to commit the act that interferes; mistake no defense)

2. **Interference with P's right of possession** (exercising dominion or control)

3. **So serious** (based on duration/extent, intent to assert a right, D's good faith, extent of harm and P's inconvenience) **that it deprives P of the use of the chattel**

4. **Damages** (full value of property or replevin)

C. **Trespass to Land**

1. **Intent** to enter land or cause physical invasion, not to trespass; transferred intent applies

2. **Physical invasion** of property

3. **Proper Plaintiff**—anyone in actual or constructive possession of land

4. **Necessity as defense**

   • **Private**—Qualified privilege for limited number of people to enter land to protect own person/property from harm; not liable for trespass but responsible for actual damages

   • **Public**—Unqualified/absolute privilege to avert imminent public disaster; not liable for damage if actions reasonable or reasonable belief that necessity existed, even if initial entry not necessary

D. **Nuisance**

1. **Private**—Substantial and unreasonable interference with another's use or enjoyment of his land

   • **Proper Plaintiff**—anyone with possessory rights in real property

   • **Interference** must be intentional, negligent, reckless, or result of abnormally dangerous conduct

   • **Substantial**—offensive to average reasonable person in the community (objective)

   • **Unreasonable**—injury caused outweighs usefulness of the action

   • **Defenses** to private nuisance

     ○ **Regulatory compliance**—incomplete defense; admissible but not determinative

     ○ **Coming to the nuisance**—does not entitle D to judgment as a matter of law but jury may consider

2. **Public**—unreasonable interference with a right common to the general public; defenses in private nuisance generally applicable

   • **Proper Plaintiff**—private citizen suffering harm **different in kind** from general public

3. **Remedies**—damages; injunctive relief (balance the equities)

4. **Abatement**

   • Private—Reasonable force permitted to abate; must give D notice of the nuisance and D refuses to act

   • Public—Absent unique injury, public nuisance may be abated only by public authority

IV. **Negligence**—Failure to exercise care a reasonable person would exercise; breach of the duty to prevent foreseeable risk of harm to anyone in the plaintiff's position; breach must be the cause of the plaintiff's injuries

   A. **Elements**

      1. **Duty** (obligation to protect another against unreasonable risk of injury)

      2. **Breach** (failure to meet that obligation)

      3. **Causation** (close causal connection between action and injury)

      4. **Damages** (loss suffered)

   B. **Duty**—owed to all foreseeable persons who may be injured by D's failure to meet reasonable standard of care; foreseeability of harm to another sufficient to create general duty to act with reasonable care

      1. **Failure to act**—Generally no duty to act

      2. **Foreseeability of harm to the plaintiff**

        • *Cardozo*—D only liable to Ps w/in the zone of foreseeable harm (*Palsgraf* majority rule)

        • *Andrews*—If D can foresee harm to anyone resulting from his negligence, D owed duty to everyone harmed (foreseeable or not) (minority rule)

      3. **Special foreseeable Ps**

        • **Rescuers**—D liable for negligently putting rescuer/rescued party in danger

           o Can apply comparative responsibility if rescuer's efforts are unreasonable

           o Emergency professionals barred from recovery if injury results from risk of the job ("firefighter's rule")

        • **Fetuses**—duty of care owed to fetuses viable at time of injury

      4. **Affirmative duty to act—Exceptions to general rule that there is no duty to act**

        • Assumption of duty

        • Placing another in peril

        • By contract

        • By authority

        • By relationship (e.g., employer-employee, parent-child, common carrier-passenger)

   C. **The Standard of Care**

      1. **Reasonably prudent person—objective standard**

        • Physical (not mental) characteristics are considered in determining reasonableness

        • Voluntarily intoxicated person held to same standard as sober person

        • Child—reasonable child of similar age, intelligence, and experience

           o But child engaged in high-risk adult activity held to adult standard

           o Children under age of five generally found incapable of negligent conduct

      2. **Custom**

        • Evidence of custom is admissible but not conclusive in establishing proper standard of care

- **Professionals**—expected to show same skill, knowledge, and care as other practitioners in same community; specialists may be held to higher standard
- **Physicians**
  - Many jurisdictions have changed to national standard—average qualified practitioner
  - Failure to comply with **informed consent** requirement is medical negligence (malpractice) unless risk is commonly known, patient is unconscious, patient waives or is incompetent, or disclosure too harmful

3. **Negligence per se**
   - Criminal or regulatory statute imposes a specific duty for protection of others
   - D neglects to perform the duty
   - D liable to **anyone in the class** of people intended to be protected by statute
   - For **harms of the type** the statute was intended to protect against
   - That were proximately caused by D's violation
   - Defenses—
     - Compliance impossible or more dangerous than noncompliance
     - Violation reasonable under the circumstances
     - Statutory vagueness or ambiguity

4. **Standards of care for specific classes of defendants**
   - **Common carriers (planes, trains, buses)**—highest duty of care consistent with practical operation of the business (majority)
   - **Innkeepers**—ordinary negligence (majority); "slight negligence" (common law)
   - **Automobile drivers**—absent "guest statute" (minority—refrain from wanton & willful misconduct), ordinary care to guests as well as passengers (majority)
   - **Bailor**—duty to warn all bailees of known dangerous defects; duty to warn bailee for hire of defects bailor should have known about with reasonable diligence
   - **Bailee**—gratuitous bailee liable only for gross negligence; bailee for hire must exercise extraordinary care; bailee for mutual benefit must take reasonable care
   - **Sellers of real property**—duty to disclose known, concealed, unreasonably dangerous conditions; liability to third parties continues until buyer has a reasonable opportunity to discover and remedy defect

5. **Standard for possessors of land**
   - **Trespassers (traditional/majority approach)**—refrain from willful, wanton, reckless or intentional misconduct towards trespassers; no "spring-guns"
     - **Discovered**—warn or protect against concealed, dangerous, artificial conditions
     - **Undiscovered**—generally no duty unless owner should reasonably know that trespassers are entering land, then same duty owed a licensee (majority)
     - **Attractive nuisance**—liable for injuries to trespassing children if artificial condition poses unreasonable risk of serious bodily injury, children cannot appreciate the danger, burden of eliminating danger slight compared to risk of harm, and owner fails to exercise reasonable care to protect children

- **Invitee (traditional approach/majority)**—Invited to enter for purposes for which the land is held open or for business purposes
  - Reasonable care to inspect, discover dangerous conditions, and protect invitee from them; non-delegable duty
  - Duty does not extend beyond scope of the invitation
  - **Recreational land use (some juris.)**—possessor who opens land to public for recreation generally not liable for injuries sustained by recreational land users unless (i) charges a fee or (ii) acts willfully, maliciously, or with gross negligence
- **Licensee (traditional approach/majority)**—enters land of another with permission or privilege (social guest; emergency personnel)
  - Warn of concealed dangers that are known or should be obvious.
  - Use reasonable care in conducting activities on the land
  - No duty to inspect
- Modern and Third Restatement Approach (minority)
  - Reasonable care under all circumstances; no invitee/licensee distinction
  - Fact of trespass considered by jury in determining reasonable care
  - Duty not to act in intentional, willful, or wanton manner causing physical harm is only duty owed to **flagrant trespasser** (Third Restatement)
- Landlords and tenants
  - Landlord liable for injuries occurring in common areas resulting from hidden dangers about which landlord fails to warn, on premises leased for public use, as a result of a hazard caused by negligent repair, or involving a hazard landlord agreed to repair
  - Tenant liable for injuries to third parties due to conditions w/in tenant's control
- Off-premises victims
  - No duty for harm by **natural** condition (except rotting trees in urban areas)
  - Duty to prevent unreasonable risk of harm caused by **artificial** condition

D. Breach or Violation of Duty of Care

1. **Burden of proof** (preponderance of the evidence)
   - Greater probability than not that D failed to meet standard of care (as shown by custom/usage, statutory violation, or res ipsa loquitur)
   - Failure was proximate cause of injury and P suffered damages

2. **Traditional approach**—compare D's conduct with what **reasonably prudent person** would do under the circumstances (objective)

3. **Modern and Restatement approach (cost-benefit analysis)**—consider (i) foreseeable **likelihood** that D's conduct would cause harm, (ii) foreseeable **severity** of resulting harm, and (iii) D's **burden** in avoiding the harm

4. **Res ipsa loquitur** (circumstantial evidence; doesn't change standard of care; establishes an inference of negligence sufficient to avoid dismissal)
   - P's harm wouldn't have occurred if D used ordinary care (no injury would typically occur in absence of negligence)

- P not responsible for injury (loosely applied in most comparative fault jurisdictions)
- P's injury under D's exclusive control
  - Modern trend favors generous interpretation of exclusivity
  - Many courts ignore exclusivity for product liability if manufacturer wrapped the package or it is clear that negligence took place during production
  - If many medical personnel had access to P during surgery in malpractice claim, some jurisdictions presume each D has breached a duty of care unless each D rebuts

E. Causation

1. **Cause in fact/actual cause**—"but for" D's act/omission, injury wouldn't have occurred; most courts require causal link; substantial-factor test for multiple causes/Ds; if unclear, burden shifts to multiple Ds to prove each did not cause P's harm

   - **Joint and several liability**—may apply if 2+ Ds are each a factual cause of indivisible injury or Ds acted with common plan or design
   - **Loss of Chance**—applies in some juris. if P's chance of recovery was <50% before D's conduct; can recover percentage of total damages equal to difference between chance of recovery before and after D's negligence

2. **Proximate cause/scope of liability**

   - Limitation on liability
     - **Foreseeability**—D liable for reasonably foreseeable consequences of a foreseeable type (majority); D liable for all direct consequences (minority/Andrew's test)
     - **Ps who can recover**—P can recover if P was a foreseeable victim of D's conduct (majority) or P's harm was w/in scope of liability of D's conduct (minority)
     - **Eggshell skull rule**—Extent of damages need not be foreseeable
   - Intervening and superseding causes
     - Direct cause—uninterrupted chain of events from D's act to P's injury—foreseeability of type of harm does not necessarily preclude liability (majority)
     - Intervening cause—a cause of P's harm that occurs after D's tortious act
     - Superseding cause—breaks the chain of proximate causation; D not liable; **unforeseeable** intervening cause is a superseding cause ("Act of God;" criminal act; intentional tort of third party); **negligent** intervening acts are **foreseeable** (medical malpractice) and may lead to joint and several liability

F. Damages

1. **Actual damages**—must prove actual injury (personal injury or property damage), not just economic loss; nominal damages and attorney's fees not permitted in negligence actions

   - **Parasitic damage**—if tort caused physical harm, may add emotional distress damages (e.g., NIED claims)

2. **Compensatory damages**—make the victim whole

3. **Duty to mitigate**—not a duty to D, but may reduce P's recovery

4. **Personal injury**—past/future pain and suffering, medical expenses, lost wages/reduced future earnings; "eggshell skull" rule applies (liable for full extent of P's injuries; may be increased because of preexisting condition)

5. **Property damage**—generally, difference between fair market value before injury and immediately after; most courts allow cost of repair as alternative if cost of repair does not exceed value of property, or cost of replacement for household items

6. **Collateral source rule**—benefits from outside source not credited against liability (traditional); statutes have eliminated or substantially modified rule (modern trend); payments from D's insurer not a collateral source and are credited against D's liability

7. **Punitive damages**—clear/convincing evidence, malicious, willful & wanton, or reckless behavior

G. Special Rules of Liability

1. **NIED**—D's negligence creates foreseeable risk of injury to P and D's action causes a threat of physical impact that causes emotional distress

   - Threat of physical impact directed at P or someone in immediate presence of P

     o Negligent misdiagnosis causing physical symptoms, mishandling of corpses, and common carriers falsely reporting relative's death may not require threat of impact

   - Bystander must be w/in zone of danger; if not, may be allowed if close relationship to injured person, present at scene, & personally observed injury

   - Majority rule—physical symptoms generally required

2. **Wrongful death**—recoverable damages include loss of support, companionship, society, and affection, but not pain/suffering of P; recovery limited to what decedent could recover

3. **Survival actions**—survival statute may permit representative of decedent's estate to pursue any claims decedent would have had at time of death; may include pain/suffering

   - If survival and wrongful death actions permitted, no double recovery allowed

4. **Loss arising from injury to family member**—loss of consortium for spouses; loss of services for injured child

5. **Wrongful life**—minority allows action by child for failure to perform contraceptive procedure or diagnose congenital defect; damage limited to those attributable to disability

6. **Wrongful birth**—if birth due to failed contraceptive procedure or diagnosis of defect, many states permit parents to recover medical expenses for caring for disabled child; some states allow mother to recover pain/suffering damages and medical expenses for labor

H. Vicarious Liability

1. **Liability of employer for employee's torts**

   - Generally only liable if w/in employer's **right to control** (otherwise, see IC)

   - Tort w/in **scope of employment** (acts employee is employed to do or acts intended to profit or benefit employer); not liable for intentional torts unless force inherent to job (i.e., bouncer), or authorized to act/speak for employer and position provided opportunity for the tort (i.e., fraudulent contract as employer's agent);

   - Employer may be liable for **detour** (minor deviation from scope) but not **frolic** (unauthorized and substantial deviation)

   - **Not vicarious liability**—negligent hiring, supervision, entrustment, or retention of employee is primary negligence not vicarious liability

2. **Independent contractors (IC)**—employers not liable for IC's torts except for:
   - Negligent selection of independent contractor (primary negligence, not vicarious)
   - Vicarious liability for non-delegable duty, or
   - Vicarious liability for IC engaged in inherently dangerous activity

3. **Partners with a common purpose and mutual right of control**—liable for tortious conduct of each other if committed w/in scope of business purposes

4. **Car owners**
   - **Negligent entrustment** of car or other object with potential for harm (if D knows/should know of driver's or user's negligent propensities)
   - **Family-purpose doctrine** (D liable for family members driving with permission) **versus owner liability statutes** (liable for anyone driving with permission)

5. **Parent/child**—vicarious liability only if child acted as parent's agent, state statute applies, or if assumed liability on child's driver's license application for negligent driving
   - Primarily negligent if fails to exercise reasonable care to prevent minor child from intentionally or negligently harming third party if parent (i) can control child and (ii) knows or should know the necessity and opportunity for exercising such control

6. **Dram-Shop liability**—many states recognize cause of action against seller of intoxicating beverages when a third party is subsequently injured due to buyer's intoxication; most states only allow liability if buyer was minor or intoxicated at time of sale; many states extend to social hosts for injuries to intoxicated guest and/or third parties

I. **Limitation of Liability Due to Defendant's Identity or Relationships (Immunities)**

1. **Government**
   - **Federal**—traditionally immune, but now immunity is limited by FTCA
     - Sovereign immunity not waived for enumerated torts, discretionary functions, gov't contractor product liability (unless failed to warn or conform with gov't specifications), and most traditional gov't activities
     - Immunity waived for intentional torts committed by law-enforcement officers
   - **State**—most states have waived sovereign immunity, at least partially, but acts vary
     - **Municipalities/local gov't agencies**—usually governed by state tort claims acts; immunity traditionally attached only to governmental functions
     - **Public-duty rule**—no liability to any one citizen for municipality's failure to fulfill a duty that owed to public at large, unless special relationship creates special duty

2. **Government officials**—immunity applies if is performing **discretionary functions** entrusted by law unless acts with malice or improper purpose; no tort immunity for carrying out **ministerial acts**
   - **Absolute immunity from personal liability**—legislators performing their legislative functions, judges performing their judicial functions, prosecutors

3. **Intra-family**—interspousal immunity extinguished in most states; parent-child immunity generally limited to core parenting activities

4. **Charitable**—eliminated or capped in most states

J. Sharing Liability Among Multiple Defendants

1. **Joint & several liability**—each D found liable for single indivisible harm liable for the entire harm

2. **Pure several liability**—(majority rule) each D liable only for his proportionate share

3. **Satisfaction & release**—no double recovery

4. **Contribution**—tortfeasor who paid more than fair share of common liability can recover excess of fair share from joint tortfeasor; can recover no more than the joint tortfeasor would be liable to P for; not generally available for intentional tortfeasors

5. **Indemnification**—shifting of loss from vicariously liable tortfeasor to primarily responsible party; may be based on agreement, equity, subsequent additional harm, or strict product liability

K. Defenses to Negligence

1. **Contributory negligence**

   - P's negligence is complete bar to recovery (common law/traditional rule)

   - Not a defense to an intentional tort, gross negligence, or recklessness

   - **Last clear chance rule**—abolished in most jurisdictions; P may mitigate legal effect of own fault if D had last clear chance to avoid injuring P; D's actual knowledge of P's inattention required for liability to inattentive P; D liable to helpless P if knew or should have known of P's helpless peril

2. **Comparative fault**

   - **Pure**—not a complete bar to recovery; P's damages reduced by proportion that P's fault bears to total harm

   - Partial

     o If P is less at fault than Ds combined, P's recovery reduced by percentage of fault

     o If P is more at fault than Ds combined, P recovers nothing

     o If P and D are equally at fault, P recovers 50% of his total damages (in minority jurisdictions P recovers nothing if equally at fault)

   - Comparative fault will not reduce P's recovery for intentional torts

3. **Assumption of the risk (A/R)**

   - Traditionally—unreasonably proceeding in face of known, specific risk bars recovery

   - Contributory negligence jurisdiction—no recovery

   - Comparative fault jurisdiction—merely reduces recovery

   - Exculpatory clauses in contracts—unenforceable if (i) disclaims liability for reckless or wanton misconduct or gross negligence;(ii) gross disparity of bargaining power (iii) exculpated party offers services of great importance or practical necessity to public; (iv) subject to typical contractual defenses; or (v) against public policy

     o Generally, common carriers, innkeepers, and employers cannot disclaim liability for negligence.

V. **Strict Liability (S/L)—DAD** (**D**angerous activities, **A**nimals, and **D**efective/dangerous products)

    A. **Elements**

        1. **Absolute duty to make P's person or property safe**

        2. **Breach**

        3. **Actual & proximate causation**

        4. **Damages**

    B. **Abnormally Dangerous Activities**

        1. Not commonly engaged in; inherent, foreseeable, and highly significant risk of harm (look to gravity of harm, inappropriateness of place, limited value of activity)

        2. S/L limited to harm expected from activity

    C. **Animals**

        1. **Wild animals**—not by custom devoted to the service of humankind where it is being kept

          • Owner is S/L for harm done by wild animal despite owner's precautions to prevent harm, as long as harm arises from dangerous propensity characteristic of animal or about which owner has reason to know

          • Owner S/L for reasonably foreseeable damage caused by trespassing animal

          • Owner S/L for injuries caused by P's fearful reaction to unrestrained wild animal

          • Owner not S/L to undiscovered trespasser except for injuries by vicious watchdog

        2. **Domestic animals**

          • Owner S/L for injuries if knows or has reason to know of dangerous propensities and harm results

          • Owner S/L for reasonably foreseeable damage caused by trespassing household pets if owner knows or has reason to know that the pet is intruding on another's property in a way that has a tendency to cause substantial harm; general negligence standard applies if pet strays onto a public road and contributes to an accident there

    D. **Defenses to S/L**

        1. **Contributory negligence not a defense** in contributory negligence jurisdictions—does not bar recovery

        2. **Contributory negligence** may reduce P's recovery in most comparative fault jurisdictions under a S/L claim (Third Restatement approach); courts divided, some do not allow reduction

        3. **Assumption of Risk/"Knowing contributory negligence"**—bars recovery

        4. **Statutory privilege**—no S/L for D performing essential public services

VI. **Products Liability**

    A. **Negligence**

        1. **Duty**—reasonable care owed to any foreseeable P by commercial manufacturer/distributor/retailer/seller

        2. **Breach**—failure to exercise reasonable care in inspection/sale of product (i.e., defect would have been discovered if D wasn't negligent)

        3. **Causation**—factual & proximate

4. **Damages**—actual injury/property damage, not pure economic loss

5. **Defenses**—contributory/comparative negligence and A/R

B. **Strict Products Liability**

1. **Elements**

- Product was defective (in manufacture, design, or failure to warn)

- Defect existed when it left D's control

- Defect caused P's injury when used in a reasonably foreseeable way

2. **Defective product** (res ipsa may apply)

- **Manufacturing defect**—product does not conform to D's own specifications

- Design defect

   o Consumer expectation test—dangerous beyond expectation of ordinary consumer

   o Risk-utility test—risks > benefits and reasonable alternative design (economically feasible) available; failure to use that design rendered product unreasonably safe

- Failure-to-warn defect

   o (i) Foreseeable risk of harm, (ii) not obvious to ordinary user of product, and (iii) risks could have been reduced or avoided w/ reasonable instructions or warnings

   o **Learned-intermediary rule**—manufacturer of prescription drug typically satisfies duty to warn by warning prescribing physician of problems with the drug, unless (i) manufacturer knows drug will be dispensed without personal intervention or evaluation of a healthcare provider, or (ii) in the case of birth control pills.

3. **Plaintiff**—not required to be in privity of contract; anyone foreseeably injured may recover

4. **Defendants**—must be in the business of selling (includes manufacturer, distributor, and retail seller)

- If D provides both products and services, generally liable if product is consumed, not if product is only used (i.e., hospital not generally liable as a distributor of implants)

- Casual sellers and auctioneers generally not S/L

5. **Damages**—personal injury or property damage, pure economic loss must be brought under warranty action

6. **Defenses**

- Comparative fault—P's negligence reduces recovery as will A/R (majority)

- Contributory negligence—P's negligence not a defense if P misused product in reasonably foreseeable way or negligently failed to discover defect

- A/R—complete bar to recovery in contributory-negligence jurisdictions; in most comparative-fault jurisdictions A/R only reduces recovery

- Unforeseeable misuse, alteration, or modification by the user precludes (most contributory-negligence states) or reduces (most comparative-fault states) recovery

- Compliance with governmental safety standards—not conclusive evidence that product is not defective, but may be considered

- State-of-the-art standard—product conforms with level of scientific/technological/safety knowledge existing and reasonably feasible when product was distributed; compliance with state-of-the-art standard will only bar recovery in some states; n/a to manufacturing defect claims

- Statute of limitations—begins to run against P with personal injury when P discovers, or should discover w/ reasonable care, his injury and its connection to the product

C. **Warranties** (against seller, manufacturer, and distributor of product)

1. **Implied warranties**

- **Merchantability**—product is generally acceptable and reasonably fit for ordinary purpose

- **Fitness**—product fit for particular purpose; seller must know purpose and buyer must rely on seller's skill or judgment in supplying product

- Privity requirements

  o Alternative A (majority)—allows only purchaser or member of his family/household to recover for personal injury (not property damage or pure economic loss)

  o Alternative B—anyone reasonably expected to use, consume, or be affected by the product may recover for personal injury

  o Alternative C—Alternative B + recovery for property damage and economic loss

- **Damages**—personal injury; property damage; pure economic loss

2. **Express warranties**

- Affirmation of fact or a promise about product; part of the basis of bargain

- Seller liable for any breach of express warranty, regardless of fault

3. **Defenses**

- Disclaimers

  o Consumer goods—limitation of consequential damages for personal injury is unconscionable

  o Express warranties—valid only if consistent with warranty (usually not)

- Comparative fault and A/R—same as in S/L claims

- Contributory negligence—not a bar except when it overlaps A/R

- Misuse—prevents recovery under the implied warranty of merchantability when the product is warranted to be fit for ordinary purposes (majority)

- Claim generally fails if P fails to provide seller with notice of breach of warranty within the statutorily required time period or "a reasonable period of time"

VII. **Defamation, Invasion of Privacy, and Business Torts**

A. **Defamation**

1. **Elements**

- **Defamatory language**—diminishing respect, esteem, or goodwill toward P

- **Of or concerning P**—reasonable third party believes language refers to particular P

- **Publication**—intentional or negligent communication to third party; republication identifying original speaker and uncertainty as to accuracy of the statement still may satisfy this element
- **Falsity** (public concern)
  - If statement relates to matter of **public concern** or P is a **public figure**, P must prove defamatory statement is **false**
  - **Private** P suing on a statement that does **not** involve matter of public concern not required to prove falsity; D may prove truth as an affirmative defense
  - **Opinion** only basis for defamation if **implies knowledge of facts**
- **Fault**
  - Public figure—actual malice (D knows of falsity/reckless disregard of truth)
  - Private figure/matter of public concern—D acted with fault; either negligence or actual malice
  - Private figure/not matter of public concern—at least negligence

2. **Libel/Slander Distinguished**

- **Libel**—written, printed or otherwise recorded in permanent form; general damages that compensate P for harm to reputation (generally includes radio and television)
  - Common law allowed recovery for presumed damages
  - Libel per quod—if defamatory statement requires proof of extrinsic facts to show it is defamatory, P must prove either special damages or a category of slander per se
- **Slander**—spoken word, gesture, or any form other than libel; special damages required; third party heard comments and acted adversely to P; usually, but not always, economic loss
- Slander per se—no special damages required if accused of committing a crime, conduct that reflects poorly on P's trade or profession, loathsome disease, sexual misconduct; general damages then permitted as parasitic damages

3. **Constitutional limits on damages**

- Public figure—can only recover actual proven damages
- Private person/matter of public concern—actual damages but if actual malice proven, punitive or presumed damages also permitted
- Private person/not public concern—general, including presumed, damages without proving actual malice

4. **Defenses**

- **Truth**—complete defense
- **Consent**—cannot exceed scope
- **Absolute privilege**—for remarks during judicial/legislative proceedings, between spouses, or in required publications
- **Qualified privilege**—affecting important public interest, in the interest of D or third party; privilege is lost if abused; burden on D to prove privilege exists; burden on P to prove privilege abused and lost

B. **Invasion of Privacy—I FLAP** (Intrusion, False Light, Appropriation, Private facts)

1. **Applies only to individuals, terminates upon death**

   - **Intrusion upon seclusion**—D's act of intrusion into P's private affairs, objectionable to a reasonable person (no publication required)

   - **False light**—publication of facts about P or attributing views/actions to P that place him in false light objectionable to a reasonable person under circumstances; truth not always a defense; in matters of public interest, P must show malice

   - **Misappropriation**—unauthorized use of P's picture or name for D's advantage; lack of consent; injury (some states allow action to survive death)

   - **Public disclosure of private facts**—public disclosure of private facts (even if true) about P that would be highly offensive to a reasonable person and is not of legitimate concern to the public; in tension with First Amendment—disfavored tort

2. **Damages**—proof of emotional/mental distress enough, special damages not required

3. **Defenses**—Absolute/qualified privilege for false light/public disclosure; consent applies to all types of privacy torts, but any mistake re: consent negates defense; truth not a defense

C. **Intentional Misrepresentation**

1. **False representation of material fact**—generally no duty to disclose

2. **Scienter**—knowledge or reckless disregard of truth

3. **Intent to induce** P to act or refrain in reliance on misrepresentation

4. **Causation**—actual reliance

5. **Justifiable reliance**—not justifiable if statement obviously false or lay opinion

6. **Damages**—actual economic loss/consequential damages, no nominal damages

D. **Negligent Misrepresentation**

1. **D** (accounting firm or other supplier of commercial information)

2. Provides **false information** to P as a result of D's **negligence** in the course of D's business or profession

3. P **justifiably relies** on the information and incurs **pecuniary damages** as a result

   - P must be in contractual relationship with D or D knows P is a member of a limited group for whose benefit the information is supplied

   - Information must be relied on in a transaction that D intends to influence or knows recipient intends to

4. **Defenses**—standard negligence defenses

5. **Damages**—reliance and consequential

E. **Intentional Interference with Business Relations**

1. **Intentional interference with contract**

   - D knew of valid contractual relationship between P and third party (not "at-will")

   - D intentionally interfered with contract in a way that substantially exceeds fair competition and free expression, resulting in a breach and

   - Breach caused damages to P

- Defenses—justified if motivated by health, safety, or morals; contract is terminable at will; D is business competitor

2. **Interference with prospective economic advantage** (no contract)

   - More egregious conduct required for liability, should be independently tortious; violates federal or state law; improper conduct per balancing analysis

   - Business competitor will not be liable for encouraging switching business

3. **Theft of trade secrets**

   - P owns valid trade secret (provides a business advantage)

   - Not generally known

   - Reasonable precautions to protect

   - D took secret by improper means

F. Injurious Falsehoods

1. **Trade libel**—malicious publication of derogatory statement relating to P's title to business property/quality of products, and interference or damage to business relationships; proof of special damages required and mental suffering damages unavailable; truth and fair competition are valid defenses

2. **Slander of title**—publication of false statement derogatory to P's title to real property; malice; special damages as a result of diminished value in the eyes of third parties

G. Wrongful Use of Legal System

1. **Malicious prosecution**—intentional & malicious institution of legal proceeding for improper purpose; no probable cause; action dismissed in favor of the person against whom it was brought

   - Damages can include legal expenses, lost work time, loss of reputation, emotional distress

   - Judges and prosecutors have absolute immunity from liability

2. **Abuse of Process**—use of legal process against P in a wrongful manner to accomplish a purpose other than that for which the process was intended; willful act; proof of damages required

Milestone Exam One

MILESTONE EXAM ONE

TIME: 81 MINUTES

Welcome to Milestone Exam One. This exam consists of 45 questions in the areas of Contracts, Real Property, and Torts. This exam will take approximately 81 minutes (an average of 1.8 minutes per question). After you have completed this exam, log in to your course to submit your answers, view detailed answer explanations, and compare your performance to other Themis students.

Name: _____ Date: _____

Start Time: _____ End Time: _____

1. [A] [B] [C] [D]	26. [A] [B] [C] [D]
2. [A] [B] [C] [D]	27. [A] [B] [C] [D]
3. [A] [B] [C] [D]	28. [A] [B] [C] [D]
4. [A] [B] [C] [D]	29. [A] [B] [C] [D]
5. [A] [B] [C] [D]	30. [A] [B] [C] [D]
6. [A] [B] [C] [D]	31. [A] [B] [C] [D]
7. [A] [B] [C] [D]	32. [A] [B] [C] [D]
8. [A] [B] [C] [D]	33. [A] [B] [C] [D]
9. [A] [B] [C] [D]	34. [A] [B] [C] [D]
10. [A] [B] [C] [D]	35. [A] [B] [C] [D]
11. [A] [B] [C] [D]	36. [A] [B] [C] [D]
12. [A] [B] [C] [D]	37. [A] [B] [C] [D]
13. [A] [B] [C] [D]	38. [A] [B] [C] [D]
14. [A] [B] [C] [D]	39. [A] [B] [C] [D]
15. [A] [B] [C] [D]	40. [A] [B] [C] [D]
16. [A] [B] [C] [D]	41. [A] [B] [C] [D]
17. [A] [B] [C] [D]	42. [A] [B] [C] [D]
18. [A] [B] [C] [D]	43. [A] [B] [C] [D]
19. [A] [B] [C] [D]	44. [A] [B] [C] [D]
20. [A] [B] [C] [D]	45. [A] [B] [C] [D]
21. [A] [B] [C] [D]	46. [A] [B] [C] [D]
22. [A] [B] [C] [D]	47. [A] [B] [C] [D]
23. [A] [B] [C] [D]	48. [A] [B] [C] [D]
24. [A] [B] [C] [D]	49. [A] [B] [C] [D]
25. [A] [B] [C] [D]	50. [A] [B] [C] [D]

Themis
BarReview

Score ( ) Rescore ( )

1. In need of money, the owner of a ring prepared an email one evening proposing to sell the ring to a friend for $500, but only if he responded within 24 hours. Unable to bring herself to send the email, the owner, who normally was a teetotaler, began drinking. When she was thoroughly intoxicated, she sent the email without realizing it. After the owner sobered up the following afternoon, she called her friend and said that she had never meant to send the email, but her friend informed her that he had already responded by email, agreeing to the transaction.

Does a valid contract exist?

A. Yes, because the friend accepted the owner's offer to sell the ring.
B. Yes, because the friend had 24 hours in which to respond.
C. No, because the owner lacked capacity at the time that she made the offer.
D. No, because the contract was executory.

2. A wife owned a pistol, which she kept loaded in a locked safe in her bedroom. Unbeknownst to the wife, her husband took the pistol, fired it at a pesky squirrel until it was empty, and returned the empty pistol to the safe. Shortly thereafter, the wife returned home to find her husband and sister alone in the house. The wife, having long harbored jealousy over the close relationship between her husband and sister, decided to teach them a lesson. She got the pistol, pointed it at her husband and sister, and threatened to shoot them. She never intended shoot them, but merely to scare them. The husband and sister have sued the wife for assault.

Is either the husband or sister likely to prevail in an action for assault?

A. No, neither will prevail because the wife did not intend to shoot either the sister or husband.
B. No, neither will prevail because the pistol was unloaded.
C. Yes, the sister alone will prevail because she did not know the pistol was unloaded.
D. Yes, both plaintiffs will prevail because they can each prove the elements for assault.

3. An attorney was sued by a client for malpractice. The client obtained a judgment against the attorney and, by filing the judgment in the county in which the attorney rented an office, created a lien that was valid against any real property then owned or subsequently acquired by the attorney for up to 10 years. Three years later, the attorney purchased a residence in the same county. The attorney financed the purchase with a loan from a bank, which was secured by a mortgage on the residence. Two years later, the attorney failed to make the required mortgage payments. The bank initiated foreclosure proceedings, joining the client as a party. The jurisdiction has adopted the following statute: "No conveyance or mortgage of real property shall be good against subsequent purchasers for value and without notice unless the same be recorded according to law." In addition, the jurisdiction treats a mortgage as a lien against the real property.

Who has priority to the proceeds from the foreclosure sale?

A. The client, because the lien was first in time.

B. The client, because the lien was recorded first.

C. The bank, because the lien is not affected by the foreclosure sale.

D. The bank, because the mortgage was a purchase money mortgage.

4. Twenty years ago, a property owner deeded his house to a charitable organization. The warranty deed stated that the house was transferred to the organization "provided that the organization uses the premises as a halfway house for troubled teenagers; otherwise, the owner may reenter the property." Nine years after the property was transferred, the charitable organization ceased running a halfway house, and began using the house as its administrative office. Recently, upon the death of the property owner, all of his real property passed by will to his daughter. The time period for adverse possession in the state where the house is located is 10 years.

Does the charitable organization have a current possessory interest in the house?

A. No, because the charitable organization ceased to use the house as a halfway house.

B. No, because the owner devised his interest in the house to his daughter.

C. Yes, because the charitable organization has outright ownership of the house through adverse possession.

D. Yes, because the right of re-entry has not been exercised.

5. A homeowner devised her home to her best friend, "but if [the best friend] predeceases me, to her heirs." The best friend died shortly before the homeowner did. The best friend is survived by her daughter, and the homeowner is survived by her son. The best friend's daughter claims that she should take the home, while the homeowner's son claims that it should pass with the rest of the homeowner's estate.

The applicable jurisdiction has an anti-lapse statute. Who should receive the homeowner's home?

A. The best friend's daughter, because of the anti-lapse statute.
B. The best friend's daughter, because the homeowner left the home to the best friend and her heirs.
C. The homeowner's son, because the gift lapsed.
D. The homeowner's son, because the homeowner and the best friend were not related by blood.

6. A baker and a bride-to-be entered into a contract in which the baker agreed to bake the wedding cake for the bride's wedding at a cost of $2,500. The contract contained a clause that read: "An express condition of Bride's performance under the Contract is Baker's satisfaction of Bride's aesthetic expectations in the design of her wedding cake." In keeping with the wedding's butterfly theme, the baker constructed an elegant cake accented with colorful butterflies, flowers, and caterpillars. At the wedding reception, the guests were enthralled by the cake. The bride, however, upset over the inclusion of the caterpillars, to which she had a genuine aversion, refused to pay the baker. The baker sued the bride to enforce the contract.

Should the court enforce the contract?

A. Yes, because the cake was aesthetically pleasing to the wedding guests.
B. Yes, because the baker substantially performed.
C. No, because the bride was personally and honestly dissatisfied with the cake.
D. No, because no contract was formed between the parties.

7. A country club hosted a celebrity golf tournament to raise money for a local hospital. The country club had a strict policy of requiring any person not currently engaged in a golf match to stay off the course while a tournament is in session. The country club made an announcement to this effect, adding that entering the course during play could result in serious injury. An adult club member, who was aware of the policy, walked onto the course during a match in order to procure the signature of a famous golf star. While on the course, the member was struck in the head with a golf ball and injured.

In a suit against the country club by the member to recover for his injuries, how will the court likely hold?

A. Liable, because the club member was a business invitee.

B. Liable, because the presence of famous golf stars constituted an attractive nuisance.

C. Not liable, because the country club enjoys charitable immunity.

D. Not liable, because the country club did not breach its duty to the club member.

8. A buyer agreed in writing to purchase sports memorabilia related to a legendary sports figure, which was on display at a museum, from the owner for $500,000. The agreement called for the payment to be made and the memorabilia handed over at the end of the display period, 60 days after the agreement was signed by both parties. Forty-five days later, a record held by the sports legend was broken and the fair market value of the memorabilia dropped to $275,000. The buyer repudiated the contract. The following week, before the owner could locate another buyer, the memorabilia, on loan for public display, was destroyed without the fault of either the buyer or the owner. The owner had only insured the memorabilia for $100,000.

How much is the owner likely to recover from the buyer?

A. $500,000.00

B. $400,000.00

C. $275,000.00

D. $225,000.00

9. A homeowner called a septic cleaning company and made arrangements for the company to remove the waste from the septic tank on the homeowner's property. After completing the job, the company mailed the homeowner a bill for $500, the fair market value of the services rendered by the company. The bill indicated that payment was due in 60 days. Upon receiving the bill, the homeowner called the company and informed it that, since he had lost his job due to an accident, he would not be paying the company's bill. The following day the company filed suit for breach of contract. Ten days later, the homeowner moved to dismiss the suit. The court granted the motion, dismissing the suit without prejudice.

Is the court's dismissal proper?

A. No, because the parties' dealings created an implied-in-fact contract.

B. No, because the homeowner has repudiated the contract.

C. Yes, because the vendor failed to demand assurances.

D. Yes, because the vendor's complaint is premature.

10. A homeowner borrowed money from a bank in order to install a deck at her residence. The bank loan, which was evidenced by a note that contained an acceleration clause, was secured by a five-year mortgage on the residence. The bank promptly recorded this mortgage. Two years later, the homeowner sold the residence to a buyer. The agreement between the homeowner and the buyer provided for the buyer to assume the mortgage. The bank was not a party to this agreement and did not provide any consideration to the buyer for entering into this agreement. Six months after the buyer took possession of the residence, the buyer stopped making payments on the loan. The bank initiated an action against the buyer for the outstanding balance due on the home improvement loan.

Is the buyer liable to the bank for the outstanding balance?

A. Yes, because the buyer agreed to assume the homeowner's mortgage obligation.

B. Yes, because the buyer is in possession of the residence.

C. No, because the bank was not a party to agreement between the homeowner and buyer.

D. No, because the buyer did not receive consideration from the bank for agreeing to assume the loan obligation.

11. A hardware store owner observed a customer looking at a display of chain saws. The customer asked the owner which of two brands he would recommend. The owner said, "I swear by Brand X. In my opinion they make the best chain saws." In making this statement, the owner had no intent to offer the customer a warranty. The customer purchased a Brand X chain saw. On the customer's sales receipt, was printed, "All warrantees, express or implied, are hereby disclaimed." The chain saw malfunctioned, resulting in serious injury to the customer. The customer sued the store owner for breach of an express warranty.

Of the following, which would be the store owner's best defense?

A. The store owner did not use the words "warranty" or "guarantee."

B. The store owner did not intend to offer a warranty.

C. Any express warranty was disclaimed by the sale receipt.

D. The store owner's words constituted his opinion.

12. A tool distributor sold a retailer an assortment of tools on credit. Immediately prior to the sale, the distributor, concerned about the retailer's financial health, telephoned the retailer to ask if the retailer would be able to pay for the tools. The retailer assured the distributor that it was solvent, even though the retailer knew it might not be before it paid for the tools. Twelve days after the retailer received the tools, the distributor learned that the retailer was insolvent and immediately sought to reclaim the tools.

Can the distributor do so?

A. No, because the retailer had retained the tools for twelve days.

B. No, because the retailer had received the tools.

C. Yes, because the retailer had falsely assured the manufacturer that it was solvent.

D. Yes, because the retailer acted immediately upon learning that the retailer was insolvent.

13. A son went to visit his father, who was very ill. The father and son reminisced about hunting trips they had taken on property owned by the father. The father told the son that he wanted the son to have the property after the father died. The son did not know that the father had sold the property earlier that month to a farmer who owned and lived on adjacent property. Shortly after the father died, the son took a trip to hunt on the property. While the son was hunting, the farmer approached the son and correctly told him that the father had sold the land to the farmer. The son, bursting into tears, pointed his rifle at the farmer. The son told the farmer that he would shoot the farmer for telling lies about the father. The farmer's wife, who was watching the exchange, approached the son from behind and hit him over the head with a shovel. The son died from his injuries, and his estate has sued the farmer's wife.

Is the son's estate likely to succeed in a suit against the farmer's wife?

A. No, because the farmer's wife is protected by the privilege of necessity.
B. No, because the wife had a reasonable belief that the farmer would be entitled to use self-defense.
C. Yes, because only the farmer would be entitled to use force against the son.
D. Yes, because the son reasonably believed that the farmer was trespassing on the son's land.

14. An unscrupulous landowner sold undeveloped land to two different buyers and then disappeared with the proceeds. Each buyer paid fair market value for the land and neither buyer was aware of the landowner's transaction with the other buyer. Subsequently, the first buyer, upon learning of the second conveyance, recorded her deed. The second buyer did not record his deed.

The applicable recording act reads: "A conveyance of any interest in land shall not be valid against any subsequent purchaser for value, without notice thereof, unless the conveyance is recorded."

In action brought by the first buyer against the second buyer, who is entitled to ownership of the land?

A. The first buyer, pursuant to the "first in time, first in right" rule, because the recording act does not apply since the second buyer did not record his deed.
B. The first buyer, pursuant to the recording act, because she alone recorded her deed.
C. The second buyer, pursuant to the recording act, because he paid fair market value for the land without notice of the first conveyance.
D. The second buyer, pursuant to the recording act, because the first buyer knew of the second conveyance prior to recording her deed.

15. A homeowner financed the purchase of his residence with a $200,000 loan from a bank. The loan, which was to be repaid over twenty years, was secured by a mortgage on the residence. The bank promptly recorded the mortgage. The following year, the homeowner borrowed $50,000 from a credit union to start a business. The credit union loan, which had a two-year term, was secured by a mortgage on the residence, which the credit union immediately recorded. The next year, the homeowner obtained a two-year loan from the bank for $25,000 to pay for his daughter's wedding. The homeowner agreed to increase the mortgage on the residence as security for this loan. The bank recorded the modified mortgage.

The homeowner defaulted on all three loans. The bank initiated foreclosure proceedings, to which the credit union was named as a party. The proceeds from the foreclosure sale were sufficient to repay the bank in full for its residential purchase loan and either the credit union's business loan or the bank's wedding loan, but not both.

Who should be paid in full?

A. The bank, because the bank's mortgage was recorded before the credit union's mortgage.

B. The bank, because the bank initiated the foreclosure proceedings.

C. The credit union, because the credit union's mortgage was recorded before the bank modified its mortgage.

D. The credit union, because the bank's modification of its mortgage prejudiced the credit union.

16. A customer at a bakery ordered a cake, which the bakery stated was made by an independent third party. The cake contained small shards of metal. The metal was not detected by the bakery, even though the bakery conducted a reasonable inspection of the cake and otherwise had no reason to suspect that the cake contained the metal. The customer ate the cake and immediately incurred serious injuries from eating the shards of metal.

The customer brought suit against the bakery based on strict products liability for injuries suffered from eating the cake. Who will prevail?

A. The customer, because the bakery was a commercial supplier of the dessert.

B. The customer, because the bakery failed to warn him of the presence of the metal in the dessert.

C. The bakery, because the bakery did not bake the cake.

D. The bakery, because the metal was not detectable by reasonable inspection.

17. Two farmers who own adjacent farms decided to construct a small road that straddles their common property line. They entered into a written agreement whereby each granted to the other a right of access over his property in accord with the dimensions and location of the road and each promised that he, his heirs, devisees, assignees, and successors would equally share the repair and maintenance of the road with the neighboring property owner. This agreement was promptly and properly recorded. After the road was built, one of the farmers sold his farm in fee simple absolute to a rancher. A year ago, the other farmer died. His property passed by intestacy to his son. Through an oral agreement, the son leased the inherited farm to another farmer for a one-year term. The son told the new farmer of the shared maintenance agreement with the rancher, but otherwise did not discuss the maintenance of the road with the new farmer. This past spring, due to heavy flooding, the maintenance of the road was costly. When the new farmer contacted the rancher, the rancher, noting that he rarely used the road and preferred the public highway that abutted his property, refused to reimburse the farmer for the maintenance expenditures.

Under which of the following theories can the new farmer successfully recover half of the costs for maintenance from the rancher?

A. The agreement contains a covenant that runs with the land.

B. Detrimental reliance on the son's revelation of the shared maintenance agreement.

C. The agreement contains an easement.

D. The agreement contains an equitable servitude.

18. A consumer purchased a ladder from a hardware store for use around the house. Due to a defect in the design of the ladder, the consumer fell from the ladder and was seriously injured. The manufacturer of the ladder had affixed a notice to the ladder that limited consequential damages from any defect in the ladder or from a breach of the implied warranty of merchantability. The consumer had read the notice prior to purchasing the ladder. The consumer brought an action based on both a products liability claim and breach of the implied warranty of merchantability claim against the manufacturer to recover damages for his personal injuries.

Can either claim support the consumer's recovery?

A. No, as to either type of claim.

B. Yes, as to the products liability claim, but no, as to the implied warranty of merchantability claim.

C. Yes, as to the implied warranty of merchantability claim, but no, as to the products liability claim.

D. Yes, as to both types of claims.

19. A child was playing mini-golf at a recreation center when she went into an artificial creek to retrieve a lost ball. A high fence with a childproof lock surrounded the creek, but, the child's mother opened the lock to let her daughter into the creek area to quickly retrieve the ball. When the girl reached into the creek, she was electrically shocked by a live wire from a motorized windmill that had fallen in the creek. She suffered long-term disability because of the electric shock. The family of the child filed a claim against the recreation center. The recreation center filed a response claiming it was not liable for the accident because it posted warnings that the creek was dangerous and surrounded it with a high fence that could not be opened without the intervention of an adult.

Under the traditional approach, is the recreation center likely to be successful in defending the suit?

A. Yes, because the child entered the prohibited area.

B. Yes, because the creek was surrounded by a locked fence with warnings.

C. No, because the creek was abnormally dangerous.

D. No, because the creek was an attractive nuisance.

20. A university ordered scientific equipment from a manufacturer for prompt shipment. The manufacturer accepted the order. Several days later, prior to identification of the equipment, the manufacturer became insolvent. Upon learning of the manufacturer's insolvency, the university did not seek reasonable assurances of performance from the manufacturer. Although the university could have placed an order with another company for the same equipment, the university chose instead to tender the purchase price to the manufacturer. When the manufacturer refused to accept the tendered price and ship the equipment, the university filed an action to force the manufacturer to fill the order.

Is it likely that the university can compel the manufacturer to supply the scientific equipment?

A. No, because the equipment was neither identified nor unique.

B. No, because the university did not seek reasonable assurances of performance from the manufacturer.

C. Yes, because the manufacturer is insolvent.

D. Yes, because the university is a buyer and the manufacturer is in breach of the contract.

21. The plaintiff was driving on a city street when a car swerved in front of him, forcing the plaintiff to slam on his brakes to avoid a collision. The defendant was driving the car behind the plaintiff. Because the defendant was speeding, he was unable to slow down quickly enough to avoid hitting the plaintiff. The plaintiff sustained severe whiplash as a result of the collision.

The plaintiff has sued the defendant. The evidence at trial shows that both the defendant and the driver of the car that swerved in front of the plaintiff were negligent, and that the negligence of each caused the plaintiff's injuries. The defendant has moved for a directed verdict, arguing that the plaintiff did not establish causation.

Is the court likely to grant the defendant's motion?

A. No, because the defendant's conduct was the cause of the plaintiff's injury.

B. No, because the plaintiff can prove proximate causation, even if he cannot prove actual causation.

C. Yes, because a plaintiff may not recover against a single defendant when multiple individuals contributed to the plaintiff's injury.

D. Yes, because the defendant can prove that his negligence would not have resulted in the plaintiff's injury had the other car not swerved.

22. A thief stole an expensive vase from the home of the vase's owner. The owner later acquired information that the vase was being stored in a warehouse on the other side of town. The owner went to the warehouse and broke a window to enter the premises. There, he encountered the thief, standing next to the vase. The owner brandished a gun, and said, "Hand over the vase, or else." The owner had no intention of actually firing a shot, but his finger slipped and pulled the trigger. The thief was hit by a bullet in the chest. While the thief writhed on the floor, the owner found and seized the vase, and exited the premises through the front door. The thief survived the attack, and sued the owner for battery.

Is he likely to prevail?

A. Yes, because the thief suffered serious injury.

B. Yes, because the owner intended to place the thief in fear.

C. No, because the owner's conduct was privileged.

D. No, because the shooting was accidental.

23. A testator's will provided for a devise of the testator's residence to the testator's daughter and a devise of $100,000 to the testator's son. At the time of the testator's death, the testator owned the residence in fee simple absolute. The residence was not subject to any encumbrances. The testator's only other asset at the time of her death was a bank account that had a balance of $5,000. The personal representative of the testator's estate applied to the money in the bank account to the satisfaction of the testator's outstanding debts and transferred title of the testator's residence to the daughter. The son filed an action in probate court challenging the personal representative's distribution of the testator's residence to the daughter. The son asserted that the personal representative should have sold the residence and divided the proceeds between the testator's daughter and himself.

Which of the following legal concepts provides the best support for personal representative's action?

A. Abatement.

B. Ademption.

C. Exoneration.

D. Lapse.

24. A couple orally agreed that, after they were married, the husband would move into the wife's house, the husband would transfer $20,000 to the wife, and the house would be retitled under joint ownership. After the couple was married, the husband moved into the wife's house and transferred $20,000 to the wife's separate bank account, but before the wife had time to retitle the house under joint ownership, she died. Upon the wife's death, the husband petitioned the personal representative of his wife's estate to honor the couple's pre-marital agreement in determining the distribution of the wife's estate.

Of the following, which is best argument that the personal representative can advance to deny the husband's petition?

A. Marriage was a condition of the contract.

B. The agreement was not in writing.

C. The wife's death terminated her contractual obligation.

D. The wife had not breached her obligation to retitle the house under joint ownership.

25. Based on an honest belief, an employer terminated a bookkeeper for embezzlement. The employer also threatened to file a criminal complaint unless the bookkeeper agreed to repay the stolen funds. The bookkeeper, seeking to avoid criminal prosecution, agreed, and signed a promissory note payable to the employer in the amount of the embezzled funds. The bookkeeper subsequently admitted to having embezzled the money.

Can the bookkeeper avoid the promissory note?

A. No, because the bookkeeper admitted to embezzling from her employer.

B. No, because the employer's threat was based on an honest belief that the bookkeeper was an embezzler.

C. Yes, because the bookkeeper signed the note under duress.

D. Yes, because the employer terminated the bookkeeper.

26. The owner of a small parcel of undeveloped land conveyed the right to construct and use a road across the parcel to a corporation that owned a sizable tract of undeveloped adjacent land. The landowner was aware that the corporation intended to construct a factory on that tract of land and understood that the corporation intended to use the road to provide access to the factory. Before beginning construction of the factory, the corporation changed its plans and acquired additional contiguous property from a third party. As a consequence, the corporation planned to build a factory that was slightly larger than the one originally planned on both this newly acquired property and the property the corporation originally owned. There would be a modest increase in the traffic using the road associated with this modification. Upon learning of the corporation's change in plans, the individual sued to enjoin the corporation from building and using the road to provide access to the factory.

Should the court grant the injunction?

A. No, because the individual was aware of the purpose of the road.

B. No, because the increase in usage of the road was modest.

C. Yes, because there was no preexisting road on the parcel.

D. Yes, because the easement would benefit property acquired after the easement was granted.

27. The owner of a new and unnamed store selling musical instruments was talking by telephone with a famous violinist who was known for her signature red violin. The owner asked whether the violinist would be able to perform at the store's opening and the violinist agreed. The next day, the owner and the violinist executed a valid written contract for the violinist to perform at the opening. The contract contained a clause stating that the contract was the complete and final agreement between the parties. When the violinist appeared at the store to perform, the owner refused to let her play. The violinist sued the owner for breach of contract. The owner moved to introduce evidence that during the telephone conversation, the owner had told the violinist that he would need her services only if he was able to secure the rights to use "theredviolin.com" as the domain name of the store; the violinist objected that the evidence was inadmissible. The contract contains no mention of this condition.

Is the court likely to admit evidence of the conversation regarding the domain name?

A. Yes, because the conversation is evidence of a condition precedent to the existence of the contract.

B. Yes, because this evidence does not contradict the written contract.

C. No, because the parol evidence rule prohibits the introduction of prior extrinsic evidence.

D. No, because the written contract was a complete integration of the parties' agreement.

28. A couple owned a home with a large backyard in which they hosted raucous parties, with extremely loud music and bright lights. These parties often occurred during weekdays and went until dawn. Despite multiple complaints, the couple continued to host these parties. The couple had the following three neighbors: an elderly woman who was abnormally sensitive to loud noises; a teacher who thought the parties were hilarious, as they reminded him of his fraternity days; and a mother who found the parties highly annoying and disruptive to her and her family but never addressed the issue with the couple.

Who would be barred from recovering from the couple in a nuisance action?

A. The elderly woman, because she has special sensitivities.

B. The teacher, because he is not offended by the actions.

C. The mother, because she has not made the couple aware of the effect of their parties on her family.

D. All of the above may recover.

29. An individual purchased a residence with the aid of a bank loan. In exchange, the individual signed a document giving the bank a security interest in the residence. A bank employee filed this mortgage document with the proper governmental entity, but did not file any of the other documents related to the loan, including the note that evidenced the individual's obligation to repay the loan. Subsequently, the individual sold the residence to a buyer who purchased the residence for its fair market value without actual knowledge of the mortgage. The buyer properly filed the deed. The individual later defaulted on the bank loan. A statute in the applicable jurisdiction provides, "No conveyance or mortgage of real property shall be good against subsequent purchasers for value unless the same be first recorded according to law."

Can the bank foreclose on its mortgage on the residence?

A. No, because the buyer purchased the residence for its fair market value.

B. No, because the bank did not record the other loan documents, including the note.

C. Yes, because the buyer had record notice of the mortgage.

D. Yes, because the bank recorded its mortgage before the buyer's purchase.

30. An attorney entered into a valid contract with a client to provide legal services for a set fee of $5,000. The contract provides that rather than paying the attorney, the client is to pay the fee to the attorney's daughter. The daughter, upon learning of the contract from her father, decided to donate this money to a local animal shelter. She told the manager of a local animal shelter that she planned to donate $5,000 to the shelter. The manager, relying on this, purchased $5,000 worth of pet supplies and medicine. The lawyer rendered the legal services, but the client ultimately failed to pay the daughter, who in turn did not donate the money to the shelter. The animal shelter files suit against the client for breach of contract.

Will the animal shelter prevail in its action against the client?

A. Yes, because of the animal shelter's detrimental reliance.

B. Yes, because the shelter is a donee beneficiary.

C. No, because the attorney had no intention to benefit the animal shelter.

D. No, because delegation of duties is not permitted under a services contract.

31. Two cousins received a residence as tenants in common when their grandmother left it to them in her will. The older cousin lived out of state, so the cousins both agreed that the younger cousin would live in the residence. While the younger cousin lived in residence, she paid the property taxes on the residence, an amount far less than the fair rental value of residence. She also paid for the maintenance of the residence, including substantial repairs to the plumbing after a pipe burst. The older cousin fell on hard times. He told his younger cousin that she owed him rent for the time she had been living in the residence. The younger cousin denied owing the older cousin any rent, and claimed that the older cousin owed her for reimbursement for taxes and repairs she had made on the residence throughout the years.

Neither cousin has requested a partition or accounting. Do either of the cousins owe the other money with respect to the residence?

A. The older cousin owes the younger cousin money for his share of taxes and repairs, and the younger cousin owes the older cousin rent.

B. The older cousin owes the younger cousin money for his share of taxes and repairs, but the younger cousin does not owe the older cousin any money for rent.

C. The younger cousin owes the older cousin money for rent, but the older cousin does not owe the younger cousin any money for his share of taxes and repairs.

D. The younger cousin does not owe the older cousin any money for rent, and the older cousin does not owe the younger cousin any money for his share of the taxes and repairs.

32. A manufacturer entered into a 30-year lease with the owner of a building zoned for commercial use. The lease contained a term that gave the manufacturer the right of first refusal if the owner ever decided to sell the building. Ten years later, the owner entered into a contract to sell the building to a third party. The owner has refused to honor the manufacturer's right of first refusal, contending that it violates the Rule Against Perpetuities. The jurisdiction recognizes the common-law Rule Against Perpetuities and the majority rule regarding its application to rights of first refusal.

Which of the following is the manufacturer's best argument that the Rule Against Perpetuities does not apply to the manufacturer's right of first refusal?

A. The right of first refusal was granted in conjunction with a lease.

B. The right of first refusal was granted as part of a commercial transaction.

C. There is no life in being against which the right of first refusal is measured.

D. The manufacturer exercised the right of first refusal before the expiration of the 21-year period.

33. Two individuals entered into a written contract for the sale of a moped for $475. The contract required delivery of the moped on July 1 and provided that oral modification of the contract was prohibited. On June 25, the seller called the buyer and asked if the seller could deliver the moped on July 2, explaining that the seller was overseas and could not return until July 2 due to work commitments that he could not change. The buyer agreed. On June 30 the buyer called the seller, informing him that he was disregarding the modification and demanding delivery of the moped on July 1. The seller delivered the moped on July 2, but the buyer refused to accept or pay for it.

Has the buyer breached the contract?

A. Yes, because the buyer agreed to the modification.

B. Yes, because the buyer waived the July 1 delivery requirement.

C. No, because the buyer did not receive consideration for the modification.

D. No, because the modification was not in writing.

34. Two brothers owned a pasture as joint tenants with the right of survivorship. The older brother had one child, a daughter. The younger brother was a bachelor. Together the brothers deeded a 20 percent interest in the land to the older brother's daughter. Recently, the older brother gave his daughter an additional 10 percent interest in the land.

Under a traditional joint-tenancy analysis, what are the current ownership interests in the land?

A. The two brothers have a 70 percent interest, and the daughter has a 30 percent interest, each as joint tenants with the other two.

B. The two brothers have a 70 percent interest as joint tenants, and the daughter has a 30 percent interest as a tenant in common with her father and uncle.

C. The two brothers each have a 35 percent interest and the daughter has a 30 percent interest, each as a tenant in common with the other two.

D. The younger brother has a 40 percent interest, the daughter has a 30 percent interest, and the older brother has a 30 percent interest, each as a tenant in common with the other two.

35. A woman underwent gall bladder surgery, which was performed by the hospital's head surgeon. An intern observed the surgery and provided time updates to the surgical team, since the team had a limited time in which to complete the operation. The woman experienced significant pain following the surgery, and returned to her doctor. An x-ray revealed that a hemostat, which is an instrument typically used in gall bladder surgery, had been left in the woman's gall bladder. After the hemostat was removed, the woman continued to experience pain due to permanent injuries caused by the hemostat. The woman sued the head surgeon and the intern involved in her surgery. At trial, the woman did not provide any direct evidence that the surgeon or the intern had left the hemostat in her gall bladder. At the close of evidence, the intern moved for a directed verdict. The judge granted the motion.

What is the most likely reason that the judge granted the intern's motion?

A. A negligence plaintiff must provide direct evidence of negligence.

B. The doctrine of res ipsa loquitur is inapplicable to medical malpractice claims.

C. The head surgeon was vicariously responsible for the intern's actions.

D. The intern did not have exclusive control over the hemostat.

36. In response to a phone query by a manufacturer of fans, a supplier of motors offered to sell the manufacturer up to 10,000 motors at the price of $15 each. The supplier assured the manufacturer before ending the call that this price was good for 60 days. One month later, the manufacturer ordered 5,000 motors from the supplier. The supplier informed the manufacturer that the price was now $20 per motor.

Of the following, which is the manufacturer's weakest argument that the price is $15 per motor?

A. The supplier's assurance of the $15 price was irrevocable for 60 days.

B. A month is a reasonable time in which to accept the offer.

C. The supplier could reasonably foresee that the manufacturer would rely on the supplier's offer.

D. The supplier had not revoked its offer.

37. The owner of a building leased a portion of the ground floor for two years at a fixed monthly rent to a chef who opened a restaurant. Eight months later the chef, due to a souring of the local economy, informed the owner that she was closing the restaurant. She vacated the premises and stopped paying rent, which prior to that time she had timely paid. The owner unsuccessfully sought to rent the unoccupied space on behalf of the chef for the following four months before bringing suit against the chef for breach of the lease.

What is the maximum amount of rent to which the owner is entitled?

A. Sixteen months' rent.
B. Twelve months' rent.
C. Four months' rent.
D. Nothing.

38. A personal ad appeared in a pornographic magazine that was published and distributed nationwide. The ad stated that an individual was willing to perform various, specified deviant sexual acts. At the end of the ad, the individual was identified by her first and last name. As a consequence, the individual received lewd and offensive communications from strangers. The individual filed an action based on invasion of privacy due to the public disclosure of private facts and the publication of facts placing her in a false light, both recognized in the jurisdiction. In the complaint, the individual alleged that she had neither submitted the ad to the magazine publisher nor had any desire to perform such acts and that the publisher had published the ad with reckless disregard for its truthfulness. The publisher moved to dismiss the complaint.

How should the court rule on this motion?

A. Grant the motion as to both counts.
B. Grant the motion as to the public disclosure of private facts and deny it as to the publication of facts placing her in a false light.
C. Grant the motion as to the publication of facts placing her in a false light and deny it as to the public disclosure of private facts.
D. Deny the motion as to both counts.

39. At the beginning of the month, an aunt called her niece who lived in a distant city. During the conversation, the aunt promised to give a family heirloom worth $50,000 to her niece if the niece came to the aunt's home to retrieve it. The niece promised to come. The following day the niece bought an airline ticket to fly to the city where her aunt lived at the end of the month. The day before the niece was to make the trip, her aunt died. Under the terms of the aunt's will, the heirloom was left to someone else.

Can the niece acquire the heirloom by enforcing her aunt's promise against the aunt's estate?

A. Yes, under the doctrine of promissory estoppel.

B. Yes, because there was an exchange of promises.

C. No, because the aunt's promise was oral.

D. No, because the aunt promised to make a gift.

40. The owner of a tract of vacant land granted a power-line easement over the land to the electric company. The easement, which was granted in a properly executed written agreement, was never recorded. Several years later, the owner sold the tract of land. The buyer, who planned to sell hot air balloon rides on the property, bought the property sight unseen. After the buyer purchased the property, he discovered the power lines, which would make hot air balloon rides on the property prohibitively dangerous. The applicable jurisdiction has the following recording statute: "No conveyance or mortgage of real property shall be good against subsequent purchasers for value and without notice unless the same be recorded according to law."

Can the buyer successfully challenge the easement?

A. Yes, because the buyer had no actual notice of the easement.

B. Yes, because the easement was not recorded.

C. No, because the buyer had inquiry notice of the easement.

D. No, because with the easements, the land is not suited for the buyer's purpose.

41. As part of a fraternity dare, a college student stood in the middle of a road while drinking a beer. The driver of a car, tired of the fraternity pranks throughout the town, saw the student standing in the road, and reduced his speed but decided not to stop or swerve, saying to himself, "Well, he shouldn't be in the road anyway. He had better get out of the way, and if I hit him, it's his own fault." The intoxicated student could not get out of the way quickly enough, and the driver ran over his foot.

If the student sues the driver for negligence in a pure contributory negligence jurisdiction, is the driver liable for the injuries that the student sustained to his foot?

A. The driver would be liable only for part of the student's damages.
B. The driver would not be liable for the student's damages due to the student's contributory negligence.
C. The driver would be liable for all of the student's damages.
D. The driver would be liable only if he intended to cause injury to the student.

42. At an auction without reserve, the auctioneer called for bids for an antique chair. The first bidder, a consumer without specialized knowledge about antique furniture, bid $10,000. Her bid was acknowledged by the auctioneer. The second bidder bid $11,000, which was also acknowledged by the auctioneer. Before the auctioneer announced the sale of the item to the second bidder, she withdrew her bid. The auctioneer then announced that the chair was sold to the first bidder for $10,000.

Can the first bidder successfully challenge this sale?

A. Yes, because the first bidder was not a merchant.
B. Yes, because the withdrawal of the highest bid did not reinstate the next lowest bid.
C. No, because the auctioneer accepted the first bidder's bid.
D. No, because the auction was without reserve.

43. A client entered into a written contract with his lawyer for the lawyer to provide legal services with regard to the purchase of land. The contract specified that the lawyer was to be paid a flat fee of $2,000 for his services. Prior to completion of the purchase, the lawyer orally assigned his interest in the contract to a third-party landscaper, in exchange for services the landscaper had performed for the lawyer. The lawyer then rendered the legal services necessary for the completion of the purchase of the land.

Can the third-party landscaper collect the lawyer's fee from the client?

A. No, because the assignment was not in writing.

B. No, because the contract between the client and the lawyer was for services.

C. Yes, because the assignment was supported by consideration.

D. Yes, because the lawyer assigned his interest to the third party.

44. The defendant purchased a tiger in the hopes of achieving his life's ambition of performing in a Las Vegas show. The defendant kept the tiger locked in a cage specifically designed for such animals. Unbeknownst to the defendant, however, there was a manufacturing defect in the cage that caused the lock to spring open. The tiger escaped from the cage and ran onto the defendant's yard, where the plaintiff, a painter hired by the defendant, was on a ladder painting the exterior of the defendant's home. The plaintiff panicked when he saw the tiger, causing him to fall off the ladder. The tiger ran off the property without approaching the plaintiff. The plaintiff sustained significant injuries as the result of his fall. The plaintiff has sued the defendant. At trial, the defendant has provided evidence that he exercised reasonable care in containing the tiger. The jurisdiction recognizes the doctrine of contributory negligence.

Is the plaintiff likely to prevail at trial?

A. No, because the plaintiff's own negligence on the ladder contributed to his injuries.

B. No, because the tiger was not a direct cause of the plaintiff's injury.

C. Yes, because the painter was an invitee, and was thus owed the highest duty of care.

D. Yes, because the defendant is strictly liable for the plaintiff's injury.

45.   A pharmaceutical company hired an experienced sales person. Their employment agreement stated that the sales person would be provided with a company car, and that the car could be used for both personal and business use. Prior to finalizing the agreement, the company checked the sales person's driving record and learned that he had no history of tickets or accidents. During his first week on the job, the sales person used his company car to attend a client meeting. After the meeting, the sales person met some friends at a bar, where he had several drinks. The sales person then drove his company car home. On the way, the sales person hit a pedestrian, breaking both the pedestrian's legs. The pedestrian has sued the sales person and the pharmaceutical company for negligence.

Is the company likely to be held liable on a theory of vicarious liability?

A. No, because the company had no reason to know of the sales person's negligent propensities.

B. No, because the sales person was not acting within the scope of his employment.

C. Yes, because the company agreed to let the sales person use a company car for personal use.

D. Yes, because the sales person was on his way home from a meeting with a client.

ANSWER KEY

Remember to log in to your course to submit your answers and view detailed answer explanations.

Item	Answer	Subject	Chapter	Section
1	A	CONTRACTS	FORMATION OF CONTRACTS	Mutual Assent
2	C	TORTS	INTENTIONAL TORTS INVOLVING PERSONAL INJURY	Assault
3	D	REAL PROPERTY	DISPUTES ABOUT OWNERSHIP IN LAND	The Land Sale Contract
4	D	REAL PROPERTY	OWNERSHIP	Present Estates
5	B	REAL PROPERTY	DISPUTES ABOUT OWNERSHIP IN LAND	Conveyance by Will and by Operation of Law
6	C	CONTRACTS	CONDITIONS AND PERFORMANCE	Satisfaction of Conditions
7	D	TORTS	NEGLIGENCE	Duty
8	B	CONTRACTS	BREACH OF CONTRACTS AND REMEDIES	Remedies Under the UCC
9	D	CONTRACTS	BREACH OF CONTRACTS AND REMEDIES	Anticipatory Repudiation
10	A	REAL PROPERTY	DISPUTES ABOUT OWNERSHIP IN LAND	The Land Sale Contract
11	D	CONTRACTS	FORMATION OF CONTRACTS	Warranties in Sale-of-Goods Contracts
12	A	CONTRACTS	BREACH OF CONTRACTS AND REMEDIES	Remedies Under the UCC
13	B	TORTS	DEFENSES TO INTENTIONAL TORTS INVOLVING PERSONAL INJURY	Defense of Others
14	C	REAL PROPERTY	DISPUTES ABOUT OWNERSHIP IN LAND	Delivery and Recording of Deed

Item	Answer	Subject	Chapter	Section
15	D	REAL PROPERTY	DISPUTES ABOUT OWNERSHIP IN LAND	The Land Sale Contract
16	A	TORTS	PRODUCTS LIABILITY	Strict Products Liability
17	A	REAL PROPERTY	DISPUTES ABOUT THE USE OF LAND	Covenants Running with the Land
18	D	TORTS	PRODUCTS LIABILITY	Warranties
19	B	TORTS	NEGLIGENCE	The Standard of Care
20	A	CONTRACTS	BREACH OF CONTRACT AND REMEDIES	Remedies Under the UCC
21	A	TORTS	NEGLIGENCE	Causation
22	B	TORTS	INTENTIONAL TORTS INVOLVING PERSONAL INJURY	Battery
23	A	REAL PROPERTY	DISPUTES ABOUT OWNERSHIP IN LAND	Conveyance by Will and by Operation of Law
24	B	CONTRACTS	STATUTE OF FRAUDS	Types of Contracts Within the Statute of Frauds
25	C	CONTRACTS	FORMATION OF CONTRACTS	Defenses to Formation
26	D	REAL PROPERTY	DISPUTES ABOUT THE USE OF LAND	Easements
27	A	CONTRACTS	PAROL EVIDENCE RULE	When the Parol Evidence Rule is Inapplicable
28	D	TORTS	HARMS TO PERSONAL PROPERTY AND LAND	Nuisance
29	D	REAL PROPERTY	DISPUTES ABOUT OWNERSHIP IN LAND	Delivery and Recording of Deed
30	C	CONTRACTS	THIRD-PARTY BENEFICIARY CONTRACTS	Intended and Incidental Beneficiaries

Item	Answer	Subject	Chapter	Section
31	D	REAL PROPERTY	OWNERSHIP	Concurrent Estates
32	A	REAL PROPERTY	DISPUTES ABOUT OWNERSHIP IN LAND	The Land Sale Contract
33	D	CONTRACTS	FORMATION OF CONTRACTS	Consideration
34	D	REAL PROPERTY	OWNERSHIP	Concurrent Estates
35	D	TORTS	NEGLIGENCE	Breach or Violation of Duty of Care
36	A	CONTRACTS	FORMATION OF CONTRACTS	Mutual Assent
37	C	REAL PROPERTY	LANDLORD AND TENANT	Duties of Tenant
38	B	TORTS	DEFAMATION, INVASION OF PRIVACY, AND BUSINESS TORTS	Invasion of Privacy
39	D	CONTRACTS	FORMATION OF CONTRACTS	Consideration
40	C	REAL PROPERTY	DISPUTES ABOUT OWNERSHIP IN LAND	Delivery and Recording of Deed
41	C	TORTS	NEGLIGENCE	Defenses to Negligence
42	B	CONTRACTS	FORMATION OF CONTRACTS	Mutual Assent
43	D	CONTRACTS	ASSIGNMENT OF RIGHTS AND DELEGATION OF DUTIES	Assignment of Rights
44	D	TORTS	STRICT LIABILITY	Animals
45	B	TORTS	NEGLIGENCE	Vicarious Liability

Milestone Exam Two

MILESTONE EXAM TWO

TIME: 99 MINUTES

Welcome to Milestone Exam Two. This exam consists of 55 questions in the areas of Civil Procedure, Constitutional Law, Criminal Law & Procedure, and Evidence. This exam will take approximately 99 minutes (an average of 1.8 minutes per question). After you have completed this exam, log in to your course to submit your answers, view detailed answer explanations, and compare your performance to other Themis students.

Name: _____ Date: _____

Start Time: _____ End Time: _____

1 ⊏A⊐ ⊏B⊐ ⊏C⊐ ⊏D⊐   26 ⊏A⊐ ⊏B⊐ ⊏C⊐ ⊏D⊐   51 ⊏A⊐ ⊏B⊐ ⊏C⊐ ⊏D⊐
2 ⊏A⊐ ⊏B⊐ ⊏C⊐ ⊏D⊐   27 ⊏A⊐ ⊏B⊐ ⊏C⊐ ⊏D⊐   52 ⊏A⊐ ⊏B⊐ ⊏C⊐ ⊏D⊐
3 ⊏A⊐ ⊏B⊐ ⊏C⊐ ⊏D⊐   28 ⊏A⊐ ⊏B⊐ ⊏C⊐ ⊏D⊐   53 ⊏A⊐ ⊏B⊐ ⊏C⊐ ⊏D⊐
4 ⊏A⊐ ⊏B⊐ ⊏C⊐ ⊏D⊐   29 ⊏A⊐ ⊏B⊐ ⊏C⊐ ⊏D⊐   54 ⊏A⊐ ⊏B⊐ ⊏C⊐ ⊏D⊐
5 ⊏A⊐ ⊏B⊐ ⊏C⊐ ⊏D⊐   30 ⊏A⊐ ⊏B⊐ ⊏C⊐ ⊏D⊐   55 ⊏A⊐ ⊏B⊐ ⊏C⊐ ⊏D⊐
6 ⊏A⊐ ⊏B⊐ ⊏C⊐ ⊏D⊐   31 ⊏A⊐ ⊏B⊐ ⊏C⊐ ⊏D⊐
7 ⊏A⊐ ⊏B⊐ ⊏C⊐ ⊏D⊐   32 ⊏A⊐ ⊏B⊐ ⊏C⊐ ⊏D⊐
8 ⊏A⊐ ⊏B⊐ ⊏C⊐ ⊏D⊐   33 ⊏A⊐ ⊏B⊐ ⊏C⊐ ⊏D⊐
9 ⊏A⊐ ⊏B⊐ ⊏C⊐ ⊏D⊐   34 ⊏A⊐ ⊏B⊐ ⊏C⊐ ⊏D⊐
10 ⊏A⊐ ⊏B⊐ ⊏C⊐ ⊏D⊐   35 ⊏A⊐ ⊏B⊐ ⊏C⊐ ⊏D⊐
11 ⊏A⊐ ⊏B⊐ ⊏C⊐ ⊏D⊐   36 ⊏A⊐ ⊏B⊐ ⊏C⊐ ⊏D⊐
12 ⊏A⊐ ⊏B⊐ ⊏C⊐ ⊏D⊐   37 ⊏A⊐ ⊏B⊐ ⊏C⊐ ⊏D⊐
13 ⊏A⊐ ⊏B⊐ ⊏C⊐ ⊏D⊐   38 ⊏A⊐ ⊏B⊐ ⊏C⊐ ⊏D⊐
14 ⊏A⊐ ⊏B⊐ ⊏C⊐ ⊏D⊐   39 ⊏A⊐ ⊏B⊐ ⊏C⊐ ⊏D⊐
15 ⊏A⊐ ⊏B⊐ ⊏C⊐ ⊏D⊐   40 ⊏A⊐ ⊏B⊐ ⊏C⊐ ⊏D⊐
16 ⊏A⊐ ⊏B⊐ ⊏C⊐ ⊏D⊐   41 ⊏A⊐ ⊏B⊐ ⊏C⊐ ⊏D⊐
17 ⊏A⊐ ⊏B⊐ ⊏C⊐ ⊏D⊐   42 ⊏A⊐ ⊏B⊐ ⊏C⊐ ⊏D⊐
18 ⊏A⊐ ⊏B⊐ ⊏C⊐ ⊏D⊐   43 ⊏A⊐ ⊏B⊐ ⊏C⊐ ⊏D⊐
19 ⊏A⊐ ⊏B⊐ ⊏C⊐ ⊏D⊐   44 ⊏A⊐ ⊏B⊐ ⊏C⊐ ⊏D⊐
20 ⊏A⊐ ⊏B⊐ ⊏C⊐ ⊏D⊐   45 ⊏A⊐ ⊏B⊐ ⊏C⊐ ⊏D⊐
21 ⊏A⊐ ⊏B⊐ ⊏C⊐ ⊏D⊐   46 ⊏A⊐ ⊏B⊐ ⊏C⊐ ⊏D⊐
22 ⊏A⊐ ⊏B⊐ ⊏C⊐ ⊏D⊐   47 ⊏A⊐ ⊏B⊐ ⊏C⊐ ⊏D⊐
23 ⊏A⊐ ⊏B⊐ ⊏C⊐ ⊏D⊐   48 ⊏A⊐ ⊏B⊐ ⊏C⊐ ⊏D⊐
24 ⊏A⊐ ⊏B⊐ ⊏C⊐ ⊏D⊐   49 ⊏A⊐ ⊏B⊐ ⊏C⊐ ⊏D⊐
25 ⊏A⊐ ⊏B⊐ ⊏C⊐ ⊏D⊐   50 ⊏A⊐ ⊏B⊐ ⊏C⊐ ⊏D⊐

Themis
Bar Review

SCORE   RESCORE

1. The user of a power tool sued the tool's manufacturer in state court. The action was based on a strict product liability claim that the manufacturer's failure to adequately warn the user of a defect in the power tool caused the user's injury. The manufacturer properly removed the case to federal court. The applicable law of the state that governs the existence of the strict product liability claim also recognizes a rebuttable heeding presumption. This presumption assumes that an injured plaintiff would have heeded an adequate warning if one had been given. Under state law, this presumption does not shift the burden of persuasion on this issue to the manufacturer.

The manufacturer did not present evidence that the user would not have heeded a different warning had it been given. The court instructed the jury that it must apply the presumption that the warning, if given, would have been heedeD.

Is the court's instruction correct?

A. No, because the jury may, but is not required to, apply the presumption.
B. No, because state law presumptions are not recognized in a federal diversity action.
C. Yes, because the manufacturer failed to offer evidence to rebut the presumption.
D. Yes, because the Federal Rules of Evidence apply the bursting bubble approach to presumptions.

2. After a female politician is injured in a riot following a heated, public debate, a state enacts the following statute: "Any words targeting women or minorities likely to produce violence or rioting are prohibited on any public property."

Is the statute constitutional?

A. No, because the statute punishes only speech targeting specific groups.
B. No, because the state cannot restrict speech in public forums.
C. Yes, because the state can prohibit fighting words.
D. Yes, because laws affecting women and minorities receive heightened scrutiny.

3. The defendant, a college student, attended a lecture for his history class regarding the first moon landing. The defendant, who had a history of mental illness, believed that the evidence of the moon landing was the result of a conspiracy by the U.S. government, and that a human had never set foot on the moon. Irate at the professor's lecture, the defendant started yelling his theories at the class. When the professor asked the defendant to leave the class, he became furious and hit the professor with his textbook. The defendant has been charged with battery, and has pleaded not guilty by reason of insanity due to his history of mental illness. The evidence at trial shows that the defendant's mental illness caused him to hit the professor and that although he knew it was wrong, he could not resist the impulse to harm her. The jurisdiction follows the M'Naughten test regarding criminal insanity.

May the defendant be convicted of battery?

A. Yes, because the defendant's loss of control was not sudden.
B. Yes, because the defendant appreciated the wrongfulness of his actions.
C. No, because the defendant lacked the capacity for self-control.
D. No, because the defendant's unlawful act was the product of his mental defect.

4. A witness testified in a federal case on behalf of a criminal defendant. On cross-examination, the government sought to impeach the witness with a state court conviction for felony assault nine years prior. The witness had started a ministry for other prisoners during his short time in prison, and became an active religious and community leader following his release. He has not had any arrests or convictions since being released from prison, and he was previously pardoned by the outgoing governor based on his efforts on behalf of the community. The defense has filed a motion to exclude evidence of the conviction. When presented with the motion, the judge noted that the conviction was probative of the veracity of the witness, and would have little prejudicial effect.

Is the judge likely to allow evidence of the assault conviction to be admitted?

A. Yes, because the conviction is less than 10 years old.
B. Yes, because the probative value of the conviction is not outweighed by its prejudicial effect.
C. No, because assault is not a crime of dishonesty or false statement.
D. No, because the witness was pardoned and has not been convicted of another felony.

5. A retailer incorporated in State A sued the publisher of a newsletter for libel in a State C state court. The retailer's complaint sought $1 million in damages in good faith. The retailer, which had its headquarters in State B, did business throughout the United States, but had its largest warehouse in State C where it also operated more stores than any other state. The publisher of the newsletter, which had subscribers in every state, was an individual who lived most of the year abroad, but continued to be domiciled in State C. The publisher timely filed a petition to remove the libel action to a State C federal district court.

Should the federal court deny this petition?

A. No, because diversity jurisdiction exists.

B. No, because the newsletter is published nationwide.

C. Yes, because the retailer and publisher are citizens of the same state for diversity purposes.

D. Yes, because the publisher is a citizen of the forum state.

6. Two gang members orchestrated a plan to scare a local priest who was organizing after school programs to keep kids off the street. They planned to go into the priest's office with a gun, threaten him, and steal any money in the church offices. One gang member went into the office with the gun while the other stood outside as a lookout. When the priest approached the gang member with the gun in an attempt to reason with him, the gang member panicked and shot the priest, who died instantly. The prosecution charged both gang members with conspiracy and murder, but offered a deal to each in exchange for his testimony against the other. The shooter accepted the deal, while the defendant, who was the lookout, decided to proceed to trial.

Is the defendant likely to be convicted of murder?

A. No, because the defendant did not conspire to murder the priest.

B. No, because the defendant's co-conspirator will not be tried.

C. Yes, because the Wharton Rule allows the defendant to be convicted without his co-conspirator.

D. Yes, because the murder was committed in furtherance of the conspiracy.

7. The defendant robbed an elderly woman at gunpoint. An off-duty police officer witnessed the incident from a distance while walking his dog. He chased down the defendant and placed him under arrest. After being informed of his Miranda rights, the defendant immediately invoked his right to counsel. The defendant was taken to the police station, and before the defendant's attorney arrived, the defendant was placed in a lineup. The defendant did not object to being placed in the lineup. The elderly woman immediately identified the defendant as the robber. The defendant's attorney moved to suppress the identification because it was conducted without the attorney present.

Is the defendant's motion likely to be granted?

A. No, because the defendant waived his right to have counsel present.
B. No, because the defendant was not entitled to the presence of counsel.
C. Yes, because the defendant invoked his right to counsel.
D. Yes, because the lineup was a corporeal identification.

8. A supplier sued a commercial customer for nonpayment of its bill. The customer, contending that it had paid the supplier, produced and authenticated a printed version of a receipt purportedly prepared by the supplier showing a payment made by the customer. The receipt had been scanned by the customer into its computer databank. The customer had intentionally discarded the original receipt in the normal course of its business practice to reduce recordkeeping costs. Contending that the original receipt had been a forgery, the supplier objected to the admission of the printed version of the receipt into evidence. The judge ruled in favor of the supplier, and prohibited the admission of the receipt. The customer then sought to call its employee to testify that he had personally sent the payment reflected in the receipt to the supplier.

Should the court, over the supplier's objection, permit the customer's employee to testify about the payment?

A. No, because the supplier called into the question the authenticity of the original receipt.
B. No, because the customer had intentionally discarded the original receipt.
C. Yes, because the printed version of the receipt constituted a duplicate.
D. Yes, because the employee had personal knowledge of the payment.

9. During the defendant's cross-country road trip, he was involved in a car accident with the plaintiff in the state where the plaintiff lived. Following the accident, the plaintiff sued the defendant in federal court located in the state where the accident occurred. Prior to the accident, the defendant had never been to the forum state. The defendant flew home from the forum state directly following the accident, and has not been back to the forum state since that time. Before filing a responsive pleading, the defendant filed a motion to dismiss, arguing that the court lacked personal jurisdiction. The court denied the defendant's motion.

What is the most likely basis for the exercise of jurisdiction over the defendant in this case?

A.   General jurisdiction.

B.   In rem jurisdiction.

C.   Quasi-in rem jurisdiction.

D.   Specific jurisdiction.

10. The plaintiff resides in a city in the Southern District of State C. The plaintiff credibly alleges that her federal legal rights were violated in a city in the Western District of State D by two defendants. The first defendant resides in a city in the Northern District of State C. The second defendant resides in a town in the Central District of State C, where the plaintiff's employer is located.

In which of the following districts would venue be proper as to all the parties?

A. The Western District of State D, the Northern District of State C, or the Southern District of State C

B. The Western District of State D, the Central District of State C, or the Southern District of State C.

C. The Western District of State D, the Northern District of State C, or the Central District of State C.

D. The Western District of State D, the Northern District of State C, the Central District of State C, or the Southern District of State C.

11. Congress passed a law allowing the Secretary of Transportation to designate speed limits on all interstate highways "at whatever speed prudent in the interests of both safety and efficiency." The Secretary of Transportation felt that each state was in the best position, based on their studies of their own highway systems, to determine the appropriate speed limit within that state, so he collaborated with each state's department of transportation to determine each state's limit. As a result of an increasing number of high-speed car accidents, one state decided to lower its speed limit. A driver was ticketed for driving over the state's newly-lowered speed limit. The driver challenged the validity of the statute giving the Secretary of Transportation power to designate the speed limits.

Should the statute be found invalid or valid?

A. Invalid, because Congress exceeded its authority to delegate this matter to the Secretary of Transportation.
B. Invalid, because the legislation did not contain sufficiently intelligible standards by which to guide the Secretary of Transportation.
C. Valid, because the legislation was a proper exercise of Congress's power to delegate to the executive branch.
D. Valid, because the Secretary of Transportation consulted each state's department of transportation to guide his decision.

12. The State H federal district court chose a representative for a class of 67 patients who were allegedly injured by negligent medical care at a hospital in State H and collectively suffered damages of $3,000,000. After correctly asserting diversity jurisdiction, the court certified the class upon finding that the four basic requirements for a class action have been met and that prosecution of the claims through separate actions would impair the interests of other class members. The court posted on the courthouse bulletin board its certification order, which (1) described the action, the class, and the legal claims; and (2) informed class members that they may appear through an attorney and may request an exclusion, but otherwise are bound by the class judgment. Most members of the class never see this notice, including one patient who suffered especially severe damages as a result of the hospital's negligence. After the class action trial is almost finished, the patient, who is unaware of the trial, filed a separate suit in the State H federal district court against the hospital.

Should the court allow that suit?

A. Yes, because the contents of the notice did not meet the requirements of the federal class action rule.
B. Yes, because the patient never received appropriate notice of the class action.
C. No, because the Class Action Fairness Act prohibits such suits.
D. No, because the court properly certified the class and was not required to provide notice of the class action.

13. A homeowner was selling illegal drugs out of his house, which was located in a well-heeled, suburban neighborhood. A customer, knowing that the homeowner likely had a large amount of cash from selling drugs, knocked on the homeowner's door. When the homeowner opened the door upon recognizing the customer, the customer pulled out a toy pistol that looked like a real gun and demanded money. The customer followed the homeowner inside and over to a table with a drawer in the entryway, in which the homeowner told the customer there was money. Instead, the homeowner pulled a gun out of the drawer and shot and killed the customer. The homeowner is arrested and charged with murder. The jurisdiction does not follow the retreat doctrine.

Should the homeowner be convicted of the customer's murder?

A. No, because it was reasonable for the homeowner to believe that his life was at risk.

B. No, because the jurisdiction does not follow the retreat doctrine.

C. Yes, because the customer was not armed with a deadly weapon.

D. Yes, because the homeowner was committing a crime by selling the drugs and therefore was not privileged to use self-defense.

14. A witness was making a deposit at a local bank when the bank was robbed. The witness observed the robber closely and subsequently gave the police a detailed written description of the robber and the events that occurred in the bank. Following the robber's arrest and subsequent release on bail, the robber appeared at the witness's home, telling him to leave the state immediately and not appear at the trial or he would be killed. The witness telephoned the police to report the threat, but also told them that he was afraid for his life. At trial, the witness, who had left the state, did not appear and failed to respond to a subpoena. The prosecution now seeks to introduce the witness's written statement into evidence. The defendant objects to the introduction of the evidence.

Should the judge admit the written statement over the objection of the defendant?

A. Yes, as a prior statement of identification.

B. Yes, because the robber forfeited any right to object as a result of his threat against the witness.

C. No, as it is hearsay not within any exception.

D. No, because the witness's absence is voluntary and therefore does not constitute unavailability.

15. A plaintiff brought a products liability action against an out-of-state manufacturer seeking $125,000 in damages due to personal injuries received while using a tool made by the manufacturer. Pursuant to the permissive joinder rule, the plaintiff's spouse joined in the action, which was filed in federal court, seeking damages of $5,000 for loss of consortium.

Does the court have subject-matter jurisdiction over the spouse's claim?

A. No, because the spouse's claim does not satisfy the amount-in-controversy requirement.

B. No, because the court's jurisdiction over plaintiff's claim is not based on federal question jurisdiction.

C. Yes, because the spouse's claim forms part of the same case or controversy as the plaintiff's claim.

D. Yes, because the plaintiffs are related.

16. A woman sought to kill her husband. She developed an elaborate plan that involved cutting the brake lines on his automobile while his car sat in his office parking lot. On the morning of the planned killing, the woman walked with her husband to the garage. Watching as her husband began to pull his car out of the garage, the woman activated the switch to shut the garage door. The switch malfunctioned and as result the garage door came crashing down on the car and crushed the husband to death.

For which crime could the woman properly be found guilty?

A. Murder.

B. Voluntary manslaughter.

C. Involuntary manslaughter.

D. None of the above.

17. A plaintiff brought suit against a defendant for injuries she sustained in a car accident that she accused the defendant of negligently causing. Prior to filing suit, the plaintiff's attorney had the plaintiff visit a physician to determine the extent of her injuries for purposes of determining the damages to be claimed in the lawsuit. After the plaintiff's examination, while the attorney, plaintiff, and physician were discussing the extent of the plaintiff's injuries, the plaintiff admitted that she may have had a few beers right before the accident. At trial, the defendant's counsel sought to call the doctor to testify about the statement. The plaintiff properly objected to the introduction of this testimony.

How should the judge rule on the plaintiff's objection?

A. Sustain the objection, as the attorney-client privilege is applicable.
B. Sustain the objection, as the physician-patient privilege is applicable.
C. Overrule the objection, as the statement was made by an opposing party.
D. Overrule the objection, as the physician would constitute an expert witness.

18. A man borrowed his friend's truck in order to move to a new apartment and promised to return the truck two days later, following the completion of the move. After finishing the move, the man instead sold the truck to a used car dealer in order to pay off the back rent he owed to his landlord on his former apartment, which was his intention at the time he borrowed the truck.

With which of the following crimes should the man be charged?

A. Larceny by trick.
B. Embezzlement.
C. False pretenses.
D. No crime.

19. After violence against a specific religious minority becomes an epidemic in the United States, Congress enacts hate crime legislation pertaining to those of that religious faith and also establishes that no public entity may discriminate against this group unless such discrimination is the least restrictive means to achieve a compelling interest.

What is the most likely reason for the invalidity of this law?

A. Congress is improperly creating hate crime legislation coupled with civil rights legislation.

B. Congress is improperly creating new equal protection rights.

C. The law should apply intermediate scrutiny to discrimination by a public entity to a group.

D. Congress does not have a sufficiently compelling state interest in enacting the legislation.

20. An investor brought an action in federal district court for damages based on a violation of federal securities law. The defendant, a foreign corporation, received service of process by proper means in its country of incorporation. While the defendant's contacts with the state in which the forum court sits do not satisfy the "minimum contacts" test, the defendant's contacts with the entire United States satisfy this test.

Of the following, which additional fact must the investor establish in order for the court to exercise personal jurisdiction over the defendant?

A. No state court could exercise jurisdiction over the foreign corporation.

B. The district court is located in the state in which the investor is domiciled.

C. The applicable federal securities law provides for nationwide service of process.

D. The court has personal jurisdiction over the defendant under the long-arm statute of the forum state.

21. A police officer received an anonymous tip that the defendant was manufacturing methamphetamine in his basement. Based solely on the tip, the officer obtained a warrant to search the defendant's basement for drugs and related manufacturing equipment. The officer and his partner went to the defendant's home to execute the warrant. Believing the defendant was not home, the officers did not knock on the door, but simply opened the unlocked door. In searching the defendant's basement, the officers found large quantities of methamphetamine, related manufacturing equipment, and a notebook that said "Ledger" across the cover. The notebook contained a ledger, with the names of the defendant's clients and statements of their accounts. The officers seized all these items. The defendant seeks to suppress the evidence seized by the officers.

What is the defendant's best argument in favor of suppressing the notebook?

A. The notebook was not named in the warrant.
B. The notebook was in the nature of a personal diary.
C. The officers failed to "knock and announce" their presence.
D. The warrant was invalid.

22. Congress enacted a statute called the "Anti-Sweatshop Law" (ASL) making it a federal felony punishable by fines or imprisonment for an individual or private business to knowingly employ two or more workers and keep them in involuntary employment based on physical or legal threats made by the employer. The ASL's text and legislative history indicated that in enacting the ASL, Congress intended to regulate purely private behavior regardless of whether the behavior affected interstate commerce.

If the Supreme Court upholds the statute against a constitutional challenge, which of the following amendments, taken alone, would be sufficient to support the holding?

A. The Twelfth Amendment.
B. The Thirteenth Amendment.
C. The Fourteenth Amendment.
D. The Fifteenth Amendment.

23. A plaintiff sued a defendant for damages resulting from an automobile accident. At trial, the defendant sought to offer into evidence a properly authenticated letter from the plaintiff that stated, "I know I might have been partially at fault, so I am willing to accept half of my original request in order to avoid a lengthy trial." The plaintiff objected to the introduction of the letter.

May the court admit the letter over the plaintiff's objection?

A. Yes, because it constitutes a statement against interest.

B. Yes, because it constitutes an admission by a party opponent.

C. No, because it was made as part of an offer to settle the dispute.

D. No, because it is hearsay not within any exception.

24. As part of a divorce decree, a father was ordered to make monthly child support payments to his son's mother. The father failed to make such payments. At a criminal contempt hearing regarding the father's failure to comply with the child support order, the father's attorney presented evidence as to the father's inability to make such payments, which evidence was disputed by the mother. Under state law, there is a presumption that, with regard to enforcement of a child support order, the parent obligated to make child support payments has the ability to make such payments, since such ability was determined by the court at the time that the order was issued. In addition, the highest state court has ruled that, with regard to imposition of criminal contempt for a failure to make child support payments, the burden of proof as to the inability to make such payments is placed on the father. The court, finding that the father had not met this burden, held the father in criminal contempt and sentenced him to six months in prison. The father has appealed this decision as unconstitutional.

Which of the following is the father's best argument in support of his challenge to the constitutionality of this decision?

A. A presumption in a criminal trial violates the Due Process Clause of the Fourteenth Amendment.

B. The Due Process Clause of the Fourteenth Amendment does not permit the burden of proof to be placed on the person on whom the criminal penalty would be imposed.

C. The ability to make child support payments is an element of criminal contempt.

D. The father's right to trial by jury was violated.

25. On August 1, the plaintiff, a citizen of one state, sued the defendant, a citizen of another state, in the federal district court in the defendant's home state. The plaintiff's complaint credibly alleges that (1) the defendant breached a contract with the plaintiff that resulted in $150,000 in damages, and (2) the court has diversity jurisdiction. On November 15, the plaintiff served process on the defendant by sending the summons and complaint to the defendant's residence via Overnight Express Mail, a form of service authorized by the law of the forum state. The defendant moves to dismiss the complaint based on insufficient service of process.

Should the court grant this motion?

A. Yes, because the Federal Rules authorize service only on a defendant personally, on a person of suitable age and discretion at defendant's usual abode, or on an agent authorized by a defendant or by law to receive service.

B. Yes, because the service of process was not timely.

C. No, because under the *Erie* doctrine, the federal court must apply state law.

D. No, because the Federal Rules allow service that follows state law governing courts in the state where the federal district court is located.

26. A state enacts a statute prohibiting semi-truck drivers from using cellular phones while operating their vehicles. There is no general statute applying the same prohibition to regular drivers in the state. A truck driver in the state sues in federal court after he receives a citation for using his cellular phone while operating his vehicle. He claims he is being unfairly targeted.

Which of the following would govern the analysis of the driver's claim?

A. Substantive Due Process.

B. Privileges and Immunities Clause.

C. Dormant Commerce Clause.

D. Procedural Due Process.

27. The defendant was arrested for the murder of his wife. Following his arrest, the defendant was handcuffed and placed in a police car by two police officers. The officers did not provide the defendant with Miranda warnings. During the drive to the police station, the officers began questioning the defendant about his whereabouts the night of the murder. The defendant stated that he was home alone all night waiting for his wife, who never arrived home. At trial, the prosecution offered evidence showing that the wife was murdered in the home she shared with the defendant. The defendant took the stand in his own defense and testified that, on the night of the murder, he was at his brother's house watching a movie, and that he spent the night there. The prosecution seeks to introduce the defendant's earlier statement to the police that he was home alone.

Is the defendant's statement to the police admissible?

A. No, because the defendant was not advised of his Miranda rights.

B. Yes, but only to impeach the defendant's credibility.

C. Yes, but only to prove that the defendant was home on the night of the murder.

D. Yes, both to impeach the defendant's credibility and to prove that he was home on the night of the murder.

28. In a breach of contract action, the defendant denied that her signature appears on the contract. At trial, the plaintiff called the defendant's secretary as a witness to testify that, having worked for the defendant for several years, she had seen the defendant's signature many times and that the signature on the contract is the signature of the defendant. The defendant objected to the witness's testimony.

Should the court overrule the objection?

A. No, because the identification of handwriting requires expert testimony and the secretary has not been qualified as an expert.

B. No, because the jury must compare the signature in question with another signature of the defendant that has been proven to be genuine in order to authenticate it.

C. Yes, because a lay witness with prior personal knowledge of a person's handwriting may testify as to whether the document is in that person's handwriting.

D. Yes, because the secretary can be considered an expert with specific knowledge of her employer's handwriting and signature.

29. A mother, upon learning that her son had been assaulted by his middle school teacher, filed a suit on behalf of her son against the school district, claiming that it had negligently hired the teacher. At trial, the mother sought to introduce the testimony of one of the teacher's former students from when the teacher had worked in a different school district. The witness would testify that the teacher had beaten her. The mother had further evidence that this incident had been included in the teacher's personnel file.

Is the former student's testimony likely to be admitted?

A. No, because character evidence is generally not admissible in civil cases.

B. No, because character may not be proved by evidence of specific instances of conduct.

C. Yes, because the teacher's character is an essential element of the mother's claim.

D. Yes, because character evidence is generally admissible in civil cases.

30. A consumer sued a lawn mower manufacturer in a federal district court sitting in diversity jurisdiction, alleging that the consumer suffered damages due to a defect in the manufacture of a lawn mower. Prior to commencing suit, the consumer consulted two experts, a design expert and a manufacturing expert, about the lawn mower that was the source of the consumer's injuries. After filing the complaint, the consumer, in making his required disclosures, identified the manufacturing expert as an expert expected to be called at trial. The design expert is not expected to testify. The manufacturer sent an interrogatory to the consumer requesting the identity of any other experts consulted with regard to the case.

Is the consumer required to identify the design expert in his answer to the interrogatory?

A. No, because the design expert is not expected to testify at trial.

B. No, because the information is protected by the work product doctrine.

C. Yes, because the manufacturer has specifically requested the identity of all experts consulted by the plaintiff.

D. Yes, because no privilege or other protection applies.

31. In response to recent unusual earthquake activity, a large city has enacted an ordinance requiring the permanent placement of seismographic equipment in the basement of 20 randomly selected commercial buildings throughout the city as part of the creation of an early warning network. Although the owners of the buildings will not be compensated, the cost of the purchase and installation of the equipment is to be borne by a private university that will operate the early warning network. The owner of one building that has been randomly selected as a site for this equipment has challenged this law as unconstitutional.

Should the court rule in favor of the owner?

A. No, because the economic impact on the owner would be slight.

B. No, because the owner's building was randomly selected.

C. Yes, because the city will not operate the network.

D. Yes, because the equipment will reside permanently in the building.

32. Congress enacted immigration legislation that provided for special preferences for admitting into the United States an alien with a family member who is a United States citizen. In defining "family members" for this purpose, the statute included a natural mother and her illegitimate child, but made no similar provision for a natural father and his illegitimate child due to the greater administrative difficulty in ascertaining the existence of this relationship. A United States citizen who was the natural father of an illegitimate child filed an action in federal court challenging the constitutionality of the exclusion of a natural father and his illegitimate child from the definition of "family members."

Can the father successfully challenge this statute as unconstitutional?

A. No, because the father has not suffered an economic injury, thus does not have standing.

B. No, because the exclusion is not arbitrary and unreasonable.

C. Yes, because the statute discriminates on the basis of gender.

D. Yes, because illegitimacy is a quasi-suspect class.

33. A man overheard his co-worker make a pass at his wife at an office party. The man was furious and went outside to collect his thoughts. A few minutes later, he returned to the party and joined his wife and his co-worker in their conversation. When the man's co-worker excused himself to go to the restroom, the man followed him into the restroom and hit him over the head with a beer bottle. Although the man did not intend to kill his co-worker, the co-worker fell into a coma and died a week later.

What is the most serious crime, listed in order of increasing seriousness, for which the man could properly be convicted?

A. Aggravated battery.
B. Involuntary manslaughter.
C. Voluntary manslaughter.
D. Murder.

34. A plaintiff secured a default judgment for breach of contract against a defendant in a diversity action brought in federal district court in State X. The defendant, a natural person, was not domiciled in State X, but had sufficient contacts with the state to satisfy the minimum contacts test. The defendant was properly served with process but elected not to contest the action. The plaintiff has, pursuant to statute, registered the judgment with a federal district court located in State Y. The defendant has a bank account in State Y, but otherwise has no property or contacts with the state. The plaintiff has sought a court order permitting a levy against the defendant's bank account to satisfy the judgment. The defendant has challenged this order on grounds that the federal district court in State Y lacks personal jurisdiction over the defendant.

How should the court rule on the defendant's challenge?

A. Uphold the challenge, because the defendant did not litigate the matter in the federal district court in State X.
B. Uphold the challenge, because the defendant lacks minimum contacts with State Y.
C. Deny the challenge, because of the Full Faith and Credit Clause in Article IV of the U.S. Constitution.
D. Deny the challenge, because the minimum contacts test does not apply.

35. A police officer saw a man who was a convicted drug dealer walking down the street. The officer temporarily detained the man based on a reasonable suspicion that the man was illegally carrying a weapon. The officer conducted a pat-down of the man and felt an indeterminate lump in the man's jacket pocket. The officer removed the object, which turned out to be a pocket Bible. Protruding from the Bible was a plastic bag containing a white powder. The officer recognized the powder as heroin, and immediately arrested the man. Later tests confirmed that the powder was heroin. At trial, the man's attorney moved to exclude evidence of the heroin.

How should the judge rule?

A. Deny the motion, because the evidence was discovered during a valid Terry stop.

B. Deny the motion, because the officer had reasonable suspicion that the man was carrying a weapon.

C. Grant the motion, because the pocket Bible did not immediately resemble a weapon or contraband.

D. Grant the motion, because the officer did not have probable cause to stop the man and conduct a pat-down.

36. A state government official was murdered by the defendant. In response to the murder, the state legislature passed and the governor signed into law a statute that made it a crime to use a handgun to inflict serious bodily injury or death on a state government official. Subsequently, the defendant was arrested, prosecuted, and convicted of common-law murder and violation of the handgun statute. The defendant was sentenced to 20 years in prison for the murder and five years in prison for the handgun offense, to be served concurrently. On appeal, the defendant argued that his conviction for the handgun offense was unconstitutional. This argument had been rejected by the trial court.

Should the appellate court affirm the defendant's conviction for this offense?

A. No, because it constitutes a bill of attainder in violation of Article 1, section 10.

B. No, because it constitutes an ex post facto law in violation of Article 1, section 10.

C. Yes, because the defendant's sentence for the handgun offense ran concurrently with his sentence for common-law murder.

D. Yes, because the law was in existence before the defendant's arrest.

37. In a negligence action in a jurisdiction that had adopted comparative negligence, a jury rendered a verdict that the plaintiff suffered $90,000 in damages and was 10 percent at fault. The plaintiff's attorney had presented evidence and argued in his closing argument that the plaintiff's damages were $100,000. Immediately after the verdict, the plaintiff, with permission from the court, discussed the case with all six of the jurors together before they left the courtroom. The plaintiff discovered that each of the jurors thought, contrary to the court's instructions, that the damage amount was the amount that the plaintiff would receive, rather than the amount from which 10 percent would be deducted. The plaintiff seeks to offer testimony from each juror to that effect in order to increase the amount of the verdict to $100,000.

Is the testimony of the jurors admissible?

A. Yes, because a mistake was made by the jury in rendering its verdict.

B. Yes, because the jury misunderstanding was related to the applicable law, rather than the facts.

C. No, because a juror cannot be questioned about a verdict in the presence of the other jurors.

D. No, because a juror cannot testify as to any juror's mental processes concerning a verdict.

38. A state anticipates a possible reduction of its native oyster population due to a variety of factors, including non-customary weather patterns and polluted waters. To discourage excessive fishing until oyster numbers are confirmed for the season, the state enacts a statute raising the cost of oyster-fishing licenses for all out-of-state residents to twenty times that of in-state residents. The statute does not distinguish between commercial and recreational oyster fishing. An out-of-state commercial oyster fisherman files suit in federal court to have the statute struck down.

Is the statute constitutional?

A. No, because the statute violates the Privileges and Immunities Clause of Article IV.

B. No, because the statute violates the Privileges or Immunities Clause of the Fourteenth Amendment.

C. Yes, because the statute does not discriminate against out-of-state commerce.

D. Yes, because the statute also applies to recreational oyster fishing.

39. A pharmacist was charged with conspiracy to knowingly defraud the government with regard to Medicare payments. The prosecutor called a physician to testify regarding a prescription written by the physician that was filled by the pharmacist. During the defense attorney's cross-examination of the physician, the judge asked the physician, "What did the pharmacist think about this prescription?" The defense attorney immediately objected to the question.

Should the court overrule this objection?

A. Yes, because a judge may question a witness for the purpose of clarifying a witness's testimony.

B. Yes, because the answer to the question is relevant and not overly prejudicial.

C. No, because a judge may not question a witness.

D. No, because the question calls for an unsupported conclusion.

40. A plaintiff brought an injunctive action in federal court under the federal Clean Water Act, based on alleged pollution of a stream. The stream is located in a state in which both parties are citizens. The complaint also contained a nuisance claim based on state law arising from the same set of circumstances as the federal claim. The plaintiff sought injunctive relief only with respect to the nuisance claim. The defendant has filed a motion to dismiss the nuisance claim for lack of subject-matter jurisdiction.

Must the court grant this motion?

A. Yes, because the defendant did not seek monetary damages.

B. Yes, because there is no diversity of citizenship between the parties.

C. No, because the court may exercise supplemental jurisdiction over this claim.

D. No, because the court has general equity jurisdiction to issue an injunction.

41. A prosecutor convened a grand jury to bring criminal charges against a pharmaceutical corporation. The charges were related to a new drug that was linked to several deaths. The prosecutor served a subpoena on a corporate employee who oversaw the testing of new drugs and kept the records related to such testing, requiring the production of all records related to testing done on the new drug. The employee refused to produce the records on Fifth Amendment grounds, asserting that the production of the records might incriminate him personally.

Is the employee likely to be required to produce the records?

A. No, because the Fifth Amendment privilege applies to corporations.

B. No, because the production of the records would incriminate the employee personally.

C. Yes, because the Fifth Amendment privilege does not apply in grand jury proceedings.

D. Yes, because the Fifth Amendment privilege does not extend to the custodian of corporate records.

42. After the defendant murdered his neighbor, the victim's family members lined the street when the defendant was taken away by police and screamed, "Murderer! Murderer!" At the trial for wrongful death, the plaintiffs' attorney sought to have the evidence of the family's statements admitted to show the initial impact the crime had on these family members, who had always been quiet and private members of the community. He intended to provide even more evidence to demonstrate increasing the damages suffered by the victim's family.

Is the evidence admissible for these purposes?

A. Yes, because the statements are not being used to establish that the defendant murdered the neighbor.

B. Yes, because the statements are relevant to the plaintiffs' argument.

C. Yes, because the statements are being used in a civil trial.

D. No, because the statements are hearsay.

43. A state law authorizes the state department of education to conduct an audit and to assign ratings to all public schools in the state based on graduation rates, test scores, and teacher attrition. The law also prohibits students from transferring to another school until at least the following school year in order to maintain the accuracy of statistics related to each school. The only exception allows the transfer of students whose families relocate to communities in other school districts, but requires that even students who relocate to other communities must continue to attend a public school in the new district. Three students in a single family relocated to another public school district; the public schools in that district were known to be struggling with high dropout rates and low test scores. The parents of these students applied to a local parochial school, and their children were accepted by the school, but the school was forced to deny the children admission based on the state law. The school then filed suit in federal court and asserted that the students have a right to attend the parochial school. Neither the students nor their parents were joined as plaintiffs in the suit.

How should the court proceed?

A. Hear the merits of the case and rule in favor of the state.

B. Hear the merits of the case and rule in favor of the school.

C. Dismiss the case, because the school does not have standing to sue.

D. Dismiss the case, because only the students would have standing to sue.

44. A defendant is acquitted of murder. Subsequently, the family members of the victim bring a wrongful death action against the defendant. The defendant seeks to introduce a properly authenticated, certified copy of the final judgment to show that the defendant did not wrongfully kill the victim. The victim's family members object to the introduction of the judgment.

May the defendant introduce the copy of the final judgment from his criminal case?

A. No, because a judgment in a criminal case is inadmissible in a subsequent civil action.

B. No, because the judgment is inadmissible hearsay.

C. Yes, because the copy of the judgment satisfies the original document rule.

D. Yes, because the level of proof in a civil action is less than that in the murder case.

45. On August 1, the plaintiff properly filed a complaint in federal court against the defendant for violating federal water pollution laws in a way that damaged the plaintiff's waterfront property. The defendant did not waive service of process. On August 7, the plaintiff properly served the defendant with the summons and complaint. On August 16, the plaintiff amended her complaint to add a claim under state nuisance law and, that same day, properly served the amended complaint on the defendant.

When is the latest date that the defendant can submit his answer?

A. 21 days after the complaint was filed (August 22).
B. 21 days after the complaint and summons were served (August 28).
C. 14 days after the amended complaint was served (August 30).
D. 21 days after the amended complaint was served (September 6).

46. Two siblings own real property located in State A as tenants in common. The brother was a citizen of State B; his sister was a citizen of Canada who was domiciled in State C. The oil and mineral rights to the property had been leased to a citizen of State C. The siblings initiated a breach-of-lease action against the lessee in a State A federal district court. In the complaint, each sibling asserted in good faith that damages suffered individually as a lessor of a half-interest in the mineral rights equaled $40,000. Shortly after the case was filed, the brother died. His property interests passed by will to his son who was a citizen of State C. Upon receiving title to the property and prior to trial, the son's motion to substitute himself as a party was granted. At trial, the defendant-lessee moved to dismiss the case for lack of subject matter jurisdiction.

For which of the following reasons should the court grant the defendant's motion?

A. Diversity jurisdiction does not exist because the amount-in-controversy requirement has not been met.
B. Diversity jurisdiction does not exist because an alien cannot bring a federal action against an American citizen.
C. Diversity jurisdiction does not exist because the sister and the lessee are both domiciled in State C.
D. Diversity jurisdiction does not exist because the son and the lessee are both citizens of State C.

47. During a period of exceptionally high unemployment, a group of students in a major city began protesting the salary of some of the highest paid businessmen in the country. Coincidentally, many of those businessmen reside in the city where the students intend to protest. The students organized peacefully on the sidewalks in front of the homes of the individual businessmen for two hours each morning during the workweek. They held signs, chanted quietly, and left without much fanfare, though they did create a substantial amount of traffic, media interest, and disruption to the daily routines of the businessmen. The students were subsequently arrested under a state statute that bans picketing in front of individual residences.

Is the state statute prohibiting this speech constitutional as applied to the students' actions?

A. No, but only because their demonstration is not inciting any lawless action.

B. No, because the sidewalk constitutes a public forum.

C. Yes, but only because the regulation is content-neutral.

D. Yes, because they are focusing the protests on particular residences.

48. A small, struggling, formerly industrial city in one state was only 30 miles from the border of the neighboring state, and only 40 miles from a booming city in the neighboring state. In an effort to entice more citizens of the neighboring state to come to the small city to shop, dine, and otherwise spend money, the small city passed an ordinance relieving out-of-state citizens from paying the city's sales tax. A group of small-city citizens properly brought a suit against the city, challenging the ordinance.

Of the following constitutional provisions, which would be the basis on which the citizens could most effectively challenge the ordinance?

A. The Due Process Clause of the Fifth Amendment.

B. The Equal Protection Clause of the Fourteenth Amendment.

C. The Privileges and Immunities Clause of Article IV, Section 2.

D. The Privileges or Immunities Clause of the Fourteenth Amendment.

49. A property owner constructed a fence along what he thought was the boundary to his property. A year later, a neighbor who was selling adjoining property had a survey conducted. As a consequence of the survey, the neighbor brought an action against the property owner seeking removal of the fence.

At trial, the neighbor testified that he had orally objected to the property owner about the placement of the fence at the time it was constructed. After the neighbor left the witness stand, the property owner sought to introduce into evidence a certified copy of the official judgment and conviction of the neighbor for perjury. The neighbor was convicted 11 years ago and released from prison nine years ago. The property owner had not asked the neighbor about the conviction while the neighbor was on the stand.

Should the court permit the introduction of the judgment for the purpose of impeaching the neighbor's testimony?

A. No, because the neighbor was convicted of perjury more than 10 years ago.

B. No, because the neighbor was not questioned about the conviction while the neighbor was on the witness stand.

C. Yes, because a conviction used to impeach a witness's character for truthfulness may be proved by extrinsic evidence.

D. Yes, because a witness in a civil case may not be impeached with a previous conviction.

50. On March 1, the plaintiff sued the defendant, a citizen of a different state, in the appropriate federal court and credibly alleged that the defendant negligently injured her in a car accident, requested $100,000 in damages, and invoked diversity jurisdiction. The plaintiff did not demand a jury trial, and she properly served the defendant on March 1. On March 20, the defendant served his answer, making a general denial. On April 1, the defendant served the plaintiff with a demand for jury trial.

Should the court grant the defendant's demand?

A. Yes, because the defendant has made a timely demand for a jury trial.

B. Yes, because there is a constitutional right to a jury trial in any legal action for damages in excess of $75,000.

C. No, because there is no right to a jury trial in a civil action.

D. No, because only a plaintiff has the right to demand a jury trial.

51. Three plaintiffs sued as representatives of a class of 75 individuals allegedly injured by a defectively designed product in federal district court. The three plaintiffs asserted product liability claims under state law, and alleged that they each suffered injuries resulting from the defectively designed product. Two of the named plaintiffs, as well as the unnamed plaintiffs, suffered relatively minor injuries, and asserted damages ranging from $10,000 to $25,000. The third named plaintiff, who suffered severe physical injuries, sought damages of $200,000. None of the named plaintiffs are domiciled in the state where the manufacturer is incorporated and has its principal place of business. The defendant manufacturer has asserted that the federal district court lacks subject-matter jurisdiction.

What is the plaintiffs' best argument that the court may exercise jurisdiction over their claims?

A. As long as one plaintiff in a putative class asserts a good faith claim over $75,000, a court may exercise supplemental jurisdiction over the remaining claims.

B. The amount-in-controversy requirement for diversity jurisdiction is satisfied for all claims of a putative class if any putative class member asserts a good faith claim over $75,000.

C. The claims of the putative class members may be aggregated to satisfy the amount-in-controversy requirement for diversity jurisdiction.

D. There is no amount-in-controversy requirement for class actions if there is complete diversity between the parties.

52. In state court, an employee was tried and convicted of embezzling funds from her employer. Pursuant to the criminal statute, the employee was ordered to make restitution of the embezzled funds, but not otherwise subjected to imprisonment or a fine for her conduct, even though both were statutorily permitted. The employee successfully appealed her conviction due to improperly admitted evidence. Upon retrial, the employee was again found guilty. In addition to ordering the defendant to make restitution, the judge, commenting that she had wasted valuable judicial resources by appealing her prior conviction, also fined her $50,000. On appeal, the employee contends that her punishment was unconstitutional.

Should the appellate court vacate her sentence?

A. Yes, because the constitutional prohibition against double jeopardy prevents the imposition of a harsher sentence upon retrial of defendant after a successful appeal of a conviction.

B. Yes, because the imposition of a fine violated the Due Process Clause of the Fourteenth Amendment.

C. No, because the constitutional prohibition against double jeopardy does not apply to fines, but only to imprisonment.

D. No, because a defendant may be retried after an appeal results in the defendant's conviction being overturned due to trial errors.

53. A plaintiff filed suit against a defendant supermarket for injuries he sustained when he slipped on a piece of lettuce in the supermarket's produce aisle. A supermarket employee who witnessed the plaintiff's fall prepared a written summary of the events that had occurred in order to alert the supermarket's management. At trial, the supermarket's lawyer called the employee as a witness and, after her testimony, asked her to read her summary to the jury. The plaintiff objected to the testimony.

May the court admit the testimony at this time over the plaintiff's objection?

A. Yes, if the employee is unable to remember the actual events.

B. Yes, because the employee is on the witness stand and can be cross-examined.

C. No, because it is hearsay not within any exception.

D. No, because such testimony may only be offered into evidence by an adverse party.

54. A secretary was angry at her boss for not granting her a raise. The secretary decided to "teach the boss a lesson" by breaking into the boss's house and stealing the boss's personal computer. That evening, the secretary waited until she was sure the boss had gone to sleep and then used a key the boss had given her to the house for emergencies in order to enter the house. She took the personal computer and then left the house.

The secretary is subsequently arrested and charged with burglary in a jurisdiction that follows the common law. Should the woman be convicted?

A. No, because she did not break into the house.

B. No, because she did not intend to commit a felony in the house.

C. Yes, because the boss was in the house at the time the secretary entered.

D. Yes, because she entered the house that evening during a non-emergency situation to steal the computer.

55. A state enacted a statute requiring that prior to voting in a local primary election, a resident must reside within the state for six months. The intent behind the statute is to prohibit transient residents from affecting the long-term affairs of the state. A resident of the state has been a registered voter in another state for many years but has only lived and worked in the state for 90 days. On the day of the primary, the resident tried to vote at a polling station but was banned from doing so by an elections official citing the above statute. The resident then filed suit in federal district court to challenge the constitutionality of the statute.

Which of the following reflects the proper burden of persuasion in this suit?

A. The resident must demonstrate that the statute is not necessary to achieve an important state interest.

B. The resident must demonstrate that the statute is not rationally related to a legitimate state interest.

C. The state must demonstrate that the statute is the least restrictive means of achieving a compelling state interest.

D. The state must demonstrate that the statute is rationally related to a legitimate state interest.

ANSWER KEY

Item	Answer	Subject	Chapter	Section
1	C	EVIDENCE	PRESENTATION OF EVIDENCE	Burdens and Presumptions
2	A	CONSTITUTIONAL LAW	FREEDOM OF EXPRESSION AND ASSOCIATION	Regulation of Content
3	B	CRIMINAL LAW	GENERAL PRINCIPLES	Responsibility
4	D	EVIDENCE	WITNESSES	Impeachment
5	D	CIVIL PROCEDURE	SUBJECT MATTER JURISDICTION	Removal Jurisdiction
6	D	CRIMINAL LAW	INCHOATE CRIMES	Conspiracy
7	B	CRIMINAL PROCEDURE	PRETRIAL PROCEDURES	Eyewitness Identification Procedures
8	D	EVIDENCE	TANGIBLE EVIDENCE	Best Evidence Rule
9	D	CIVIL PROCEDURE	PERSONAL JURISDICTION	In Personam Jurisdiction
10	C	CIVIL PROCEDURE	VENUE	Local and Transitory Actions
11	C	CONSTITUTIONAL LAW	FEDERAL INTERBRANCH RELATIONSHIPS	Delegation of Legislative Power
12	D	CIVIL PROCEDURE	MULTIPLE PARTIES AND CLAIMS	Class Actions
13	A	CRIMINAL LAW	DEFENSES	Specific Defenses
14	B	EVIDENCE	HEARSAY EXCEPTIONS	Declarant Unavailable as a Witness
15	C	FEDERAL CIVIL PROCEDURE	SUBJECT MATTER JURISDICTION	Supplemental Jurisdiction
16	D	CRIMINAL LAW	GENERAL PRINCIPLES	Mens Rea- State of Mind
17	A	EVIDENCE	PRIVILEGES AND OTHER POLICY EXCLUSIONS	Privileges

Item	Answer	Subject	Chapter	Section
18	A	CRIMINAL LAW	OTHER CRIMES	Crimes Against Property
19	B	CONSTITUTIONAL LAW	THE POWERS OF CONGRESS	Power to Enforce the Thirteenth, Fourteenth, and Fifteenth Amendments
20	A	CIVIL PROCEDURE	PERSONAL JURISDICTION	In General
21	D	CRIMINAL PROCEDURE	FOURTH AMENDMENT: APPLICATION TO ARREST	Search and Seizure
22	B	CONSTITUTIONAL LAW	THE POWERS OF CONGRESS	Commerce
23	C	EVIDENCE	PRIVILEGES AND OTHER POLICY EXCLUSIONS	Public Policy Exclusions
24	C	CRIMINAL PROCEDURE	TRIAL	Due Process
25	D	CIVIL PROCEDURE	PLEADINGS	Service of Process
26	A	CONSTITUTIONAL LAW	SUBSTANTIVE DUE PROCESS	Standard of Review
27	B	CRIMINAL PROCEDURE	FIFTH AMENDMENT RIGHTS AND PRIVILEGES	Fifth Amendment in Police Interrogation Context
28	C	EVIDENCE	TANGIBLE EVIDENCE	Authentication
29	C	EVIDENCE	RELEVANCE	Character Evidence
30	A	CIVIL PROCEDURE	PRETRIAL PROCEDURE AND DISCOVERY	Discovery Scope and Limits
31	D	CONSTITUTIONAL LAW	TAKINGS CLAUSE	Types of Takings
32	C	CONSTITUTIONAL LAW	EQUAL PROTECTION	Suspect Classifications
33	D	CRIMINAL LAW	HOMICIDE	Types of Homicide
34	D	CIVIL PROCEDURE	PERSONAL JURISDICTION	In Personam Jurisdiction

Item	Answer	Subject	Chapter	Section
35	C	CRIMINAL PROCEDURE	FOURTH AMENDMENT: APPLICATION TO ARREST, SEARCH AND SEIZURE	Search and Seizure
36	B	CONSTITUTIONAL LAW	PROHIBITED LEGISLATION	Ex Post Facto Laws
37	D	EVIDENCE	WITNESSES	Competence
38	A	CONSTITUTIONAL LAW	PRIVILEGES AND IMMUNITIES CLAUSE	Article IV
39	D	EVIDENCE	PRESENTATON OF EVIDENCE	Mode and Order of Presentation of Evidence
40	C	CIVIL PROCEDURE	SUBJECT MATTER JURISDICTION	Supplemental Jurisdiction
41	D	CRIMINAL PROCEDURE	FIFTH AMENDMENT RIGHTS AND PRIVILEGES	The Privilege Against Compulsory Self-Incrimination
42	A	EVIDENCE	HEARSAY	What is Hearsay
43	B	CONSTITUTIONAL LAW	JUDICIAL POWER	Judicial Review in Operation
44	B	EVIDENCE	HEARSAY EXCEPTIONS	Declarant's Availability Immaterial
45	C	CIVIL PROCEDURE	PLEADINGS	Amendments and Supplemental Pleadings
46	C	CIVIL PROCEDURE	SUBJECT MATTER JURISDICTION	Diversity Jurisdiction
47	D	CONSTITUTIONAL LAW	FREEDOM OF EXPRESSION AND ASSOCIATION	Regulation of Time, Place, and Manner of Association
48	B	CONSTITUTIONAL LAW	EQUAL PROTECTION	General Considerations
49	C	EVIDENCE	WITNESSES	Impeachment
50	A	CIVIL PROCEDURE	TRIAL PROCEDURE	Jury Trial
51	A	CIVIL PROCEDURE	SUBJECT MATTER JURISDICTION	Diversity Jurisdiction
52	B	CRIMINAL PROCEDURE	POST-TRIAL CONSIDERATIONS	Double Jeopardy

Item	Answer	Subject	Chapter	Section
53	A	EVIDENCE	HEARSAY EXCEPTIONS	Declarant's Availability Immaterial
54	D	CRIMINAL LAW	OTHER CRIMES	Crimes Against Property
55	C	CONSTITUTIONAL LAW	SUBSTANTIVE DUE PROCESS	Fundamental Rights

Simulated MBE

SIMULATED MULTISTATE BAR EXAMINATION

TIME: SIX HOURS

This simulated Multistate Bar Exam (MBE) is presented in the same format that the MBE will appear when you take it. We recommend that you take this exam under actual exam conditions. That is, you should schedule two consecutive **uninterrupted** 3-hour blocks of time (with an hour-long break in between) in which to complete this exam.

During the actual exam, your score will be based on the number of questions you answer correctly. It is therefore to your advantage to try to answer as many questions as you can. Use your time effectively. Do not hurry, but work steadily and as quickly as you can without sacrificing your accuracy. If a question seems too difficult, go on to the next one. Give only one answer to each question; multiple answers will not be counted.

After you have completed this simulated exam, you may grade your work using the answer key provided. In order to fully understand each question and answer, we recommend that you review the explanatory answers in the myThemis™ Learning Portal as well as view the Simulated MBE Analysis lectures, which discuss each question and answer in detail.

Please do not take this exam until your myTo-Do List has prompted you to do so. (Flex study students: Be sure you have completed all MBE lectures and practice sessions, as well as the first two Milestone Exams, before beginning this exam.)

SIMULATED MBE: AM

Name: _____   Date: _____

Start Time: _____   End Time: _____

1 ⊏A⊐ ⊏B⊐ ⊏C⊐ ⊏D⊐   26 ⊏A⊐ ⊏B⊐ ⊏C⊐ ⊏D⊐   51 ⊏A⊐ ⊏B⊐ ⊏C⊐ ⊏D⊐   76 ⊏A⊐ ⊏B⊐ ⊏C⊐ ⊏D⊐
2 ⊏A⊐ ⊏B⊐ ⊏C⊐ ⊏D⊐   27 ⊏A⊐ ⊏B⊐ ⊏C⊐ ⊏D⊐   52 ⊏A⊐ ⊏B⊐ ⊏C⊐ ⊏D⊐   77 ⊏A⊐ ⊏B⊐ ⊏C⊐ ⊏D⊐
3 ⊏A⊐ ⊏B⊐ ⊏C⊐ ⊏D⊐   28 ⊏A⊐ ⊏B⊐ ⊏C⊐ ⊏D⊐   53 ⊏A⊐ ⊏B⊐ ⊏C⊐ ⊏D⊐   78 ⊏A⊐ ⊏B⊐ ⊏C⊐ ⊏D⊐
4 ⊏A⊐ ⊏B⊐ ⊏C⊐ ⊏D⊐   29 ⊏A⊐ ⊏B⊐ ⊏C⊐ ⊏D⊐   54 ⊏A⊐ ⊏B⊐ ⊏C⊐ ⊏D⊐   79 ⊏A⊐ ⊏B⊐ ⊏C⊐ ⊏D⊐
5 ⊏A⊐ ⊏B⊐ ⊏C⊐ ⊏D⊐   30 ⊏A⊐ ⊏B⊐ ⊏C⊐ ⊏D⊐   55 ⊏A⊐ ⊏B⊐ ⊏C⊐ ⊏D⊐   80 ⊏A⊐ ⊏B⊐ ⊏C⊐ ⊏D⊐
6 ⊏A⊐ ⊏B⊐ ⊏C⊐ ⊏D⊐   31 ⊏A⊐ ⊏B⊐ ⊏C⊐ ⊏D⊐   56 ⊏A⊐ ⊏B⊐ ⊏C⊐ ⊏D⊐   81 ⊏A⊐ ⊏B⊐ ⊏C⊐ ⊏D⊐
7 ⊏A⊐ ⊏B⊐ ⊏C⊐ ⊏D⊐   32 ⊏A⊐ ⊏B⊐ ⊏C⊐ ⊏D⊐   57 ⊏A⊐ ⊏B⊐ ⊏C⊐ ⊏D⊐   82 ⊏A⊐ ⊏B⊐ ⊏C⊐ ⊏D⊐
8 ⊏A⊐ ⊏B⊐ ⊏C⊐ ⊏D⊐   33 ⊏A⊐ ⊏B⊐ ⊏C⊐ ⊏D⊐   58 ⊏A⊐ ⊏B⊐ ⊏C⊐ ⊏D⊐   83 ⊏A⊐ ⊏B⊐ ⊏C⊐ ⊏D⊐
9 ⊏A⊐ ⊏B⊐ ⊏C⊐ ⊏D⊐   34 ⊏A⊐ ⊏B⊐ ⊏C⊐ ⊏D⊐   59 ⊏A⊐ ⊏B⊐ ⊏C⊐ ⊏D⊐   84 ⊏A⊐ ⊏B⊐ ⊏C⊐ ⊏D⊐
10 ⊏A⊐ ⊏B⊐ ⊏C⊐ ⊏D⊐   35 ⊏A⊐ ⊏B⊐ ⊏C⊐ ⊏D⊐   60 ⊏A⊐ ⊏B⊐ ⊏C⊐ ⊏D⊐   85 ⊏A⊐ ⊏B⊐ ⊏C⊐ ⊏D⊐
11 ⊏A⊐ ⊏B⊐ ⊏C⊐ ⊏D⊐   36 ⊏A⊐ ⊏B⊐ ⊏C⊐ ⊏D⊐   61 ⊏A⊐ ⊏B⊐ ⊏C⊐ ⊏D⊐   86 ⊏A⊐ ⊏B⊐ ⊏C⊐ ⊏D⊐
12 ⊏A⊐ ⊏B⊐ ⊏C⊐ ⊏D⊐   37 ⊏A⊐ ⊏B⊐ ⊏C⊐ ⊏D⊐   62 ⊏A⊐ ⊏B⊐ ⊏C⊐ ⊏D⊐   87 ⊏A⊐ ⊏B⊐ ⊏C⊐ ⊏D⊐
13 ⊏A⊐ ⊏B⊐ ⊏C⊐ ⊏D⊐   38 ⊏A⊐ ⊏B⊐ ⊏C⊐ ⊏D⊐   63 ⊏A⊐ ⊏B⊐ ⊏C⊐ ⊏D⊐   88 ⊏A⊐ ⊏B⊐ ⊏C⊐ ⊏D⊐
14 ⊏A⊐ ⊏B⊐ ⊏C⊐ ⊏D⊐   39 ⊏A⊐ ⊏B⊐ ⊏C⊐ ⊏D⊐   64 ⊏A⊐ ⊏B⊐ ⊏C⊐ ⊏D⊐   89 ⊏A⊐ ⊏B⊐ ⊏C⊐ ⊏D⊐
15 ⊏A⊐ ⊏B⊐ ⊏C⊐ ⊏D⊐   40 ⊏A⊐ ⊏B⊐ ⊏C⊐ ⊏D⊐   65 ⊏A⊐ ⊏B⊐ ⊏C⊐ ⊏D⊐   90 ⊏A⊐ ⊏B⊐ ⊏C⊐ ⊏D⊐
16 ⊏A⊐ ⊏B⊐ ⊏C⊐ ⊏D⊐   41 ⊏A⊐ ⊏B⊐ ⊏C⊐ ⊏D⊐   66 ⊏A⊐ ⊏B⊐ ⊏C⊐ ⊏D⊐   91 ⊏A⊐ ⊏B⊐ ⊏C⊐ ⊏D⊐
17 ⊏A⊐ ⊏B⊐ ⊏C⊐ ⊏D⊐   42 ⊏A⊐ ⊏B⊐ ⊏C⊐ ⊏D⊐   67 ⊏A⊐ ⊏B⊐ ⊏C⊐ ⊏D⊐   92 ⊏A⊐ ⊏B⊐ ⊏C⊐ ⊏D⊐
18 ⊏A⊐ ⊏B⊐ ⊏C⊐ ⊏D⊐   43 ⊏A⊐ ⊏B⊐ ⊏C⊐ ⊏D⊐   68 ⊏A⊐ ⊏B⊐ ⊏C⊐ ⊏D⊐   93 ⊏A⊐ ⊏B⊐ ⊏C⊐ ⊏D⊐
19 ⊏A⊐ ⊏B⊐ ⊏C⊐ ⊏D⊐   44 ⊏A⊐ ⊏B⊐ ⊏C⊐ ⊏D⊐   69 ⊏A⊐ ⊏B⊐ ⊏C⊐ ⊏D⊐   94 ⊏A⊐ ⊏B⊐ ⊏C⊐ ⊏D⊐
20 ⊏A⊐ ⊏B⊐ ⊏C⊐ ⊏D⊐   45 ⊏A⊐ ⊏B⊐ ⊏C⊐ ⊏D⊐   70 ⊏A⊐ ⊏B⊐ ⊏C⊐ ⊏D⊐   95 ⊏A⊐ ⊏B⊐ ⊏C⊐ ⊏D⊐
21 ⊏A⊐ ⊏B⊐ ⊏C⊐ ⊏D⊐   46 ⊏A⊐ ⊏B⊐ ⊏C⊐ ⊏D⊐   71 ⊏A⊐ ⊏B⊐ ⊏C⊐ ⊏D⊐   96 ⊏A⊐ ⊏B⊐ ⊏C⊐ ⊏D⊐
22 ⊏A⊐ ⊏B⊐ ⊏C⊐ ⊏D⊐   47 ⊏A⊐ ⊏B⊐ ⊏C⊐ ⊏D⊐   72 ⊏A⊐ ⊏B⊐ ⊏C⊐ ⊏D⊐   97 ⊏A⊐ ⊏B⊐ ⊏C⊐ ⊏D⊐
23 ⊏A⊐ ⊏B⊐ ⊏C⊐ ⊏D⊐   48 ⊏A⊐ ⊏B⊐ ⊏C⊐ ⊏D⊐   73 ⊏A⊐ ⊏B⊐ ⊏C⊐ ⊏D⊐   98 ⊏A⊐ ⊏B⊐ ⊏C⊐ ⊏D⊐
24 ⊏A⊐ ⊏B⊐ ⊏C⊐ ⊏D⊐   49 ⊏A⊐ ⊏B⊐ ⊏C⊐ ⊏D⊐   74 ⊏A⊐ ⊏B⊐ ⊏C⊐ ⊏D⊐   99 ⊏A⊐ ⊏B⊐ ⊏C⊐ ⊏D⊐
25 ⊏A⊐ ⊏B⊐ ⊏C⊐ ⊏D⊐   50 ⊏A⊐ ⊏B⊐ ⊏C⊐ ⊏D⊐   75 ⊏A⊐ ⊏B⊐ ⊏C⊐ ⊏D⊐   100 ⊏A⊐ ⊏B⊐ ⊏C⊐ ⊏D⊐

Themis
Bar Review

SCORE   RESCORE

SIMULATED MBE: PM

Name: _____   Date: _____

Start Time: _____   End Time: _____

101 ⊏A⊐ ⊏B⊐ ⊏C⊐ ⊏D⊐	126 ⊏A⊐ ⊏B⊐ ⊏C⊐ ⊏D⊐	151 ⊏A⊐ ⊏B⊐ ⊏C⊐ ⊏D⊐	176 ⊏A⊐ ⊏B⊐ ⊏C⊐ ⊏D⊐
102 ⊏A⊐ ⊏B⊐ ⊏C⊐ ⊏D⊐	127 ⊏A⊐ ⊏B⊐ ⊏C⊐ ⊏D⊐	152 ⊏A⊐ ⊏B⊐ ⊏C⊐ ⊏D⊐	177 ⊏A⊐ ⊏B⊐ ⊏C⊐ ⊏D⊐
103 ⊏A⊐ ⊏B⊐ ⊏C⊐ ⊏D⊐	128 ⊏A⊐ ⊏B⊐ ⊏C⊐ ⊏D⊐	153 ⊏A⊐ ⊏B⊐ ⊏C⊐ ⊏D⊐	178 ⊏A⊐ ⊏B⊐ ⊏C⊐ ⊏D⊐
104 ⊏A⊐ ⊏B⊐ ⊏C⊐ ⊏D⊐	129 ⊏A⊐ ⊏B⊐ ⊏C⊐ ⊏D⊐	154 ⊏A⊐ ⊏B⊐ ⊏C⊐ ⊏D⊐	179 ⊏A⊐ ⊏B⊐ ⊏C⊐ ⊏D⊐
105 ⊏A⊐ ⊏B⊐ ⊏C⊐ ⊏D⊐	130 ⊏A⊐ ⊏B⊐ ⊏C⊐ ⊏D⊐	155 ⊏A⊐ ⊏B⊐ ⊏C⊐ ⊏D⊐	180 ⊏A⊐ ⊏B⊐ ⊏C⊐ ⊏D⊐
106 ⊏A⊐ ⊏B⊐ ⊏C⊐ ⊏D⊐	131 ⊏A⊐ ⊏B⊐ ⊏C⊐ ⊏D⊐	156 ⊏A⊐ ⊏B⊐ ⊏C⊐ ⊏D⊐	181 ⊏A⊐ ⊏B⊐ ⊏C⊐ ⊏D⊐
107 ⊏A⊐ ⊏B⊐ ⊏C⊐ ⊏D⊐	132 ⊏A⊐ ⊏B⊐ ⊏C⊐ ⊏D⊐	157 ⊏A⊐ ⊏B⊐ ⊏C⊐ ⊏D⊐	182 ⊏A⊐ ⊏B⊐ ⊏C⊐ ⊏D⊐
108 ⊏A⊐ ⊏B⊐ ⊏C⊐ ⊏D⊐	133 ⊏A⊐ ⊏B⊐ ⊏C⊐ ⊏D⊐	158 ⊏A⊐ ⊏B⊐ ⊏C⊐ ⊏D⊐	183 ⊏A⊐ ⊏B⊐ ⊏C⊐ ⊏D⊐
109 ⊏A⊐ ⊏B⊐ ⊏C⊐ ⊏D⊐	134 ⊏A⊐ ⊏B⊐ ⊏C⊐ ⊏D⊐	159 ⊏A⊐ ⊏B⊐ ⊏C⊐ ⊏D⊐	184 ⊏A⊐ ⊏B⊐ ⊏C⊐ ⊏D⊐
110 ⊏A⊐ ⊏B⊐ ⊏C⊐ ⊏D⊐	135 ⊏A⊐ ⊏B⊐ ⊏C⊐ ⊏D⊐	160 ⊏A⊐ ⊏B⊐ ⊏C⊐ ⊏D⊐	185 ⊏A⊐ ⊏B⊐ ⊏C⊐ ⊏D⊐
111 ⊏A⊐ ⊏B⊐ ⊏C⊐ ⊏D⊐	136 ⊏A⊐ ⊏B⊐ ⊏C⊐ ⊏D⊐	161 ⊏A⊐ ⊏B⊐ ⊏C⊐ ⊏D⊐	186 ⊏A⊐ ⊏B⊐ ⊏C⊐ ⊏D⊐
112 ⊏A⊐ ⊏B⊐ ⊏C⊐ ⊏D⊐	137 ⊏A⊐ ⊏B⊐ ⊏C⊐ ⊏D⊐	162 ⊏A⊐ ⊏B⊐ ⊏C⊐ ⊏D⊐	187 ⊏A⊐ ⊏B⊐ ⊏C⊐ ⊏D⊐
113 ⊏A⊐ ⊏B⊐ ⊏C⊐ ⊏D⊐	138 ⊏A⊐ ⊏B⊐ ⊏C⊐ ⊏D⊐	163 ⊏A⊐ ⊏B⊐ ⊏C⊐ ⊏D⊐	188 ⊏A⊐ ⊏B⊐ ⊏C⊐ ⊏D⊐
114 ⊏A⊐ ⊏B⊐ ⊏C⊐ ⊏D⊐	139 ⊏A⊐ ⊏B⊐ ⊏C⊐ ⊏D⊐	164 ⊏A⊐ ⊏B⊐ ⊏C⊐ ⊏D⊐	189 ⊏A⊐ ⊏B⊐ ⊏C⊐ ⊏D⊐
115 ⊏A⊐ ⊏B⊐ ⊏C⊐ ⊏D⊐	140 ⊏A⊐ ⊏B⊐ ⊏C⊐ ⊏D⊐	165 ⊏A⊐ ⊏B⊐ ⊏C⊐ ⊏D⊐	190 ⊏A⊐ ⊏B⊐ ⊏C⊐ ⊏D⊐
116 ⊏A⊐ ⊏B⊐ ⊏C⊐ ⊏D⊐	141 ⊏A⊐ ⊏B⊐ ⊏C⊐ ⊏D⊐	166 ⊏A⊐ ⊏B⊐ ⊏C⊐ ⊏D⊐	191 ⊏A⊐ ⊏B⊐ ⊏C⊐ ⊏D⊐
117 ⊏A⊐ ⊏B⊐ ⊏C⊐ ⊏D⊐	142 ⊏A⊐ ⊏B⊐ ⊏C⊐ ⊏D⊐	167 ⊏A⊐ ⊏B⊐ ⊏C⊐ ⊏D⊐	192 ⊏A⊐ ⊏B⊐ ⊏C⊐ ⊏D⊐
118 ⊏A⊐ ⊏B⊐ ⊏C⊐ ⊏D⊐	143 ⊏A⊐ ⊏B⊐ ⊏C⊐ ⊏D⊐	168 ⊏A⊐ ⊏B⊐ ⊏C⊐ ⊏D⊐	193 ⊏A⊐ ⊏B⊐ ⊏C⊐ ⊏D⊐
119 ⊏A⊐ ⊏B⊐ ⊏C⊐ ⊏D⊐	144 ⊏A⊐ ⊏B⊐ ⊏C⊐ ⊏D⊐	169 ⊏A⊐ ⊏B⊐ ⊏C⊐ ⊏D⊐	194 ⊏A⊐ ⊏B⊐ ⊏C⊐ ⊏D⊐
120 ⊏A⊐ ⊏B⊐ ⊏C⊐ ⊏D⊐	145 ⊏A⊐ ⊏B⊐ ⊏C⊐ ⊏D⊐	170 ⊏A⊐ ⊏B⊐ ⊏C⊐ ⊏D⊐	195 ⊏A⊐ ⊏B⊐ ⊏C⊐ ⊏D⊐
121 ⊏A⊐ ⊏B⊐ ⊏C⊐ ⊏D⊐	146 ⊏A⊐ ⊏B⊐ ⊏C⊐ ⊏D⊐	171 ⊏A⊐ ⊏B⊐ ⊏C⊐ ⊏D⊐	196 ⊏A⊐ ⊏B⊐ ⊏C⊐ ⊏D⊐
122 ⊏A⊐ ⊏B⊐ ⊏C⊐ ⊏D⊐	147 ⊏A⊐ ⊏B⊐ ⊏C⊐ ⊏D⊐	172 ⊏A⊐ ⊏B⊐ ⊏C⊐ ⊏D⊐	197 ⊏A⊐ ⊏B⊐ ⊏C⊐ ⊏D⊐
123 ⊏A⊐ ⊏B⊐ ⊏C⊐ ⊏D⊐	148 ⊏A⊐ ⊏B⊐ ⊏C⊐ ⊏D⊐	173 ⊏A⊐ ⊏B⊐ ⊏C⊐ ⊏D⊐	198 ⊏A⊐ ⊏B⊐ ⊏C⊐ ⊏D⊐
124 ⊏A⊐ ⊏B⊐ ⊏C⊐ ⊏D⊐	149 ⊏A⊐ ⊏B⊐ ⊏C⊐ ⊏D⊐	174 ⊏A⊐ ⊏B⊐ ⊏C⊐ ⊏D⊐	199 ⊏A⊐ ⊏B⊐ ⊏C⊐ ⊏D⊐
125 ⊏A⊐ ⊏B⊐ ⊏C⊐ ⊏D⊐	150 ⊏A⊐ ⊏B⊐ ⊏C⊐ ⊏D⊐	175 ⊏A⊐ ⊏B⊐ ⊏C⊐ ⊏D⊐	200 ⊏A⊐ ⊏B⊐ ⊏C⊐ ⊏D⊐

Themis
Bar Review

SCORE

RESCORE

Directions: Each of the questions or incomplete statements below is followed by four suggested answers or completions. You are to choose the best of the stated alternatives. Answer all questions according to the generally accepted view, except where otherwise noted.

For the purposes of this test, you are to assume the application of (1) the amendments to the Federal Rules of Civil Procedure through 2012; and (2) the sections of Title 28 to the U.S. Code pertaining to jurisdiction, venue, and transfer. Assume also that Articles 1 and 2 of the Uniform Commercial Code have been adopted. You are also to assume relevant application of Article 9 of the UCC concerning fixtures. The Federal Rules of Evidence are deemed to control. The terms "Constitution," "constitutional," and "unconstitutional" refer to the federal Constitution unless indicated to the contrary. You are to assume that there is no applicable statute unless otherwise specified; however, survival actions and claims for wrongful death should be assumed to be available where applicable. You should assume that joint and several liability, with pure comparative negligence, is the relevant rule unless otherwise indicated.

1. A collector owned a painting that needed professional restoration. The collector brought the painting to a restorer and, after examining the painting, the restorer quoted the collector a price for the restoration. The restorer told the collector that since she was going on a vacation and would be unreachable, the collector had a month to make his decision. Two days later, the collector mailed a letter to the restorer accepting the restorer's price. Through no fault of the collector, this letter was lost in the mail and never delivered. The next day, the collector learned of another person who would do the restoration for a lower price and would begin immediately. The collector mailed a second letter to the restorer that stated that he did not require her services. On arriving home from her vacation, the restorer received the collector's second letter. As a consequence, she contacted another art owner and began restoration work for that owner. In the meantime, the collector became dissatisfied with the work of the second restorer. He contacted the original restorer and demanded that she begin the restoration work on his painting, which she refused to do. The collector is suing the restorer for breach of contract in a jurisdiction that follows the mailbox rule.

Will the collector prevail?

(A) No, because the restorer relied on the collector's rejection.

(B) No, because the restorer never received the collector's acceptance.

(C) Yes, because the collector had timely accepted the restorer's offer.

(D) Yes, because the "mailbox rule" does not apply when both a rejection and an acceptance are sent.

2. The defendant's attorney in a fraud case called a witness to testify as to the defendant's character. On cross-examination, the prosecutor asked the witness whether he had ever been arrested for writing bad checks. In fact, the witness had been arrested two years ago for writing bad checks, but the charges had been dropped due to a lack of evidence that the witness had committed the crime. The defendant's attorney objects to the question.

Should the prosecutor be allowed to ask the question?

(A) No, because a witness who is not the defendant may not be cross-examined about prior bad acts.

(B) No, because the witness was never charged with the crime.

(C) Yes, because writing bad checks is probative of the witness's untruthfulness.

(D) Yes, because the arrest occurred only two years ago.

3. A company owned and operated a private golf course. One of the fairways on the course ran parallel to a navigable body of water. The company was aware that golfers frequently but unintentionally hit golf balls into the water when playing that hole because there were no barriers to prevent the balls from going into the water. A 12-year-old child, while sailing on the water, was struck by one such ball and suffered a serious physical injury.

The injured child's parent has filed a public nuisance action against the company, on behalf of his child, to recover for his injuries.

Is the plaintiff precluded from recovering?

(A) No, because the child was seriously injured while on navigable water due to the company's negligence.

(B) No, because of the attractive nuisance doctrine.

(C) Yes, because the child did not have an ownership interest in land.

(D) Yes, because the golfer's action was unintentional.

4. A plaintiff brought a negligence action in federal court to recover damages for injuries suffered as an audience member at an event held by the defendant. The defendant was a citizen of the forum state; the plaintiff was a citizen of the neighboring state in which the event was held. Under the forum state's choice-of-law rules, the negligence law of the neighboring state applied to this action. Under the negligence law of the neighboring state, the defendant owed a duty to the plaintiff. Under the negligence law of the forum state, the defendant did not owe a duty to the plaintiff. Which law should the court apply in deciding this action?

(A) The negligence law of the forum state, because that is the law of the state in which the federal court sits.

(B) The negligence law of the forum state, because choice-of-law rules are procedural rules.

(C) The negligence law of the neighboring state, because of the forum state's choice-of-law rules.

(D) The negligence law of the neighboring state, because the plaintiff is a citizen of this state.

5. Under his will, a bachelor devises his farm to his brother. The language of the devise makes no mention of the need of the brother to survive the testator. The will contains a residuary clause that leaves all property not otherwise devised by the will to the bachelor's sister. The bachelor's brother dies more than a year before the bachelor, but the brother has two children, both of whom survive the bachelor.

There is an anti-lapse statute that applies to a devise by a testator to a relative who is a descendant of the testator, the testator's parents, or the testator's grandparents.

Are the brother's children entitled to their uncle's farm?

(A) No, because their father did not survive his brother.

(B) No, because the will contained a residuary clause.

(C) Yes, because the language of the will did not require the brother to survive the testator.

(D) Yes, because the anti-lapse statute operates to save the lapsed devise.

6. During a trial for injuries a plaintiff sustained in a car accident with the defendant, the plaintiff's attorney called a witness to the stand to testify that the witness, a 25-year-old woman, saw the defendant run a stop sign and crash into the plaintiff's car. The witness was not associated with the defendant in any way. The plaintiff's attorney questioned the witness in an attempt to get her to testify that she saw the defendant run the stop sign, but she would not do so, and seemed to be deliberately avoiding the topic. Finally, the plaintiff's attorney asked that the witness be treated as hostile, and asked her, "Did you see the defendant run the stop sign on the day in question?" The defendant's attorney objected to the form of the question.

How is the court likely to rule on the defendant's objection?

(A) Overrule it, because a party may generally ask leading questions of his own witnesses.

(B) Overrule it, because a leading question was necessary to develop the witness's testimony.

(C) Sustain it, because a party may not treat his own witness as hostile.

(D) Sustain it, because leading questions are not appropriate for this witness.

7. A man and his girlfriend spent the afternoon at the beach, where each of them consumed a significant quantity of alcohol. The man saw one of the town's wealthiest residents arrive at the beach, spread out a beach towel, put down a large cloth bag on the towel, drop what looked like a wallet into the bag, and run into the ocean. The man told his girlfriend what he had seen the wealthy man do. She didn't respond, but walked over to the bag and opened it. The bag did not contain the man's wallet, but it did contain an expensive ring. She took the ring, and closed the bag. The wealthy man's companion, who was just coming onto the beach, observed the girlfriend's actions. The girlfriend was arrested. Soon thereafter, the man was arrested as well.

The man is charged with conspiracy to commit larceny, among other crimes. The applicable jurisdiction has adopted a conspiracy statute based on the Model Penal Code. Which of the following is the weakest argument that the man can advance in defense of the charge?

(A) The man's statement to his girlfriend was inadequate to form a conspiracy agreement.

(B) The theft of the ring was beyond the scope of the conspiracy.

(C) The man did not perform an overt act to advance the conspiracy.

(D) The man's intoxicated state prevented him from forming the intent necessary to commit the crime.

8. A state feared abuse of its statute providing for welfare benefits, which was administered by its department of public assistance. The department believed that a particular man who had been receiving welfare payments for the past year was not eligible for them because he had adequate means of support. The department informed the man in writing of its decision to terminate his welfare benefits. The department also informed the man that he could schedule an administrative hearing, which would be held in approximately one month, to contest that decision and to present any evidence on his own behalf.

If the man challenges this termination on constitutional grounds, will he likely be successful?

(A) Yes, because the man had a Due Process right to a notice and hearing before his welfare benefits were terminated.

(B) Yes, because the department of public assistance has impaired the obligations of its contract with the man in violation of the Contracts Clause.

(C) No, because the department has provided the man with notice and a hearing sufficient to satisfy the Due Process Clause.

(D) No, because a state can establish the procedures for terminating an interest that the state itself has created, as distinguished from a purely private interest.

9. A retail furniture store ordered ten sofas from a manufacturer at $1,000 each, plus shipping, to be delivered and paid for in five equal monthly installments. With the first shipment of two sofas, the manufacturer sent an invoice to the retailer, billing the retailer $2,000 plus shipping. The invoice also noted that the manufacturer retained a security interest in all sofas shipped until the purchase price for all sofas ordered was paid in full.

Not happy with the security interest term, the retailer immediately notified the manufacturer that this term was unacceptable. After sending payment for the first two sofas, the retailer told the manufacturer not to send any more sofas. The manufacturer sued the retailer for breach of contract.

In the breach of contract action by the manufacturer against the retailer, what will be the result?

(A) The manufacturer will prevail, because both parties are merchants.

(B) The manufacturer will prevail, but can only enforce the terms of the original offer.

(C) The retailer will prevail, because the knock-out rule voids the contract.

(D) The retailer will prevail, because the additional terms materially affected the bargain.

10. A developer purchased a 60-acre parcel of wooded land and divided the parcel into 20 three-acre lots. The developer advertised the rustic character of the lots and the intent to sell the lots for development as single-family residences. This was in conformity with the zoning restrictions on the land, which required that the land be used for residential purposes and that the size of each lot not be less than two acres. Over a period of several years, the developer sold 15 of the lots.

The deed for each of these lots contained the following provision:

This deed is subject to the condition that the property may only be used for residential purposes and may not be subdivided but must be sold in its entirety. This condition shall be a covenant running with the land and shall be binding on all owners, their heirs, devisees, successors, and assignees.

The deed for each lot was promptly and properly recorded.

The developer, facing financial difficulty, sold the remaining five lots to a land speculator. The deeds to these lots did not contain the character and size provision that the developer had inserted into the other deeds, nor did the speculator have actual knowledge of the developer's advertising related to the character and size of the lots. The land speculator, acting in response to a zoning change that reduced the minimum permissible size of a lot to only one acre, has obtained governmental approval to divide each of the five remaining lots in thirds and is now offering the 15 lots for sale.

An owner of one of the three-acre lots has brought suit against the speculator seeking an injunction to prevent him from selling the lots in less than three-acre parcels. Can the speculator successfully defend against this lawsuit?

(A) Yes, because the speculator's deeds did not contain the character and size provision.

(B) Yes, because the speculator has obtained governmental approval to subdivide the lots.

(C) No, because the lots purchased by the speculator are subject to an implied servitude.

(D) No, because the speculator purchased the lots for commercial rather than residential purposes.

11. A couple sought to purchase a particular house in large part because they believed, based on their research, that a certain historical figure had lived in it. The owner, having not previously heard about this association, neither confirmed nor denied their belief, merely shrugging his shoulders in response to their inquiries about it. The owner did not investigate the matter. The couple purchased the house from the owner. Later, the couple found out that the historical figure had not in fact lived in the house.

If the couple sues to void the contract, will they prevail?

(A) Yes, because the owner's failure to investigate the historical figure's connection with the house constituted a breach of the duty of good faith.

(B) Yes, because the couple's purpose in entering into the contract was frustrated by the mistake.

(C) No, because the risk of this unilateral mistake was borne by the couple.

(D) No, because the fact that the historical figure did not live there did not materially affect the bargain.

12. Congress passed the Equality in Employment Act ("EEA"), which was co-sponsored by both senators from a particular state and enjoyed the support of all of that state's federal representatives. Section 1 of the EEA required every state, within 18 months of passage, to enact legislation prohibiting employment discrimination based on sexual orientation. Section 2 of the EEA provided that any state that enacted such legislation before the deadline would receive $20 million in federal funding for programs designed to eliminate employment discrimination against gays and lesbians. Two years after passage of the act, the state had not enacted a statute prohibiting such discrimination.

If the United States sues the state for violating this act, what would be the most likely decision by the Supreme Court with regard to these two sections?

(A) Strike down Section 1 as exceeding Congress's power under the Commerce Clause, but uphold Section 2 as a proper exercise of the Spending Power.

(B) Strike down Section 1 as a "commandeering" of state legislatures to enact laws, but uphold Section 2 as a proper exercise of the Spending Power.

(C) Uphold Section 1 as a proper exercise of Congress's power under the Commerce Clause, but strike down Section 2 as an improper exercise of the Spending Power.

(D) Uphold Sections 1 and 2 against any federalism-based challenge because the state's own congressional delegation supported the EEA and thus consented to any possible infringement on the state's sovereignty.

13. A witness to an armed robbery identified a suspect in a proper police lineup that was not attended by the suspect's attorney. Charges were brought against the suspect, but the witness, a tourist from out of the country, had returned to her home country before the trial began. At trial, the prosecutor seeks to introduce the witness's prior statement of identification into evidence. The defendant objects to the introduction of the evidence.

Should the court allow the prior statement of identification into evidence?

(A) Yes, it should be admissible as nonhearsay.

(B) Yes, because the witness is unavailable, so the statement of identification falls under a hearsay exception.

(C) No, because the defendant's attorney was not present at the identification.

(D) No, because the witness is unavailable.

14. A witness who was not a defendant invoked his Fifth Amendment right to remain silent during a federal criminal trial for insider trading. After being given derivative-use immunity, the witness testified. Several weeks later, the witness was a defendant in a state-law civil fraud proceeding based on his previous testimony in the federal trial. He moved to dismiss the case on the grounds that the previous grant of immunity protected him against a future action against him.

Will the defendant's motion be granted?

(A) Yes, because a grant of immunity can be given to a witness who is not a defendant.

(B) Yes, because the defendant was given derivative-use immunity.

(C) No, because the defendant's immunity was limited to federal prosecution.

(D) No, because the defendant's immunity does not extend to a subsequent civil trial.

15. A law makes it a crime to "knowingly sell, distribute, or barter a sexually explicit film featuring actors younger than the age of majority." The owner of an adult video store sold explicit videos in her store that featured 18-year-old actors, but she took reasonable steps to ensure that no videos featuring younger actors were sold in her store. The video store owner, however, incorrectly believed that the age of majority in the jurisdiction was 18; in fact, the age of majority was 19 years old.

The owner was arrested and charged with violating the statute in a jurisdiction that has adopted the Model Penal Code. The prosecution does not contest that her error was made honestly. Should she nonetheless be convicted?

(A) Yes, because the owner's error was a mistake of law, which is not a valid defense.

(B) Yes, because the owner knowingly sold the illegal videos.

(C) No, because the owner's error negated the requisite *mens rea*.

(D) No, because the owner's conscious objective was not to engage in selling the illicit videos.

16. A patient, a citizen of state A, had a severe allergic reaction to a prescription drug approved by the federal Food & Drug Administration (FDA). The patient was hospitalized for many days and missed a number of days of work. She filed suit in the U.S. District Court in the city of her residence against the manufacturer of the drug. The manufacturer is incorporated in State B, but has its principal place of business in State A. The patient claims that the manufacturer violated both State A tort law and the federal Safe Drug Act (SDA), which provides that "persons who reasonably believe that they may have been injured by a prescription drug have a cause of action in the appropriate U.S. District Court." State A law is unsettled on the issue of whether obtaining FDA approval shields a drug manufacturer from tort liability. The patient requests damages of $40,000 for medical expenses, $20,000 for lost pay, and $15,000 for pain and suffering.

Should the U.S. District Court exercise jurisdiction?

(A) Yes, because the court has federal-question jurisdiction.

(B) Yes, because the court has diversity jurisdiction.

(C) No, because the federal court should abstain from exercising jurisdiction until the State A courts decide the unsettled issue of state law.

(D) No, because by adding an uncertain state-law cause of action, the patient did not present a well-pleaded complaint.

17. The maker of a prescription drug provides physicians who prescribe the drug with detailed instructions regarding its use. The instructions include a warning about the possibility of an allergic reaction that could result in serious physical harm if the drug is taken with a common over-the-counter medication. However, the allergic reaction is only likely to occur in a very small portion of the population, so the drug maker does not provide this warning to consumers of the drug.

A physician who had received the detailed instructions from the drug maker prescribed the drug for a patient. The physician did not warn the patient about the possible allergic reaction. The patient experienced an allergic reaction from taking the drug in combination with the over-the-counter medication and suffered a debilitating injury.

The patient brought a strict products liability action against the drug maker based on its failure to warn the patient of the possibility of an allergic reaction. Who will prevail?

(A) The patient, because the drug maker failed to warn the patient of the allergic reaction.

(B) The patient, because the drug maker, as a commercial supplier, is liable for harm done by the drug.

(C) The drug maker, because it warned the prescribing physician of the allergic reaction.

(D) The drug maker, because the number of persons at risk was very limited.

18. A plaintiff filed a complaint in federal district court in the state where the plaintiff was domiciled. The plaintiff asserted that the defendant, who lived in a neighboring state, was liable for damages the plaintiff sustained in a car accident that took place in the neighboring state. The plaintiff had the defendant personally served by a process server while the defendant was traveling through the forum state, which was his only contact with the forum state. Nineteen days after being served with the complaint, the defendant served an answer in which he denied that he was responsible for the car accident. The next day, the defendant filed a motion to dismiss, arguing that the court lacked personal jurisdiction over him.

Is the court likely to grant the defendant's motion?

(A) Yes, because the defendant raised the issue of personal jurisdiction within 21 days of being served with the complaint.

(B) Yes, because the defendant did not have sufficient minimum contacts with the forum state.

(C) No, because the defendant waived any objection to personal jurisdiction.

(D) No, because the defendant was personally served with process while in the forum state.

19. The owner of a chain of retail stores built a warehouse that was financed by a loan from a bank. In exchange for the loan, the bank took a mortgage on the warehouse.

Several years later, a thief broke into the warehouse by cutting a hole in the roof. The owner hired a contractor to repair the roof but, due to the contractor's shoddy work, the roof leaks whenever it rains, making a large portion of the warehouse unusable. Due to a contraction in the owner's business, the remaining usable space of the warehouse is sufficient for the owner's needs, but the unusable space impairs the bank's security interest.

Learning of the condition of the warehouse, the bank requested that the owner repair the warehouse roof. The owner refused. The bank brought an action to compel the owner to properly repair the roof.

The mortgage provides that it was made with recourse to the personal liability of the owner. Neither the mortgage nor the deed contains a covenant requiring the owner to maintain or repair the premises. The owner is not in default with respect to the mortgage payments. The jurisdiction follows a lien theory with regard to ownership of a mortgage and does not have an anti-deficiency statute.

Will the bank succeed?

(A) No, because the owner is not liable for waste.

(B) No, because the owner is not in default with respect to the required mortgage payments.

(C) Yes, because the mortgaged property is not residential.

(D) Yes, because the condition of the roof impairs the bank's security interest.

20. A large clothing retailer contracted with a firm that specialized in custom printing to print the logo of a major sporting event onto 5,000 jerseys. The logo was coupled with an identifying landmark of the city in which the event was to take place. The retailer planned to sell the jerseys as souvenirs at the event. As called for in the contract, the retailer supplied the firm with the jerseys and paid half the contract price. Shortly before the event and before any shirts had been printed, the stadium where the game was to be held was damaged by an earthquake. As a consequence, the event was moved to another city.

The retailer demanded the return of its payment and the jerseys. The supplier, claiming that it was entitled to the benefit of its bargain, kept its anticipated profit of $2,000 but returned the jerseys and the remainder of the payment to the retailer. The retailer filed a lawsuit seeking rescission of the contract and return of the $2,000.

What is the retailer's best argument in support of its suit?

(A) Performance of the contract has become impracticable because the relocation of the sporting event was an unforeseeable occurrence.

(B) The relocation of the sporting event has made enforcement of the contract on its original terms unconscionable.

(C) The contract is void due to mutual mistake, as both parties were mistaken as to an essential element of the contract.

(D) The retailer's contractual duties are discharged because the game's relocation frustrated the purpose of the contract.

21. On a winter day, a youth, seeking refuge from the cold, entered a small neighborhood grocery store without the knowledge of the store's owner, who was standing at the cash register. Shortly thereafter, the only other person in the store approached the register and requested an item located on a shelf behind the owner. As the owner turned to retrieve the requested item, the individual drew a gun and commanded the owner to give him the money in the register. As the owner turned back toward the customer, the customer fired the gun at her and missed. The owner grappled with the customer and succeeded in knocking the gun out of the customer's hand. As the customer retrieved his gun, the owner grabbed her own gun, for which she had a valid license. They fired at each other, each missing the other. Although the owner's actions did not create an unreasonable risk of harm to the youth, the bullet from the owner's gun nevertheless struck and killed the youth.

The estate of the youth filed a wrongful death action against the store owner. Who will prevail?

(A) The store owner, because the owner acted in self-defense.

(B) The store owner, because the owner's shooting of the youth was not negligent.

(C) The estate of the youth, because the youth was an invitee.

(D) The estate of the youth, because the youth was not a co-conspirator with the robber.

22. An organization against drunk driving sought permission from the owner of a mall to pass out leaflets in favor of tougher drunk driving laws in front of a liquor store. The mall owner denied the organization permission. The organization, filing an action in an appropriate court, sought an injunction permitting the organization to pass out its leaflets in accord with its free speech rights.

The state's highest court, interpreting the state constitution, permits the exercise of free speech rights on private property that is regularly held open to the public. Of the following reasons, which is the best argument for granting the injunction?

(A) Leafleting is a form of speech that is protected by the First Amendment of the United States Constitution.

(B) The reason for leafleting was related to the place where the organization sought to leaflet.

(C) The leafleting was permitted by the state constitution.

(D) By admitting members of the general public, the mall constituted a limited public forum.

23. The plaintiff attended a professional baseball game, where he was hit by a foul ball. He was rushed to a hospital and diagnosed with a head bruise. The injury was minor, and the plaintiff's pain went away after three days. However, such a blow to the head, in one out of every 500,000 cases, can lead to serious brain injuries many years later. The plaintiff sued the defendant baseball team for negligence and requested $1,000,000 in damages. The federal court properly exercised diversity jurisdiction. The jury's verdict was that the defendant was liable for negligence, based on evidence that the ball that hit the plaintiff went through a hole in protective netting that the team failed to repair. The jury awarded the plaintiff $15,000 for medical expenses and three days of lost wages, plus $985,000 for "pain and suffering," primarily for the mental anguish of not knowing whether a brain injury would develop later. In similar cases, the highest award for pain and suffering was $50,000. The defendant moved for a new trial. The court concluded that the damages awarded were excessive and ordered a new trial limited to the issue of damages. The plaintiff properly appealed the court's order. Should the appellate court rule in his favor?

(A) Yes, because the district court should have ordered a new trial on all the issues, not on the issue of damages alone.

(B) Yes, because the district court failed to give the plaintiff the option of remittitur instead of a new trial.

(C) No, because a district court with diversity jurisdiction is required to order a new trial whenever the "pain and suffering" component of a damages award is more than ten times the plaintiff's tangible losses.

(D) No, because the district court had discretion to order a new trial on the issue of damages.

24. In a criminal trial for arson, a prosecution witness testifies under oath that she saw the defendant set fire to the victim's home. The defendant's attorney does not cross-examine the witness, but seeks to admit testimony that the witness gave at a deposition several months before the trial. At the deposition, the witness testified under oath that she did not see the defendant set fire to the victim's home.

Should the court admit the deposition testimony?

(A) The court should admit the witness's deposition testimony for impeachment purposes, but not as substantive evidence.

(B) The court should admit the witness's deposition testimony for impeachment purposes and as substantive evidence.

(C) The court should not admit the witness's deposition testimony because the defendant's attorney did not allow the witness the chance to explain her inconsistent testimony.

(D) The court should not admit the witness's deposition testimony because it is hearsay.

25. A man whose terminally ill aunt had promised to devise an undeveloped parcel of land to him sold the parcel to a friend. The friend purchased the property based on the nephew's false assertion that he owned the parcel; the friend was unaware of the aunt's ownership of the parcel. The friend did not perform a title search and did not record the deed, which was a general warranty deed.

Subsequently, the aunt died. As promised, she devised the parcel to her nephew. The personal representative of the estate executed and recorded a deed transferring title to the parcel to the nephew. After the aunt's death, no one paid the property taxes on the parcel. Eventually, the state seized the parcel and sold it through a tax sale. Before expiration of the redemption period that is statutorily permitted to the owner of the real property, the friend learned of the sale of the parcel for delinquent taxes. Claiming ownership of the parcel, the friend sought to pay the delinquent taxes and other costs and fees associated with the sale and thereby redeem the parcel. The buyer of the parcel at the tax sale, who had no prior knowledge of the friend's claim with respect to the parcel, objected.

In an action to determine ownership of the parcel, if the court finds for the friend, what is the likely reason?

(A) The friend was record owner of the parcel.

(B) The friend purchased the parcel for value and without notice.

(C) Under the doctrine of equitable conversion, the friend is the owner of the parcel.

(D) Title to the parcel vested in the friend upon the nephew's acquisition of the parcel.

26. The owner of an electronics store brought a civil suit for the value of stolen electronics against one of his former employees, who had previously been convicted in a criminal court for the theft of the same goods. During the civil trial, the plaintiff-owner called a witness whom he hoped would testify that she saw the defendant in possession of the stolen goods the day after the electronics store was robbed. The witness, however, testified that she did not see the defendant in possession of the goods, and that she was actually out of town the day after the robbery. The plaintiff seeks to introduce the witness's testimony in the criminal case, in which she testified that she saw the defendant in possession of the goods the next day. The defendant objects to the introduction of the statement.

Should the court allow the testimony into evidence?

(A) Yes, for impeachment only.

(B) Yes, as substantive evidence only.

(C) Yes, for both impeachment and as substantive evidence.

(D) No, not for any reason.

27. In a bicycle race with a $5,000 prize for the winner, a cyclist was leading by a significant margin. A spectator at the race was married to the second place rider. Sensing that her husband would not win unless she took action, the spectator drove to a point two miles ahead on the course, scattered several nails in the middle of the course, and then left the area. Soon thereafter, the cyclist approached the area and noticed the nails. He attempted to swerve around the obstruction but a nail punctured his tire. He fell off his bike, suffered significant physical injuries, and was unable to complete the race.

If the cyclist sues the spectator, under what theory is the cyclist least likely to recover maximum punitive damages?

(A) Assault

(B) Intentional infliction of emotional distress

(C) Trespass to chattels

(D) Battery

28. An artist who had designed a sculpture to be made out of steel went to the website of a merchant that sold specialized tools. Using the chat feature, the artist explained to an employee of the merchant that the artist wanted to purchase a tool that could cut through steel. The employee suggested that the artist purchase a particular saw. The employee, pointing out that the website's description of the saw indicated that it could cut through most metals, added that the saw "should cut through steel with no problem." The artist purchased the saw from the merchant's website for a total cost of $450. Conspicuously appearing on the page where the artist had to indicate his consent in order to purchase the saw was the following: "There are no implied warranties provided with this product other than the general warranty of merchantability." The tool failed to cut through the steel that the artist intended to use for his sculpture. The artist sued the merchant for damages attributable to breach of the implied warranty of fitness for a particular purpose.

Which party is likely to prevail?

(A) The merchant, because the merchant disclaimed the warranty of fitness for a particular purpose.

(B) The merchant, because warranties do not apply to goods valued under $500.

(C) The artist, because the merchant's employee knew that the artist wanted a saw that would cut steel and relied on his judgment that the saw would do so.

(D) The artist, because the implied warranty of fitness for a particular purpose cannot be disclaimed by a merchant.

29. A 15-year-old male was being tried in state court as an adult for murder. At voir dire, the prosecutor exercised all of his peremptory challenges to exclude persons under the age of 30 from the jury. The defendant's attorney timely raised the issue as to whether the prosecutor had utilized his peremptory challenges in an unconstitutional manner. In response to questioning by the court, the prosecutor stated that it was his intent to exclude persons who, because of their age, would be sympathetic to the defendant. The judge found that the prosecutor's reason was genuine and not pretextual.

Should the judge sustain the defendant's objection?

(A) Yes, because the prosecutor's use of peremptory challenges violates the defendant's Sixth Amendment right to trial by an impartial jury.

(B) Yes, because the defendant was a member of the affected class.

(C) No, because the prosecutor is permitted to exercise peremptory challenges for any rational reason.

(D) No, because the prosecutor's use of peremptory challenges does not violate the Equal Protection Clause.

30. Concerned with protecting the use of federal funds from the deleterious effects of bribery, Congress enacted a statute criminalizing the acceptance of a bribe by a state or local official where the state or local government received at least $10,000 in federal funds.

A county government, in exchange for its agreement to permit the housing of federal prisoners in the county's jail, received a payment of federal funds for each prisoner. The total amount received by the county government for housing federal prisoners exceeded $100,000 annually. A federal prisoner housed in the county jail agreed to transfer title to a pickup truck to a prison guard in exchange for the guard permitting the prisoner to receive illegal conjugal visits. The prison guard was charged with violating the statute. Is the application of the statute to the guard's taking title to the prisoner's truck constitutional?

(A) No, because the bribe did not directly relate to the federal funds.

(B) No, because a federal statute that criminalizes noneconomic behavior must have a significant impact on interstate commerce.

(C) Yes, because the statute was a valid congressional exercise, pursuant to the Necessary and Proper Clause, of ensuring that its power to appropriate money for the general welfare was not thwarted.

(D) Yes, because the statute was a valid congressional exercise of its inherent police powers.

31. A farmer was diagnosed by his doctor with a terminal illness. Upon arriving home immediately after having received the news, the farmer wrote the following, "I, farmer, now transfer my farm, Blackacre, to my son." The farmer, who owned Blackacre in fee simple absolute, then signed and dated the document. The farmer neither discussed the document nor its contents with anyone else, but simply placed it with his personal papers.

Soon thereafter, the farmer died. Among the farmer's personal papers, in addition to the document, was a will. The farmer had executed the will in compliance with the required formalities 10 years prior to his death. Under the terms of the will, the farm was devised to the farmer's daughter. The daughter and son were the farmer's only heirs.

After learning of the document and the will, the son and daughter each claimed ownership of Blackacre outright.

In an appropriate action to determine ownership of the farm filed by the personal representative of the farmer's estate after admission of the will to probate, who is entitled to ownership of the farm?

(A) The daughter, because the unwitnessed document is not a valid deed and therefore the farm passed to her by the terms of the will.

(B) The daughter, because the document, which was neither delivered to nor accepted by the son prior to the farmer's death, was not a valid deed and therefore the farm passed to her by the terms of the will.

(C) The son, because the document was a deed that took effect during the farmer's lifetime.

(D) The son, because the document was executed after the will and therefore superseded the will.

32. Engrossed in a cell phone conversation, a pedestrian in a rural area failed to look out for traffic while crossing a road. The driver of an oncoming car noticed the pedestrian and began to brake, which caused a cake sitting on the front passenger seat to slide off the seat and onto the floor of the car. Distracted by the cake, the driver, who was 17 years old and properly licensed to operate the car without supervision, momentarily forgot about the pedestrian. When the driver's attention returned to the road, the driver did not have sufficient time to avoid striking the pedestrian, who suffered serious physical injuries as a result.

The applicable jurisdiction has adopted a modified comparative negligence statute.

The pedestrian brings a negligence action against the driver for damages stemming from the pedestrian's physical injuries, which total $200,000. The jury determines that the driver was 80% at fault and the pedestrian was 20% at fault.

How much will the pedestrian be permitted to recover?

(A) Nothing, because the pedestrian was negligent.

(B) $160,000, because the pedestrian's damages are reduced by the percentage that the pedestrian was at fault.

(C) $200,000, because the driver had the last clear chance to avoid the accident.

(D) $200,000, because the driver was engaged in an adult activity.

33. A testator's will contained a devise of the testator's residence to the testator's daughter and bequeathed $100,000 to the testator's son. At the time of her death, the testator owned the residence in fee simple absolute. The residence was not subject to any encumbrances. The testator's only other asset at the time of her death was a bank account that had a balance of $5,000. The personal representative of the testator's estate applied the money in the bank account to the satisfaction of the testator's outstanding debts and transferred title of the testator's residence to the daughter.

The son filed an action in probate court challenging the personal representative's distribution of the testator's residence to the daughter. The son asserted that the personal representative should have sold the residence and divided the proceeds between the two children.

Which of the following legal concepts provides the best support for the personal representative's action?

(A) Abatement

(B) Ademption

(C) Exoneration

(D) Lapse

34. A plaintiff properly filed a complaint in state court seeking an injunction because the defendant was violating a state law that protected trade secrets. The defendant timely filed an answer asserting a defense based on federal patent law. The next day the defendant, who was not a citizen of the forum state, timely filed a notice of removal with the federal district court located in the forum state. In response, the plaintiff filed a motion to remand the case to state court, arguing that the federal court lacked federal question jurisdiction.

Should the federal district court grant the plaintiff's motion?

(A) Yes, because the defendant failed to file the notice of removal before filing an answer.

(B) Yes, because the complaint was based on state law.

(C) No, because the defendant's answer raised a defense based on federal law.

(D) No, because the defendant was not a citizen of the forum state.

35. A man decided to master the art of throwing knives. He practiced for several years, until he had perfected his skills and was able to hit a spot no larger than a dime with confidence. After demonstrating his prowess to a friend, the man convinced the friend to stand against a wall while the man threw knives at her. The man threw three knives extremely close to the friend, but the fourth knife struck the friend, injuring her slightly. Although the friend's injury was minor, unbeknownst to the man, she had a rare blood disorder that caused her to bleed to death.

The crimes below are listed in ascending order of seriousness. What is the most serious common law crime for which the man can be convicted?

(A) Battery

(B) Involuntary manslaughter

(C) Voluntary manslaughter

(D) Murder

36. A pregnant mother and a soccer coach of the mother's young child were involved in a serious verbal altercation. The argument continued escalating until the coach suddenly punched the mother in the face and pushed her to the ground. The coach immediately fled the area. The mother did not suffer serious physical injury. Nonetheless, the incident greatly traumatized her. In the weeks following the attack, she had many sleepless nights and suffered several panic attacks.

The mother brought suit against the coach for intentional infliction of emotional distress. The coach filed a motion for summary judgment. How should the court rule on the motion?

(A) Grant the motion, because the coach did not intend to cause severe emotional distress.

(B) Grant the motion, because the mother did not suffer a significant physical injury.

(C) Deny the motion, because a jury could find that the coach was reckless as to the risk of causing emotional distress.

(D) Deny the motion, because the doctrine of transferred intent applies.

37. A plaintiff sued the owner of a small clothing store for injuries she sustained when she slipped and fell while shopping in the defendant's store. The defendant wants to introduce into evidence a written record of the event made by one of his employees. The record detailed the fact that the plaintiff slipped on her own drink that she had spilled without reporting to anyone. It also included the plaintiff's threat to sue the store, and the store owner's instructions to the employee to immediately write a report, so that there was a record of what happened in the event that the plaintiff sued. The employee is unavailable to testify. The plaintiff objects to the introduction of the document.

Should the court sustain the plaintiff's objection to the introduction of the document?

(A) Yes, because the document violates the best evidence rule.

(B) Yes, because the document is hearsay not within any exception.

(C) No, because the document is a business record.

(D) No, because the employee is unavailable to authenticate the record.

38. A college student entered the back yard of a zoology professor to attend a social gathering for students that was to be held there. The professor was cleaning out the cage of his pet porcupine and had carelessly allowed the porcupine to roam free. The porcupine, well camouflaged in a pile of leaves, was sunning itself. The student didn't see the porcupine, tripped over it, and broke his hand.

The applicable jurisdiction permits the keeping of a porcupine as a pet.

In a strict liability action by the student against the professor, who will prevail?

(A) The student, because the professor possessed a wild animal.

(B) The student, because the professor, aware that students were coming to a social gathering, failed to act with reasonable care.

(C) The professor, because the student was only a licensee, not an invitee.

(D) The professor, because the student was not injured as a consequence of a dangerous propensity of the animal.

39. The defendant declined to enter into a contract to sell her house for $200,000 to the plaintiff. The next day, the defendant executed a contract to sell her house to another individual for $201,000. The plaintiff sued the defendant in the appropriate federal court and claimed that the defendant's decision was based on the plaintiff's ethnicity and thus violated a federal statute. The court granted summary judgment for the defendant. The plaintiff then sued in the same federal court, claiming that the defendant's decision was based on the defendant's disability, in violation of another federal statute. Can the plaintiff pursue this action if challenged by the defendant?

(A) Yes, because the second claim of disability discrimination was based on a different federal statute than the first claim.

(B) Yes, because the court decided the prior claim of discrimination based on ethnicity through summary judgment, rather than upon a full consideration of the merits.

(C) No, because the doctrine of collateral estoppel precludes the second case.

(D) No, because the claim of disability discrimination was precluded, as it arose out of the same transaction as the prior claim of discrimination based on ethnicity.

40. A publishing company entered into a contract to purchase a newspaper company. The contract specified that "it shall be a condition precedent to buyer's obligation to pay that the newspaper shall have 200,000 subscribers by December 31 of this year." In anticipation of the purchase, the publishing company purchased $200,000 of new equipment to be used in printing the newspaper; the newspaper was aware of the investment.

At the end of the business day on December 31, the newspaper had only 199,750 subscribers, and had no justification for the shortfall. The publishing company immediately redirected $100,000 of the new equipment to print one of its magazines, but the other $100,000 of equipment was custom-made for the newspaper and could not be used elsewhere. The publishing company refused to go through with the sale, and then sued the newspaper company for $100,000. Is the publishing company likely to prevail?

(A) Yes, because the newspaper company did not comply with the condition precedent.

(B) Yes, because the publishing company mitigated its damages to the maximum extent reasonably possible.

(C) No, because the newspaper company substantially complied with the condition precedent.

(D) No, because failure of a condition precedent does not give rise to damages.

41. An attorney represents a corporation in a federal securities case. As the attorney reviewed her files before court, she discovered that—despite her diligence—a memo marked "PRIVILEGED AND CONFIDENTIAL" had inadvertently been included in a folder containing public financial documents. The attorney knew that she had copied this folder and produced it in its entirety to opposing counsel during discovery. However, the memo is detrimental to her client's case. The attorney immediately contacted opposing counsel and requested that the memo be returned to her, that all copies be destroyed, and that the information within the memo not be used at trial; she included the judge on this correspondence. Opposing counsel refused to return the memo, and informed the attorney that they did plan to use it at trial. The memo in question was from the corporation's chief executive officer to the attorney, and contained the chief financial officer's thoughts and questions regarding the attorney's trial strategy.

Should the court allow the defendant to introduce the memo into evidence at trial?

(A) Yes, because the attorney waived the privilege when she disclosed the memo to opposing counsel.

(B) Yes, because the memo was not privileged to begin with.

(C) No, because the attorney did not waive the privilege.

(D) No, because all documents from clients to attorneys are privileged.

42. A buyer purchased a newly constructed house from a builder for use as a residence. The buyer did not perform an inspection of the house prior to the purchase. Neither the contract nor the deed contained any warranties as to the condition of the house.

Six months later, during a heavy downpour, the basement flooded. Since that time, whenever there has been a substantial rain, there has been water in the basement. The source of the problem has been identified as several cracks in the foundation wall that surrounds the basement. An expert hired by the buyer has opined that the cracks formed due to settling after the home was built and could have been prevented by adherence to proper construction methods. The builder has repeatedly refused to address the problem.

Just before the first anniversary of the purchase, the buyer filed suit against the builder for the defective foundation wall and the resulting damages. There are no applicable state statutes that address the issue.

Who will prevail?

(A) The builder, because the builder did not give the buyer a written warranty as to the condition of the house.

(B) The builder, because the buyer failed to conduct a home inspection.

(C) The buyer, because the builder of a residence is liable for any material defects in the house.

(D) The buyer, because the builder breached the warranty of fitness or suitability.

43. A significant number of colleges were located in a small state. Local police departments constantly received complaints about the conduct of college students, especially those who lived together off-campus. Due to constant pressure from citizens of the college towns, the state legislature enacted a statute preventing more than four unrelated men under the age of 25 from living together in any privately owned house, apartment, or condominium. A group of five unrelated men between the ages of 18 and 23 attempted to lease a house together but were refused on the basis of this law. The men have challenged the constitutionality of the law in court.

Which of the following is the group's best argument for declaring the statute unconstitutional?

(A) The statute is not rationally related to a legitimate state interest.

(B) The statute unconstitutionally discriminates against the men based on their gender.

(C) The statute unconstitutionally discriminates against the men based on their age.

(D) The statute denies the group the fundamental right to live together.

44. During a severe storm, a horse came onto a rancher's property. The rancher discovered the horse the next morning, and saw a serious wound on one of its legs. The rancher paid a veterinarian to examine and treat the horse, and the rancher then provided the horse with food and shelter.

Two weeks later, the horse's owner arrived at the rancher's home and asked for the return of his horse. The rancher returned the horse to its owner, and asked the owner for reimbursement for the veterinary visit and for the expenses incurred in feeding and sheltering the horse. The horse's owner refused to pay.

The rancher sued the horse's owner for the costs of veterinary care, food, and shelter. Is he likely to prevail?

(A) Yes, because the rancher's conduct created an implied-in-fact contract.

(B) Yes, because the horse's owner would be unjustly enriched if he were not forced to pay the rancher's expenses.

(C) No, because a valid contract was never formed between the rancher and the horse's owner.

(D) No, because the horse's owner never engaged in any conduct to signify that he assented to the rancher's expenditures.

45. A plaintiff sued a defendant for injuries sustained when the defendant ran a red light and struck the plaintiff as she crossed the street. The defendant denies that he ran the red light. The intersection where the accident took place features a camera that automatically captures a series of images of vehicles passing through the intersection when the light is red. During discovery, the plaintiff's attorney subpoenaed the city for copies of the photographs. The city printed two sets of the requested photographs directly from the camera, and sent one set to the plaintiff's counsel and the other set to the defendant's counsel. After laying a proper foundation, the plaintiff's attorney plans to introduce her set of the pictures into evidence. The defense attorney objects.

Is the plaintiff's set of photographs taken by the camera admissible?

(A) Yes, because the set of photographs is relevant and not excluded by a specific rule or law.

(B) Yes, because photographic evidence is always admissible.

(C) No, because of the best evidence rule.

(D) No, because there is no photographer to testify.

46. The United States Supreme Court, overruling *Roe v. Wade* and *Planned Parenthood v. Casey*, held that women do not have a constitutional right to abortion. Congress responded by passing the Abortion Rights Restoration Act (ARRA), which restored the essential holdings of *Roe* and *Casey* by prohibiting any government from unduly burdening a woman's exercise of the constitutional right to abortion.

In a constitutional challenge to the validity of ARRA, is a federal court likely to strike down the act?

(A) No, because Congress had a rational basis for concluding that abortions are a commercial activity that, considered in the aggregate, substantially affect interstate commerce.

(B) No, because Congress is defining constitutional rights more expansively than the Supreme Court, not restricting them.

(C) Yes, because Congress is not remedying the violation of a judicially recognized constitutional right, but rather is attempting to create a new constitutional right.

(D) Yes, because it violates the constitutional principle of federalism.

47. Police officers have a reasonable suspicion, but not probable cause, that the defendant committed a robbery. The police officers, acting without a warrant, went to the defendant's home and requested that he come to the stationhouse for fingerprinting. The defendant refused until the police officers threatened him with arrest. The defendant, reasonably believing that he was not free to deny the officers' request, accompanied the police officers to the stationhouse, where he was fingerprinted. His fingerprints matched those taken from the scene of the crime. Consequently, the defendant was arrested and charged with the robbery. At his trial, the defendant moved to suppress the fingerprint evidence. Should the judge grant this motion?

(A) Yes, because the police officers' action constituted an unlawful seizure and evidence seized as a consequence must be excluded.

(B) Yes, because the procedure violated the defendant's Fifth Amendment privilege against self-incrimination.

(C) No, because fingerprinting is a reliable form of scientific evidence that would assist the trier of fact.

(D) No, because the police officers' reasonable suspicions justified the defendant's warrantless detention for the purpose of fingerprinting.

48. A buyer purchased a residence from an individual seller. Within the buyer's deed, which was not recorded, was a provision that the buyer, his heirs, assignees, and successors promised to adhere to the community association guidelines and to recognize the association's right to enforce those guidelines. Among the guidelines issued by the community association was the following: "No fence greater than six feet in height shall be installed or maintained by any homeowner." The community association has rigorously enforced this guideline.

The buyer subsequently died and devised the residence to her husband for life and then to her son. The husband, without actual knowledge of the guidelines or their contents, installed an eight-foot-high fence. The local zoning ordinance permits fences no greater than eight feet in height to be constructed in the residential neighborhood.

The community association has sought an injunction against the husband to compel him to remove the fence. Who will prevail?

(A) The community association, because the provision in the buyer's deed creates an equitable servitude.

(B) The community association, because the fence constitutes waste.

(C) The husband, because he only possesses a life estate.

(D) The husband, because neither he nor his wife acquired the residence from the community association.

49. A middle-aged farmer who lived by himself in a rural area had surgery to correct an orthopedic problem. Since his recovery would take about a year, he contacted a retired nurse about serving as his caretaker. While the farmer was still in the hospital, the two reached an agreement, the terms of which were specified in two letters. The letter written by the nurse identified the farmer by name and stated, "I agree to take care of your medical needs for a period of one year, starting when you leave the hospital." The letter written by the man identified the nurse by name and stated, "I agree to pay you $10,000 per month." Each letter was signed by its drafter. Before his discharge from the hospital, the man found out that the hospital had a less expensive program for home care, and cancelled the contract.

Unable to find other employment, the nurse brought a breach of contract action against the man. Based solely on the letters, will the nurse be able to establish the existence of a contract?

(A) Yes, because this agreement can be performed within one year.

(B) Yes, because the writings, taken together, sufficiently state the essential terms of the agreement.

(C) No, because the Statute of Frauds precludes enforcement.

(D) No, because the writings do not evidence a valid offer and acceptance.

50. A small restaurant utilized the same beverage supplier for many years. The owner of the restaurant had developed a very strong working relationship with the supplier's employees. The contract between the supplier and the restaurant only obligated the supplier to provide beverages, but the supplier's employees frequently performed repairs on the restaurant's soda dispensers, and were available to fill emergency orders even late at night and on weekends. Furthermore, the restaurant received a commission for each beverage sold at its restaurants, which the beverage supplier, unlike many other suppliers, paid in cash. The restaurant received lucrative offers to switch to other distributors, but repeatedly chose to stay with its supplier because of the personalized service.

The beverage supplier decided that it would be advantageous to concentrate its business solely on larger accounts. Without obtaining approval from the restaurant, the supplier "assigned all rights and delegated all duties" arising under its contract with the restaurant to a second beverage distributor. The second distributor did not pay any consideration for this transfer. While there was no anti-assignment clause its contract with the original supplier, the restaurant was not pleased with the assignment, and refused service from the new distributor.

The new distributor filed suit against the restaurant, claiming breach of contract. What is the restaurant's strongest argument in defense?

(A) While rights under a contract may normally be assigned, delegations of contractual duties are generally not permitted.

(B) The new distributor's failure to pay any consideration to the original supplier makes the assignment unenforceable.

(C) The failure to seek the restaurant's approval of the transfer of contractual rights and duties means that the restaurant is not bound by the transfer.

(D) The restaurant has a substantial interest in having the original beverage supplier perform the contract.

51. An employee at a toy store intervened in a dispute between two unrelated customers, a mother and a grandfather, over who was entitled to a particular hard-to-come-by doll, which was the only remaining one at the store. The employee arbitrarily determined that the mother had possession of the doll first and awarded her the right to purchase the doll. When the grandfather protested the employee's decision, the mother threatened to inflict physical harm on the grandfather and raised her arm to strike him. Fearful that the mother would do so, the grandfather looked to the employee for help. The employee, who because of his size could easily have forestalled the mother's attack, simply shrugged his shoulders. Before the mother made contact with the grandfather, he crumpled to floor, the victim of a stroke caused by the mother's threat.

The grandfather initiates a lawsuit against the mother, the employee, and the owner of the store on the grounds of assault for damages attributable to his stroke.   The owner of the store moves to dismiss the complaint against herself for failure to state a cause of action. How should the court rule?

(A) Deny the motion, because the grandfather was reasonably apprehensive of an immediate battery.

(B) Deny the motion, because the employee failed to act to protect the grandfather.

(C) Grant the motion, because the owner is not vicariously liable for assault by one customer upon another.

(D) Grant the motion, because *respondeat superior* does not apply to an employee's intentional torts.

52. The plaintiff and the defendant were involved in a physical altercation, and the plaintiff sustained serious injuries to his hand. Several weeks later, the defendant inherited a valuable piece of real estate from a distant relative in a state several thousand miles away. The defendant had never been to the state where the property was located. The plaintiff heard about the defendant's inheritance, and filed suit against the defendant in the state where the property was located. In his complaint, the plaintiff asserted a claim of battery against the defendant, alleging $100,000 in damages.   Before filing a responsive pleading, the defendant, who was properly served, filed a motion to dismiss, arguing that the court lacked jurisdiction over both parties. The forum state has adopted a long-arm statute that extends jurisdiction up to the constitutional limits.

Is the court likely to grant the motion to dismiss?

(A) Yes, because personal jurisdiction is improper over both parties.

(B) Yes, because personal jurisdiction is improper over the defendant.

(C) No, because personal jurisdiction is proper under the doctrine of in rem jurisdiction.

(D) No, because personal jurisdiction is proper under the doctrine of attachment jurisdiction.

53. A city often required persons seeking building permits to agree to aesthetic and environmental conditions in order to obtain such permits.

A company applied for a permit to construct a 300,000 square foot warehouse on its land in the city. The city conditioned the permit on the company's agreement to plant 45 trees on the property and to limit the building's height to 70 feet. The city had imposed similar conditions on other property owners. The effect of these conditions was to reduce the value of the company's property by three percent, but they did not prevent the construction of a warehouse on the land.

The company sued, claiming that the imposition of these conditions violated its constitutional rights. Would a court be likely to strike down these conditions?

(A) Yes, because they constitute an unconstitutional taking of private property for public use.

(B) Yes, because they are not substantially related to an important governmental interest.

(C) No, because, under the Takings Clause, they advance a legitimate government interest and do not deny the company the economically viable use of its land.

(D) No, because, under the Takings Clause, they are valid restrictions, but the court should require the city to compensate the company for the three percent reduction in its property value.

54. The plaintiff, the maker of an electronic device, filed a declaratory judgment action in federal district court against the defendant, the maker of a similar electronic device. The plaintiff sought a judgment that his device did not infringe on the defendant's patent. The court's subject matter jurisdiction was based on a federal question.

The plaintiff was a citizen of the state in which the federal district court was located. The defendant, who was a citizen of a neighboring state, lived less than 100 miles from the forum court. Despite the defendant's proximity to the forum court, the defendant was not subject to service of process in her home state for this action under the laws of the forum state. A process server employed by the plaintiff personally served the complaint and summons on the defendant in her home state. Federal patent law does not contain special service of process provisions.

Does this service of process confer personal jurisdiction over the defendant on the federal district court?

(A) Yes, because the court's subject matter jurisdiction is based on a federal question.

(B) Yes, because the "bulge provision" of Rule 4 of the Federal Rules of Civil Procedure applies.

(C) No, because this is a declaratory judgment action.

(D) No, because the defendant was not subject to service of process under the laws of the state in which the court is located.

55. An individual acquired a newly constructed house with a purchase money mortgage. Although the deed was recorded, through an oversight by the mortgagee, the mortgage was not.

Several years later, the individual sold the house at its fair market value to a couple who obtained a purchase money mortgage through another mortgagee. Both the deed and the mortgage were recorded. Neither the couple nor the second mortgagee was aware of the prior mortgage.

Shortly thereafter, the couple was killed in an accident, survived by their two young children. The couple did not leave a will. Under the law of intestate succession, the young children are the rightful heirs of their parents. The children's financial guardian, having been contacted by both mortgagees, has filed an appropriate action to determine ownership of the house.

The jurisdiction is a lien state with regard to mortgages. In addition, the applicable recording act reads, "No conveyance or mortgage of real property shall be good against subsequent purchasers for value and without notice unless the same be recorded according to law."

Who is entitled to priority with respect to the house?

(A) First mortgagee, second mortgagee, children

(B) Second mortgagee, first mortgagee, children

(C) Second mortgagee, children, first mortgagee

(D) First mortgagee, children, second mortgagee

56. To remedy past discrimination against women in college athletics, Congress required state colleges and universities to achieve "gender equity" in funding athletics. The percentage that each school must allocate to women's athletics was based on a formula that took into account the average percentage of athletic department funds allocated to men's and women's programs over a five-year period. Depending on the school's past record, this allocation could be greater than the percentage of women enrolled in the school. A state with any schools out of compliance forfeited a percentage of its federal educational funding.

A state military college first admitted women five years ago. Only 10% of its student body is currently female. To comply with the federal funding formula, the college must allocate 25% of its athletic budget to women's sports.

A male student, whose wrestling program is being discontinued because of the budget allocation, filed suit in an appropriate federal court challenging the federal law's constitutionality. Is he likely to prevail?

(A) Yes, because the government will be unable to prove that the law's discriminatory funding requirements are necessary to achieve a compelling government interest.

(B) Yes, because principles of federalism prohibit the federal government from dictating the budget allocations of state educational institutions.

(C) No, because the government will be able to prove that the law's funding requirements are substantially related to the important government objective of remedying past discrimination.

(D) No, because remedying past discrimination is a legitimate government interest, and the law's funding requirements are rationally related to that interest.

57. A prosecutor called a witness to testify in a battery trial. The witness, a friend of the defendant, behaved in a hostile manner to the prosecutor, refusing to testify that the defendant was the initial aggressor in the altercation at issue, as the prosecutor believed he would. The prosecutor decided to call a second witness to minimize any damage done by the first witness's testimony. This second witness, who was the first witness's sister, testified that because her brother had been in a fight similar to the one in question, it was her opinion that he was not a good witness. The defendant's attorney objects to the sister's testimony.

Should the prosecutor be allowed to ask the sister about the fight?

(A) Yes, because the credibility of a witness may be attacked by reputation or opinion evidence.

(B) Yes, because the first witness put his character at issue by testifying.

(C) No, because a party cannot impeach his own witness.

(D) No, because the altercations have no bearing on the first witness's character for untruthfulness.

58. Seeking to protect its small wine industry, a state passes a law prohibiting a large out-of-state corporation that engaged in the wine business in the state from entering into any new business deals within the state. The corporation sues in an appropriate federal court to enjoin state officials from enforcing this law.

On which of the following grounds would the court hold that the state's law is unconstitutional?

(A) The Dormant Commerce Clause of Article I, Section 8

(B) The Privileges and Immunities Clause of Article IV, Section 2

(C) The Privileges or Immunities Clause of the Fourteenth Amendment

(D) The Contracts Clause of Article I, Section 10

59. One summer night, a man attended a party at one of the most lavish homes in town. Midway through the party, the man asked the host if he could use the restroom, and the host directed him to a restroom on the second floor of the house. After using the restroom, the man became curious about the other rooms upstairs, and wondered if they were as beautiful as the rest of the house. His curiosity got the best of him, and he turned the handle and opened a door, which turned out to be the master bedroom. He stepped inside the room and immediately saw a large pearl necklace on the vanity table. He walked over to the table, grabbed the pearls, put them in his pocket, left the room, and went downstairs. Later in the evening, the party host saw the pearls slip out of the man's pocket. She immediately confronted the man and called the police.

If the man is later charged with common-law burglary, what is the man's best defense to the charge?

(A) The man did not break and enter the home.

(B) The man did not intend to steal anything when he entered the room.

(C) The man did not use any force to enter the bedroom.

(D) The man did not leave the premises with the pearls.

60. A plaintiff filed a complaint in federal district court. The plaintiff is a citizen of the forum state and the defendant is a citizen of another state. The cause of action is based on the defendant's alleged conversion of the plaintiff's rare and expensive coin collection. According to the complaint, the conversion took place while the plaintiff attended a rare coin convention held in the state in which the defendant is domiciled. The plaintiff has asserted that the court has personal jurisdiction over the defendant based on a certificate of deposit (CD) inherited by the defendant from his mother and issued by a bank in the forum state. The amount in the CD is less than the amount of damages sought by the plaintiff. The defendant has no other contacts with the forum state. The long-arm statute of the forum state provides for jurisdiction over a nonresident to the extent permitted by the Due Process Clause of the U.S. Constitution. The defendant has timely filed a motion to dismiss the action for lack of personal jurisdiction.

How should the court rule?

(A) Grant the motion, because the amount of the CD is less than the amount of damages sought by the plaintiff.

(B) Grant the motion, because the defendant does not have sufficient minimum contacts with the forum state.

(C) Deny the motion, because domicile is not the only means by which a court can acquire personal jurisdiction over a defendant.

(D) Deny the motion, because the defendant's banking activity in the forum state suffices to establish minimum contacts.

61. A defendant was charged with fraud in a state-law civil proceeding. During cross-examination, he was asked to state whether a note being entered into evidence was in his handwriting. Since the note contained a material false statement on which the plaintiff had relied, the defendant invoked his Fifth Amendment privilege against self-incrimination to avoid answering the question. The judge upheld the defendant's assertion of the privilege.

Was the judge correct in permitting the defendant to invoke his Fifth Amendment privilege against self-incrimination?

(A) Yes, because handwriting evidence is always testimonial in nature.

(B) Yes, because the defendant's answer is testimonial evidence.

(C) No, because the defendant may not invoke his Fifth Amendment privilege in a civil proceeding.

(D) No, because the Fifth Amendment privilege against self-incrimination is not applicable in state-law proceedings.

62. Two defendants were on trial for conspiracy to commit robbery. The prosecution would like to introduce the testimony of a security guard at the store that was to be robbed. The security guard caught one of the defendants trying to sneak in a back entrance of the store the day before the robbery was to take place, hoping to "scope out" the store. In a panic, the defendant had said, "We haven't even done anything wrong yet! We weren't going to do anything until tomorrow!" The prosecutor would like to introduce this statement against both defendants as evidence of their intent to rob the store the next day. The defendants object.

Against which defendant should the statement be admitted?

(A) Against both defendants.

(B) Against the declarant-defendant only.

(C) Against the non-declarant defendant only.

(D) Against neither defendant.

63. The owner of a ring advertised its sale over the internet. A buyer purchased the ring from the owner, paying by check. The check was dishonored by the bank upon its presentment by the owner. The buyer sold the ring to a third party who purchased the ring in good faith for cash. The owner, unable to recover damages from the buyer due to the buyer's insolvency, learned of the third party's possession of the ring and sought its return from the third party. When the third party refused, the owner filed an action to recover the ring from the third party. None of the parties was a merchant.

Will the owner prevail?

(A) Yes, because the buyer did not give value for the ring since the check was dishonored by the bank.

(B) Yes, because the buyer was not a merchant to whom the owner had entrusted the ring.

(C) No, because the third party was a good faith purchaser of the ring.

(D) No, because the third party was not a merchant.

64. A prosecutor called a child who witnessed a murder to testify at trial. The child was having trouble remembering all of the events surrounding the murder. Shortly after the child had witnessed the murder, a child psychologist, who helped the child cope with the experience, asked the child to draw a series of pictures depicting what he had seen. To help the child with his testimony, the prosecutor handed the child the pictures. After looking at them, the child was able to recollect the details of the murder scene, and was able to testify to them. The defendant's attorney had previously seen the pictures, and objected to their use.

How should the court rule on the defense's objection?

(A) Sustain it, because the pictures are covered by the psychotherapist-patient privilege.

(B) Sustain it, because the pictures are inadmissible.

(C) Overrule it, because a child witness may be afforded assistance that other witnesses are not.

(D) Overrule it, because the pictures refreshed the witness's recollection of events.

65. A landowner subdivided his land into two parcels, retaining the parcel on which his residence was located and selling the other parcel to a stranger. In the deed, the landowner retained the right to use a path that accessed a river running through the parcel sold to the stranger. The stranger recorded the deed. After the sale, the landowner regularly made use of the path and maintained it as a path.

Several years later, the landowner's daughter, over her father's objections, purchased the parcel from the stranger. Upon the landowner's death shortly thereafter, the parcel retained by the landowner passed by will to his daughter. Within a year, she gave this parcel to her son and sold the other parcel to a third party. The deeds conveying the parcels were recorded but made no reference to the right of access.

After the father's death, no one made use of the path for four years. Recently, the son, remembering hikes to the river with his grandfather, cleared and began using the path again. Upon learning of the son's actions, the third party objected to the son's use of the path.

The son has consulted a lawyer as to his use of the path. Should the lawyer advise the son that he has the right to use the path?

(A) No, because the right of access had been abandoned.

(B) No, because the right of access had been lost through merger.

(C) Yes, because the right of access was an express easement.

(D) Yes, because the right of access was an implied easement.

66. A manufacturer of hot water heaters contacted a supplier of plastic resin about using the resin in the manufacturing of a heater. The supplier gave the manufacturer technical advice about how to mold the resin into a hot water tank. The supplier told the manufacturer that, in order to withstand the temperatures specified by the manufacturer, the resin would need to be at least one inch thick. The manufacturer ordered the resin from the supplier. The manufacturer designed and made the tank for its hot water heaters three-quarters of an inch thick using the supplier's resin.

A homeowner purchased a hot water heater made by the manufacturer from a local plumbing supply store. Due solely to the walls of the tank being too thin, the tank melted when used by the homeowner. The homeowner did not suffer physical injury, but experienced substantial property damage as a consequence of the melted tank.

The homeowner initiated a strict products liability action against the plastic supplier for damages suffered as a consequence of the melted hot water tank. Who will prevail?

(A) The homeowner, because the supplier was a commercial seller of the plastic resin.

(B) The homeowner, because the melting of the material provided by the supplier caused the homeowner's harm.

(C) The supplier, because the homeowner did not suffer a physical injury.

(D) The supplier, because the defect in the hot water heater was not attributable to the supplier.

67. A series of burglaries was committed while the inhabitants were away from their homes. A police officer, relying in good faith on a valid search warrant for evidence related to these burglaries, knocked on the door of the residence specified in the warrant but did not identify himself as a police officer. Without waiting for the door to be opened by the inhabitants, the officer pried it open with a crowbar, even though he had no specific reason to believe that evidence would be destroyed or that he was in danger. The officer did not find any evidence related to the burglaries, but did find a cache of illegal drugs in plain view.

The applicable statute provides that an officer can break into a house "if, after notice of his authority and purpose, he is refused admittance."

Prior to the trial of the homeowner for possession of the illegal drugs found during the search, the homeowner moved to exclude the drugs as evidence. Should the court grant this motion?

(A) No, because the officer relied in good faith on the search warrant.

(B) No, because the officer had a valid search warrant and the drugs were in plain view.

(C) Yes, because the drugs were not covered by the search warrant.

(D) Yes, because the search was illegal.

68. A manufacturer entered into a contract with a forklift supplier to purchase 10 new forklifts for use in the manufacturer's warehouse. The contract specified that the forklifts were to be delivered within 45 days of the execution of the contract.

The day after entering into the contract, the supplier was told by a reliable source that the manufacturer was in a precarious financial position. That day the supplier, reasonably relying on the information, which was in error, sent a written notice to the manufacturer demanding assurance of the manufacturer's ability to pay.

Thirty-five days after receiving the notice, the manufacturer sent the supplier its most recent financial statements, which adequately demonstrated that the manufacturer was not in a precarious financial position and had the funds to pay for the forklifts, along with a statement of its willingness to receive the shipment of the forklifts. Immediately upon receiving the manufacturer's correspondence the following day, the supplier called the manufacturer's CEO and demanded his personal guarantee of payment for the forklifts before the supplier would deliver the forklifts. When the manufacturer's CEO declined, the supplier refused to deliver the forklifts. The manufacturer then purchased forklifts from another distributor at a higher price.

The manufacturer sued the forklift supplier for breach of contract. Should the manufacturer prevail?

(A) Yes, because the supplier breached the contract by failing to deliver the forklifts.

(B) Yes, because the supplier's information regarding the manufacturer's financial position was in error.

(C) No, because the manufacturer failed to provide adequate assurances in a timely manner.

(D) No, because the manufacturer's CEO refused to guarantee payment of the forklifts.

69. A widower owned a residence in fee simple absolute. He contracted to sell it to a couple. The couple did not record the contract. The contract did not require either party to acquire or maintain casualty insurance on the premises, and neither party did so.

After the parties entered into the contract, the widower continued to occupy the residence. A week before closing, the residence was completely destroyed by a fire caused by a lightning strike.

On whom does the risk of loss fall?

(A) The couple, because they failed to record the contract.

(B) The couple, because of the doctrine of equitable conversion.

(C) The widower, because he, as possessor of the residence, had a duty to insure it.

(D) The widower, because he retained possession of the residence.

70. A 14-year-old girl suffered from pelvic pain, but did not want to go to a gynecologist. Her 19-year-old boyfriend, who reasonably believed that the girl was 16 years old, told her that having sexual intercourse with him would cure the problem. The boyfriend knew that his statement was false. Relying on his statement, the girl gave her consent, and the two had sexual intercourse. Later, the girl learned that intercourse could not and did not cure her problem, and notified the police.

Rape is defined by statute as "sexual intercourse with a person against that person's will or with a person under the age of 14 years old." Rape is a second-degree felony unless (i) in the course thereof the actor inflicts serious bodily injury upon anyone, (ii) the victim is under the age of 14, or (iii) the victim is 14 or 15 years old and the actor is at least four years older, in which cases the offense is a first-degree felony.

The boyfriend was convicted of first-degree rape of the girl. The boyfriend has appealed the conviction, contending that he is not guilty of the crime of rape. Should the appellate court overturn the conviction?

(A) Yes, because the intercourse was not against the girl's will and she was 14 years old.

(B) Yes, because the boyfriend was at least four years older than the girl was.

(C) No, because the boyfriend obtained the girl's consent through fraudulent means.

(D) No, because lack of knowledge as to the age of the victim is not a defense.

71. The defendant lives in State A. He commutes to work in nearby State B, where he does most of his shopping (State B has no sales tax). The defendant spends a month each summer vacationing in State C. While driving from home to State C, Defendant traveled through State D for the first time, where he negligently hit and totaled the $100,000 sports car of the plaintiff, a State D citizen. The defendant continued on to State C, where he vacationed for several weeks. The day after the accident, the plaintiff filed a complaint in federal court and sought to serve process on the defendant the next day, either personally or by mail. States A, B, C, and D all have statutes authorizing personal jurisdiction over anyone who engages in activity within the state, to the extent permissible under the U.S. Constitution. Assuming subject-matter jurisdiction is proper, in which state is the plaintiff least likely to find personal jurisdiction over the defendant?

(A) State A.

(B) State B.

(C) State C.

(D) State D.

72. A man played in a recreational ice hockey league that had a well-known reputation for aggressive play. The games often became quite physical, and injuries were common. In one game, the man scored the winning goal as time expired in the game. After the referee had blown his whistle, ending play, the man launched into a particularly exuberant celebration. An opposing player, angered by the celebration, hit the man on the forearm with a hockey stick, but did not intend to cause serious injury. The man collapsed in pain; tests later revealed that he suffered a severe forearm fracture as a result of the incident.

If the man sues the opposing player for battery, will the man prevail?

(A) Yes, because the opposing player's conduct was willful and wanton.

(B) Yes, because the opposing player intended to bring about a harmful or offensive contact.

(C) No, because the man impliedly consented to rough play.

(D) No, because the opposing player did not intend to break the man's arm.

73. A medical supply company made transfers of property to a state hospital after the company became insolvent. Subsequently, the company filed for bankruptcy in federal bankruptcy court. The bankruptcy trustee, acting pursuant to the federal Bankruptcy Act, sought to recover those transfers. The state hospital, refusing to comply with the trustee's request, asserted that, as a state entity, it was immune from suit by a private individual, despite a provision in the Bankruptcy Act that expressly abrogated state immunity with respect to such transfers.

Can the trustee force the state to turn over the transferred property?

(A) Yes, because Congress was acting pursuant to the Bankruptcy Clause of Article I, Section 8, Clause 4, in subjecting the state to the Bankruptcy Act.

(B) Yes, because the action was brought in federal court.

(C) No, because the Eleventh Amendment protects a state entity from suit by a private individual for damages in federal court.

(D) No, because Congress lacks the power to abrogate state immunity.

74. An auto collector hired a restorer to refurbish a classic car she had purchased at an auction. The written restoration agreement was signed by the collector and the restorer, and contained only an identification of the vehicle, an enumerated list of the work that was to be done, and the price for the job. The agreement specified, among other things, that the car's engine was to be replaced. When the collector was shown the restored car, she was upset that the engine that was in the car when it was purchased had not been rebuilt, since the complete replacement of the car's engine lowered the value of the car as a classic. The collector refused to pay the agreed-upon price for the restoration, and instead filed suit against the restorer for breach of contract.

At trial, the collector seeks to introduce a note in her handwriting that she had shown to the restorer prior to the execution of the agreement that contained the phrase "rebuild engine." Is this note admissible?

(A) Yes, because the agreement was only partially integrated.

(B) Yes, because the parol evidence rule only applies to oral communications.

(C) No, because of the parol evidence rule.

(D) No, because the Uniform Commercial Code does not apply to this transaction.

75. In order to finance the purchase of a property, the buyer received a loan and in return gave the lender a promissory note secured by a mortgage on the property. Subsequently, the buyer divided the property into two parcels, retaining one of the parcels and selling the other to a friend. The friend took the parcel subject to the mortgage. The buyer and the friend agreed that each would be liable for one-half of the outstanding mortgage. One year later the buyer disappeared. Since the buyer was no longer paying one-half of the mortgage obligation, the lender threatened to foreclose on the property. The friend paid off the outstanding balance of the loan.

The applicable jurisdiction recognizes the lien theory of mortgages.

Can the friend bring a foreclosure action against the buyer's parcel?

(A) Yes, because the friend is subrogated to the lender's rights in the parcel.

(B) Yes, because the friend obtained ownership rights in his own parcel by purchase.

(C) No, because the friend does not have an ownership interest in the parcel since the jurisdiction adheres to the lien theory of mortgages.

(D) No, because the friend was not under a legal duty to pay the buyer's portion of the mortgage.

76. A car was parked in front of a man's house for a week without being moved. The man honestly but unreasonably believed that the car had been abandoned. He found a spare key attached to the underside of the car and, using that key, drove the car into his driveway, intending to make it his own. Several days later, the car's owner returned. Seeing his car in the man's driveway, the owner notified the police. The man was charged with larceny. Taking abandoned property is not a crime under the laws of the jurisdiction.

Should the man be convicted of larceny?

(A) No, because taking abandoned property is not a crime.

(B) No, because the man's mistake was honestly made.

(C) Yes, because an honest mistake of law does not negate the man's *mens rea*.

(D) Yes, because the man's mistake was unreasonable.

77. In a civil trial regarding a store owner's negligence in clearing ice from his front walkway, the defendant store owner testified on direct examination that he had cleared the ice from his front walkway on the morning of the plaintiff's injury. On cross-examination, the plaintiff's attorney asked the defendant if he was sure that he cleared all of the ice off the walkway, without missing any, and the defendant replied that he had. The plaintiff's attorney then sought permission to ask the defendant about two prior incidents in the last three winters in which the defendant's customers claimed to have fallen on patches of ice that the defendant failed to clear. The defendant's attorney objected to the introduction of this evidence.

Should the court allow the plaintiff's attorney to question the defendant about the prior incidents?

(A) Yes, because the two prior incidents serve as evidence that the defendant has a habit of failing to clear ice from his front walkway.

(B) Yes, because the two prior incidents bear on the defendant's credibility, since he claims to have cleared all the ice in this case.

(C) No, because failing to clear ice on the two prior incidents does not bear on the defendant's credibility and does not contradict his testimony in this case.

(D) No, because there is no evidence here as to the outcome of the prior claims.

78. A defendant was convicted of murder. During the trial, his lawyer made a strategic judgment call to refrain from introducing certain mitigating evidence. The defendant was convicted and sentenced to a long prison term. The lawyer's decision with respect to the mitigating evidence and her overall performance did not fall below an objective standard of competence for attorneys in a similar situation.

After the trial, the defendant's lawyer apologized to the defendant for not introducing the evidence, saying that in hindsight she was wrong not to have done so. The defendant now seeks to reverse his conviction on the grounds that he received ineffective assistance of counsel.

Will the defendant succeed?

(A) No, because decisions regarding trial strategy rest solely with the lawyer.

(B) No, because the defendant's lawyer's performance met the objective standard of care.

(C) Yes, because the lawyer's performance fell below the lawyer's subjective standard, and the defendant was actually prejudiced by the result.

(D) Yes, because the defendant was actually prejudiced by the result of his lawyer's performance.

79. To preserve the environment and enhance the quality of life, a city located on an ocean had restrictive property regulations. The city limited non-residential buildings to its major thoroughfare. In residential areas, single-family dwellings were strongly preferred. People could apply for "special use" permits in residential areas, but they were denied 99% of the time.

An organization that operated day-care centers for developmentally disabled children applied for a special-use permit to build and operate, in a residential area, a 7,000 square foot day care center for 15 children. The city denied the application, based primarily upon the increased traffic and noise the center would generate, which would disturb the tranquil quality of life and the environment of the residential neighborhood. The city routinely denied special-use permits to a variety of other groups on similar grounds.

On behalf of the disabled children, the organization brought an action against the city based on a constitutional claim in an appropriate federal court. Will this organization prevail?

(A) Yes, because the city's stated reasons for denying the permit do not constitute a compelling interest sufficient to justify an action that discriminated against the developmentally disabled.

(B) Yes, because the city's reasons for denying the permit do not constitute an important government interest sufficient to justify an action that discriminated against the developmentally disabled.

(C) No, because the city has a compelling interest in preserving the environment and enhancing the quality of life by protecting the tranquility of residential neighborhoods.

(D) No, because the developmentally disabled are not members of a suspect classification, and the city had a rational basis for denying the special-use permit.

80. A telephone company was removing wooden utility poles on a residential street and replacing them with new steel poles. The old poles were approximately 25 feet tall, and weighed several tons each. One morning, telephone company employees were removing an old pole. As a 10-year-old boy walked past the construction site, the old utility pole fell and crushed him to death. When the news was conveyed to the boy's mother, who was at work several miles away, she immediately fainted. For the next 48 hours, the mother was unable to function due to shock over the event. In the following months, the mother had difficulty sleeping due to nightmares as a result of the incident.

The mother sued the telephone company for negligent infliction of emotional distress stemming from her son's death. She produced evidence at trial conclusively establishing that the telephone company was negligent in allowing the old utility pole to fall. The applicable jurisdiction has abandoned the zone of danger requirement for this type of action. Which party is likely to prevail?

(A) The mother, because she was closely related to the boy.

(B) The mother, because she suffered severe emotional distress.

(C) The telephone company, because the mother was not present at the scene of the accident.

(D) The telephone company, because its actions were not extreme and outrageous.

81. During a personal injury trial, the plaintiff called an eyewitness to testify. On cross-examination, the defense attorney asked the witness about a previous conviction. Seven years ago, when the witness was 16 years old, she was tried as a juvenile and convicted of check fraud. The plaintiff objected to the introduction of evidence of this conviction, but the defense attorney maintained that he could introduce it for impeachment purposes.

Is evidence of the witness's conviction admissible?

(A) No, because the witness is testifying in a civil trial.

(B) No, because the conviction constitutes a prior bad act.

(C) Yes, because it was a conviction of a crime involving fraud or deceit.

(D) Yes, because the conviction is less than 10 years old.

82. A homeowner hired a contractor to finish her basement. They agreed on a price of $20,000 for the job. During the final stages of the remodeling, the contractor discovered that there was mold in the basement, the existence of which had been unknown to either party. The contractor refused to complete the job unless the homeowner paid an additional $2,000 to the contractor for removal of the mold. The homeowner reluctantly agreed, and the contractor finished the basement in accord with the modified contract. The homeowner paid the contractor $20,000.

In a breach of contract action to recover the $2,000, will the contractor prevail?

(A) No, because a contractual modification is not enforceable without consideration.

(B) No, because the unforeseen circumstances did not rise to the level of impracticability.

(C) Yes, because the homeowner agreed to the price increase.

(D) Yes, because the modification was based on a mutual mistake.

83. Two parked vehicles, a luxury car and a pickup truck, were seriously damaged when a light pole fell on them. The owners of the vehicles jointly sued the installer of the pole in federal district court, alleging that the damage to their vehicles was caused by the defendant's negligent installation of the pole. The owner of the car claimed $75,000 in damages and the owner of the truck claimed $15,000 in damages. The defendant was a citizen of the forum state. Each plaintiff was a citizen of the same neighboring state. Contending a lack of subject matter jurisdiction, the defendant timely filed a motion to dismiss the action. The court granted the motion. Did the court err in granting the motion?

(A) No, because the plaintiffs are citizens of the same state.

(B) No, because the amount-in-controversy requirement was not met.

(C) Yes, because the defendant is a citizen of the forum state.

(D) Yes, because the plaintiffs' claims arose out a common nucleus of operative fact.

84. In a particular state in the United States, a mortgagee routinely required the mortgagor to convey title to the secured land to the mortgagee via a deed absolute; the mortgagee would reconvey title only upon complete repayment of the loan. The deed absolute transaction also allowed the mortgagee to dispose of the land immediately upon the mortgagor's default, thereby avoiding the cost and delay of foreclosure proceedings.

A new election in this state brought into power a majority of pro-consumer legislators. The legislature enacted a statute that immediately outlawed use of the deed absolute and declared that all such deeds would be considered mere liens against the secured property. The statute applied not only to future loans, but also to loans already in existence—even though many of those outstanding loans never would have been made without the extra security provided by the deed absolute.

Mortgagees who had loaned money secured through deeds absolute challenged the constitutionality of the new statute. What is their best argument?

(A) As applied to loans made after the statute was enacted, the law substantially and unreasonably impairs the mortgagees' contract rights in violation of the Contracts Clause.

(B) As applied to loans outstanding at the time the statute was enacted, the law substantially and unreasonably impairs the mortgagees' contract rights in violation of the Contracts Clause.

(C) The statute violates the freedom of contract protected by the Fourteenth Amendment Due Process Clause.

(D) The statute violates the Fourteenth Amendment's Equal Protection Clause by discriminating against mortgagees.

85. A potential renter, a resident of State A, was searching for an apartment. The renter completed an application for a lease at an apartment complex located in State A, which was owned and managed by an apartment management company. The apartment management company's principal place of business was in State A, but it was incorporated in State B. The renter fulfilled all the requirements detailed in the application, yet the management company refused to offer her a lease. Suspecting that the management company refused to rent to her because of her ethnicity, the renter filed a claim under the Federal Fair Housing Act in State A state court seeking damages of $100,000.

If the management company seeks to remove the action to the federal district court located in State A, will it be successful?

(A) Yes, because the federal district court has original federal question jurisdiction.

(B) Yes, because the federal district court has original diversity jurisdiction.

(C) No, because, as a landlord-tenant dispute, the case is properly in state court.

(D) No, because when the state courts and federal courts have concurrent jurisdiction, the plaintiff holds the right to choose where to file the claim.

86. An avid runner was diagnosed with a serious heart condition. The runner's doctor advised her to avoid strenuous physical activity, including running, as such activity would create a substantial risk of cardiac arrest. The runner refrained from such activity for a month, but in that time she gained 15 pounds and felt very unhealthy. Deciding that the health benefits of running outweighed the risk involved, one morning she set out on her normal running path—the shoulder of a flat rural road. Five miles into the run, the runner suffered a heart attack, collapsed, and lapsed into a coma.

Two minutes later, the runner's feet and legs—which were partially sticking out into the travel lane—were run over by a car. The driver of the car, who had been traveling at a reasonable speed, was aware of the runner but was unable to avoid her due to a locking up of the car's brakes that the driver had negligently failed to have repaired.

The runner survived, but suffered serious injuries to both of her legs. The runner sued the driver for those injuries in a jurisdiction that applies traditional contributory negligence rules. Is the runner likely to prevail?

(A) No, because the runner was contributorily negligent.

(B) No, because the driver was aware of the runner's predicament before the accident occurred.

(C) Yes, because of the runner's helpless peril at the time of the accident.

(D) Yes, because the driver was negligent in driving the car with brakes in need of repair.

87. A mother made a gift of unimproved real property to her son. The son promptly and properly recorded the deed, but did not inspect the property nor otherwise make use of it by building structures or making other improvements. The son, however, did pay the real estate taxes imposed on the property.

Subsequently, the mother, forgetting about her conveyance of the property, sold it at its fair market value. The buyer promptly and properly recorded the deed. The buyer, who was not aware of the son's ownership of the property, began to construct a house on the property. Upon learning about the buyer's construction activities, the son, unaware of his mother's transaction with the buyer, brought an appropriate legal action to halt the buyer's activities and declare title to the property.

Will the buyer be successful in defending against the son's lawsuit?

(A) Yes, because the recording act does not protect a donee of real property.

(B) Yes, because the son did not make productive use of the real property.

(C) No, because the son recorded his deed before his mother made the subsequent conveyance to the buyer.

(D) No, because the son paid the real estate taxes on the property.

88. A father and son are charged with burglary. Prior to the trial, the prosecutor approached the son and asked him if he would be willing to testify against his father in exchange for a reduced sentence. After discussing the son's role in the burglary and some negotiation, the prosecutor and the son's defense attorney reached a settlement agreement. The son pleaded guilty, and was called to testify against his father. On cross-examination of the son, the father's attorney brought up the fact that the son was also originally charged with the burglary, and asked whether it was true that he received a lesser sentence for agreeing to testify against his father. The prosecutor objected to this line of questioning.

How should the court rule on the prosecutor's objection?

(A) The objection should be sustained, because the response calls for hearsay.

(B) The objection should be sustained, because it is against public policy to introduce evidence of a plea agreement.

(C) The objection should be overruled, because the question concerns bias.

(D) The objection should be overruled, because the son's sentence is irrelevant to the father's guilt.

89. A state maintained its departments, including its Fish and Game Department, through tax revenues collected primarily from its residents. The department required all recreational deer hunters (i.e., those who hunt purely for sport) to obtain a deer hunting license. The license fee was $25 a year for state residents and $150 a year for out-of-state residents. An out-of-state resident wanted to go deer hunting for sport. He objected to paying a license fee that was six times the fee paid by in-state residents. He sued in an appropriate federal court.

Will the court hold that the licensing fee scheme for recreational deer hunting is unconstitutional?

(A) Yes, because the scheme violates the Equal Protection Clause by discriminating against out-of-state hunters.

(B) Yes, because the scheme violates Article IV's Privileges and Immunities Clause by failing to accord out-of-state residents the same rights as state residents.

(C) No, because the scheme is constitutionally valid under the Dormant Commerce Clause, as the subject of the fees, deer hunting, is a recreational activity, not a commercial one.

(D) No, because the scheme is constitutionally valid under Article IV's Privileges and Immunities Clause, as recreational deer hunting is not a fundamental right, and a state may charge its residents a lower fee because their taxes support the Fish and Game Department.

90. The owner of a lakefront home in a retirement community that greatly restricts access by nonresidents was aware that her dock needed repair, but was unable to afford the considerable expense to do so. The owner placed a large heavy chair at the entrance to the dock with a sign that read, "Please do not enter. Dock in need of repair."

Two children, a six-year-old boy and a ten-year-old girl, entered the property without permission from, or knowledge of the owner. The children quickly discovered the dock. The girl read the sign aloud to the boy and advised him, "You shouldn't go out on the dock." The boy, responding "But it's not dangerous," climbed over the chair and walked out onto the dock. As the boy ran to the end of the dock, a rotten plank on which the boy stepped gave way, and he fell into the lake and drowned.

As permitted by the applicable jurisdiction, the boy's parents sued the owner in a wrongful death action alleging that her negligence with respect to the dock caused the boy's death. At trial, the boy's parents argued that the dock constituted an attractive nuisance.

Which of the following may protect the owner from liability that otherwise would arise under this doctrine?

(A) The owner lives in a retirement community that greatly restricts access by nonresidents.

(B) The boy was not attracted to the property by the presence of the dock.

(C) The boy was a trespasser.

(D) The boy was aware of the owner's warning.

91. A uniformed police officer learned about a possible burglary of a home and went to investigate. When the officer arrived, she attempted to get into the home through the front door, but found it locked. Going to the back of the home, the officer found a door slightly open. Drawing her gun, she entered the home and announced that she was a police officer. The homeowner, honestly but unreasonably fearing that the officer was the person who had broken into the home earlier, shot and killed the officer.

The homeowner was charged with murder of the police officer. The jurisdiction recognizes "imperfect" self-defense. Can the homeowner be convicted of this crime?

(A) Yes, because homeowner killed the police officer.

(B) Yes, because the homeowner's use of deadly force was unreasonable.

(C) No, because the homeowner had no duty to retreat before using deadly force.

(D) No, because the homeowner honestly believed that the police officer threatened him with death or serious bodily injury.

92. A plaintiff filed an action in state court against a defendant for breach of contract. The plaintiff, who was a citizen of the forum state, sought $100,000 in damages. The defendant, who was a citizen of a neighboring state, filed an unrelated counterclaim against the plaintiff based in negligence. The defendant sought $250,000 in damages. The plaintiff timely filed a petition to remove the case to a federal district court in the same state as the action was originally filed. The defendant has filed a motion to remand the case to state court. Should the court grant the defendant's motion?

(A) No, because both claims satisfy the amount-in-controversy requirement.

(B) No, because the action satisfies the diversity-of-citizenship requirement.

(C) Yes, because the plaintiff is a citizen of the forum state.

(D) Yes, because the plaintiff cannot remove a state action to federal court.

93. A retail store that specialized in glass objects entered into a written contract to purchase 100 hand-blown glass ornaments from an artisan. Because of the artisan's popularity, the store paid in full for the ornaments at the time that the contract was executed. The contract specified that the store would pick up the ornaments after notification that they were ready. The contract contained no other terms related to delivery of the ornaments and did not allocate the risk of loss. When the ornaments were ready, the artisan notified the store. The parties arranged for the store to pick up the packaged ornaments no later than 2:00 pm the next day. The employee assigned by the store to make the pickup did not arrive until 6:00 pm. In the late afternoon just before the store employee arrived, a short but intense storm caused a large, healthy tree on the artisan's property to fall over and destroy all the ornaments. Neither party had insured the ornaments against such a loss.

Who bears the risk of the loss with respect to the ornaments?

(A) The store, because the artisan had tendered delivery of the ornaments to the store prior to the loss.

(B) The store, because the artisan's insurance did not cover the loss.

(C) The artisan, because the store had not taken possession of the ornaments.

(D) The artisan, because the store was a merchant.

94. One rainy afternoon a car and motorcycle collided. The motorcyclist filed a negligence action against the driver of the car in a federal district court located in the state in which the accident occurred. In his complaint, the motorcyclist alleged that the driver of the car failed to yield the right-of-way; the motorcyclist sought damages totaling $88,000. The driver of the car filed a counterclaim based in negligence against the motorcyclist for $12,000 in damages. The driver alleged that the motorcyclist was traveling at an excessive speed for the weather conditions. The motorcyclist is a citizen of the United States; the driver of the car is a citizen and resident of a foreign country. The motorcyclist moved to dismiss the counterclaim for lack of subject matter jurisdiction. Can the court deny this motion?

(A) Yes, because the counterclaim arose from the same transaction as the original claim.

(B) Yes, because the accident occurred in the forum state.

(C) No, because the driver's counterclaim does not exceed $75,000.

(D) No, because the driver is a citizen and resident of a foreign country.

95. In a murder trial, the prosecutor plans to call an eyewitness to the stand to testify that he saw the defendant kill the victim. However, the witness recently suffered a severe head injury that seriously affected his memory. The witness can no longer remember witnessing the murder. Prior to the witness's injury, he testified to what he saw before the grand jury. The prosecutor would like to introduce the witness's grand jury testimony as substantive evidence that the defendant committed the murder. The defendant objects to the introduction of the evidence.

Should the court admit the witness's grand jury testimony into evidence?

(A) Yes, because the witness is unavailable to testify.

(B) Yes, if used to refresh the witness's recollection.

(C) No, because the witness does not meet the "unavailability" standard.

(D) No, because the former testimony exception does not apply to these facts.

96. In the Labor Management Relations Act, Congress expressly authorized the president to seize plants to avert a labor shutdown if the president determined that a shutdown would threaten national security.

In response to a threatened national strike by America's steel workers, the president ordered the government to seize and operate steel mills to ensure steel production that the president deemed vital to the War on Terrorism and hence to national security. Subsequent to the order, Congress did not explicitly approve or disapprove of the president's action.

One of the companies affected by the president's order filed a suit in an appropriate federal court claiming that the order violated the Constitution. What is the most likely ruling?

(A) Congress unconstitutionally delegated its legislative power to the president because the statutory standard—that a shutdown would "threaten national security"—does not provide a specific, intelligible standard.

(B) The president lacked power as Commander-in-Chief to take this action because it involved domestic affairs, not military decisions in the foreign theater of war.

(C) The president had Article II power to take this action.

(D) The president's action would be lawful only if Congress explicitly approved it.

97. The owner of a rural, wooded property devised half of the property to his daughter and the other half to his son. At the time of the devise, the only public road in the area ran along one side of the son's property, but did not adjoin the daughter's property. The daughter, wanting to build a cabin on her property, sought permission from the son to build a road on the son's property to connect with the public road, but the son refused.

In an action by the daughter to compel the son to permit her access across his land to the public road, who will prevail?

(A) The daughter, because access across the son's property is necessary for access to her land.

(B) The daughter, because she sought permission from the son before filing her court action.

(C) The son, because the son never owned the entire wooded property.

(D) The son, because there has been no prior use of his property in the manner that the daughter proposes.

98. A recidivism statute calls for a mandatory life sentence for a defendant who is convicted of three felonies. The defendant was convicted of felony theft three separate times and was sentenced to life in prison after his conviction for the third theft. In each case, the defendant stole the items from stores when nobody was watching. He did not use any weapons, nor was he violent. The defendant challenges the sentence on constitutional grounds.

Will the defendant succeed?

(A) Yes, because the sentence violates the Eighth Amendment prohibition on cruel and unusual punishment because the defendant's crimes were non-violent.

(B) Yes, because the sentence violates the Double Jeopardy Clause.

(C) No, because the Eighth Amendment prohibition on cruel and unusual punishment only applies to degrading or painful sentences involving the use of force.

(D) No, because the recidivism statute is constitutional even when applied to non-violent offenders.

99. A homeowner hired a contractor to paint the homeowner's residence. The written contract stated that it was the parties' final and complete agreement and that all prior agreements between the parties merged into the written document. Prior to executing the contract, the contractor noted debris in the gutters of the residence. The contractor stated that to prevent such debris from adversely affecting the painting, the gutters should be cleaned. The contractor offered to do this prior to undertaking the painting for $600. The homeowner orally agreed. The homeowner and the contractor then signed the written contract, which did not mention cleaning the gutters. The contractor performed all of the work called for in the written contract as well as cleaning the gutters. The homeowner paid the amount specified in the written contract, but refused to pay an additional $600 for the cleaning of the gutters.

In a breach of contract action by the contractor against the homeowner to recover the $600 payment, which of the following is the strongest argument that the homeowner can make to prevent the contractor from recovering?

(A) The agreement regarding cleaning the gutters only serves to supplement the terms of the written contract.

(B) Since the amount sought for cleaning the gutters was more than $500, it can only be evidenced by a writing.

(C) The contract was a complete integration of the agreement between the contractor and the homeowner.

(D) The parol evidence rule bars evidence about an oral agreement between the parties to a written contract.

100. The fee simple owner of land devised it to a private educational institution "for so long as the land herein conveyed is used for educational purposes; if the land is not so used, then to my daughter and her heirs." At the time of the owner's death, the owner's spouse was deceased and the owner's only two children, a son and a daughter, were alive. The owner devised all of his other real property interests to his son. The daughter died shortly after her father, devising her real property's interests to her only child, who was alive at the time of her death.

Immediately after the owner's death, the institution constructed a classroom building on the land and has held classes in the building each year thereafter.

Thirty years after the owner's death, the educational institution seeks to sell the land to a developer who intends to construct single-family homes on the land. Both the son and daughter's child, who are the owner's only living heirs, are alive.

The applicable jurisdiction has adopted the following statute: "A nonvested property interest is invalid unless when the interest is created, it is certain to vest or terminate no later than 21 years after the death of an individual then alive, or the interest either vests or terminates within 90 years after its creation."

The applicable jurisdiction does not impose time limitations on the exercise of interests that follow a defeasible fee property interest.

In order to convey marketable title to the developer, whom must the institution convince to agree to the transfer?

(A) No one, because the institution owns the land in fee simple.

(B) The daughter's child, because she holds an executory interest in the land.

(C) The son, because he holds a possibility of reverter in the land.

(D) The son and the daughter's child, because they are the owner's living heirs.

STOP.
IF YOU FINISH BEFORE TIME IS CALLED, CHECK YOUR WORK ON THIS TEST.

Directions: Each of the questions or incomplete statements below is followed by four suggested answers or completions. You are to choose the best of the stated alternatives. Answer all questions according to the generally accepted view, except where otherwise noted.

For the purposes of this test, you are to assume the application of (1) the amendments to the Federal Rules of Civil Procedure through 2012; and (2) the sections of Title 28 to the U.S. Code pertaining to jurisdiction, venue, and transfer. Assume also that Articles 1 and 2 of the Uniform Commercial Code have been adopted. You are also to assume relevant application of Article 9 of the UCC concerning fixtures. The Federal Rules of Evidence are deemed to control. The terms "Constitution," "constitutional," and "unconstitutional" refer to the federal Constitution unless indicated to the contrary. You are to assume that there is no applicable statute unless otherwise specified; however, survival actions and claims for wrongful death should be assumed to be available where applicable. You should assume that joint and several liability, with pure comparative negligence, is the relevant rule unless otherwise indicated.

101. At trial, in an effort to prove that the defendant suffers from a mental defect, a criminal defense attorney seeks to introduce evidence that his client told several people that he believed he was the President of the United States. The prosecutor contends that the evidence is inadmissible.

Is evidence of the defendant's statement admissible?

(A) No, because the statement constitutes hearsay.

(B) No, because the statement does not meet the requirements of the "state of mind" exception to the hearsay rule.

(C) Yes, because the statement is being offered as circumstantial evidence of the defendant's state of mind.

(D) Yes, because the statement is being introduced by a defense attorney in a criminal trial.

102. An indigent defendant was indicted for driving under the influence of alcohol, a misdemeanor. The lawyer who had been appointed to represent the defendant suffered a fatal heart attack on his way to the courthouse on the day scheduled for the trial. In discussing the absence of the defendant's lawyer with the defendant, the trial judge learned from the defendant that he intended to plead guilty. The judge indicated that, in exchange for the defendant's guilty plea, the defendant would not serve time in prison. The defendant agreed and was sentenced to two months in prison, with the sentence suspended.

The defendant appealed his conviction, contending that he was denied his Sixth Amendment right to counsel at trial.

Should the judge reverse the defendant's conviction?

(A) No, because the defendant was convicted of a misdemeanor.

(B) No, because the defendant's prison sentence was suspended.

(C) Yes, because the defendant was convicted of a crime for which a sentence of incarceration was imposed.

(D) Yes, because the defendant was convicted of a crime that was punishable by imprisonment.

103. An auto dealership sold a limited-production luxury vehicle as part of its business. It typically sold very few of the vehicles per year, but continued the business because it earned $25,000 in profit on each sale. The vehicles sold at retail for $150,000. A car buyer entered into a contact with the dealership to purchase one of these vehicles with the color scheme and options she desired, which the dealership ordered from the manufacturer. She signed a written order form and put down a $50,000 deposit on the vehicle. The form specified that, in the event that the buyer failed to purchase the vehicle, the deposit was non-refundable, representing liquidated damages that did not constitute a penalty.

Later, the car buyer found a better price on an identical vehicle at another dealership, and purchased that vehicle. She demanded the return of her deposit, but the dealership refused. The dealership had difficulty selling the car, and eventually had to sell it at the discounted price of $100,000.

The car buyer filed a lawsuit seeking to void the non-refundable deposit provision of the order form and seeking the return of her deposit. Is she likely to prevail?

(A) Yes, because the amount of the deposit was not reasonable in relation to the damages that could have been anticipated at the time the order form was signed.

(B) Yes, because the vehicle was not a unique good.

(C) No, because the woman signed the order form, which clearly stipulated that the deposit was not to be interpreted as a penalty.

(D) No, because the deposit was reasonable in relation to the actual damages the dealership suffered.

104. A corporation entered into an agreement with an accountant to audit the corporation's books pending a sale of all of the company's assets. The agreement specified that the accountant would perform "all services relating to the sale of assets of the corporation." The agreement was fully integrated, but did not contain a merger clause. The day after the agreement was executed, the corporation and the accountant amended the agreement to include the evaluation of prospective buyers, for $2,000 per buyer. The accountant evaluated two corporations who were potential buyers. The corporation refused to pay the additional $4,000.

In a breach of contract action, will evidence of the evaluation agreement be excluded?

(A) No, because the agreement regarding the evaluation of prospective buyers was entered into after the execution of the writing.

(B) No, because the amendment was supported by new consideration.

(C) Yes, because the agreement was fully integrated.

(D) Yes, because the second agreement dealt with the same subject matter as the first agreement.

105. The president of the United States received reliable information from federal law enforcement authorities that (1) a known terrorist group was planning a terrorist attack on America which would occur within the next two weeks, (2) the terrorists, all of whom were fluent in a particular dialect, were already in America, and (3) the terrorist group's leaders would provide to these terrorists certain details regarding the attack through coded messages contained in a U.S. newspaper published in the particular dialect. There were four such newspapers—in New York, Washington, Los Angeles, and Detroit. The president immediately ordered all four newspapers to shut down for two weeks and notified the newspapers that they were to be fully compensated for any losses they incurred because of the closure order. The newspapers immediately challenged the order as unconstitutional. Which of the following is the president's best argument is that the order should be upheld?

(A) It is not a prior restraint on speech or the press.

(B) The federal government can always suppress subversive speech as long as it pays just compensation to the person whose expression has been suppressed.

(C) The words that would be published constitute a clear and present danger to national security.

(D) Because national security is at issue, the burden is on the newspapers to establish the right to publish the information.

106. In order to purchase undeveloped land, the buyer sought a 10-year loan from a third-party lender. The buyer executed a promissory note and mortgage on the property. The lender promptly and properly recorded the mortgage. As part of the transaction, the lender also required the buyer to execute a quitclaim deed to the property to the lender, which the buyer was to give to an independent escrow agent. Under the terms of the escrow arrangement, the agent was to record the quitclaim deed to the lender upon notification that the buyer had defaulted on the loan. The escrow agreement also provided that, upon recording, the buyer's rights in the property would cease.

The buyer made installment payments on the loan, as required by its terms, for two years, but subsequently was unable to make the required loan payments. The lender notified the escrow agent of the buyer's default and the escrow agent recorded the quitclaim deed. The lender, choosing not to foreclose on the mortgage, has advertised the property for sale at an amount significantly higher than the outstanding balance in the mortgage.

Shortly thereafter, the buyer, receiving a sizeable inheritance, offered to pay the lender the full amount of the outstanding mortgage debt, which was more than 85% of the original mortgage loan. The lender refused to accept the buyer's payment. The buyer has filed an action to compel the lender to accept the payment, release the mortgage, and to void the quitclaim deed.

The applicable jurisdiction has the following statute: "No conveyance or mortgage of real property shall be good against subsequent purchasers for value and *without notice* unless the same be recorded according to law."

Who should prevail?

(A) Buyer, because the lender had notice of the previously recorded mortgage.

(B) Buyer, because the escrow arrangement has clogged the buyer's equity of redemption.

(C) Lender, because, as owner of the property pursuant to the quitclaim deed, the lender is free to sell the property.

(D) Lender, because the buyer had not paid at least half of the original mortgage loan.

107. A man shopping in a department store found a suit that he liked but could not afford. He noticed that the store had a system for identifying sale merchandise: all merchandise with a sticky red label on the tag was 50% off the original price. The man then went to an office supply store and purchased a set of identical labels. He returned to the department store with one of the labels, and placed the label on the suit's price tag. The man then took the suit to the register, paid the reduced price for the suit, and took the suit home.

Of which one of the following crimes should the man be convicted?

(A) Forgery

(B) Embezzlement

(C) Larceny by trick

(D) False pretenses

108. In December, a contractor was hired by a power utility company to perform repair work on a large transformer. The contractor performed the work negligently and as a result severely damaged one of the conducting coils in the transformer. The damage resulted in a two-day power outage in a town with a large industrial park. An electronics manufacturer was a tenant in the industrial park, and the power outage crippled its ability to meet the strong demand for its products during the critical holiday buying season. While none of the electronic manufacturer's machines were damaged, it can prove with certainty that the power outage directly caused it to lose $750,000 in business.

The electronics manufacturer sued the power utility company and the contractor for negligently causing its sales losses. If, at the end of the plaintiff's case, both defendants move for summary judgment, and all the foregoing facts are undisputed, how should the court rule on the motions?

(A) Deny both motions, because both parties were substantial factors in the electronics manufacturer's loss.

(B) Deny both motions, because the burden of proof has shifted to both defendants to exonerate themselves.

(C) Grant the motion as to the contractor, but deny the motion as to the power utility company, because liability is assigned to the principal under the *respondeat superior* doctrine.

(D) Grant both motions, because the electronics manufacturer suffered no tangible injury to its equipment or employees.

109. A federal statute provides that "all persons within the United States shall have the same right in every state to make and enforce contracts as is enjoyed by white persons." The Supreme Court interpreted this statute as applying to all contracts, including private contracts.

A black citizen of a state in the United States claims that an appliance store in her state violated this statute by refusing to enter into a sales contract with her because of her race. The appliance store defended on the ground that the statute is unconstitutional.

A federal court would be most likely to uphold this statute by relying upon which provision of the Constitution?

(A) The Thirteenth Amendment

(B) The Contracts Clause

(C) The General Welfare Clause

(D) The Equal Protection Clause of the Fourteenth Amendment

110. A mother and her son were both injured at a construction site. They brought a negligence action in federal court against the construction company for failure to exercise reasonable care with respect to their presence at the site. The mother alleged in good faith that she suffered $55,000 in damages; her son alleged in good faith $200,000 in damages. Subsequently, they permissively joined as a defendant under Rule 20 an individual whose intentional actions in tampering with warnings posted by the construction company also allegedly caused their injuries. The mother and her son are citizens of the forum state; the two defendants are citizens of other states. The individual defendant has moved to dismiss the mother's claim against it for lack of subject matter jurisdiction. How should the court rule?

(A) Grant the motion, because the mother's claim was asserted against a defendant who was permissively joined under Rule 20.

(B) Grant the motion, because supplemental jurisdiction does not apply to a claim for which diversity jurisdiction does not exist.

(C) Deny the motion, because there is complete diversity between the parties.

(D) Deny the motion, because the court has supplemental jurisdiction over the mother's claim.

111. The owner of an undeveloped lot agrees to sell the lot to a buyer. The written agreement identifies the parties, describes the property in sufficient detail, specifies the price to be paid, and spells out the payment terms. The agreement is signed by the owner. In accord with the agreement, the buyer pays the required down payment to the owner. Subsequently, the buyer constructs a garage on the lot as the first step towards building a three-story residence, but, due to a financial reversal, abandons his construction efforts.

May the seller bring an action to compel the buyer to complete the purchase?

(A) No, because of the Statute of Frauds.

(B) No, because the owner's remedy at law is adequate.

(C) Yes, because of the doctrine of part performance.

(D) Yes, because of the doctrine of detrimental reliance.

112. A fisherman who lived next to a lake owned a large sport-utility vehicle equipped with a trailer hitch. He used the vehicle primarily to tow his large fishing boat. One afternoon, a neighbor asked if she could borrow the fisherman's vehicle for a short time in order to tow her boat back from the dock, as her car was at the repair shop. The fisherman agreed to let the neighbor use the vehicle to tow her boat, but asked her to return the vehicle immediately afterward. The neighbor drove the vehicle to the dock and towed her boat back without incident.

Before returning the vehicle, the neighbor decided to buy a gift for the fisherman as a token of appreciation. While the neighbor was driving the vehicle to the store to buy the gift, she was involved in a serious accident. The neighbor was not seriously hurt, but the vehicle was a total loss.

If the fisherman sues his neighbor for conversion, will he prevail?

(A) Yes, because the neighbor exceeded the scope of consent.

(B) Yes, because the neighbor's use of the vehicle constituted a frolic rather than a mere detour.

(C) No, because the neighbor was acting for the fisherman's benefit.

(D) No, because the fisherman had consented to the activity and the damage was accidental.

113. A man carried a handgun for protection, but failed to register it. In the applicable jurisdiction, possession of an unregistered handgun is a felony. The man had little experience with firearms, and negligently carried the gun in a holster designed to fit a different handgun model. While the man was shopping for groceries one day, the gun slipped out of the holster, fell to the floor, and accidentally discharged. The bullet struck a fellow shopper, who died as a result of the incident.

The crimes below are listed in descending order of seriousness. Which is the most serious homicide crime for which the man can be convicted?

(A) Felony murder

(B) Voluntary manslaughter

(C) Involuntary manslaughter

(D) No crime

114. Congress enacted the Health Care Act (HCA) "to ensure all Americans access to health care at a reasonable cost." Congress delegated to an executive agency, the Department of Health & Human Services (HHS), responsibility for promulgating regulations to implement the HCA. The HCA further provided that a joint House/Senate committee can repeal or revise the HHS regulations if the committee determines that they inadequately fulfill the HCA's purpose. Would a court be likely to hold that the HCA is unconstitutional?

(A) Yes, because it delegates legislative power to an executive agency.

(B) Yes, because it contains a legislative veto provision.

(C) No, because Congress is reasonably trying to vindicate its Article I legislative power by ensuring the accountability of executive agencies that make law.

(D) No, because the joint committee action to repeal or revise an HHS regulation would not constitute the exercise of executive power.

115. A man became intoxicated after drinking at a neighborhood bar for several hours. He left the bar and went to a party at a friend's house, where he struck up a conversation with a woman at the party. After a few minutes, the man grabbed the woman's arm, pulled her into an empty room, and attempted to have sexual intercourse with her. The woman struggled with the man, and, before intercourse occurred, was able to break free and exit the room. The man was arrested and charged with attempted rape. At trial, the man testified that at the time of the incident he believed that the woman had consented to sexual intercourse with him.

If the jury believes the man's testimony, should he be convicted?

(A) No, because the man's intoxication prevented him from understanding the wrongfulness of his act.

(B) No, because the man believed that the woman had consented to intercourse.

(C) Yes, because the man's intoxication was voluntary.

(D) Yes, because rape is a crime of malice and intoxication is not a defense to malice crimes.

116. A famous jazz pianist and a nightclub owner executed a contract that called for the pianist to perform at the nightclub five times per week for six months. The contract prohibited the pianist from giving public performances during the contract period at any other venue located within a specified distance of the nightclub.

Three months into the contract term, the pianist received a more lucrative offer to play a series of shows at a restaurant located within the contractually prohibited area. The pianist accepted the offer. Upon learning about this arrangement, the nightclub owner filed a suit seeking an injunction to prevent the pianist from performing at the restaurant. The nightclub owner has made no attempt to hire another performer to replace the pianist. The judge determines that the contract restriction on the pianist is reasonable. Is the judge likely to grant the injunction?

(A) No, because the pianist's contractual duties are in the nature of a personal service, and hence enforcement would constitute unconstitutional involuntary servitude.

(B) No, because the nightclub owner has failed to seek a replacement entertainer.

(C) Yes, because the restriction is a valid non-compete clause.

(D) Yes, because an injunction generally may be sought as an alternative to damages in a breach of contract action.

117. A defendant on trial for forging checks took the stand in his own defense. On direct examination, the defendant denied having forged any checks; he stated that before he graduated from college the year before, he worked in his university's academic records office, indicating that he was "a trustworthy person." On cross-examination, the prosecutor asked the defendant if he had falsified records while working in the academic records office. The defendant denied that he had done so. The prosecutor then wanted to call to the stand his former supervisor from the university to testify that she had to investigate the defendant after allegations of misconduct, and that when questioned, he had admitted to her that he had falsified records. The defendant was removed from his position, but no formal charges had been brought against him.

Should the prosecutor be allowed to call the defendant's former supervisor to the stand to testify as to the falsified records?

(A) Yes, in order to impeach the defendant and to present propensity evidence.

(B) Yes, but only to impeach the defendant.

(C) No, because the testimony would contain hearsay.

(D) No, because the testimony would be extrinsic.

118. An automotive enthusiast owned a sports car that was the fastest production car available in the United States. The enthusiast was friendly with a neighbor, who was 25 years old and had a clean driving record. The neighbor wanted to borrow the sports car to drive to a social event and impress some clients. The enthusiast allowed the neighbor to borrow the sports car, but told him very clearly and sternly that he was to drive very carefully, that he was not to exceed the speed limit, and that he was to bring the sports car back as soon as the event concluded.

After the event concluded, the neighbor drove the car around for an additional two hours, often at very high speeds. Eventually, he slammed into another car while driving over 100 miles per hour. The driver of the other car survived, but sustained serious injuries in the accident.

The driver of the other car sued the enthusiast in a jurisdiction without an owner liability statute, claiming that the enthusiast negligently entrusted his neighbor with the vehicle. The foregoing facts are undisputed. If the enthusiast files a motion for a directed verdict, which party is likely to prevail?

(A) The enthusiast, because his specific instructions regarding use of the car were ignored.

(B) The enthusiast, because the neighbor had no history of negligent behavior.

(C) The other driver, because the jurisdiction does not have an owner liability statute.

(D) The other driver, because the neighbor's negligent behavior is imputed to the enthusiast.

119. In order to purchase her residence, a homeowner gave a lender a promissory note in exchange for a loan. The note was secured by a mortgage on the residence. Five years later, the homeowner gave a second lender a promissory note in exchange for a loan, in order to add another room to the residence. This note was also secured by a mortgage on the residence. Three years later, the homeowner gave a third lender a promissory note in exchange for a loan in order to construct a deck on the residence. This note was also secured by a mortgage on the residence. Each mortgage was properly recorded promptly after execution.

Recently, the homeowner has failed to make timely payments with regard to the first mortgage. The first lender has declared the homeowner in default and, in accord with the terms of the mortgage, accelerated the obligation. The first lender forecloses on the mortgage. At the foreclosure sale, the third lender purchases the residence.

To which of the following mortgages is the residence now subject?

(A) Only the first mortgage.

(B) Only the second mortgage.

(C) Both the first and the second mortgages.

(D) Neither the first nor the second mortgages.

120. A city fire department required all firefighter applicants to pass a demanding physical fitness test. The test was designed to ensure that firefighters could handle the physical rigors of the job, such as lifting heavy equipment, carrying injured people, and withstanding intense heat. Asian American applicants failed this physical fitness test at twice the rate of white applicants. Moreover, in this particular city, people of Asian descent were historically the victims of many forms of discrimination.

An Asian American man applied to be a firefighter but was rejected because he failed the physical fitness test. He sued the fire department based on a constitutional claim of discrimination. Will he prevail?

(A) Yes, because the fire department's physical fitness test had a negative disparate effect on Asian American applicants.

(B) Yes, because the unusually high current failure rate of Asian Americans on this test most likely has resulted from past intentional governmental discrimination.

(C) No, because the plaintiff failed to establish that he had any property interest in potential employment with the fire department that has been denied because of the test.

(D) No, because there is no evidence that the fire department used the test to intentionally discriminate against Asian Americans.

121. A patron at a resort ranch took part in a supervised horseback trail ride. Prior to the ride, the patron executed a valid release that enumerated the inherent risks of horseback riding and, by its terms, relieved the resort from liability from any loss, damage, or injury to the guest's person or property suffered during the ride attributable to the negligence of the ranch or its employees. The patron was injured by a fall from the horse. The horse reared in response to negligent behavior of another rider who was also a patron at the ranch.

The patron filed suit against the ranch and the other rider for damages resulting from his injuries that totaled $400,000. At trial, it was determined that the ranch was 75% at fault for the patron's injuries due to its selection and training of the horse, and that the other rider was 25% at fault.

The applicable jurisdiction recognizes the validity of such releases and has enacted both a modified comparative negligence statute and a pure several liability statute.

How much can the patron recover from the ranch?

(A) Nothing

(B) $100,000

(C) $300,000

(D) $400,000

122. A class action was filed in federal court against an insurance company by its policyholders. The complaint, alleging that the company had violated state law, asserted that the court had subject matter jurisdiction pursuant to the Class Action Fairness Act of 2005. The complaint sought total damages of $4 million. The individual damages for the 900 class members ranged from $100 to $10,000. Of the five named plaintiffs, one is a citizen of the same state as the company; the other four are citizens of other states. The company filed a motion to dismiss this action for lack of subject matter jurisdiction. Which of the following reasons supports this motion?

(A) There is not complete diversity of citizenship between the parties.

(B) The aggregate amount-in-controversy does not meet the statutory requirement.

(C) No member of the class has a claim that exceeds $75,000.

(D) The number of class members does not meet the statutory requirement.

123. A homeowner who sought to sell his home entered into an agreement with a real estate agent to market the home. The agreement specified that the agent was entitled to a commission if the agent procured a buyer who was "ready, willing, and able" to purchase the home in accord with the contract terms.

The agent found a buyer who agreed to pay the seller's asking price for the home and who pre-qualified for a loan to finance the purchase. The buyer and seller entered into a contract of sale. Among the provisions in the contract was a home inspection clause, which permitted the buyer to enter the property and conduct an inspection of the home. After conducting the inspection, during which the buyer learned of the antiquated nature of the electrical system that did not satisfy the electrical code for newly constructed homes, the buyer, in accord with the inspection clause, presented the seller with a request to upgrade the electrical wiring. Because of the cost of such an upgrade, the seller refused. Under the terms of the inspection clause, the inability of the buyer and seller to agree resulted in the voiding of the contract.

Is the agent entitled to a commission to be paid by the homeowner?

(A) No, because the contract was subject to a condition precedent that was not satisfied.

(B) No, because the buyer who demanded the seller upgrade the electrical wiring was responsible for the termination of the contract.

(C) Yes, because the buyer entered into a contract to purchase the home.

(D) Yes, because the seller, by refusing to upgrade the wiring for economic reasons, was responsible for the termination of the contract.

124. A concert violinist received an offer by mail to play a concerto with a local symphony orchestra. She checked her schedule, and thinking that she had the date free, mailed a letter to the symphony orchestra accepting the offer. Later that day, as she was checking her calendar about another matter, she realized that she had a rehearsal for another performance on that date. The violinist called the orchestra manager and declined the offer to play the concerto.

In a breach of contract action by the orchestra against the violinist, will the orchestra prevail?

(A) Yes, because the acceptance was sent before the rejection phone call was made.

(B) Yes, because the phone call was not a proper means of rejecting a written offer under the "mirror image" rule.

(C) No, because the agreement constitutes an unenforceable personal service contract.

(D) No, because the "mailbox rule" does not apply to a rejection.

125. A defendant was convicted of bank robbery in federal court. Subsequently, the defendant was indicted in the state where the bank was located for the crimes of robbery and conspiracy to commit robbery. The defendant moved to dismiss the state prosecution of these offenses on double jeopardy grounds.

Should the defendant's motion be granted?

(A) Yes, as to both offenses.

(B) Yes, as to the robbery offense only.

(C) Yes, as to the conspiracy offense only.

(D) No, as to either offense.

126. A labor union, an unincorporated association with its principal place of business located in State A, sued an employer in federal district court in an action based on violations of federal employment discrimination laws. In the complaint, the union sought damages of $75,000, and averred the statutory right to recover attorney's fees, if successful. The employer was incorporated in State B and its principal place of business was in State C. Union members live and work in 47 states, including states A, B, and C. The employer challenged the court's subject matter jurisdiction. Should the court sustain this challenge?

(A) No, because the court has federal question jurisdiction.

(B) No, because the court has diversity jurisdiction.

(C) Yes, because the amount-in-controversy requirement is not met.

(D) Yes, because diversity of citizenship is not met.

127. Article I, § 4 of the Constitution provides: "The times, places and manner of holding elections for Senators and Representatives shall be prescribed by each state legislature, but Congress may . . . make or alter such regulations." Congress enacted a statute requiring every state to allow voters to register to vote in federal elections either by mail or at a state motor vehicle department. If a state refuses to comply with the statute and is sued by the federal government, will the state likely prevail?

(A) Yes, because Congress cannot "commandeer" state legislatures to enact statutes.

(B) Yes, because Congress cannot "commandeer" state executive officials to carry out federal programs.

(C) No, because Article I, § 4 permits Congress to require states to change their laws regarding federal elections.

(D) No, because the statute, which applies to federal elections only, does not interfere with a traditional government function.

128. During a trial for attempted murder, the prosecutor seeks to introduce into evidence the victim's properly-authenticated emergency room report. The report describes the victim's stab wounds and treatment. The report also includes a statement that the victim made to his doctor during a check-up the following day, naming the defendant as his assailant. The prosecutor wants to introduce the record to prove the extent of the victim's injuries, and as evidence that the defendant was responsible for the victim's harm.

Is the victim's emergency room report admissible?

(A) The report is admissible under the business records exception, but the victim's statement within it is not.

(B) The report is admissible as a whole, because it falls under the business records exception.

(C) The report is admissible under the business records exception, and the statement within it is admissible as a statement made for the purpose of medical treatment.

(D) Neither the report nor the statement is admissible, because the victim is alive and available to testify.

129. A plaintiff sued a defendant for state law negligence in a federal district court sitting in diversity jurisdiction. The plaintiff was injured after tripping and falling at the defendant's place of business and is seeking damages for injuries resulting from the fall. The defendant has liability insurance that would cover any judgment that the plaintiff might win in the case. There have been no agreements between the parties or orders by the court regarding discovery in the case.

What is the defendant's obligation with regard to the disclosure of the defendant's liability insurance?

(A) The defendant's liability insurance agreement is not subject to discovery.

(B) The defendant need only provide a copy of the liability insurance agreement to the plaintiff if the plaintiff makes a request for production of documents concerning such agreements.

(C) The defendant need only provide information to the plaintiff concerning any insurance agreement if the insurer is joined as a party to the litigation.

(D) The defendant must make the insurance agreement available to the plaintiff even if the plaintiff does not ask for it.

130. A buyer purchased a motor home from a private seller. After taking possession of the motor home, the buyer discovered that the bedroom of the motor home was infested with bed bugs, and pest control treatments were unsuccessful in eradicating the problem. The buyer honestly claims that he would not have purchased the motor home had he known of the infestation.

At the time of the sale, the seller knew of the infestation but did not disclose the condition to the buyer. When the buyer commented to the seller at the time of the sale that the buyer assumed that the motor home did not have bed bugs, the seller simply did not respond. The buyer was justified in relying on the seller's silence as an assertion that the mobile home did not contain bed bugs. The seller's actions violated her duty of good faith and fair dealing. What is the best description of the status of the contract between the buyer and the seller?

(A) The contract is voidable by only the buyer.

(B) The contract is voidable by either the buyer or the seller.

(C) The contract is voidable by neither the buyer nor the seller.

(D) The contract is void.

131. The owner of a residence devised it to his wife for her life and remainder to his son. The son, after his father's death, regularly stopped by the residence to look after his mother and the residence. On some of the visits, the son would perform routine maintenance on the property, such as changing the air filter for the heating and air conditioning unit. When the mother permitted a companion to occupy the residence with her, the son became estranged from his mother and stopped visiting her.

Recently, a neighbor who had visited the mother called the son. The neighbor indicated that mother was in good health, but that the condition of the premises was deplorable. The son contacted his mother. She asked him to come over, which he did, but denied him access to the premises when he arrived.

Can the son gain entry to the residence to inspect the premises?

(A) No, because the right to possess the premises belongs to the mother.

(B) No, because the mother has denied him entry to the residence.

(C) Yes, because he has a license coupled with an interest.

(D) Yes, because the mother, by permitting someone else on the premises, is estopped from denying her son permission to enter the premises.

132. A woman took her car to an unscrupulous auto mechanic's garage for a tune-up. The woman's car had a new and expensive set of tires that the mechanic coveted. The woman left her car at the garage overnight. Later that night, after the woman had left the premises, the mechanic took the tires off the woman's car, put them into a back room of his garage, and replaced the tires with a cheap, old set. That same evening, the woman's friend told her about the mechanic's unscrupulous nature, and that he had a habit of stealing tires. The woman went back to the garage the next morning. Noticing that the tires on her vehicle were different, she demanded that the new, expensive tires be put back on the vehicle. The mechanic complied, and the woman left the premises.

The woman reported the mechanic to the police, and the mechanic is charged with larceny. Based on the foregoing facts, should he be convicted of the crime?

(A) Yes, because the mechanic moved the tires from the car to the back room.

(B) Yes, because the mechanic had a present intent to permanently deprive the woman of the tires.

(C) No, because the car was left with the mechanic by consent.

(D) No, because the tires were returned to the woman before she was permanently deprived of them.

133. A man and his friend attended their 10-year high school reunion party. There, the two struck up a conversation with a woman who had been a classmate. Neither the man nor his friend had seen her since high school. At the end of the reunion party, the three decided to walk to a nearby bar. As they were walking to the bar, the friend suggested a shortcut through an alley. In the alley, the friend grabbed the woman and began making unwanted sexual advances towards her. The man, despite the woman's pleas to help her, continued walking on towards the bar. Once there, the man ordered a beer and watched a sporting event on television, while his friend raped the woman in the alley.

The man was charged as an accomplice to rape. Should he be convicted of the crime?

(A) No, because the man did not commit an *actus reus* for which he could be criminally liable.

(B) No, because there was no agreement between the man and his friend to rape the woman.

(C) Yes, because the man's actions aided and abetted the friend in committing the rape.

(D) Yes, because the man was aware that the woman did not consent to his friend's sexual advances.

134. Based on an advertisement in a local newspaper, a state resident bought a cross-country roundtrip ticket on a national airline for $450. The ad did not mention that the airline charged $75 for any changes to a ticket. Because of illness, the state resident had to change her return flight, and the airline charged her $75. The state resident refused to pay, citing a state law that required any ad for the sale of tickets for any event or trip to clearly disclose any monetary penalties for changing tickets.

The airline sued the state resident in federal court for the unpaid fee, arguing that the state law is invalid, citing a federal statute prohibiting states from enforcing any law "relating to the rates, routes, or services" of any airline. Will the airline prevail?

(A) Yes, because, under the Freedom of Press Clause of the First Amendment, the content of commercial speech may not be regulated.

(B) Yes, because Congress has occupied the field of airline rates, routes, and service and hence has preempted the state law.

(C) No, because the court will apply the presumption against preemption.

(D) No, because the state law does not conflict with the federal statute.

135. In a case properly brought in federal district court, the plaintiff alleges that the state police, acting under a longstanding custom of using excessive force against people of a certain ethnicity in traffic stops, beat him up during a routine traffic stop. The plaintiff requests $100,000 in damages to remedy this injury and, fearing that the state police are targeting him, also requests preliminary and permanent injunctions prohibiting the police from using excessive force against him. The court issues an order refusing to grant the plaintiff a preliminary injunction and setting the case for trial. Three weeks later, the plaintiff appeals this order to the appropriate U.S. Court of Appeals. Can the appellate court hear this appeal?

(A) Yes, if the appellate court, in the exercise of its discretion, concludes that an appeal is warranted.

(B) Yes, as a matter of right.

(C) No, because the district court's order is not a final judgment.

(D) No, because the appeal was not filed in a timely manner.

136. A defendant on trial for battery arising from a barroom brawl sought to introduce the testimony of his grandmother, who would testify that the defendant had a reputation in her church community for being a "helpful and trustworthy person." Further, the grandmother would offer her testimony regarding an incident that took place when the defendant was 13 years old wherein he refused to engage in a schoolyard fight with one of his classmates. The prosecution objects to the grandmother's testimony in its entirety.

Should the court allow the grandmother to testify?

(A) Yes, the grandmother's testimony should be admissible in its entirety, because the defendant is allowed to present evidence of his own good character.

(B) The grandmother should be allowed to testify as to the schoolyard incident, but not as to the defendant's reputation.

(C) The grandmother should be allowed to testify as to the defendant's reputation, but not as to the schoolyard incident.

(D) No, the grandmother should not be allowed to testify as to either of these issues, because the testimony is not relevant.

137. A biotech start up firm secured a loan from a private investor to purchase land and to build a laboratory facility on that land with a mortgage on the land and the facility. Subsequently, the firm sold the developed property to a partnership. The deed stated that the partnership took the property subject to the mortgage. Later, the partnership sold the developed property to a corporation. Each deed was properly recorded promptly after its applicable closing. Immediately after closing, the president of the corporation, in exchange for adequate consideration, orally promised the partnership that the corporation would assume the mortgage.

For four months, neither the corporation nor the previous owners of the facility made the required monthly payments on the mortgage obligation to the lender. The lender has filed an action against the corporation for the past due amounts.

Is the corporation liable for these amounts?

(A) No, because, since the partnership was not personally liable for the obligation, the corporation is protected by the shelter principle from personal liability.

(B) No, because the corporation's assumption agreement was not in writing.

(C) Yes, because the corporation assumed the mortgage.

(D) Yes, because the loan was tied to a purchase money mortgage.

138. A defendant is on trial for cocaine possession. The cocaine was found during a warrantless search of the defendant's car by a police officer. The search occurred immediately after the defendant was arrested for driving a car with an inoperative taillight, a misdemeanor punishable only by a fine. The defendant had been placed in a police car prior to the search. The cocaine was found inside a closed bag on the back seat of the passenger compartment of the defendant's car. The defendant now moves to suppress the cocaine.

Will the defendant's motion be granted?

(A) Yes, because the defendant was in the police car at the time of the search.

(B) Yes, because the arrest was unreasonable and the cocaine seized was a fruit of the poisonous tree.

(C) No, because the police may search a car without a warrant under the automobile exception.

(D) No, because the search was a lawful search incident to arrest.

139. At the defendant's trial on a narcotics charge, the prosecution introduced the former testimony of a co-conspirator who had testified against the defendant at a preliminary hearing; the evidence was sufficiently corroborated. The co-conspirator has since fled the country to a jurisdiction with no extradition treaty with the United States. The defendant's attorney now seeks to impeach the credibility of the co-conspirator.

Which of the following types of evidence is the court most likely to admit?

(A) Testimony by a witness that at the time the co-conspirator testified against the defendant, he was doing so in exchange for a deal with the prosecutor for a lesser sentence.

(B) Evidence that the co-conspirator had misdemeanor convictions for public intoxication, disorderly conduct, and vandalism.

(C) Reputation evidence by a witness that the co-conspirator is a violent person.

(D) Evidence that the co-conspirator was convicted of a narcotics-related felony 11 years ago.

140. An adult woman was vacationing at a friend's house on a lake. One afternoon, the woman watched her friend maneuver his motorized personal watercraft around the lake; the friend took a particularly violent spill that temporarily knocked the wind out of him but left him otherwise unharmed. The next morning, without the friend's knowledge, she decided to take the personal watercraft out on the lake herself. Due to her inability to control the vehicle, it flipped over. As a consequence, the woman suffered serious physical injuries.

The woman brought a lawsuit against the friend to recover damages for her injuries. The applicable jurisdiction has adopted comparative negligence rules.

Prior to the submission of the case to the jury, the friend requested that the court specifically instruct the jury on the assumption of the risk defense. Should the court grant this request?

(A) Yes, because the woman voluntarily assumed the risk of being injured.

(B) Yes, because assumption of the risk is an absolute bar to recovery.

(C) No, because the defendant did not have the requisite knowledge for this defense.

(D) No, because assumption of the risk is not recognized as a separate defense.

141. Concerned about problems caused by overpopulation, a state legislature enacted a statute imposing criminal penalties on any person who is the biological parent of more than two children. The stated purpose of the statute was to preserve the state's natural resources and improve the quality of life for the state's residents.

After the statute took effect, a married couple who already had two children conceived a third. After the wife gave birth to this child, the couple was arrested and convicted under the statute. Which of the following is the strongest argument for voiding their convictions?

(A) The statute is an invalid exercise of the state's police power because there is no rational basis for concluding that the statute would further the government's stated interests.

(B) The statute places an unconstitutional burden on the fundamental privacy and procreative rights of married persons.

(C) The statute grants too much discretion to a prosecutor to determine who will be permitted to bear children.

(D) The statute denies the couple their Equal Protection rights.

142. In January, a garden center contacted a farmer who owned a greenhouse about growing seedlings for sale in the spring. The garden center promised in writing to buy, at a fixed price, all of the seedlings that the farmer raised in his greenhouse. As a consequence, the farmer purchased containers and seeds and hired a worker to prepare the containers, plant the seeds, and tend to the seedlings. Just prior to the delivery of any seedlings, the garden center notified the farmer that it would not purchase any of the seedlings. The farmer sold the seedlings at a price far below the price set by the garden center.

The farmer filed a breach of contract action to recover damages. Will the farmer likely succeed?

(A) Yes, because the farmer accepted the garden center's offer by beginning performance.

(B) Yes, because the doctrine of promissory estoppel made the offer irrevocable.

(C) No, because the garden center revoked its offer before it was accepted by farmer.

(D) No, because the garden center did not receive consideration for its promise to buy the farmer's output.

143. A homebuyer was discussing the purchase of a house with the seller. Of particular concern to the buyer was whether the house had a termite problem. The seller, aware of the buyer's concern, ordered an inspection from a licensed inspection company. The company issued a report stating that the house was free of termites. In fact, the company's inspector was negligent, and the house's foundation had a modest termite problem. Relying on the report, the seller told the buyer that the house was free of termites.

The buyer is seeking to avoid the contract. Will he prevail?

(A) Yes, because the buyer reasonably relied on the misrepresentation.

(B) Yes, because enforcing the contract would be unconscionable.

(C) No, because the misrepresentation did not rise to the level of a mutual mistake.

(D) No, because the inspector, not the seller, was negligent.

144. Eleven years ago, the owner of a condominium unit located in another state bequeathed the condominium unit to his wife for her life and then to their son. A year after the owner's death, the wife had a stroke that left her incapacitated. The son sought and was granted both personal and financial guardianship over his mother. Six months later the son suddenly died. By will, the son devised his real property to his daughter, who was unaware of the condominium unit and took no action with regard to it. The daughter assumed guardianship over her grandmother who remains alive but unable to care for herself.

Shortly after the owner's death, the wife granted an acquaintance the right to occupy the condominium unit for the following month. At the end of that month, the acquaintance tried unsuccessfully to obtain the wife's permission to remain longer. Deciding to remain despite the lack of permission, the acquaintance, since that time, has resided in the unit, maintaining it as well as paying the annual condominium fees and real estate taxes on it.

The applicable statutory period to acquire title by adverse possession is 10 years.

The acquaintance brings an appropriate action to determine title to the condominium unit. What type of ownership interest in the condominium unit will the acquaintance be found to possess?

(A) Fee simple absolute

(B) A life estate measured by the wife's life

(C) A remainder interest

(D) None

145. The plaintiff, a State A citizen, sues the defendant, a State B citizen, in State B federal court and credibly claims breach of contract resulting in damages of $106,000. The contract was executed in State C and contains a clause providing that "in a litigated dispute, the laws of State D shall govern." The State B federal court properly asserts jurisdiction. The key issue is the parol evidence rule. States A, B, C, and D take four different approaches to this rule, which typifies the division among the other 46 states. State B law also provides that, in contract cases, its courts should apply the law of the state specified by the parties in their contract. State C has the identical choice-of-law rule. State B's rules are valid under the U.S. Constitution's Full Faith & Credit and Due Process Clauses. The court should apply the parol evidence rule of which state?

(A) State A.

(B) State B.

(C) State C.

(D) State D.

146. After consuming too much alcohol, an actor tripped over his own feet and smashed face first into a sidewalk. The actor delayed seeking medical attention for his facial injuries for several days, which aggravated those injuries. When the actor finally sought treatment from a plastic surgeon, the plastic surgeon negligently performed the operation on the actor's face. After surgery, the actor failed to follow the surgeon's post-operative instructions. All of the actor's actions coupled with the surgeon's negligence contributed to the actor's permanent facial scarring.

The actor received reimbursement for some of his medical expenses from an insurer under a health insurance policy.

The actor sued the plastic surgeon for damages attributable to the surgeon's medical treatment of the actor's facial injuries. The applicable jurisdiction has not modified the common-law collateral source rule.

Assuming that the monetary effect of each of the following can be established with reasonable certainty, which can be taken into account to reduce the damages to which the actor would otherwise be entitled due to the surgeon's negligence?

(A) The plaintiff's negligent behavior that initially led to his facial injuries.

(B) The plaintiff's failure to promptly seek medical care.

(C) The plaintiff's failure to follow the surgeon's post-operative instructions.

(D) The reimbursement for medical expenses received by the plaintiff.

147. The defense attorney in a criminal rape case wants to introduce testimony that the alleged victim has a reputation in the community for promiscuity. The testimony will come from one of the victim's past sexual partners. The prosecutor objects to the introduction of the testimony, but the defense maintains that because consent is at issue in the case, the testimony is relevant.

Should the court allow the testimony?

(A) Yes, because reputation testimony is an admissible form of character evidence.

(B) Yes, because the victim's past sexual behavior can be used to prove consent.

(C) No, because evidence of a victim's past sexual behavior is inadmissible.

(D) No, because this evidence of the victim's other sexual behavior is not relevant.

148. While driving in State A, the driver of a car ran a stop sign and struck a pedestrian, a citizen of State A. The driver, a citizen of State B, had never before been in State A and has not been since. The driver was passing through the state in response to a summons to testify as a victim at a criminal trial being conducted in a neighboring state. The pedestrian filed a negligence action against the driver in federal district court in State A. The driver of the car was served with process in her home state in accordance with the federal service of process rules. The driver has timely filed a motion to dismiss this action for lack of personal jurisdiction.

State A has a long-arm statute that permits a state court to exercise personal jurisdiction to the extent permitted by the Due Process Clause of the Fourteenth Amendment to the U.S. Constitution. State A also has a statute that prohibits the service of process on a defendant who is passing through the state in response to a summons to testify at a trial held in another state.

Should the court grant the motion to dismiss for lack of personal jurisdiction?

(A) No, because the accident occurred in State A.

(B) No, because a state statute that restricts or prohibits the service of process is not applicable in a federal action.

(C) Yes, because the accident occurred while the driver was passing through State A in response to a summons to testify in another state.

(D) Yes, because the driver is not a citizen of State A.

149. A pest control company fumigated one of two buildings in an apartment complex with a toxic gas in order to eliminate unwanted insects. Even though the company exercised reasonable care, the gas escaped into the other building, which adjoined the fumigated building, where the gas caused serious illness to a tenant in that building. The tenant had received a written advance notice about the fumigation that advised the tenant of the need to vacate his apartment during the hours the fumigation was conducted. The tenant chose instead to remain there in order to watch a favorite television program.

The applicable jurisdiction treats fumigation as an ultrahazardous activity.

The injured tenant filed an action against the pest control company. Who will prevail?

(A) The tenant, because the pest control company is strictly liable for the harm that resulted from the fumigation.

(B) The tenant, because the pest control company was negligent in conducting the fumigation.

(C) The pest control company, because the tenant was not a resident of the fumigated building.

(D) The pest control company, because the tenant assumed the risk.

150. A physician entered into a written agreement to purchase land from his aunt. The agreement, which was secured by not only the land itself but also all future improvements, required the physician to make annual installment payments to the aunt. The deed from the aunt to the physician was recorded, but it made no mention of this agreement. The agreement itself was not recorded.

The following year, the physician obtained a loan from the local bank to build a house on the land in exchange for a mortgage on the property and any structures built on it. The physician informed the bank about the agreement with his aunt. The bank required the aunt to sign an agreement subordinating her loan to the bank's loan. The mortgage agreement was recorded, but the agreement between the bank and the aunt was not recorded.

After the house was built, a patient successfully sued the physician for malpractice. The judgment was promptly and properly recorded so that it became a lien against the residence of the physician. The patient was unaware of the physician's financial dealings with his aunt or the bank.

The physician failed to make timely payments on the mortgage. In accord with the terms of the mortgage, the bank declared the full mortgage obligation due and properly foreclosed on the property. At the time of the foreclosure sale, which was properly conducted, the physician's outstanding balance with regard to the agreement with his aunt was $100,000, and with regard to the mortgage was $500,000. The total amount owed with respect to the judgment was $400,000. After expenses, the sale of the mortgaged property netted only $550,000.

The applicable jurisdiction has the following two statutes:

"Every conveyance not recorded is void as against any subsequent purchaser or mortgagee in good faith and for valuable consideration from the same vendor whose conveyance is first duly recorded."

"Any judgment properly filed shall, for twelve years from filing, be a lien on the real property then owned or subsequently acquired by any person against whom the judgment is rendered."

What is the amount due to the aunt from the sale?

(A) $100,000, because the aunt's interest predated the other interests.

(B) $100,000, because the aunt's interest was a seller-financed purchase money security interest.

(C) $50,000, because the aunt's interest has priority over the patient's judgment lien, but not the bank's mortgage.

(D) Nothing, because both the patient's judgment lien and the bank's mortgage have priority over the aunt's interest.

151. In a state known for its game fish, there are many guide-led fishing expeditions marketed to tourists. The state enacted a statute that required all fishing guides who charge a fee to have a license. The purpose of the statute is to protect the state's game fish from overfishing. The license costs $100 for in-state residents and $300 for out-of-state residents.

If an out-of-state resident challenges the constitutionality of this statute, what is the most likely result?

(A) The statute will be struck down under the Privileges and Immunities Clause of Article IV, Section 2.

(B) The statute will be struck down under the Equal Protection Clause.

(C) The statute will be upheld because engaging in fishing is not a fundamental right.

(D) The statute will be upheld because regulation of fishing is traditionally a state, rather than national, function.

152. A defendant is on trial for robbery. A witness picked the defendant's picture out of a photo array that was conducted by a police officer at the police station after the defendant's arrest. The photo array was impermissibly suggestive. No counsel was present for the defendant at the photo array. Later, at trial, the witness identified the defendant. Because of the witness's extended opportunity to view the defendant at the time of the crime, this identification was reliable.

The defendant moves to suppress the identification.

Should the court grant this motion?

(A) Yes, because the defendant's right to counsel was violated.

(B) Yes, because the identification procedure was impermissibly suggestive.

(C) No, because the identification was reliable.

(D) No, because the photo array was conducted by a police officer at a police station.

153. In a trial for murder in which the defendant asserted the affirmative defense of self-defense, the defendant's attorney introduced evidence that the victim had a reputation as a violent person. In turn, the prosecutor wanted to introduce the testimony of a witness, the victim's wife, who would testify that in her opinion, the victim was a peaceful person who would not have provoked a fight. Additionally, the prosecutor wanted to introduce evidence that the defendant has a reputation for being violent.

Should the court allow the prosecutor's evidence to be admitted?

(A) Yes, as to both.

(B) No as to the testimony regarding the victim, because the victim's character is not relevant to the defendant's actions, but yes as to the testimony regarding the defendant's reputation.

(C) No, as to the testimony regarding the defendant's reputation, because the defendant did not "open the door" by putting his own character at issue, but yes as to the testimony regarding the victim.

(D) No, as to both.

154. The driver of a truck was involved in an accident with a car driven by a citizen of a foreign country. The truck driver filed suit in a federal district court in the state in which the accident occurred, where the truck driver was domiciled. The driver of the car was a permanent legal resident of the United States and was domiciled in this state as well. The truck driver alleged damages of $35,000 in good faith due to personal injuries and damages of an additional $50,000 due to property losses. As permitted by state law under a direct action statute, the suit named only the insurer of the car as a defendant. The insurer was incorporated in a neighboring state and had its headquarters in a distant state. The insurer timely moved to dismiss the action due to lack of subject matter jurisdiction. How should the court rule on this motion?

(A) Grant the motion, because alienage jurisdiction does not exist.

(B) Grant the motion, because diversity of citizenship does not exist.

(C) Deny the motion, because the amount in controversy exceeds $75,000.

(D) Deny the motion, because the insurer is not a citizen of the forum state.

155. The owner of an office building leased space to a physician in general practice for a term of five years. The physician's written lease with the owner restricted use of the space to a doctor's office, but permitted the assignment of the office with the written permission of the owner, which, according to the terms of the lease, could be withheld for any reason.

At the end of second year of the lease, the physician decided to move to another building and rented the space to a lawyer for one year. The lawyer's monthly payments were the same as those called for in the lease between the owner and the physician. The owner's permission was not sought, but the owner accepted rental payments directly from the lawyer.

At the end of the third year of the lease, the physician found a psychiatrist to rent the space for a year. As with the lawyer, the psychiatrist's monthly payments were to be the same as those called for in the lease between the owner and the physician. When contacted by the physician, the owner at first orally agreed, and then, upon learning the identity of the psychiatrist, refused due to personal animosity towards the psychiatrist.

Can the owner be compelled to accept the psychiatrist as a tenant?

(A) Yes, because the lease does not restrict the physician from subletting the office space.

(B) Yes, because the owner has waived the right to object by accepting the physician's previous sublet of the office space.

(C) No, because the physician did not obtain the owner's written permission.

(D) No, because the owner properly exercised his right to reject the psychiatrist as a tenant.

156. A toy company specialized in producing high-end toy racecars. Three months prior to the holiday shopping season, the toy company received an order of 50,000 racecars from a major retailer. The toy company immediately contracted with two of its major suppliers, a metalworking company and a paint company, to provide essential parts and paint for the racecars. The metalworking company and the paint company both were extremely busy with orders from other manufacturers, but agreed to supply needed parts and paint for the racecars.

One month later, the metalworking company, without justification, informed the toy company that it would not be able to perform the contract. The toy company found a replacement metal parts supplier, but the new supplier was only able to provide 25,000 parts. Consequently, the toy company reduced its order with the paint company by 25,000 units.

The paint company then sued the metalworking company, seeking the profits it lost because of the reduced order. The contract between the toy company and the metalworking company was silent on the issue of third-party liability. Is the paint company entitled to such relief?

(A) Yes, because the paint company is a volume seller of paint.

(B) Yes, because the paint company has a vested right to enforce the contract between the toy company and the metalworking company.

(C) No, because the paint company is not an intended beneficiary of the contract between the toy company and the metalworking company.

(D) No, because the contract between the toy company and the metalworking company did not explicitly grant third-party rights in the paint company.

157. An American helicopter manufacturer contracted with a foreign hospital located in a severely war-torn region to sell five helicopters specially outfitted for medical use. The helicopter manufacturer, in turn, contracted with a subcontractor to provide five flight systems for use in the helicopters. The subcontractor was not informed about the contract between the helicopter manufacturer and the foreign hospital, nor the location where the helicopters would be used.

After the two contracts were formed, the country in which the hospital was located descended deeply into civil war. The United Nations imposed an embargo against all shipments to that country. The helicopter manufacturer directed the subcontractor to stop all work on the contract, and to place any completed systems into storage. At that point, the subcontractor had finished three of the five flight systems called for by the subcontract. The systems were custom-built, and could not be used for any other purpose.

The subcontractor sued the helicopter manufacturer for breach of contract. Is the subcontractor likely to prevail?

(A) Yes, because the subcontractor was a vested third-party beneficiary of the contract between the helicopter manufacturer and the foreign hospital.

(B) Yes, because the helicopter manufacturer assumed the risk of the failure of the contract.

(C) No, because the contract was rendered impracticable by the United Nations embargo.

(D) No, because the failure of the contract between the helicopter manufacturer and the foreign hospital frustrated the purpose of the subcontract.

158. A father was an avid golfer who often practiced chipping the ball in his backyard. To facilitate this practice, he always left a golf club, a wedge, and a bucket of golf balls inside the house next to the back door. One afternoon, the father's 15-year-old son—an experienced golfer—came home from school, saw the golf club next to the back door, and decided to take some practice swings. On the son's second swing, the golf club slipped out of his hands, flew into the next yard, and struck a neighbor in the head. The neighbor collapsed in pain, and was later diagnosed with a concussion.

If the neighbor sues the father for his son's actions, which party should prevail?

(A) The neighbor, because the son breached his duty of care for a child his age.

(B) The neighbor, because the father is vicariously liable.

(C) The father, because he had no duty to supervise his son.

(D) The father, because his actions were reasonable.

159.   The plaintiff, an art collector, brought a declaratory judgment action in federal district court seeking a declaration that he was the owner of a painting. In his complaint, the plaintiff alleged that he had recently purchased the painting for value and in good faith. The defendant, in her answer, did not challenge the plaintiff's assertions. The defendant, however, did allege that the painting had been owned by her mother and was fraudulently sold several years earlier by her father, without her mother's consent, to an art dealer in order to support her father's gambling habit. The defendant contended that she became the rightful owner of the painting as devisee of her mother's personal property after her mother's death. Also in her answer, the defendant asserted that the court lacked personal jurisdiction over her because she was a lifelong citizen of a state other than the forum state. The painting is hanging in the plaintiff's residence, which is located in the forum state.

Does the court have personal jurisdiction over the defendant?

(A)   Yes, because the painting is located in the forum state.

(B)   Yes, because the defendant has filed an answer.

(C)   No, because possession of the painting was allegedly lost due to fraud.

(D)   No, because the defendant is not a citizen of the forum state.

160. A state statute makes the possession of all venomous snakes unlawful. The state legislature's purpose in enacting the statute was to address the problem of a rising number of fatal snakebites occurring within the state.

A religious entity based in the state teaches that God will protect its members against all harm, and that therefore its members must handle venomous snakes during the entity's religious services to witness their true faith. An ordained minister of the entity, who sincerely believes all of the religious entity's teachings, sued in an appropriate federal court to have the statute declared unconstitutional because it prevents him from exercising his religious beliefs. Is the court likely to uphold the statute?

(A) Yes, because it is a neutral law of general applicability.

(B) Yes, because it does not have the primary effect of advancing religion and does not excessively entangle the government in religion.

(C) No, because it is not the least restrictive means of achieving the state's compelling interest in public health and safety.

(D) No, because it interferes with an integral part of the religious entity's worship services.

161. In reporting on the death of a city official whose bullet-ridden body was found in a barren apartment, a newspaper attributed the death to a "drug deal that went sour." The newspaper reporter who filed the report had serious doubts about the official's involvement with drugs. Later, the newspaper determined that the official neither used nor sold illegal drugs, but instead was killed because he had been involved in a fraud scheme that went awry.

The executor of the official's estate brought an action for defamation against the newspaper. The executor is unable to establish special damages. Who will prevail?

(A) The executor, because presumed damages are permitted for a libel action.

(B) The executor, because the newspaper acted with malice.

(C) The newspaper, because the city official was dead.

(D) The newspaper, because the statement regarding the city official's involvement in criminal activity was substantially true.

162. A local contractor entered into a valid contract with a state to repave a state highway for $3 million. In accord with the terms of the contract, the contractor was paid $500,000 immediately. The remaining amount was to be paid upon completion of the contract. After the contractor had substantially completed the paving project, the governor of the state announced that the state's budget crisis threatened all state projects and services, and decided to delay payments owed by state. With regard to the paving contract, the state, rather than paying the contractor upon completion of the project, will pay the contractor $500,000 each year for the next five years, plus the prevailing interest on the overdue amount.

If the contractor sues the state in an appropriate federal court, what is state's best argument?

(A) Under the Tenth Amendment and federalism, the state has plenary power over all matters pertaining to state road repairs.

(B) The state's action does not violate the Dormant Commerce Clause because the state is acting as a market participant.

(C) The contractor lacks Article III standing.

(D) The state's action does not substantially and unreasonably impair the contractor's contract rights.

163. A borrower owed a substantial sum of money to an unsavory lender. One afternoon, the lender knocked on the borrower's door. When the borrower opened the door, the lender was holding a baseball bat and said, "If you don't get me the money you owe within the next two hours, I'll break your legs." The borrower was extremely frightened, and immediately gave the lender the cash needed to satisfy the debt.

If the borrower later sues the lender for assault, will the borrower prevail?

(A) Yes, because the lender threatened the borrower with harmful or offensive bodily contact.

(B) Yes, because the lender intended to place the borrower in apprehension of harmful or offensive bodily contact.

(C) No, because the lender's words alone cannot give rise to an assault claim.

(D) No, because the lender gave the borrower two hours to deliver the money.

164. A buyer and seller executed a fully-integrated written contract for the sale of a car. The contract specified that the seller would deliver the car to the buyer's home within five days of the execution of the contract. The day after the contract was executed, the buyer emailed the seller suggesting that she pick up the car from the seller the following day, as she would be in the seller's neighborhood. This arrangement was more convenient for the seller, so the seller immediately responded that she agreed. Afterwards, the buyer decided not to go to the seller's neighborhood, and demanded that the seller deliver the car as originally agreed. The seller refused. The buyer threatened to sue the seller for breach of contract, and the seller responded that she would simply produce the email from the buyer in response. The buyer, a first year law student, claims that the parol evidence rule would prohibit the seller from introducing the email at trial.

Is the buyer correct in her belief that the parol evidence rule prohibits the introduction of the email?

(A) Yes, because the contract was fully integrated.

(B) Yes, because the email contradicts a term in the agreement.

(C) No, because the email was sent after the contract was executed.

(D) No, because there was no fraud or duress on the part of either party.

165. A man asked a friend to burn down the man's residence so the man could collect the fire insurance proceeds. The friend stated that she would be willing to set fire to the residence for $20,000. The man offered $10,000, but the friend refused. Later, the man set fire to an office building that he owned in order to collect the fire insurance proceeds. The man honestly, but unreasonably and incorrectly, believed that there was no one in the building when he set the fire. There was a person in the office building at the time of the fire who escaped unharmed. The man is charged with solicitation and arson.

The relevant statute defines arson as "the malicious burning of any dwelling or occupied structure."

Can the man be convicted of these crimes?

(A) No, as to both solicitation and arson.

(B) Yes, as to both solicitation and arson.

(C) Yes, as to arson only.

(D) Yes, as to solicitation only.

166. A citizen of State A properly filed a complaint in a federal district court located in State B. The common-law cause of action, based on the defendant's alleged negligence, arose in State C. The defendant, a citizen of State D, has timely filed a motion to dismiss based on lack of personal jurisdiction.

Assuming each of the states' laws is constitutionally proper, which state's personal jurisdictional statutes should the court apply in ruling on this motion?

(A) State A's, because the plaintiff is a citizen of State A.

(B) State B's, because the court is located in State B.

(C) State C's, because the cause of action arose in State C.

(D) State D's, because the defendant is a citizen of State D.

167. A plaintiff and a defendant are in settlement negotiations to resolve the plaintiff's lawsuit to recover for injuries she suffered when she fell off a horse at the defendant's stable. In exchange for the plaintiff's agreeing to drop the case, the defendant offered to pay the plaintiff $5,000, which would cover her medical expenses and leave a little extra for pain and suffering. The plaintiff counter-offered $7,000, which the defendant refused. The case went to trial. The plaintiff prayed for $20,000 in damages, and reiterated during her testimony that that amount was the least amount she could accept to make her whole. The defendant testified that the plaintiff's injuries were not severe enough to warrant a $20,000 judgment, and added, "The plaintiff was willing to settle for $7,000; it's ludicrous that she is now asking for $20,000." The plaintiff's attorney objected to the defendant's statement.

How should the court rule on the plaintiff's objection?

(A) Sustain it, because the testimony contains hearsay not within any exception.

(B) Sustain it, because the testimony discloses communications regarding a settlement offer.

(C) Overrule it, because the testimony contains a prior inconsistent statement.

(D) Overrule it, because the testimony impeaches the plaintiff's credibility.

168. The owner of a parcel of land validly devises the parcel "to my wife for life, but if she remarries, then to my son for his life; then to my son's children who attain the age of 21." At the time of the conveyance, the son has one child, a daughter.

Subsequently, the son is killed in an automobile crash. At the time of the crash, the son also has a second daughter. A year after the son's funeral, the owner's wife remarries.

The oldest daughter, who is now 21, contacts a lawyer about ownership of the parcel of land. Her sister is currently 18 years old.

The jurisdiction follows the common law Rule Against Perpetuities, has abolished the common law rule regarding the destructibility of contingent remainders, and follows the rule of convenience with regard to class gifts.

Which of the following prevents the oldest daughter from owning the entire parcel in fee simple absolute?

(A) The Rule Against Perpetuities.

(B) Her sister's interest in the parcel.

(C) Her father's death and grandmother's remarriage before she turned 21 years old.

(D) Her grandmother is still alive.

169. A widow and widower were engaged to be married. After some discussion as to how to pay for the wedding, the son of the widow and the daughter of the widower each orally agreed to give $50,000 to the other's parent as a gesture of approval of the upcoming union. The son and daughter shook hands in agreement as to the arrangement, but before either gift had been made, the two became embroiled in a serious disagreement, and both agreed to forego making the gifts. In spite of this, the son of the widow did make a gift of $50,000 to the widower at the time of the wedding.

Soon after the marriage of the widow and widower, the widower died. Subsequently, the widow learned of the arrangement and sued the daughter of widower to compel her to pay $50,000. Is the widow likely to prevail?

(A) Yes, because the widow was an intended beneficiary of the agreement between the children.

(B) Yes, because the agreement between the children was not required to be in writing.

(C) No, because the agreement between the children was unenforceable as promises to make gifts.

(D) No, because the agreement between the children was rescinded before the widow's rights vested.

170. Congress has enacted many laws regulating navigation generally, but not regarding the specific subject of water pollution by ships sailing on navigable bodies of water. A state enacted a law prohibiting any ship from discharging specified pollutants, including oil, into the navigable waterways of the state. Violation of the law was punishable by fines based on the amount of the discharge. The law is necessary to the important state interest of preventing pollution; there are no reasonable alternatives available. In addition, the benefits of the law to the state outweigh the burdens it imposes on interstate commerce.

A ship owner from another state is fined pursuant to this law for discharging oil into a waterway in the state. Will the ship owner's challenge of the state law as unconstitutional be successful?

(A) Yes, because the law regulates interstate commerce, which may be regulated only by Congress.

(B) Yes, because the fine constitutes an impermissible ad valorem tax.

(C) No, because the law is necessary to the important state interest of preventing pollution and there are no reasonable alternatives available.

(D) No, because the law does not discriminate against interstate commerce and does not impose an undue burden on interstate commerce.

171. In a well-trafficked downtown location, a voyeur concealed a video camera near a sidewalk grate. As the voyeur was aware, a natural spurt of air coming up from the grate would occasionally lift a woman's skirt and reveal her underwear. In reviewing the video taken one day, the voyeur discovered a short sequence involving a prominent female politician who at the time was not wearing underwear. The voyeur contacted the politician and demanded a substantial payment in exchange for not posting the video on the Internet.

The politician sued the voyeur in an invasion of privacy action based on intrusion upon her seclusion. The voyeur moved to dismiss the action for failure to state a cause of action. Should the court grant this motion?

(A) No, because the politician did not consent to the video.

(B) No, because the video intruded into her privacy in a manner highly offensive to a reasonable person.

(C) Yes, because the video was made in a public place.

(D) Yes, because the video was not revealed to a third party.

172. A 16-year-old entered into a written agreement to buy a car from a dealership. He made a small down payment and took out a loan from the dealership for the remainder of the purchase price. The deal was fair in every respect, and the same as the car dealership would give any other customer. After the sale was finalized, the salesman's supervisor reviewed the contract, and upon researching the matter further, discovering that the boy was only 16. He told the salesperson to call the boy and cancel the contract, which he did.

In a breach of contract action brought on behalf of the boy, the court held for the boy. What was the reason?

(A) The contract is one for necessities.

(B) The contract cannot be disaffirmed because of the boy's part performance.

(C) The contract is not voidable because the terms were fair.

(D) The dealer did not have the right to void the contract.

173. Two vehicles were involved in an automobile accident. The driver of one car ran to the other car and said, "Ma'am, are you ok? Oh my goodness, I didn't even see that stop sign. I'm calling an ambulance right now." The injured woman sued the other driver. At trial, the other driver testified that the woman was the one who ran the stop sign. The woman's attorney then seeks to introduce the other driver's statement as evidence that he ran a stop sign and caused the accident.

Upon proper objection, should the court admit the statement into evidence?

(A) Yes, both as substantive evidence and for impeachment purposes.

(B) No, because as a prior inconsistent statement, it can only be used to impeach the other driver.

(C) No, because the declarant is available to testify and subject to cross-examination.

(D) No, because the statement is hearsay not within any exception.

174. A state law provided that all police officers must have been born in the United States. The state adopted this law in order to assure that police officers can speak and understand English well enough to avoid miscommunications that can endanger public safety. An individual who was born in a foreign country and became a naturalized United States citizen resides in the state. Because of the law, he was denied a job as a police officer for which he was otherwise qualified. He challenged the constitutionality of this law in an appropriate court. What is his strongest argument that the law is unconstitutional?

(A) The law discriminates against the plaintiff based on his national origin and is not narrowly tailored to further the state's compelling interest in protecting public safety.

(B) The law deprives the plaintiff of his fundamental civil right to pursue his chosen calling in violation of the Fourteenth Amendment's Due Process Clause.

(C) The law prohibits the plaintiff from gaining a job that has a direct effect on basic functions of the state government.

(D) The law deprives the plaintiff of his First Amendment rights by limiting his freedom to speak a language other than English.

175. The plaintiff sues a large out-of-state corporation in federal court. The plaintiff claims that the corporation's widget had a defect that caused him a serious injury and requests $300,000 in damages. The corporation has a great legal department and a large group of professionals with a thorough understanding of each of its products. The plaintiff's attorney hires a widget expert, and pays her $30,000 to consult with him and to provide a report on the corporation's widgets. The report concludes that the widgets were properly designed and manufactured, although it is possible that the widget used by the plaintiff had a defect. The plaintiff's attorney decided not to have the expert testify at trial. During discovery, the corporation requested all of the plaintiff's expert reports related to the litigation. Must the plaintiff's attorney disclose the expert's report?

(A) Yes, because the expert's report is relevant to the parties' claims or defenses and is not privileged.

(B) Yes, because the benefit of the expert's report to the corporation outweighs the burden of the discovery request.

(C) No, because the corporation's request was likely calculated to harass and unduly burden the plaintiff.

(D) No, because the plaintiff's attorney hired the expert as a consultant to prepare for the trial, not to testify at the trial.

176. A hospital placed an order to purchase scalpel blades from a medical supply company. The hospital specified that the blades were to be shipped immediately. Upon receipt of the order, the supply company discovered that it did not have the type of blade ordered by the hospital, and shipped instead a different type of blade, along with a note that these blades were not the type ordered by the hospital but were sent as an accommodation. The hospital rejected and returned the shipped blades, then sued the supply company for breach of contract. Will the hospital be successful in its suit?

(A) Yes, because of the perfect tender rule.

(B) Yes, because acceptance of the hospital's order could be made by shipment as well as by a promise.

(C) No, because the hospital order could only be accepted by shipment of the type of scalpel blades ordered.

(D) No, because the medical supply company did not accept the hospital's offer.

177. A large manufacturer, seeking to trim costs, entered into an agreement with an outside contractor to provide its employees with "appropriate and safe workplace tools and equipment," and to maintain that equipment in safe working order. A rotary saw provided by the outside contractor malfunctioned as a result of improper maintenance, and severely injured one of the manufacturer's employees.

The employee sued the manufacturer for negligence. Is the employee likely to succeed?

(A) No, because the manufacturer was relieved of liability when it outsourced its activities to an independent contractor.

(B) No, because the manufacturer is free to subcontract functions that are not inherently dangerous.

(C) Yes, because a principal remains simultaneously liable for the torts of its independent contractor.

(D) Yes, because workplace safety is uniquely the responsibility of the manufacturer.

178. Despite being served with a warrant, the defendant objected to having his blood drawn to determine whether it matched blood found at the scene of a robbery. Nevertheless, the police properly executed the warrant to perform the procedure, and a doctor drew the defendant's blood. The defendant was later charged with robbery, a felony. The blood at the scene matched the sample obtained from the defendant. At his robbery trial, the defendant moved to suppress this evidence. Should the judge grant this motion?

(A) Yes, because obtaining evidence through a forced medical procedure shocks the conscience.

(B) Yes, because the procedure violated the defendant's Fifth Amendment privilege against self-incrimination.

(C) No, because the blood was obtained pursuant to a warrant and drawing blood is a reasonable, minimally invasive medical procedure.

(D) No, because the defendant was charged with a felony.

179. During a burglary trial, the prosecutor plans to put an eyewitness on the stand. The eyewitness is the burglary victim's neighbor, and she will testify that she saw the defendant climb out of the victim's window on the night of the burglary. At the time of the trial, the eyewitness can no longer recall what the person she saw climbing out of the victim's home looked like. However, she wrote a detailed description in her diary right after she called the police on the night in question. When the eyewitness is on the stand, the prosecutor asks her to read the diary entry to herself to see if it refreshes her memory. When the witness admits that it does not, the prosecutor seeks to have the witness read the diary entry to the jury and to introduce the diary entry as an exhibit. The defendant objects to both.

How should the court rule?

(A) The court should sustain the defendant's objections on both counts.

(B) The court should sustain the defendant's objection as to the witness's reading the diary entry, but should overrule the defendant's objection as to its entry as an exhibit.

(C) The court should overrule the defendant's objection as to the witness's reading it to the jury, but should sustain the defendant's objection as to the diary's entry as an exhibit.

(D) The court should overrule the defendant's objections on both counts.

180. A state amended its constitution to provide that "English is the state's official language and applies to all state employees during the performance of government business." A state employee sued the state's governor to enjoin application of this provision to her. She alleged that she worked in the state's Department of Motor Vehicles and often communicated with customers in Spanish, thereby facing possible adverse employment action in violation of her First and Fourteenth Amendment rights. The governor defends against this action by invoking the political question doctrine. Will the governor likely be successful?

(A) Yes, because the case presents a hotly contested question involving sensitive political issues.

(B) Yes, because a judicial decision would unnecessarily embarrass the governor.

(C) No, because the law does not require the judge to make any discretionary policy determinations.

(D) No, because the state constitutional provision has been properly challenged as violating individual constitutional rights.

181. Two friends, a chef and an electrician, together purchased a beachfront residence. They took title to the residence as joint owners, with the chef owning a 75% interest and the electrician a 25% interest.

The chef, during the time he used the residence, prepared elaborate meals. He advertised those meals, attracted a paying clientele, and made a net profit from them.

The electrician pointed out to the chef that the electrical system in the house was in dangerous condition. The chef, agreeing with the electrician that repair of the system was necessary, stated that he had neither the time nor the expertise to fix it himself and couldn't afford the cost of doing so. The electrician repaired it and demanded that the chef contribute to the cost of the repair. The chef refused.

The electrician brought an action for partition. The court ordered the sale of the residence. It was purchased by a third party for its appraised value.

In allocating the sale proceeds, should the court take into account either the chef's net profit from the meals or the electrician's repair of the electrical system?

(A) Only the electrician's repair of the electrical system.

(B) Only the chef's net profit from the meals.

(C) Both must be taken into account.

(D) Neither should be taken into account.

182. After a man suffered a major epileptic seizure, he reported the seizure to his state's Motor Vehicle Administration, in compliance with the following statute:

Driver's license holders diagnosed with epilepsy shall be required to report their epilepsy and seizures to the State Motor Vehicle Administration (SMVA). The SMVA shall refer their license applications to the Medical Advisory Board for review. The Board may, in its discretion, suspend or revoke a person's driver's license or refuse to renew a license for longer than 90 days if the person's driving may be adversely affected by a seizure.

Pursuant to its authority, the Medical Advisory Board revoked the man's driver's license. Nonetheless, the man kept driving his car to work, and one morning, he hit a pedestrian with his car. The pedestrian was crossing the street in a crosswalk.

There is no evidence that the man was suffering an epileptic seizure at the time of the incident. The pedestrian sued the man, and during trial, argued that the man's actions constituted negligence per se.

Will the pedestrian's argument be successful?

(A) No, because the man was not suffering a seizure at the time of the accident.

(B) No, because the harm suffered by the pedestrian was not of the type contemplated by the statute.

(C) Yes, because the man was driving in violation of the Medical Advisory Board's order.

(D) Yes, because the pedestrian is in the class of persons intended to be protected by the statute.

183. The defendant was convicted of armed robbery by a unanimous vote of a six-person jury. The applicable statute provides for a sentence of not more than 20 years' imprisonment. However, if the defendant was previously convicted of specified crimes, including felony theft, the sentence could be increased to not more than 30 years' imprisonment. Upon the introduction of evidence by the prosecution, the judge determined that the defendant had been previously convicted of a felony theft and sentenced the defendant to 25 years in prison. On appeal, the defendant has challenged both his conviction and his sentence.

Should the appellate court uphold the conviction and the sentence?

(A) Yes as to the conviction, because a six-person jury is permissible in a criminal trial, and yes as to the sentence, because it was validly imposed by the judge.

(B) Yes as to the conviction, because a six-person jury is permissible in a criminal trial, but no as to the sentence, because it was not imposed by a jury.

(C) No as to the conviction, because a six-person jury is not permissible in a criminal trial, but yes as to the sentence, because it was validly imposed by the judge.

(D) No as to the conviction, because a six-person jury is not permissible in a criminal trial, and no as to the sentence, because it was not imposed by a jury.

184. A homeowner entered into an oral agreement with a landscaper to landscape the grounds surrounding her home for $75,000 while she was away for the summer. While the homeowner had described the overall effect that she wanted the landscaper to create as "stately," she left the choice of plants and other materials and their placement up to the landscaper. In order to secure the homeowner's assent, the landscaper promised her that she would be satisfied with the job or she would not have to pay him. Upon the homeowner's return in the fall, the landscaper sought payment from the homeowner. The homeowner refused to pay because, in her honest opinion, the landscaper had failed to create the effect she desired.

The landscaper filed a breach of contract action to recover $75,000 from the homeowner. At trial, the landscaper offers evidence that the landscaping was done in conformity with standards set forth by a national organization of landscapers and testimony from several witnesses that the homeowner was being unreasonable because the grounds were stately. Will the landscaper likely prevail?

(A) No, because the homeowner was not satisfied with the landscaping.

(B) No, because the contract was not in writing.

(C) Yes, because the landscaper performed in accordance with recognized standards.

(D) Yes, because the homeowner was being unreasonable in refusing to acknowledge that the landscaping had made the grounds stately.

185. An expert witness was called by the defendant to testify in a murder trial. The expert was to testify that the defendant was not responsible for his actions due to a specific mental defect. On cross-examination, the prosecutor brought to the expert witness's attention an authoritative book on psychological conditions, judicially noted to be a reliable authority in the field. The book described the symptoms of the mental defect at issue differently than the expert witness had described them, and the prosecutor read the book's description into evidence. The prosecutor wanted the jury to be able to consider the book's description as substantive evidence, but the defendant objected that the description could be used for impeachment purposes only, and not as substantive evidence. The prosecutor further wanted to introduce the book itself into evidence; the defendant objected to this as well.

Should the court allow the jury to consider the description in the book as substantive evidence, and should the book itself be introduced as evidence?

(A) The description should be considered for impeachment purposes only, and the book should not be introduced into evidence.

(B) The description should be considered as substantive evidence, and the book should not be introduced into evidence.

(C) The description should be considered as substantive evidence, and the book should be introduced into evidence.

(D) The book should be introduced into evidence, though the description may be used only for impeachment purposes.

186. A city passed an ordinance prohibiting all "adult entertainment establishments," defined as "enterprises that sell, trade, or depict materials that are obscene or pornographic." The city justified its law on the basis of reputable studies that (i) obscene and pornographic material degrades females and increases the tendency towards anti-social behavior of people who view it; and (ii) adult entertainment establishments are linked with criminal activity such as prostitution and drug dealing. The city also emphasized that the three cities bordering it all allow adult entertainment establishments.

An entrepreneur who wishes to open an adult bookstore in the city sues the city in an appropriate federal court and claims that the ordinance is unconstitutional. Will she likely prevail?

(A) Yes, because the city's ordinance deprives her of her right to earn a living in violation of the Due Process Clause of the Fourteenth Amendment.

(B) Yes, because the First Amendment prohibits the city from banning all adult entertainment establishments.

(C) No, because the plaintiff has not been deprived of her constitutional right to earn a living, as she can open her adult bookstore in one of the three nearby cities.

(D) No, because the city has legitimate reasons for banning adult entertainment establishments that are not based on the content of the material they are selling, trading, or depicting.

187. A tenant rented an apartment in a multi-family dwelling on a month-to-month basis. Under the terms of the lease, the tenant had an absolute duty to repair the premises. At the time that the tenant rented the apartment, the landlord made the tenant aware of several housing code violations that constituted a substantial threat to the tenant's health and safety. After waiting a reasonable time for the landlord to correct the violations, the tenant, in accord with a statutory provision, placed the monthly rent payment in an escrow account, rather than submitting it to the landlord.

After failing to receive the rent for two months, the landlord filed an action seeking eviction of the tenant.

If the tenant raised the landlord's failure to correct the housing code violations as a defense, will the tenant be successful?

(A) No, because the tenant had a contractual duty to repair the premises.

(B) No, because the tenant was aware of the violations when the tenant assumed control of the premises.

(C) Yes, because of the implied warranty of habitability.

(D) Yes, because the landlord's actions constituted a constructive eviction.

188. Arriving home from work, a husband found his wife engaged in sex with his best friend. The husband flew into a rage and verbally threatened to shoot both of them, although he did not own a gun. The best friend quickly left and the husband eventually calmed down and regained his self-control after his wife promised not to see the best friend again. Nevertheless, the husband left the house to purchase a handgun. After making his purchase, he stopped by a local bar and became inebriated.

In the meantime, the best friend returned to drop off the husband's favorite hat, which the husband had left at the best friend's house the day before. Only the wife was home, but as the wife was giving the best friend a goodbye hug, the husband returned home, still inebriated. As both the wife and the best friend attempted to explain the innocent nature of their being together, the husband, his shock over their relationship returning, pulled the trigger. His shot missed the best friend and instead killed the wife.

The husband was charged with common law murder of his wife. Which of the following would be his best argument against the charge?

(A) He didn't intend to kill his wife.

(B) His intoxicated state prevented him from forming the intent necessary to commit the crime.

(C) The sight of his best friend and his wife together again reignited his feelings regarding his wife's adultery.

(D) A reasonable person would not have cooled off from the initial discovery of the adultery.

189. The federal Protect Marriage Act (PMA) provides that (1) states need not give "full faith and credit" to marriages recognized as valid in other states, (2) the United States may enforce or defend the PMA, and (3) if the United States does not do so, a specified private law firm has the right to enforce or defend the law. A man who validly married his partner under State A law moved to State B, which bans same-sex marriage and refuses to give full faith and credit to such marriages pursuant to the PMA. The man sought an injunction in federal court prohibiting State B officials from enforcing the state law and the PMA, claiming that these laws violate his constitutional rights to liberty and equality. The United States also became involved in this action to defend the PMA. A few weeks later, however, the United States withdrew because the President concluded that the PMA is unconstitutional.

If the law firm seeks to defend the PMA, it should timely file a motion that rests on which of the following doctrines?

(A) Intervention as of right.

(B) Compulsory joinder.

(C) Permissive joinder.

(D) Interpleader.

190. The Occupational Safety and Health Act of 1970 (OSHA) required all private employers in America to meet certain minimum federal standards to ensure safe and healthful work environments. Recently, Congress amended OSHA, extending its coverage requirements to state and local government employers.

A state sued in an appropriate federal court, challenging the constitutionality of this amendment. Will the court likely uphold the amendment as constitutional?

(A) No, because the amendment violates the Tenth Amendment.

(B) No, because the amendment violates fundamental principles of federalism, because Congress has directly impaired the states' ability to carry out their integral governmental functions.

(C) Yes, because the amendment merely affects the activities of states acting in their proprietary capacity.

(D) Yes, because the amendment is a valid exercise of Congress's Commerce Clause power.

191. A credit union loaned money to a married couple to enable them to purchase a mansion as their primary residence. The couple gave the credit union a mortgage on the mansion. The credit union promptly and properly filed the mortgage with the local land records office.

A little more than a year later, the homeowners financed the purchase of an expensive chandelier from a lighting supply store on credit. The couple gave the store a note and a security interest in the chandelier. Due to an employee oversight, the store failed to file the security interest with the local land records office until 15 days after the chandelier was installed in the mansion.

About two years after the purchase of the chandelier, the husband's business suffered a severe downturn, and the homeowners defaulted on their mortgage and their note to the store. The credit union initiated foreclosure proceedings and, upon learning that the store planned to remove the chandelier from the mansion, filed an action to prevent the store from doing so.

Whose rights to the chandelier are superior?

(A) The credit union, because it holds a purchase money mortgage on the mansion.

(B) The credit union, because it recorded its mortgage before the store recorded its security interest.

(C) The store, because the chandelier was a fixture.

(D) The store, because it timely and properly recorded its security interest.

192. A pedestrian was walking next to a building under construction. Suddenly, he was hit in the head by a falling brick. As a consequence, the pedestrian suffered a skull fracture and a severe brain injury.

The pedestrian sued the construction company. At trial, the pedestrian did not introduce any direct evidence of the construction company's negligence, but proved that the construction company's employees were in control of its bricks at all relevant times, and that a brick does not ordinarily fall from a building under construction without negligence. The construction company offered uncontroverted proof that the pedestrian was negligent by walking so close to an active construction site. The jurisdiction in which the lawsuit is proceeding applies pure comparative negligence rules.

At the close of all evidence, the construction company moved for a directed verdict. Should the court deny this motion?

(A) Yes, because the pedestrian's negligence does not reduce the likelihood of the construction company being negligent.

(B) Yes, because *res ipsa loquitur* requires a finding of negligence.

(C) No, because a party who is negligent may not prevail under a *res ipsa loquitur* theory.

(D) No, because the pedestrian has not produced any direct evidence of the company's culpability.

193. A plaintiff sued a defendant for injuries she sustained when she slipped on a wet floor in the defendant's restaurant. The plaintiff saw a physician and underwent physical therapy sessions to treat her injuries. During one session, the plaintiff said to her physical therapist, "You know, I saw the 'Caution, Floor is Wet' sign before I fell, but I was in such a hurry to get back to my table that I ignored it." Another patient undergoing physical therapy with another therapist overheard the statement, and informed the defendant, who happened to be his friend. The defendant wants to introduce the testimony of his friend, as whether the plaintiff had notice of the wet floor is at issue in the case. The plaintiff objects to the testimony.

Should the court allow the friend to testify as to the plaintiff's statement?

(A) No, because the statement is inadmissible hearsay.

(B) No, because the statement is privileged.

(C) Yes, because the statement is not hearsay.

(D) Yes, because the statement was made for the purposes of medical diagnosis or treatment.

194. A gas station entered into a contract with an oil distributor to purchase a specified quantity of gasoline for resale. The contract specified, per the gas station's request, that the gasoline was to be 99.5% free of impurities, as determined by industry-standard measurements. Another contract provision specified that the gasoline was to be delivered by July 31 at the latest.

The oil distributor delivered the gasoline to the gas station on July 30. Before accepting the delivery, the gas station manager checked the purity of the gasoline. The gasoline was only 99.3% free of impurities, and the manager rejected it. The oil distributor immediately informed the gas station manager that it intended to cure the defect by delivering a new shipment as soon as possible. The oil distributor delivered a new shipment of gasoline to the gas station on August 1, but the gas station manager rejected the new shipment. Both parties agree that the gasoline in the second shipment was 99.7% free of impurities.

Later, the oil distributor sued the gas station for breach of contract. Is it likely to prevail?

(A) No, because the oil distributor had no right to cure its defective tender.

(B) No, because an acceptable shipment needed to be delivered by July 31.

(C) Yes, because the second shipment was a conforming tender, and the gas station was required to accept it.

(D) Yes, because the oil distributor properly cured its defective tender within a reasonable time.

195. A chef and her friend were cooking dinner. As the friend handed a knife to the chef, the knife slipped and fell, slicing into the chef's foot. While the chef's foot was being treated at the hospital, the chef contracted a severe infection, which eventually necessitated the amputation of her foot.

The chef sued the hospital and her friend in a jurisdiction that applies traditional joint and several liability rules, allows contribution, and uses a pure comparative negligence system. The jury determined that the chef suffered $1 million in damages, and apportioned the fault as follows: 30% to the chef, 55% to the friend, and 15% to the hospital.

How much, if anything, may the chef collect from the hospital, and how much, if anything, may the hospital seek in contribution from the friend?

(A) The chef may collect $150,000 from the hospital, and the hospital may not seek contribution from the friend.

(B) The chef may collect $150,000 from the hospital, and the hospital may seek $150,000 in contribution from the friend.

(C) The chef may collect $700,000 from the hospital, and the hospital may seek $550,000 in contribution from the friend.

(D) The chef may collect $700,000 from the hospital, and the hospital may not seek contribution from the friend.

196. A homeowner held title to her residence in fee simple absolute. During her ownership, the homeowner converted a first floor room into a library. She designed floor-to-ceiling bookcases with elaborate decorative items. She contracted with a carpenter to build and install the bookcases in the room. The bookcases were affixed to the walls of the rooms with screws rather than nails so that they could be more easily removed. She intended to take the bookcases with her if she ever moved.

In the sales brochure that was prepared by the homeowner's real estate broker and approved of by the homeowner, the room was described as a library, but no specific mention was made of the bookcases.

The contract of sale did not contain a reference to the bookcases. After the contract of sale was entered into, the homeowner had the bookcases removed from the house and repaired the damage to the walls caused by their removal.

On a walk-through of the premises prior to closing, the buyer discovered that the bookcases had been removed. The buyer, after balking at the transfer of the property without the bookcases, agreed to accept the deed but reserved the right to pursue an action regarding the removal of the bookcases.

In the action based on the removal of the bookcases brought by the buyer for money damages, which of the following would not be a strong argument that the specified party could make in support of its position?

(A) The seller argues that the damage done to the room from the removal of the bookcases was repaired.

(B) The seller argues that the seller's subjective intent, at the time of installation, was to remove the bookcases if the house was ever sold.

(C) The buyer argues that the bookcases were specially designed for use in the library.

(D) The buyer argues that the bookcases were important to the function of the room as a library.

197. A woman met a man at a party at the home of a third person. The woman noticed that the man was wearing an expensive gold watch. As the party was winding down and the woman and man were alone, the woman slipped a sedative into the man's drink. Waiting until the man passed out, the woman then removed the watch from the man's wrist and left the party. Later, the party's host discovered the man asleep, and revived him. When the man discovered that his watch was missing, the man called the police. The man, who lived at home with his parents, had taken the watch from his father's dresser for the evening, without his father's permission.

The woman was arrested and charged with robbery. Can she be convicted of the crime?

(A) Yes, because the woman used force to permanently deprive the man of the watch he was wearing.

(B) Yes, because the taking took place at a dwelling.

(C) No, because the watch belonged to the man's father and the man did not have permission to use it.

(D) No, because the man was unconscious when his watch was taken.

198. Over the course of one night, an attorney went to three different bars: Bar A, Bar B, and Bar C. The attorney stayed at each bar for roughly equal amounts of time, and each bar served him enough liquor to make him legally intoxicated. At the end of the night, the attorney left Bar C and was driving home erratically. A block away from his home, the attorney lost control of his car, careened into oncoming traffic, and collided with his neighbor's car. The attorney died in the collision, and his neighbor was permanently disfigured.

The neighbor sued Bar A in a jurisdiction that has adopted standard dram shop laws. Bar A filed a motion to dismiss the suit for failing to state a claim upon which relief can be granted. How should the court rule on the motion?

(A) Deny the motion, and order Bar B, Bar C, and the attorney's estate joined as defendants.

(B) Deny the motion, because a reasonable fact finder could determine that the neighbor's injuries were a continuing consequence of Bar A's actions.

(C) Grant the motion, because the attorney's criminal act of driving drunk was a superseding cause that cut off Bar A's liability.

(D) Grant the motion, because Bar A's negligence was not the "but-for" cause of the neighbor's injuries.

199. In a valid contract, the plaintiff promised to pay the defendant $87,000 to fumigate the plaintiff's commercial office building within seven days to stop a major insect infestation. The defendant performed the fumigation, and plaintiff paid the $87,000. Two months later, the plaintiff filed a complaint in the State A federal district court, making three main allegations. First, "Plaintiff is a State Z citizen, Defendant is a State A citizen, the amount in controversy is $87,000, and the court has diversity jurisdiction." Second, "Defendant breached its contract with Plaintiff (copy attached) by failing to render adequate performance, and Plaintiff has been unable to sell his commercial office building." Third, "Plaintiff demands judgment of $87,000, the amount Plaintiff lost as a result of Defendant's breach."

What would be the defendant's best response?

(A) Filing a Rule 12(b) motion to dismiss for lack of subject matter jurisdiction.

(B) Filing a Rule 12(b)(6) motion to dismiss for failure to state a claim upon which relief can be granted.

(C) Filing an answer denying the plaintiff's allegation that the defendant breached the contract.

(D) Filing a motion for summary judgment on the grounds that there is no genuine issue of material fact and that the defendant is entitled to judgment as a matter of law.

200. In a criminal trial for attempted murder, the prosecutor seeks to introduce a statement made by the victim immediately after he was attacked by the defendant. The victim, very seriously injured, shouted the defendant's name and said, "I can't believe you shot me! I'm dying!" At the time of the trial, the victim has mostly recovered from his injuries, but suffered permanent memory loss, has no recollection of the incident at all, and has no recollection of making the statement. The prosecutor seeks to introduce the statement as a dying declaration, but the defendant objects.

Should this statement be admissible under the "dying declaration" exception to the hearsay rules?

(A) No, the statement is not admissible as a dying declaration.

(B) No, because the victim did not die.

(C) Yes, because the victim is unavailable due to his inability to remember.

(D) Yes, because the proceeding in which the statement will be introduced is a criminal trial.

STOP.
IF YOU FINISH BEFORE TIME IS CALLED, CHECK YOUR WORK ON THIS TEST.

ANSWER KEY

Item	Answer	Subject	Item	Answer	Subject	Item	Answer	Subject
1	A	CONTRACTS	33	A	REAL PROP.	65	B	REAL PROP.
2	B	EVIDENCE	34	B	CIV. PRO.	66	D	TORTS
3	A	TORTS	35	D	CRIM. LAW	67	B	CRIM. LAW
4	C	CIV. PRO.	36	C	TORTS	68	A	CONTRACTS
5	D	REAL PROP.	37	B	EVIDENCE	69	B	REAL PROP.
6	B	EVIDENCE	38	D	TORTS	70	A	CRIM. LAW
7	C	CRIM. LAW	39	D	CIV. PRO.	71	B	CIV. PRO.
8	A	CONST. LAW	40	D	CONTRACTS	72	B	TORTS
9	B	CONTRACTS	41	C	EVIDENCE	73	A	CONST. LAW
10	C	REAL PROP.	42	D	REAL PROP.	74	C	CONTRACTS
11	C	CONTRACTS	43	B	CONST. LAW	75	A	REAL PROP.
12	B	CONST. LAW	44	B	CONTRACTS	76	B	CRIM. LAW
13	D	EVIDENCE	45	A	EVIDENCE	77	C	EVIDENCE
14	D	CRIM. LAW	46	C	CONST. LAW	78	B	CRIM. LAW
15	C	CRIM. LAW	47	A	CRIM. LAW	79	D	CONST. LAW
16	A	CIV. PRO.	48	A	REAL PROP.	80	C	TORTS
17	C	TORTS	49	C	CONTRACTS	81	A	EVIDENCE
18	C	CIV. PRO.	50	D	CONTRACTS	82	C	CONTRACTS
19	D	REAL PROP.	51	C	TORTS	83	B	CIV. PRO.
20	D	CONTRACTS	52	B	CIV. PRO.	84	B	CONST. LAW
21	B	TORTS	53	C	CONST. LAW	85	A	CIV. PRO.
22	C	CONST. LAW	54	D	CIV. PRO.	86	A	TORTS
23	D	CIV. PRO.	55	C	REAL PROP.	87	C	REAL PROP.
24	B	EVIDENCE	56	C	CONST. LAW	88	C	EVIDENCE
25	D	REAL PROP.	57	D	EVIDENCE	89	D	CONST. LAW
26	C	EVIDENCE	58	A	CONST. LAW	90	A	TORTS
27	B	TORTS	59	B	CRIM. LAW	91	D	CRIM. LAW
28	A	CONTRACTS	60	B	CIV. PRO.	92	D	CIV. PRO.
29	D	CRIM. LAW	61	B	CRIM. LAW	93	B	CONTRACTS
30	C	CONST. LAW	62	A	EVIDENCE	94	A	CIV. PRO.
31	B	REAL PROP.	63	C	CONTRACTS	95	D	EVIDENCE
32	B	TORTS	64	D	EVIDENCE	96	C	CONST. LAW

Item	Answer	Subject	Item	Answer	Subject	Item	Answer	Subject
97	A	REAL PROP.	132	C	CRIM. LAW	167	B	EVIDENCE
98	D	CRIM. LAW	133	A	CRIM. LAW	168	B	REAL PROP.
99	C	CONTRACTS	134	B	CONST. LAW	169	D	CONTRACTS
100	B	REAL PROP.	135	B	CIV. PRO.	170	D	CONST. LAW
101	C	EVIDENCE	136	D	EVIDENCE	171	B	TORTS
102	C	CRIM. LAW	137	C	REAL PROP.	172	D	CONTRACTS
103	D	CONTRACTS	138	A	CRIM. LAW	173	A	EVIDENCE
104	A	CONTRACTS	139	A	EVIDENCE	174	A	CONST. LAW
105	C	CONST. LAW	140	D	TORTS	175	D	CIV. PRO.
106	B	REAL PROP.	141	B	CONST. LAW	176	D	CONTRACTS
107	D	CRIM. LAW	142	A	CONTRACTS	177	D	TORTS
108	D	TORTS	143	A	CONTRACTS	178	C	CRIM. LAW
109	A	CONST. LAW	144	B	REAL PROP.	179	C	EVIDENCE
110	A	CIV. PRO.	145	D	CIV. PRO.	180	D	CONST. LAW
111	C	REAL PROP.	146	C	TORTS	181	A	REAL PROP.
112	A	TORTS	147	D	EVIDENCE	182	A	TORTS
113	C	CRIM. LAW	148	A	CIV. PRO.	183	A	CRIM. LAW
114	B	CONST. LAW	149	D	TORTS	184	A	CONTRACTS
115	B	CRIM. LAW	150	C	REAL PROP.	185	B	EVIDENCE
116	C	CONTRACTS	151	A	CONST. LAW	186	B	CONST. LAW
117	D	EVIDENCE	152	C	CRIM. LAW	187	C	REAL PROP.
118	B	TORTS	153	A	EVIDENCE	188	C	CRIM. LAW
119	D	REAL PROP.	154	B	CIV. PRO.	189	A	CIV. PRO.
120	D	CONST. LAW	155	A	REAL PROP.	190	D	CONST. LAW
121	A	TORTS	156	C	CONTRACTS	191	D	REAL PROP.
122	B	CIV. PRO.	157	B	CONTRACTS	192	A	TORTS
123	A	REAL PROP.	158	D	TORTS	193	C	EVIDENCE
124	A	CONTRACTS	159	A	CIV. PRO.	194	B	CONTRACTS
125	D	CRIM. LAW	160	A	CONST. LAW	195	C	TORTS
126	A	CIV. PRO.	161	C	TORTS	196	B	REAL PROP.
127	C	CONST. LAW	162	D	CONST. LAW	197	A	CRIM. LAW
128	A	EVIDENCE	163	D	TORTS	198	B	TORTS
129	D	CIV. PRO.	164	C	EVIDENCE	199	B	CIV. PRO.
130	A	CONTRACTS	165	B	CRIM. LAW	200	A	EVIDENCE
131	C	REAL PROP.	166	B	CIV. PRO.			

Additional Practice

ADDITIONAL PRACTICE

This section of the book contains 100 additional practice questions covering all subject areas tested on the MBE. It is designed for students who have completed all of the assigned practice question sets in Directed Study, but would like to work additional paper-based multiple-choice questions. Like the previous sections of this book, the answers to these questions can be accessed online.

QUESTION 1

A few weeks before the beginning of a murder trial, a witness to the murder identified the defendant in a photo array as the person who killed the victim. Between the time of the photo array and the trial, the witness died. The witness was the only eyewitness to the crime, aside from the victim and the murderer, so the prosecution wants to admit at the trial the witness's identification of the defendant from the photo array. The defendant's attorney objects to the introduction of the statement, but the prosecutor claims that as a prior statement of identification, it is admissible.

Is the statement admissible as a prior statement of identification?

A. Yes, because prior statements of identification are admissible as non-hearsay.

B. Yes, because the witness is unavailable to testify.

C. No, because the witness did not testify at the present trial.

D. No, because the witness did not testify under oath at a previous trial, hearing, or deposition as to the identity of the murderer.

QUESTION 2

A man told his girlfriend that he was planning to rob a 24-hour convenience store and would split the proceeds from the robbery if she agreed to drive the getaway car. The girlfriend agreed and drove the man to the store so he could commit the robbery. While holding up the cashier in the store, the man's gun went off accidentally, killing the cashier. The man left through the exit at the back of the store, leaving the girlfriend in the car outside the store to be arrested when the police arrived.

For which of the following crimes may the girlfriend properly be convicted and punished?

A. Robbery only.

B. Murder only.

C. Both robbery and murder.

D. Neither robbery nor murder.

QUESTION 3

A state board of transportation ordered a railroad company to sell a parcel of land adjoining its railroad track. The parcel in question had been part of a much larger section of land transferred a number of years before from the state to the railroad company in exchange for the company's provision of railroad services to the citizens of the state. The state board fixed a reasonable price based on the land's fair market value to compensate the railroad company for the loss of its land. The railroad refused to sell the land to the designated buyer, a farmer's cooperative. The private cooperative planned to build a warehouse on the land in order to store its members' produce for shipment by rail and other means.

In an action to compel the railroad to comply with the order of the state board, should the court rule in favor of the state board?

A. Yes, because the railroad is a regulated by the state board of transportation.

B. Yes, because the price set by the board constitutes just compensation.

C. No, because the order violates the Fourteenth Amendment's incorporation of the Fifth Amendment.

D. No, because the order originated with a state board rather than a state legislature.

QUESTION 4

After his car broke down on the side of a country road, a driver wandered onto an adjacent property to seek the use of a telephone. Unbeknownst to the driver, the property owner bred large dogs. The particular breed has a reputation for being dangerous, and members of the breed are typically used as watchdogs. The specific dogs owned by this breeder, however, are known among nearby residents as being extremely friendly. The driver climbed over a large wooden fence to reach the property. Once the dogs spotted the driver, three of the largest dogs ran to greet him, though he assumed the dogs planned to attack. Excessively frightened, the driver attempted to jump over a nearby barbed-wire fence and severely cut his legs. When the dogs finally reached the man, they did nothing more than lick his face until their owner arrived. The driver sued the owner under a strict liability theory for the damages resulting from his injury.

Is the driver likely to succeed in his suit?

A. Yes, because the injury was caused by the driver's reaction to a dangerous propensity that is characteristic of the breed of dog.

B. Yes, because landowners are strictly liable for injuries inflicted by their animals.

C. No, because the driver was an undiscovered trespasser.

D. No, because the owner was not negligent.

QUESTION 5

The buyer of a home was unable to secure financing from a bank for the full amount of the purchase price set by the seller. The seller agreed to accept cash from the buyer for 10 percent of the purchase price and the buyer's note for 10 percent of the purchase price. Upon being informed of this arrangement, the bank agreed to loan the buyer the remaining 80 percent. Both the seller and the bank secured their interests through mortgages on the home, with the exchange of documents between all three parties at closing. The bank recorded its mortgage, but the seller did not record his mortgage. Subsequently, the buyer defaulted on both its loan obligation to the bank and the note to the seller. Both the bank and the seller joined in a foreclosure action. The proceeds do not fully cover the buyer's obligations to both the bank and the seller. The jurisdiction has enacted the following statute: "No conveyance or mortgage of real property shall be good against subsequent purchasers for value and without notice unless the same be first recorded according to law."

Which of the following statements accurately describes the priorities of the bank and the seller to the proceeds?

A. The bank has priority to the proceeds, because the seller failed to record his mortgage.

B. The bank has priority to the proceeds, because it recorded its mortgage.

C. The seller has priority to the proceeds, because the seller financed the purchase of the home.

D. The seller is entitled to 1/9 of the proceeds and the bank is entitled to 8/9 of the proceeds, because both received their mortgages in the same proceeding.

QUESTION 6

A shareholder in a closely held corporation brought an action against the corporation to compel it to make a $100,000 distribution that had been authorized by the board of directors. The shareholder filed the action in a federal district court for the state in which the corporation was incorporated and had its principal place of business. The shareholder was born and grew up in a neighboring state, but recently moved to a foreign country with the intent to live there permanently, but with no intent to surrender her United States citizenship or acquire foreign citizenship. Does the court have subject-matter jurisdiction over this action?

A. Yes, because the shareholder is domiciled in a foreign country.

B. Yes, because the shareholder is a United States citizen.

C. No, because diversity jurisdiction does not exist.

D. No, because the corporation is not a federal corporation.

QUESTION 7

While putting out a large fire in an office building downtown, firefighters discovered evidence of arson and immediately called police to the scene. The police began questioning bystanders who had gathered outside of the firefighters' perimeter in an effort to determine whether any of them had seen something suspicious that might lead to the arrest of the arsonist. Many of the bystanders were cooperative, but some declined to provide any information, and a few even chose to walk away when the police began asking them questions. One bystander who did stay and talk to the police made the police suspicious. When one of the officers detected the smell of gasoline on the suspect, the officer mentioned that whoever had set the building on fire had used gasoline as an accelerant. The suspect immediately confessed, and the police arrested him. The suspect's defense attorney filed a motion to suppress the crime scene confession, as the officer did not give the suspect his Miranda warnings before questioning him.

The court should:

A. Grant the motion, because the officer knew his statement was likely to elicit an incriminating response.

B. Grant the motion, because once the officer suspected the suspect of the crime, he should have stopped and given the suspect Miranda warnings before the interrogation began.

C. Deny the motion, because the questioning was not conducted in a police station or while the suspect was under arrest.

D. Deny the motion, because the suspect was not in the custody of the police, and was free to leave the presence of the questioning officer.

QUESTION 8

A defendant was charged with burglary. At trial, the defendant's girlfriend testified that she was at home with the defendant when the alleged burglary occurred. Following the girlfriend's testimony, the prosecution called the girlfriend's colleague to the stand. The colleague testified that he believed the girlfriend was a liar, and gave several examples of instances in which she had lied about her progress on projects that they had worked on together. The defense objected to the colleague's testimony. The judge ruled that the witness's testimony that he believed the girlfriend was a liar was admissible, but that the testimony regarding her lying about work projects was inadmissible. On cross-examination, the defense questioned the colleague about a time when the girlfriend found and returned the colleague's lost wallet. The prosecution objected, and the judge sustained the objection, excluding the testimony about the wallet.

Which of the judge's rulings was in error?

A. The judge did not err in any of the above rulings.

B. The judge erred in excluding the colleague's testimony regarding the lost wallet.

C. The judge erred in excluding the colleague's testimony that the girlfriend lied about her progress on work projects.

D. The judge erred in admitting the colleague's testimony that he believed the girlfriend was a liar.

QUESTION 9

The plaintiff, a State N citizen, properly invokes a State M federal court's diversity jurisdiction in a tort suit against the defendant, an airplane manufacturer based in State M. The plaintiff credibly alleges that he was severely injured when the defendant's airplane crashed as a result of an improperly installed engine part. During discovery, the plaintiff learns that an employee of the defendant who installed engine parts at the time the plane was manufactured was an alcoholic whose drinking may have impaired his work. The defendant fired the employee before the plane crash that injured the plaintiff. What discovery device may the plaintiff use to obtain more information from the former employee?

A. An oral deposition.

B. An interrogatory.

C. A physical examination.

D. A request for admission.

QUESTION 10

A defendant was charged with burglary of a store and faced up to 25 years of imprisonment. At the trial, the prosecution called a critical witness who had contacted the police after the burglary and supplied information for the defendant's arrest. The witness testified that he lived near the store and that he saw the defendant outside the store just after the crime occurred. On cross-examination, the defense attempted to show that the witness had a motive to lie in order to divert suspicion away from himself. The defense sought to impeach the witness by questioning him about his juvenile conviction for breaking and entering another neighborhood store two years ago, for which the witness was currently on probation.

May the defense properly question the witness about the juvenile adjudication?

A. No, because it is a juvenile adjudication.

B. No, because the witness is on probation with regard to the juvenile adjudication.

C. Yes, because the juvenile adjudication is being used to show the witness's motive.

D. Yes, because the defendant was charged with a crime that was punishable by imprisonment for more than one year.

QUESTION 11

A plaintiff sued a defendant for injuries resulting from alleged negligence by the defendant in an automobile accident. On direct examination, the plaintiff described the circumstances surrounding the accident and testified that the defendant's car was blue. On cross-examination, the defendant's attorney showed the plaintiff pictures of the accident scene taken by the police that indicate that the defendant's car was actually black. In

rebuttal, the plaintiff's attorney calls the plaintiff's boss as a witness to testify that she has known the plaintiff for ten years, and that in her opinion the plaintiff is a truthful person. The defendant objects to the introduction of this evidence.

Should the judge admit the boss's statement over the defendant's objection?

A. No, because the boss's statement does not discuss the plaintiff's reputation for truth and veracity.

B. No, because the plaintiff's character was not attacked.

C. Yes, because it is properly in the form of opinion evidence.

D. Yes, because it tends to show that the plaintiff is an honest person.

QUESTION 12

An independent truck driver often received assignments to transport cargo for a delivery company. The driver was one of the delivery company's most reliable contractors. When the driver was in need of a new truck, the delivery company contracted with a truck manufacturer to purchase the truck on an installment basis. The manufacturer retained a security interest in the truck until all payments were made. The contract between the delivery company and the manufacturer provided that the delivery company "shall not assign this contract without the prior written consent" of the manufacturer. Nonetheless, the delivery company assigned the contract, in writing, to the truck driver. The truck driver made all payments on the truck for two years until she was involved in a serious collision that destroyed the truck. The insurance proceeds on the destroyed truck were paid to the manufacturer. After the manufacturer used the proceeds to satisfy the contract balance, $20,000 remained. The truck driver delivered a copy of the assignment to the manufacturer, and demanded the remainder of the proceeds. The truck manufacturer stated that the contract was non-assignable, and that it would only pay the proceeds to the delivery company. The truck driver then filed suit to compel the truck manufacturer to pay her the proceeds.

Is she likely to succeed?

A. Yes, because the written assignment from the delivery company to the truck driver was a novation.

B. Yes, because the contract was assigned to the truck driver.

C. No, because the contract between the delivery company and the truck manufacturer was non-assignable.

D. No, because the truck driver was merely an incidental beneficiary of the contract between the delivery company and the truck manufacturer.

QUESTION 13

A business operates a daycare center for pets. Employees of the business transport pets from their homes to the center and back again. One day after obtaining a large poodle from a client's home, an employee drove the business's van back to the daycare center. Less than a mile before reaching the center, he realized the poodle vomited in the van and all over the employee's coat. Rather than returning directly to the center, the employee pulled into a carwash to clean the van, and then drove to a dry cleaner across the street from the carwash to drop off his coat before returning to work. When exiting the dry cleaner's parking lot, the employee turned around to console the sick poodle and drove into the car in front of him. He severely damaged the car, but the poodle sustained no injuries.

Would the business be liable to the car owner for the actions of the employee?

A. Yes, because the employee's trip to the dry cleaner was not a substantial deviation.

B. Yes, because the employee was within a mile of the daycare center.

C. No, because this deviation by the employee absolved the business of liability.

D. No, because the employee did not go directly to and from the client's home.

QUESTION 14

A mining company contracted with a railroad to transport 10,000 tons of coal from the company's mines to a power company at a cost of $100,000. The railroad told the mining company that the coal would arrive at the power company on June 1st, but the contract contained a clause that the railroad would not be liable for any losses suffered by the mining company as a result of a late shipment. The railroad was aware that the mining company had contracted with the power company to deliver the coal on June 1st, and pursuant to standard industry custom, the price to be paid by the power company decreased by $1 per ton for each day that the coal was late. The shipment of coal did not reach the power company until June 10, and the railroad had no justification for the 10-day delay. Because of the delay, the mining company lost $100,000 in revenue from the sale. The mining company filed suit against the railroad for breach of contract, claiming $100,000 in damages.

Is the mining company likely to succeed in its claim?

A. Yes, because the damages that the mining company would suffer from the railroad's delay were known to the railroad prior to shipment of the coal.

B. Yes, because consequential damages cannot be excluded by a merchant.

C. No, because the claimed damages are disproportionate to the original contract price between the railroad and the mining company.

D. No, because the contract between the mining company and the railroad protected the railroad from losses suffered by the mining company due to a late shipment.

QUESTION 15

A group of parents of public school students proposed a new school rule that would require teachers to begin each school day by standing for a minute of silent prayer before lessons began. The rule would not require the teachers or students to pray during the minute of silent prayer, but would require teachers to say, "Please stand for a minute of silent prayer." Students who did not wish to participate could remain seated.

Would the school rule be constitutional?

A. No, because the rule violates the Establishment Clause of the First Amendment.

B. No, because the rule is not rationally related to any neutral law of general applicability.

C. Yes, because none of the students would be required to participate.

D. Yes, because parents of the students, and not the school board, wish to implement the rule.

QUESTION 16

A large utility company was located inside State A. The company burned coal to produce electricity, some of which was used within the state, but the majority of which was provided to neighboring states. In order to fund clean-up efforts made necessary as a result of burning coal, State A taxed the electricity the utility provided to its customers based on the amount used. Accordingly, even though some tax revenue came from electricity provided to State A residents, most of the tax revenue came from out-of-state residents. Residents of neighboring State B challenged State A's tax as unconstitutional, claiming that the tax disproportionately affected nonresident individuals.

Assuming that Congress has not directly acted in the area, is the court most likely to find the tax constitutional or unconstitutional?

A. Constitutional, as a proper ad valorem tax.

B. Constitutional, as a proper state tax that comports with the Commerce Clause.

C. Unconstitutional, as a violation of the Privileges and Immunities Clause of Article IV.

D. Unconstitutional, as a violation of the Equal Protection Clause of the Fourteenth Amendment.

QUESTION 17

A 22-year-old defendant was charged with voluntary manslaughter. At the trial, the defendant testified on his own behalf. On cross-examination, in order to impeach the defendant's character for truthfulness, the prosecution sought to question the defendant about being adjudicated delinquent with respect to a burglary when he was 16 years old. If prosecuted as an adult, the defendant could have been subject to up to 25 years of imprisonment.

Should the court permit the prosecution to introduce such evidence?

A. No, because a defendant-witness's character for truthfulness may not be impeached by a juvenile adjudication.

B. No, because burglary is not a crime involving proof of a dishonest act or false statement.

C. Yes, because not more than 10 years have passed since the adjudication.

D. Yes, because an adult witness may be impeached with evidence that he was adjudicated delinquent with respect to a burglary as a minor.

QUESTION 18

An auto manufacturer contracted with a supplier to provide speakers for 10,000 vehicles at a total price of $600,000. Prior to the date fixed for delivery of the speakers, the supplier, without justification, informed the manufacturer that it could not supply the speakers. The manufacturer immediately sought quotes from other suppliers. The manufacturer received a quote from a second supplier, who had previously provided the manufacturer with speakers in a timely and satisfactory manner, to sell 10,000 speakers for $800,000. A short time later, the manufacturer received an offer from a third supplier: with whom the manufacturer had not previously worked: to supply the 10,000 speakers for $600,000. The manufacturer, reasonably concerned that the third supplier would be unable to provide the speakers in a timely and satisfactory manner, entered into a contract with the second supplier. Subsequently, the first supplier told the manufacturer that it would be able to supply the speakers by the original delivery date and, although not requested by the manufacturer, provided the manufacturer with adequate evidence that the speakers would be timely delivered. The manufacturer told the first supplier not to deliver the goods and instead acquired them from the second supplier. The auto manufacturer sued the first supplier for $200,000.

Should the auto manufacturer prevail?

A. Yes, because the auto manufacturer is entitled to recover the cost of acquiring substitute speakers.

B. Yes, because the first supplier had repudiated its contractual obligation.

C. No, because the auto manufacturer was required to mitigate its damages by accepting the third supplier's lower offer.

D. No, because the first supplier withdrew its repudiation prior to the time for performance.

QUESTION 19

A homeowner hired a roofer to install a new roof on his house. The homeowner scheduled the installation to take place during a week when he was to be on vacation. Although the contract specified that the color of the shingles was to be brown, the homeowner returned to find that the roofer instead had installed red shingles.

Although the new roof was structurally sound, the homeowner refused the pay the roofer. The roofer sued the homeowner. The fact-finder determined that the roofer had materially breached the contract.

Under what theory of damages is the roofer most likely to recover?

A. Expectancy damages

B. Restitution damages

C. Reliance damages

D. None, because the roofer materially breached the contract.

QUESTION 20

A plaintiff filed suit in federal district court under diversity jurisdiction, asserting a state-law claim against two co-defendants for civil fraud in a business transaction. Each defendant's attorney indicated that she sought to depose eight different witnesses, for a total of 16 witness depositions by the defense. The plaintiff declined to stipulate that the defendants can take more than 10 depositions.

Do the Federal Rules of Civil Procedure allow all 16 depositions?

A. Yes, the defense may automatically depose all 16 witnesses.

B. Yes, the defense may depose the 16 witnesses with the approval of the court.

C. No, the defense may not depose the 16 witnesses without the plaintiff's agreement.

D. No, the defense is subject to an absolute limit of 10 depositions in an action based on diversity jurisdiction.

QUESTION 21

A state university's discrimination policy includes a provision that no on-campus organization may discriminate against any student on the basis of race or gender by refusing to admit that student to the organization. A group of students filed paperwork with the student activities office to be approved as an on-campus organization for students of a certain religion. The organization was granted the right to organize on campus and functions for a year with the approval of the university, which audits each on-campus organization's admission procedures every six months. When the organization attempts to be recertified the following year, however, its request is denied, despite the results of a concurrent, school-wide audit determining that no discrimination of any sort had occurred within the organization over the past year. The university's reasoning is that the entire organization was comprised only of students of one race at the time of the organization's recertification application and therefore violated the university's discrimination policy.

Would the university's denial of the recertification be proper?

A. Yes, because the organization is clearly violating the university's discrimination policy.

B. Yes, because the university can deny all applications.

C. No, because there is no discrimination on the part of the organization.

D. No, because the state cannot restrict the organization's freedom of association.

QUESTION 22

The owner of a mine and a wealthy friend were having lunch in a restaurant. The owner had operated the mine as a successful business for a number of years and planned to continue to do so indefinitely, but was always boasting to friends that he could sell the business for far more than its asset value. On this occasion, the owner stated to the friend that he would sell her his business for $15 million, even though its assets were only worth $10 million. The friend responded "If that's your best offer, I can't accept it." The owner then wrote on a napkin, "I, Owner, hereby offer to sell my mining business to Friend, for $15 million." The friend took the

napkin, wrote, "I accept your offer," then signed her name and pocketed the napkin. Nothing more was said about the sale. The next day, the friend, upon learning that a valuable vein had been discovered in the mine that day, contacted the owner. The owner refused to transfer the mine to his friend.

In a breach of contract action by the friend against the mine owner, which of the following is the owner's best defense to this action?

A. The owner did not intend to sell his mining business.

B. The friend did not reasonably believe that the owner intended to sell his mining business.

C. The writing by the owner was not sufficiently definite to constitute an offer.

D. The friend had rejected the owner's offer to sell his mining business for $15 million.

QUESTION 23

An aspiring singer moved into a house in a suburban subdivision. The singer was a member or a heavy metal band, and decided to use the garage of his new house as a rehearsal space. The band members had conflicting schedules, and the only time they could all practice was between 4 a.m. and 7 a.m. Five mornings a week, the band practiced in his garage during that time. The music could be heard clearly in all of the homes on the cul-de-sac where the singer lived. Many of the singer's neighbors complained because the music kept them awake, but the singer ignored these complaints. The singer's neighbor, who was hard of hearing, could not hear the music clearly and was not woken by the music. Nonetheless, he disliked the singer and his band members, and he has sued the singer for nuisance. The singer has moved for summary judgment, arguing that the neighbor cannot prove that there was a substantial interference with his use and enjoyment of his property.

Is the singer likely to prevail in his summary judgment motion?

A. No, because the noise would be offense or annoying to a normal, reasonable person in the community.

B. No, because the utility of the conduct does not outweigh the harm.

C. Yes, because a homeowner may use his home for any purposes not prohibited by zoning ordinances.

D. Yes, because the noise is not offensive or annoying to the neighbor.

QUESTION 24

A skier was riding on a ski lift at a large resort. Passengers on the lift were seated on chairs, and were secured onto the chairs with lap bars. While riding on the lift, the skier's cell phone rang in her pocket, and she momentarily removed her lap bar to reach the phone. While the lap bar was unfastened, the ski lift suddenly malfunctioned, jerking the skier forward and out of her seat. She fell 15 feet to the ground and, as a result, suffered a broken leg. Several other passengers on the lift were also seriously injured as a result of the accident. The ski lift was manufactured, maintained, and operated by a large ski lift corporation. The skier sued the ski lift corporation in a jurisdiction that applies contributory negligence rules. At trial, the skier could produce no direct evidence of negligence on the part of the ski lift corporation, but claimed that her injury could not have occurred without their negligence.

Which of the following questions will not be at issue in this negligence action?

A. Would the skier's injury have occurred if she had not removed the lap bar?

B. Did any outside parties have access to the ski lift machinery?

C. Would the skier's injury have occurred if the ski lift corporation exercised reasonable care?

D. Were the skier's actions the primary cause of the accident?

QUESTION 25

An alien actor was under contract to film a movie in the United States. The actor was a well-known supporter of a political group in his country that had executed various attacks on United States citizens living abroad. The actor publicly stated that he did not condone violence and offered no financial support to the group following such incidents. When the actor attempted to enter the United States, he was refused entry by a federal customs officer pursuant to a federal statute that denies any supporter of the political group entry into the United States.

Is this refusal valid?

A. Yes, because aliens have no absolute right to enter the United States.

B. Yes, because aliens can be deported if a notice and hearing has occurred.

C. No, because the refusal of entry discriminates on the basis of political beliefs.

D. No, because the refusal impairs the actor's contractual obligation.

QUESTION 26

A rash of home burglaries occurred in a single neighborhood, all occurring during the week around lunchtime. Multiple neighbors of the burglary victims reported seeing a blue SUV with a cracked windshield parked outside of the residences, with someone in the driver seat of the vehicle who appeared to be acting as a look-out. Because of the increase in burglaries, the police were looking for a vehicle that matched this description. A police officer, while patrolling the neighborhood around lunchtime, spotted a blue SUV with a cracked windshield parked outside a residence with the defendant sitting in the driver's seat. The officer approached the vehicle and asked the defendant to get out. The officer then began to question the defendant about his activities. The defendant admitted that he was a look-out for his friend, who was in the residence stealing valuables. Both the defendant and his friend were arrested for burglary.

At trial, the defendant moved to suppress his confession.

Should the defendant's motion to suppress be granted?

A. No, because the police officer had probable cause to question the defendant.

B. No, because the police officer had reasonable suspicion the defendant was involved in criminal activity.

C. Yes, because the police officer did not have probable cause to detain the defendant.

D. Yes, because the police officer did not read the defendant his Miranda rights before questioning him.

QUESTION 27

An adult daughter called a local restaurant to place a large delivery order. The restaurant generally requires a credit card for all delivery orders, but the daughter's father, who is a regular at the restaurant and happened to be there when the daughter placed the order, told the clerk that, in the event the daughter failed to pay for the food, he would do so. The restaurant delivered the order to the daughter, who, having decided to order something else instead, refused to accept or pay for the food.

Can the restaurant collect from the father?

A. No, because the father's promise was made orally.

B. No, because a third party will not be held liable for the contract obligations of another.

C. Yes, because the father promised to pay.

D. Yes, because a parent is liable to pay for necessities provided to a child.

QUESTION 28

An employee sued her former employer after she was fired. At trial, the employee argued that when she was hired she had signed an employment contract that stated that she could be fired only for cause. The employer argued that the parties had never signed an employment contract, and that the employee was an at-will employee. The employer stipulated that there was not cause to discharge the employee, because she performed her job in a satisfactory manner. Rather, the CEO testified that, as part of a downsizing effort, he had approved the discharge of all at-will employees in the department where the employee worked. At trial, the employee sought to question the CEO about a conversation in which the CEO told the employee that he was happy with her performance. The employer objected to admission of the testimony.

Is the CEO's testimony likely to be admitted?

A. No, because the testimony is hearsay not within any exception.

B. No, because the evidence is not probative and material.

C. Yes, because the evidence does not constitute hearsay.

D. Yes, because the probative value outweighs any danger of unfair prejudice.

QUESTION 29

The plaintiff, a State D citizen, is a shareholder of a corporation incorporated and having its principal place of business in State D. She brought an action in the U.S. District Court in State D requesting an injunction against the corporation, which allegedly was violating a State D law that required corporations to invest only in lawful commercial paper and that gave shareholders a right to sue over alleged violations of this law. The plaintiff claims that the defendant corporation had been purchasing commercial paper that had been issued by the federal government in violation of the U.S. Constitution. The corporation denies this claim and moves to dismiss on the ground that the U.S. District Court lacks jurisdiction.

What would the court be most likely to do?

A. Exercise general federal-question jurisdiction because federal law created the plaintiff's cause of action.

B. Exercise general federal-question jurisdiction because the plaintiff has a real and substantial issue of federal law and her right to relief depends upon the resolution of this issue.

C. Dismiss for lack of jurisdiction because the plaintiff's claim arose under state law because state law created her cause of action, and there is no diversity of citizenship.

D. Dismiss for lack of jurisdiction because shareholders cannot sue their corporations in federal court, except for violations of federal securities law.

QUESTION 30

A public university adopted the following policy: In order to be recognized as a student organization with rights to school facilities and funds, an organization must permit any student to be a member regardless of the student's status or beliefs. One student organization was a local chapter of a national organization that restricted membership in local chapters to members of a particular religious sect and denied membership to homosexual individuals.

May the university apply its policy to the student religious group?

A. No, because the policy violates the First Amendment Free Exercise Clause.

B. No, because the policy violates the First Amendment Freedom of Association Clause.

C. Yes, because a public university is free to allocate its funds among student groups in any rational manner it sees fit.

D. Yes, because a public university is a limited public forum and the policy is content neutral.

QUESTION 31

Federal agents were investigating a drug trafficking ring. The agents received reliable information that the drug ring used a drug dealer's basement as the primary storage site for their drugs. Relying on this information, the agents obtained a warrant to search the drug dealer's basement for drugs and related paraphernalia. After failing to find any evidence in the basement, the agents searched the drug dealer's bedroom and seized a notebook they found on the dresser. The notebook contained a ledger, with the names of the drug dealer's suppliers and clients, as well as statements of their accounts. One of the drug dealer's suppliers named in the ledger was later arrested, charged, and tried jointly with the drug dealer. The drug dealer's supplier seeks to suppress evidence of the ledger at trial, arguing that the seizure of the ledger was illegal.

Should the judge grant the supplier's motion?

A. No, because the supplier lacks standing to challenge the seizure of the ledger.

B. No, because the ledger was seized legally.

C. Yes, because the ledger was not specifically named in the warrant.

D. Yes, because the agents exceeded the scope of the warrant when they searched the drug dealer's bedroom.

QUESTION 32

A restaurant posted a flyer in its serving room, which states: "Take the All-You-Can-Eat Challenge! Any person who can finish five entrées from our dinner menu in less than one hour dines free for a year!" A customer saw the flyer and ordered five entrées. As the customer started on his fifth entrée, the restaurant manager tore down the flyer in full view of the restaurant patrons and the customer, and said "Deal's off!" The customer finished all five entrées in 59 minutes. When the manager told the customer that he would not be able to dine free for a year, the customer refused to pay for the five entrées.

If the restaurant does not let the customer dine free for a year, does the customer have a claim against the restaurant?

A. No, because the restaurant manager effectively withdrew the offer before the customer completed the five entrées.

B. No, because the customer did not pay for the five entrées.

C. Yes, because the restaurant could not revoke its offer once the customer had commenced performance.

D. Yes, because the customer's ordering of five entrées constituted acceptance of the restaurant's offer.

QUESTION 33

The plaintiff, a State X citizen, is a stock broker in a State X branch of a brokerage firm that has its principal place of business in State Y. The plaintiff, whose performance consistently places her in the top quarter of her firm, earns $75,000 a year. She did not get promoted to a partnership at her firm, which would guarantee her a minimum compensation of $200,000 annually. Instead, she was offered a "Senior Broker" position at $100,000 a year. The plaintiff believes that the firm's decision was motivated by her ethnic background. The local office has 100 partners (96 are State A citizens), but only one partner is of the plaintiff's same ethnic background, even though over 10 percent of the local population is. She sued the firm in State X's federal district court and alleged that the firm's actions violated both (1) state contract law and (2) a federal statute granting employees a cause of action in federal court against employers who allegedly discriminate based on race or ethnicity. The firm objected on the ground that the court lacks jurisdiction.

What is the most likely result?

A. The court has federal-question jurisdiction to decide the federal law claim, but not the state contract claim, which must be brought in state court because of federalism concerns.

B. The court has diversity jurisdiction to decide the state contract claim, and federal-question jurisdiction to decide the federal law claim.

C. The court has federal-question jurisdiction to decide the federal law claim, and can assert supplemental jurisdiction over the state contract claim.

D. The court must decline to exercise jurisdiction until the state courts resolve the plaintiff's state law contract claim.

QUESTION 34

A man and his friend were at a bar when the friend confessed to the man that the friend had been secretly dating the man's sister. The man became very angry and hit his friend. The bartender quickly stepped in between the two men. The man, intending to hit his friend again, accidentally hit the bartender's arm. The bartender was left with a bruise on his arm, but did not sustain any other injury. The bartender has sued the man for battery.

Is the bartender likely to prevail in a battery action against the man?

A. No, because the bartender was not seriously injured.

B. No, because the man did not intend to hit the bartender.

C. Yes, because the man intended to hit his friend but actually hit and injured the bartender.

D. Yes, because the bartender was a foreseeable plaintiff.

QUESTION 35

A farmer purchased a tract of farmland adjacent to a factory. For months, the factory had emitted a foul-smelling chemical cloud that hovered approximately one foot over the farmland. The farmer invited the factory foreman to his farmland to show him the damage the chemical cloud was doing to his land. The foreman informed the farmer that there was nothing he could do, and that the previous landowner had not complained about the cloud. The farmer brought suit against the factory for trespass to his land.

Will the farmer's trespass suit against the factory be successful?

A. No, because nothing is physically touching the farmer's property.

B. No, because the factory was in operation and producing the cloud before the farmer purchased the land.

C. Yes, because the chemical cloud constitutes a physical invasion of the property.

D. Yes, because the factory's agent, the foreman, physically entered the farmers property.

QUESTION 36

A public school teacher's employment was terminated after she announced her pregnancy. During a post-termination hearing, the school relied on a state statute allowing for the "discharge of any employee based on physical limitations preventing full performance of his or her job duties." The teacher was only two months pregnant at the time of her announcement, and there was no indication that she would have a difficult pregnancy. The teacher sued in state court on the basis that she had no physical limitation preventing her from performing her job and that the statute was in conflict with federal law. In the court's opinion, which reinstated the teacher, the court analyzed the state statute in light of federal law regarding a variety of issues related to discrimination, employment practices, and public employment, but failed to clearly indicate the basis for its decision. On appeal, the decision was affirmed per curiam by the highest court of the state. The school district appealed the decision to the Supreme Court.

If the Supreme Court were to review this case, what would be the most likely reason allowing such review?

A. The school did not discriminate against the teacher.

B. The state court decision relied on federal law.

C. The Supreme Court is required to hear the case.

D. The state court decision incorrectly applied state law.

QUESTION 37

A brother and sister own parcels of adjacent property. Their father had owned the land in its entirety, and when the siblings graduated from college, he split his estate in two and gave each sibling a parcel. The brother's property was landlocked, so his sister granted him an easement over her property in order to access the sole public road. The easement was not recorded. Five years later, the brother, having never set foot on his parcel, sold it to his sister. The sister eventually resold this parcel to a stranger, after telling the stranger about the easement she had granted her brother. Shortly thereafter, she sold her own parcel to a colleague. The stranger seeks access over the colleague's parcel in order to reach the public road, but the colleague refuses.

Does the stranger have a right to an easement across the colleague's parcel?

A. No, because the brother's easement was not recorded.

B. No, because the brother's easement was extinguished upon the sister's acquisition of her brother's parcel.

C. Yes, because the stranger requires an easement by necessity.

D. Yes, because the colleague had notice of the brother's easement.

QUESTION 38

During military drills that occurred during a severe storm, a military jet was forced to make an emergency landing. As there were no airports nearby, the jet was forced to land on a farmer's property. The landing destroyed acres of growing crops, resulting in a substantial economic loss for the farmer. The landing destroyed not only the growing crops (which he intended to sell months later), but also the possibility of growing further crops for the rest of the season. However, the farmer will be able to plant crops the following spring as normal. The farmer filed suit under constitutional law principles on the basis that he is owed just compensation for the value he would have been able to receive months later when selling the crops. He has not yet filed any tort claim related to the destruction of his crops.

Which of the following amounts would constitute the most likely amount to be received by the farmer based on the current suit?

A. The value of the crops at the time they were destroyed, because the action constituted a taking.

B. The value of the crops at the time they would be sold, because the actions constituted a taking.

C. Nothing, because the farmer was not planning to sell the crops when they were destroyed by the landing.

D. Nothing, because the landing would not constitute a taking.

QUESTION 39

Two brothers received land when their father left it to them in his will. The will contained the following provision, "because I want each of my boys to pass his share of the land to their children upon his death, I want them to hold this land as joint tenants." Neither brother wanted to sell the property, but one brother did mortgage his interest in the property. The property is located in a lien theory state.

What kind of co-tenancy do the brothers have in the land?

A. A joint tenancy, because the father expressly created one in his will.

B. A tenancy in common by default, because the will failed to create a joint tenancy.

C. A tenancy by the entirety, because they are siblings.

D. No co-tenancy, because any co-tenancy was destroyed when one brother mortgaged his interest in the property.

QUESTION 40

A man was the owner of Blackacre, an undeveloped city lot. The owner and a buyer executed a written document in which the owner agreed to sell Blackacre to the buyer and the buyer agreed to buy Blackacre from owner for $100,000; the document did not provide for an earnest money down payment. The owner recorded the document, as authorized by statute. The owner orally gave the buyer permission to park his car on Blackacre without charge prior to the closing. Thereafter, the buyer frequently parked his car on Blackacre. Another property came on the market that the buyer wanted more than Blackacre. The buyer decided to try to escape any obligation to the owner of Blackacre. The buyer had been told that contracts for the purchase and sale of real property require consideration and concluded that because he had made no earnest money down payment, he could refuse to close and not be liable. The buyer notified the owner of his intention not to close and, in fact, did refuse to close on the date set for the closing. The owner brought an appropriate action to compel specific performance by the buyer.

If the owner wins, it will be because

A. the buyer's use of Blackacre for parking constitutes part performance.

B. general contract rules regarding consideration apply to real estate contracts.

C. the doctrine of equitable conversion applies.

D. the document was recorded.

QUESTION 41

The owner of a convenience store was in the back of his store when he heard a loud noise. When he walked to the front of the store to determine the cause of the commotion, he saw that a large pile of canned goods had just fallen. Around that time, a woman walked into the store wearing a large coat despite the warm weather outside. The woman was bedraggled and smelled of liquor. The owner correctly ascertained that the woman neither caused the canned goods to fall nor stole anything. However, he assumed that she entered the store intending to steal. The owner therefore ordered the woman to go to the back office, where he questioned her for two hours. While he left the door to both the office and the store unlocked, he continually threatened that if the woman did not comply with questioning or left the room, he would have her arrested the next time he saw her around his store. The woman was obviously confused and anxious but never left or asked to leave the room at any point.

Would the owner's actions constitute false imprisonment?

A. Yes, because the questioning lasted for over two hours.

B. Yes, because the owner's actions were not reasonable.

C. No, because the woman was not confined or restrained.

D. No, because the woman was a suspected shoplifter.

QUESTION 42

An attorney represented a client in a legal battle over a valuable necklace that had belonged to the client's deceased grandmother. The attorney told the client, who had possession of the necklace, that the client was legally required to leave the necklace with the attorney until the legal issues were resolved. In fact, there was no such requirement. Rather, the lawyer intended to sell the necklace and retire on a small island where the lawyer believed she would never be found. After the client gave the necklace to the lawyer, the lawyer sold the necklace to a jeweler. The jeweler, who had known the grandmother, later recognized the necklace as the grandmother's, and he called the police. The attorney was arrested at the airport later that day.

The attorney is guilty of which of the following crimes?

A. Embezzlement.

B. False pretenses.

C. Larceny.

D. Larceny by trick.

QUESTION 43

The defendant robbed a convenience store while wearing a ski mask to hide his identity. In an attempt to wrestle the gun from the defendant, the clerk removed the defendant's mask, saw the defendant's face, and was subsequently shot. Police apprehended the defendant, and the defendant was subsequently charged and appointed an attorney. The clerk remained hospitalized for weeks. While the clerk was in the hospital, a police officer visited the clerk. The officer asked the clerk if he would recognize the robber, and the clerk replied, "Of course. He came in to buy cigarettes almost every day." The officer told the clerk that the defendant had been arrested for the robbery, and that the police had found the gun used in the robbery in the defendant's car. The officer then showed the defendant's picture to the clerk. The clerk confirmed that the defendant was the robber. Shortly before trial, the clerk died from an infection related to the shooting. The defendant has moved to suppress the clerk's identification.

Is the defendant's motion likely to be granted?

A. No, because the clerk is unavailable to testify.

B. No, because the identification was reliable.

C. Yes, because the defendant was entitled to have his attorney present for the identification.

D. Yes, because the identification procedures were unnecessarily suggestive.

QUESTION 44

A traffic accident victim initiated a diversity action for damages stemming from an accident against a truck driver and the corporation who had hired him as an independent contractor for a one-time delivery, to fill in for their own truck driver, who had fallen ill. The victim filed the complaint, which was based on negligence with regard to the truck driver and respondeat superior with respect to the corporation, in the federal district court for State A, the state in which the accident occurred. The truck driver was transporting equipment from State B, the state of incorporation and principal place of business of the corporation, to State C, where the corporation was opening a new plant. The corporation had no business dealings in State A. The victim is a citizen of State D. The forum state has a long-arm statute that permits a state court to exercise personal jurisdiction to the extent permitted by the Due Process Clause of the Fourteenth Amendment to the U.S. Constitution.

What is the corporation's best argument that the court lacks personal jurisdiction over it?

A. The minimum contacts test cannot not be satisfied due to the corporation's lack of business dealings in State A.

B. The victim is not a citizen of State A.

C. The corporation had not purposefully availed itself of the benefits and laws of State A.

D. The truck driver was an independent contractor, rather than an employee of the corporation.

QUESTION 45

A retailer received a written firm offer signed by a supplier. The offer committed the supplier to providing the retailer with up to 10,000 tubes of toothpaste over the next 45 days at $1 a tube. Thirty days later, the supplier informed the retailer that the price per tube of toothpaste would be $1.10. The next day the retailer ordered 6,000 tubes of toothpaste from the supplier, which the supplier promptly shipped. Sixty days after the receipt of the offer, the retailer ordered another 4,000 tubes of toothpaste, which the supplier also promptly shipped.

What price is the retailer permitted to charge the supplier for the toothpaste?

A. $10,000 (10,000 * $1), because the supplier's firm offer was effective for 90 days regardless of its terms.

B. $10,400 ((6,000 * $1) + (4,000 * $1.10)), because the supplier's firm offer was effective for only 45 days.

C. $11,000 (10,000 * $1.10), because the firm offer rule does not apply where the buyer is a merchant.

D. $11,000 (10,000 * $1.10), because the supplier informed the retailer that the price was increased to $1.10 before the retailer's placement of either order.

QUESTION 46

A shareholder of a corporation brought a derivative action on behalf of the corporation against a director of the corporation for breach of her duty of loyalty. The shareholder sought to call the director's ex-husband to testify to a private conversation between the director and ex-husband while they were married, in which the director stated, "I'm going to buy that land and then resell it to the corporation. I'll make a killing."

Which of the following grounds would be the best ground upon which the director could object to the admission of this testimony?

A. Hearsay

B. Bias

C. Spousal immunity privilege

D. Marital communications privilege

QUESTION 47

A federal counterintelligence unit has been trying to locate a specific terrorist group for over a decade. A newspaper reaching an international audience gains knowledge of the unit's specific location and a plan for capturing members of the terrorist group. The plan for the capture of the terrorist group coincides with the imminent anniversary date of a prior terrorist attack by the group. Just prior to that date, the newspaper intends to publish an article that focuses on the prior attack, but in light of the plan, ends with the following words: "And to those who attacked our citizens: We know where you are, and we are coming to get you." The government files a motion for an injunction to prevent the newspaper from printing the story with that ending. The government asserts that the publication will alert the group to the impending attack and provide them with time to avoid capture. The government requests that the publisher not be allowed to publish the article as is until further notification from the counterintelligence unit. In responding to the motion, the publisher alleges that the article does not threaten national security, but fails to assert that the article is protected speech.

Which of the following would the court least likely consider in its decision?

A. The words included in the article are insufficient to cause a particular harm.

B. The publisher was given a hearing before the injunction was issued.

C. The publisher cannot publish the article within the foreseeable future.

D. The publisher did not prove that the article was protected speech.

QUESTION 48

A grocery store and a greenhouse farmer entered into a valid contract for 100 boxes of Grade 1 tomatoes, to be delivered on or before the end of the month. On the last day of the month, the farmer delivered 100 boxes of Grade 2 tomatoes to the store. Based on the price and popularity of Grade 2 tomatoes in the area, the farmer reasonably believed that the store would accept these tomatoes at a reduced price. When the grocery store refused to accept the delivery, the farmer promised to return the following morning with 100 boxes of Grade 1 tomatoes. When the farmer did, the grocery store again refused to accept the tomatoes.

Is the store's rejection of the Grade 1 tomatoes proper?

A. Yes, because their delivery was untimely.

B. Yes, because the perfect tender rule applies to sales of goods.

C. No, because the store's earlier rejection of the Grade 2 tomatoes at a reduced price was improper.

D. No, because the farmer cured the nonconforming tender.

QUESTION 49

The defendant, a private employer, summarily fired the plaintiff as a result of a negative performance review. The defendant's Employee Handbook, however, promised employees that they had 60 days to address concerns raised in performance reviews, before the defendant made a final decision on their employment. The plaintiff's attorney filed a signed complaint in federal court reciting the foregoing facts and claiming that the defendant violated the Fourteenth Amendment's Due Process Clause by failing to follow its handbook procedures before firing the plaintiff. Since this Amendment was ratified, however, the Supreme Court has consistently and unanimously held that only state—not private—actors can violate this Amendment. The attorney believes that the Court should reverse this law because it hurts parties, like his client, who are victimized by private actors' procedural mistakes. The defendant moves for Rule 11 monetary sanctions against the plaintiff.

Should the motion be granted?

A. Yes, because the plaintiff's factual contentions lack evidentiary support.

B. Yes, because the plaintiff's claims are not warranted by either existing Fourteenth Amendment law or a non-frivolous argument for reversing that law.

C. No, because the plaintiff's claims are warranted by a non-frivolous argument for reversing existing Fourteenth Amendment law.

D. No, because a court cannot impose a monetary sanction against a represented party on the ground that his claims are not warranted by existing law or a non-frivolous argument for reversing it.

QUESTION 50

A contractor purchased a furnace from a distributor of heating systems, after the distributor recommended the furnace based on the contractor's stated needs. The bill of sale between the distributor and the contractor stated, "All warrantees, express or implied, are hereby disclaimed." The contractor installed the furnace in an office building. Due to a manufacturing defect, the furnace failed to heat the building as it should have. The contractor was sued by the owner of the office building.

Can the contractor assert a claim against the distributor for breach of the implied warranty of merchantability?

A. No, because there is no implied warranty of merchantability for sales between merchants.

B. No, because the distributor disclaimed this warranty.

C. Yes, because furnace failed to heat the building.

D. Yes, because the contractor relied on the distributor's judgment.

QUESTION 51

Two neighbors owned single-story homes next door to one another. The first neighbor informed the second neighbor that he planned to make some small improvements to his home, within all applicable neighborhood rules and covenants. The second neighbor was concerned that the improvements would block her view, but the first neighbor assured her that they would not. The two neighbors orally promised one another that they would never make any improvements to their own homes or yards that would negatively affect the view or light enjoyed by the other's property. Indeed, the completed improvement had no affect on the second neighbor's view. The second neighbor then informed the first neighbor that she planned to make an improvement to her home. The first neighbor reminded the second neighbor of their agreement, which the second neighbor assured him that she would honor. The first neighbor went on an extended vacation, and when he arrived home, he was horrified to see that the second neighbor's improvements to her home completely blocked his view of a nearby woodland, and was so tall that the first neighbor's yard received very little light each day.

If the first neighbor sues the second neighbor for breach of their agreement, is the first neighbor likely to be successful?

A. No, because the agreement was more restrictive than the neighborhood rules and covenants.

B. No, because the agreement between the first and second neighbors was not in writing.

C. Yes, because the agreement between the first and second neighbors was an implied reciprocal servitude, which need not be in writing.

D. Yes, because the agreement between the first and second neighbors was a valid negative easement.

QUESTION 52

A dairy ordered a tank trailer from a commercial retailer. The contract did not identify a specific tank trailer, but did specify various features that the tank trailer should have. The contract called for the retailer to deliver the tank trailer to the dairy. Subsequently, the retailer acquired a tank trailer from a manufacturer that it believed met the requirements of the contract. Several days later, the retailer, in accordance with the contract, had the dairy's emblem painted on each side of the tank trailer, and then delivered it to the dairy. The tank trailer did not, in fact, conform to the contract.

At which time did the dairy acquire an insurable interest in the tank trailer?

A. When the contract was entered into.

B. When the retailer acquired the tank trailer from the manufacturer.

C. When the retailer had the dairy's emblem painted on the tank trailer.

D. When the retailer delivered the tank trailer.

QUESTION 53

Many years ago, the owner of an estate gave a railroad company an easement to build, operate, and maintain railroad tracks on the estate. The written easement detailed the projected dimensions of the railroad, but it was not recorded and the tracks were never laid. Ten years ago, the owner sold the underlying property to a farmer. The deed of sale mentioned the easement. Recently, the railroad company contacted the farmer to let him know that it planned to install tracks on its easement. The tracks would be six inches wider than originally projected, as the minimum size of train cars had increased since the easement was granted. The railroad company, which had since purchased a communications company, also wanted to install a fiber-optic system on the same land covered by the easement. The farmer has refused to allow the railroad company to install the tracks and the fiber optic system.

Can the railroad company install the wider railroad tracks and the fiber-optic system?

A. No as to both the wider railroad tracks and the fiber-optic cables.

B. No as to the wider railroad tracks, but yes as to the fiber-optic cables.

C. Yes as to the wider railroad tracks, but no as to the fiber-optic cables.

D. Yes as to both the wider railroad tracks and the fiber-optic cables.

QUESTION 54

A guest who had spent the night in a home offered to take out the trash for the homeowner who was late for work the next morning. The homeowner readily agreed. After the homeowner left, the guest placed drug paraphernalia into an opaque trash bag. The guest placed the bag into a metal trash can, tightly placed the lid on the can, and sat the can at the curb for pick-up by a private trash removal company. An employee of the company picked up the bag, but, as prearranged, gave it to an undercover police officer, who had been investigating the homeowner for running an illegal gambling operation. Through her fingerprint on the paraphernalia, the guest was charged with possession of drug paraphernalia. She contested the seizure of the paraphernalia as a violation of her Fourth Amendment rights.

Should the use of this paraphernalia as evidence be suppressed?

A. Yes, because the paraphernalia was not in plain view.

B. Yes, because an overnight guest in a home has a reasonable expectation of privacy with respect to the home.

C. No, because it was initially taken by an employee of a private company, not a police officer.

D. No, because the paraphernalia was found in the garbage, which was set out at the curb for pick-up.

QUESTION 55

A woman purchased a large tract of land on which she planned to build her new home. The land was adjacent to a large factory. The factory emitted large clouds of ash that coated a section of the woman's land. During this time, the woman could not use that section of the land, as the ash would burn the woman's eyes and cause severe respiratory problems. The woman informed the factory's managers of the ash, but they refused to do anything about it.

Which of the following causes of action can the woman likely successfully maintain?

A. Both nuisance and trespass.

B. Either nuisance or trespass, but not both.

C. Nuisance only.

D. Trespass only.

QUESTION 56

The defendant, an 18-year-old high school senior, was worried about his friend's attachment to a stuffed animal that the friend had slept with since childhood. The defendant formulated a plan to take the toy, hoping this would break the friend's attachment to it. While the friend and his family were out to dinner, the defendant used the spare key that the family kept under the doormat to open the front door and sneak into the friend's home. The defendant took the stuffed animal back to his own home and threw it in the trash can. The next day, the friend was distraught over the loss of the stuffed animal, and the defendant admitted what he had done. The friend retrieved the stuffed animal from the trash, washed it, and forgave the defendant.

What is the most serious crime, listed in order of increasing seriousness, for which the defendant may be convicted?

A. Attempted larceny.

B. Larceny.

C. Burglary.

D. Robbery.

QUESTION 57

In a civil trial for damages that the plaintiff sustained as the result of an automobile accident, the defendant's attorney sought to admit into evidence the journal entry of a witness to the accident to demonstrate the witness's uncertainty of the events immediately after the accident. The entry contained a sentence that stated, "I don't think the defendant was at fault." The witness claimed that she was unable to remember the event well enough to testify, even after looking at the journal entry on the witness stand. She did, however, indicate that she wrote the journal entry only 30 minutes after witnessing the accident. After the defendant's motion to admit this journal entry, the plaintiff's attorney objected to the introduction of the journal entry into evidence.

Assuming the defendant's attorney can lay the proper foundation, how should the court proceed?

A. The court should allow the journal entry to be read to the jury, but should not admit the entry as an exhibit.

B. The court should admit the journal entry as an exhibit, but should not allow it to be read to the jury.

C. The court should both allow the journal entry to be read to the jury and introduce the entry as an exhibit.

D. The court should neither allow the journal entry to be read to the jury nor introduce the entry as an exhibit.

QUESTION 58

A plaintiff sued a defendant in federal district court. The plaintiff was domiciled in the forum state; the defendant was domiciled in another state. The plaintiff asserted two unrelated causes of action against the defendant. One was based on a breach of contract, for which the plaintiff sought $60,000 in damages. The other was a personal injury claim for which $25,000 in damages was sought. The defendant, who was served with process while in the forum state, filed a timely motion to dismiss based on the lack of subject matter jurisdiction. How should the court rule?

A. Grant the motion, because the plaintiff's claims are unrelated and neither exceeds $75,000.

B. Grant the motion, because the plaintiff is domiciled in the forum state.

C. Deny the motion, because the defendant was served with process in the forum state.

D. Deny the motion, because diversity jurisdiction exists.

QUESTION 59

The owner of an antique pocket watch took it to a jeweler for a cleaning. The jeweler, who also sold watches, convinced the owner that the expensive watch had little value and fraudulently purchased it from the owner for $50. The jeweler sold the watch to a collector for $5,000 after regaling the collector with the story of its acquisition.

Does the collector have good title to the watch?

A. Yes, because the jeweler was a merchant who dealt in pocket watches.

B. Yes, because the collector did not participate in the jeweler's acquisition of the watch.

C. No, because the jeweler obtained the watch by fraud.

D. No, because the collector was not a good faith purchaser of the watch.

QUESTION 60

A retail store that specialized in crystal figurines entered into a contract to purchase 100 crystal swans at a price of $50 each from the artisan who would design and make them. The store paid for the swans at the time that the contract was executed. The contract specified that the artisan would deliver the swans personally to the store. The artisan notified the store upon completion of the swans in conformity with the contract. Unfortunately, 10 of the swans were destroyed in transit. The store refused to accept the remaining 90 swans, even though the artisan offered to reduce the purchase price by $500. The store sued the artisan for the return of the $5,000 paid to the artisan.

What will be the likely result?

A. The artisan will recover the entire contract price, because risk of loss transferred to the store upon the artisan's notification to the store of the completion of the crystal swans.

B. The artisan will prevail, but can only recover the contract price for the intact crystal swans.

C. The store will prevail, because the contract is void due to the artisan's inability to deliver 100 swans.

D. The store will prevail, because the store is not required to accept a non-conforming delivery.

QUESTION 61

Many years ago, the owner of a cattle ranch gave a utility company an easement to install underground phone lines on the ranch to service the other properties in the area. The easement was properly recorded. Five years ago, the rancher sold the underlying property to a gardener. The deed of sale did not mention the easement. Upon purchasing the ranch, the gardener spent great time and expense converting the cattle-trampled ranch into a large botanic garden. Recently, the utility company, who had never installed the phone lines, contacted the gardener to let him know that it would now like to install an underground fiber-optic system across the estate. The fiber-optic system would provide phone service and high-speed internet service to the gardener's estate and the surrounding estates, which to this point have had to depend on unreliable satellite service. The gardener refuses to allow the utility company to install the fiber optic system.

Will the utility company likely be able to enforce the easement?

A. No, because the easement was for the installation of phone lines, not fiber-optic cables.

B. No, because the utility company abandoned the easement.

C. Yes, because the easement is for public use.

D. Yes, because the easement was properly recorded.

QUESTION 62

Acting on behalf of a 13-year-old child who was struck by the defendant's car, the child's parents filed a negligence action in federal court based on diversity jurisdiction. The defendant asserted as a defense to the action that the child was contributorily negligent. The defense has placed into evidence facts that would sustain a finding that the child was contributorily negligent. The state law that governs the existence of this defense provides that a child who is at least seven years old but less than 14 years old is rebuttably presumed to be incapable of negligence.

Must the court apply the state law presumption in determining whether the child was contributorily negligent?

A. Yes, because the state law presumption must be applied when state substantive law is determinative of the existence of the contributorily negligence defense.

B. Yes, because the defendant has placed into evidence facts that would rebut the presumption.

C. No, because the Federal Rules of Evidence do not contain this specific presumption regarding a child's capacity for negligence, and the court may, but is not required to, apply the state law presumption.

D. No, because the presumption applies to a defense rather than a claim.

QUESTION 63

To celebrate finishing his psychiatric residency, a doctor went on vacation with two of his fellow residents. After having several drinks at a local bar, the doctor encountered an unconscious woman on the sidewalk. Assuming that she had suffered a heart attack, the doctor immediately began providing cardiopulmonary resuscitation. One of the other residents told the doctor that it he believes that the woman has just fainted, and that they should bring her some water. In fact, the woman has a condition that causes her to faint when she gets dehydrated. Due to his inebriated state, however, the doctor ignored the other resident and aggressively continued giving chest compressions. In the process, he accidentally broke one of the woman's ribs. When the woman regained consciousness, she was in extreme pain from the broken rib. She later sued the doctor for negligence. The doctor moves to dismiss the complaint, citing a Good Samaritan statute adopted by the state that protects medical personnel from liability for ordinary negligence when they voluntarily render emergency care.

Is the judge likely to grant the doctor's motion to dismiss?

A. No, because the doctor did not obtain informed consent.

B. No, because the Good Samaritan statute would not protect the doctor under the circumstances.

C. Yes, because the Good Samaritan statute would protect the doctor from liability.

D. Yes, because a reasonable doctor would have done the same thing.

QUESTION 64

A father was injured after sitting on a chair that was part of his daughter's tea set, which is called "Mommy and Me Princess Party." The set contained two small chairs designed for children and two larger chairs designed for adults. The injury occurred when, due to a defect, the chair collapsed underneath the father, who weighs 160 pounds and sat in one of the larger chairs in a normal fashion. The label on the box and accompanying instructions state: "This set includes chairs for the princess in all of us. Small chairs are designed for those ages 3-8, while the larger chairs are designed for mommies not exceeding 200 pounds." The father filed a claim based on a manufacturing defect against the manufacturer. The manufacturer filed a motion to dismiss on the basis that the plaintiff is male and was never meant to use the chair included in "Mommy and Me Princess Party." Evidence shows that no tampering or damage occurred to the tea set after it left the manufacturer's control and that the father's injury is directly related to his fall from the broken chair. Evidence also shows that the product as designed could safely support a person weighing up to 200 pounds.

How should the trial judge proceed?

A. Grant the motion to dismiss, because the product as designed was built to withstand the father's weight.

B. Grant the motion to dismiss, because the father's use of the chair was unreasonable in light of the product name and description.

C. Deny the motion to dismiss, because the father did not exceed the weight limitations set forth by the label.

D. Deny the motion to dismiss, because the manufacturer did not properly warn about the possible dangers of sitting in the chair.

QUESTION 65

A plaintiff properly filed suit for negligence in a federal district court against a defendant corporation. The plaintiff had worked at the corporation's industrial warehouse for the past 24 years and was recently diagnosed with a fatal disease associated with a chemical that had been used at the corporation's warehouse. Use of the chemical violated a federal law enacted to protect the health of workers. The plaintiff is aware that a supplier to the defendant corporation has documents in its possession indicating that the defendant corporation used the chemical because it was less expensive than other alternative chemicals and had purposefully concealed its use.

Can the plaintiff properly obtain the supplier's documents under the Federal Rules of Civil Procedure?

A. Yes, the plaintiff may subpoena the documents from the supplier.

B. Yes, the plaintiff may serve a request for production on the supplier.

C. No, the plaintiff must join the supplier in the suit in order to request the documents.

D. No, the plaintiff cannot obtain documents from the supplier, a non-party.

QUESTION 66

In order to purchase a building, the buyer obtained a $300,000 loan from a bank. The loan, which carried a fixed rate of interest, was secured by a mortgage on the building. The buyer is required to make quarterly interest payments, but the principle is due and payable in a lump sum at the end of three years. Two years after obtaining the bank loan, the buyer borrowed $50,000 from a credit union and gave the credit union a promissory note secured by a mortgage on the building. The loan proceeds were used for personal purposes unrelated to the building. A year later, the buyer was unable to pay the bank the principal amount that was due. The bank agreed to extend the term of the loan for an additional year if the buyer continued to make quarterly interest payments at the same interest rate. Each mortgage, as well as the extension agreement, was recorded shortly after being granted by the buyer. The state in which the building is located has adopted the following statute: No conveyance or mortgage of real property shall be good against subsequent purchasers for value and without notice unless the same be recorded according to law.

Which lender has priority?

A. The bank, because its mortgage was a purchase money mortgage.

B. The bank, because the modification of its mortgage did not prejudice the interests of the credit union.

C. The credit union, because its mortgage was recorded before the bank's mortgage was modified.

D. The credit union, because the bank had constructive notice of the credit union's mortgage prior the modification of the bank's mortgage.

QUESTION 67

At a criminal trial for rape, the prosecution seeks to admit into evidence a statement made by the defendant to his friend, acknowledging that he raped the victim. The defendant made the statement shortly after the rape, but before he knew he was a suspect. The defendant testified at trial that he did not rape the victim.

Is the statement the defendant made to his friend acknowledging the rape admissible?

A. Yes, the statement is admissible as non-hearsay.

B. Yes, the statement is admissible because it falls within the statement against interest exception to the hearsay rule.

C. No, the statement is inadmissible hearsay not within any exception.

D. No, because the statement was not against the defendant's interest at the time he made it.

QUESTION 68

Last year, Congress enacted legislation providing for funding opportunities to eligible secular and religiously affiliated colleges and universities. The funding will be available through individual counties as each county's funding limitations allow. The legislation does not require that each county apply standard guidelines nor does it provide any suggested guidelines other than a statement that "all counties should track funding and compile guidelines in the event of a federal audit." A county awards a large grant to a religiously affiliated college that employs a substantial number of residents. The grant contract, signed by representatives from both the county and the college, states as follows: "All grant monies must be used in compliance with country regulations. Further, the college must track the allocation of grant monies throughout the grant term."

Is the county's award of the grant constitutional?

A. No, because the county provided grant monies to a religiously affiliated college.

B. No, because it does not require that the aid be used only for nonreligious purposes.

C. Yes, because the college is required to track funding.

D. Yes, because the college may be the subject of a federal audit.

QUESTION 69

A tomato farmer in a small state developed a special variety of tomatoes. In addition to being delicious and standing up well during transport, these tomatoes were higher in vitamins and nutrients than other tomatoes. Due to the successful sale of these tomatoes, other farmers outside of the state began growing similar tomatoes and selling them at a lower price. The out-of-state farmers have contracts to sell their tomatoes to discount markets in the state. The out-of-state tomatoes are similar in taste and durability to the special variety, but lack the heightened nutritional value. Nevertheless, because of their lower cost, they are cutting into the sales of the special variety. Accordingly, the state legislature enacted a law "to ensure the health and vitality of its citizens by protecting them from imitation, nutritionally-deficient fruits and vegetables, and to preserve the integrity and prosperity of the state's local produce industry." Among other things, the law forbids the future sale of any tomatoes within the state that fail to meet the nutritional value of the state's own special varietal of tomatoes; no other tomato meets this requirement. The law also applies to the state's purchase of produce for public schools and other government facilities.

Is the state's law constitutional?

A.   No, because the law unduly burdens interstate commerce.

B.   No, because the law interferes with potential contracts between the tomato farmers and the discount markets.

C.   Yes, because the law furthers the legitimate state interest of preserving the health of its citizens and its farm industry.

D.   Yes, because the law falls under the market participant exception to the Dormant Commerce Clause.

QUESTION 70

A woman kept a wolf as a pet in her yard in the city. One day, the wolf escaped and wandered down the road. The woman's neighbor was walking on the same road when he saw the wolf. The wolf growled at the neighbor, which frightened the neighbor. In his attempt to get away from the wolf, the neighbor tripped and broke his leg.

Is the woman liable for her neighbor's injuries?

A.   No, because the injury the neighbor suffered is not of the type normally caused by a wolf.

B.   No, because the wolf was not on the woman's property.

C.   Yes, because the woman was strictly liable for harm caused by the wolf.

D.   Yes, because the wolf menaced the neighbor.

QUESTION 71

A man owned a residence in fee simple absolute. Upon his death, he devised the residence to his daughter for life and upon her death to his nephew. While the daughter was away, a neighbor carelessly set off fireworks that damaged the roof of the residence. The daughter placed a tarp over the damaged area of the roof, which protected the interior of the residence from the adverse consequences of the damage, but did not have the roof repaired. The residence was uninsured. The nephew has sued the daughter to compel her to repair the residence.

In the majority of jurisdictions, is the nephew likely to succeed in his suit?

A.   Yes, because a life tenant owes a duty of reasonable repair to the holder of a future interest.

B.   Yes, because the daughter failed to insure the residence.

C.   No, because the nephew failed to insure the residence.

D.   No, because the damage was caused by the neighbor's negligence.

QUESTION 72

Police set up a sobriety checkpoint after dark on a state highway. The police stopped every fourth car driving down the highway, without exercising any judgment as to whether the driver of the car was intoxicated. In the absence of any problem, a driver was detained less than a minute. The driver and only occupant of one such car stopped was an adult with a valid driver's license. The officer approached the car with a device for detecting alcohol on the driver's breath. The officer held the device, which looked like a flashlight, about 10 inches away from the driver's face, within the recommended range for the proper operation of the device. Upon obtaining a positive reading from the device, the officer asked the driver to step out of the car, even though the officer did not otherwise detect the presence of alcohol. The driver failed a field sobriety test. This provided the officer with probable cause to arrest the driver for driving while under the influence, which the officer did. The driver was taken to a police station where a breath test indicated that he was legally intoxicated.

Of the following constitutionally based arguments which would be the strongest in favor of suppression of the evidence of the driver's intoxication?

A.   Because of the brevity of the stop, it did not constitute a seizure within the meaning of the Fourth Amendment.

B.   The police officer lacked reasonable suspicion to stop the driver's car.

C.   The search for the presence of alcohol on a driver's breath by a police officer using his sense of smell violates the driver's reasonable expectation of privacy.

D.   The use of a device that is not available to the general public to detect the presence of alcohol that the officer otherwise would not have detected violated the driver's reasonable expectation of privacy.

QUESTION 73

After arresting a man on a charge of first-degree murder, the police demanded that the man provide a blood sample to determine if his DNA matched DNA found at the crime scene and provide a voice sample to compare the sound of his voice to a voice heard in the background on the victim's 911 call for help.

If the man were to challenge the police demands, which of the demands could be successfully challenged as a violation of the Fifth Amendment's protection against compulsory self-incrimination?

A.   Both the demand for the blood sample and the demand for the voice sample.

B.   Only the demand for the blood sample.

C.   Only the demand for the voice sample.

D.   Neither the demand for the blood sample nor the demand for the voice sample.

QUESTION 74

A supplier regularly sold sand to a concrete maker. The supplier knows that concrete must be made with a certain ratio of sand, water, and cement to be stable. The sand supplier correctly suspects that the concrete maker uses less sand than is necessary in the manufacture of the concrete, although the sand supplier has nothing to do with the concrete maker's blending process. A building made with the concrete maker's concrete collapses due to the improper ratio, injuring several people. The injured people sue the sand supplier for their injuries, though all parties agree that the sand itself was not defective.

Is the sand supplier liable?

A.   No, because the sand was not defective.

B.   No, because the supplier of a component part is not liable to the ultimate consumer if the final product is defective.

C.   Yes, because the supplier of a component part is strictly liable for defects in the final product.

D.   Yes, because the supplier failed to warn of the concrete's deficient quantity of sand.

QUESTION 75

A landowner filed an action in federal district court to void a contract for sale of her land to a limited partnership for $500,000. The landowner lived in the forum state. As required by state law, the limited partnership had filed a certificate of limited partnership with the Secretary of State for the forum state. The sole general partner of the limited partnership was a corporation that was incorporated in another state where it also had its principal place of business. The limited partners were citizens of various states, including at least one limited partner who was a citizen of the forum state. Does the court have subject matter jurisdiction over this action?

A. No, because the limited partnership filed a certificate of limited partnership with the Secretary of State for the forum state.

B. No, because a limited partner is a citizen of the same state as the landowner.

C. Yes, because the general partner and the landowner are citizens of different states and the amount-in-controversy requirement is satisfied.

D. Yes, because the action was filed in the state where the land was located.

QUESTION 76

After federally funded studies on the fiscal impact of mail delivery in the United States, Congress enacts the Postal Limitations Act, which attempts to decrease the amount of paper used in the mail delivery process by limiting advertisements mailed by grocery stores. The studies outlined three main conclusions. First, the paper used in grocery store advertisements destroys thousands of trees each year. Second, by limiting the amount of advertisements that are mailed each week, Congress would save millions of dollars, which would help to avoid the necessity of a bankruptcy filing by the U.S. Postal Service. Third, the studies indicate that advertisements by grocery stores were not only the most common type of unwanted mail in the country but also required substantially more paper than any other type of business. The Act limits grocery stores from sending advertisements via mail more than once per week, unless they decrease the amount of paper used to advertise to a specific, defined amount. The grocery stores are not limited in any other form of advertising, such as online advertising or advertising within the store. After one of the largest grocery stores in the country is banned from sending its daily advertisement and coupons, its representative sues in federal court to have the Act struck down.

Do the limitations set forth in the Postal Limitations Act exceed Congressional authority?

A. Yes, because the Act abridges freedom of speech.

B. Yes, because Congress cannot limit the right to send or receive mail.

C. No, because Congress has the exclusive power to establish post offices.

D. No, because Congress may impose reasonable restrictions on the use of mail.

QUESTION 77

A plaintiff sued a defendant in federal district court for the western district of a state. The plaintiff, who lived in the same city as the court was located, asserted a cause of action that arose under federal law. The defendant, a lifelong resident of a town located in the eastern federal judicial district of the state, was served with the complaint and summons at his home. The federal district court for the western district, which issued the summons, is located more than 100 miles from the defendant's home. The defendant timely filed a motion to dismiss the complaint for lack of personal jurisdiction.

How should the court rule on this motion?

A. Deny the motion, because the plaintiff and the defendant live in different judicial districts.

B. Deny the motion, because the defendant was a lifelong resident of the forum state.

C. Grant the motion, because the forum court was located more than 100 miles from the defendant's home.

D. Grant the motion, because the plaintiff and defendant are residents of the same state.

QUESTION 78

A state recently enacted a consumer protection statute preventing the in-state sale of avocados containing less than 8 percent oil to ensure that only mature avocados were marketed within the state. Pursuant to a federal law that permitted fruit growers in economically depressed areas to cooperatively fix marketing rules for the orderly and economically efficient marketing of fruit for the benefit of both the local and national economy, avocado growers in a neighboring state, an economically depressed area, determined the marketability of avocados based solely on the size and color of the avocado. In accordance with the federal law, the U.S. Secretary of Agriculture approved this marketability rule. A significant number of avocados in the economically depressed state that met the federally approved rule would be excluded from sale in the first state by that state's consumer protection statute, although no growers from the economically depressed state have yet tried to sell their avocados in the first state. The cooperative formed by these growers to oversee the marketing rules filed an action in federal court against the officials in the first state, seeking to enjoin those officials from enforcing the statute.

Which of the following arguments is the best argument for the officials in the first state?

A. The first state's statute is a valid exercise of the police power and is not preempted by federal law.

B. The Eleventh Amendment prevents this suit.

C. The cooperative lacks standing to sue.

D. The federal law is unconstitutional because Congress cannot regulate intrastate activity.

QUESTION 79

A produce wholesaler owed a sizeable debt that was past due. The lender offered, in exchange for a small parcel of land owned by the wholesaler, to reduce the amount of the debt by an amount equal to half of the fair market value of the land; the wholesaler refused. In order to compel the wholesaler to sell the land, the lender threatened to sue the wholesaler for the outstanding amount of the debt and to immediately attach a major shipment of produce to the wholesaler's most important and newly acquired client, although the wholesaler had sufficient other assets that could be attached.

The wholesaler, feeling he had no choice since he did not have the cash on hand to pay off the debt, sold the land to the lender. The wholesaler subsequently sued the lender to void the sale.

Will the wholesaler be able to avoid the sale?

A. No, because the lender's threat was economic.

B. No, because the lender owed the amount that the lender threatened to collect.

C. Yes, because the wholesaler sold the land under duress.

D. Yes, because the wholesaler had been threatened with litigation.

QUESTION 80

The plaintiff and his friend were walking on a city sidewalk. The friend jokingly pushed the plaintiff after the plaintiff started making fun of the friend's taste in music. This caused the plaintiff to trip over his own feet and stumble into the bike lane of the street. The defendant driver, who was involved in a heated argument on his cell phone, had veered into the bike lane and did not see the plaintiff. He hit the plaintiff, causing the plaintiff numerous injuries. The plaintiff has sued the defendant. The evidence at trial shows that the plaintiff's injuries were caused by the negligence of both the friend and the defendant. The state has adopted a system of pure several liability.

Is the plaintiff likely to prevail in a negligence claim against the defendant?

A. No, because the plaintiff's injuries were caused by multiple tortfeasors.

B. No, because the state does not recognize joint and several liability.

C. Yes, because the defendant and the friend were independent tortfeasors.

D. Yes, because the defendant's conduct was the actual cause of the plaintiff's injury.

QUESTION 81

A farmer selling grain went to a large commercial bakery for a meeting with the bakery's buyer. The buyer asked the farmer to wait in his office while he, the buyer, finished a meeting with a supplier who had just delivered a new forklift to the bakery. While walking to the buyer's office, the farmer noticed the forklift on the bakery's floor, and saw that the forklift's keys were on its seat. He decided to take it on a tour around the bakery. The farmer rode into an equipment room that had a "no trespassers" sign on the door. While driving in the room, he crashed into a large support beam because the forklift's steering mechanism was faulty. The beam, which was not built to withstand such sudden impact, fell on the farmer and injured him severely.

In a negligence suit against the bakery for damages stemming from the farmer's injuries, is the farmer likely to be successful?

A. No, because the farmer exceeded the scope of his invitation when he drove the forklift.

B. No, because the bakery owed no duty of care to the farmer.

C. Yes, because the bakery had a duty to warn of inherently dangerous conditions on its property.

D. Yes, because the farmer was a business invitee.

QUESTION 82

A defendant is prosecuted for robbery. The defendant is acquitted by a jury. The prosecution then seeks to charge the defendant with other crimes arising out of the same transaction.

With which of the following can the prosecution charge the defendant without violating the Double Jeopardy Clause?

A. Felony murder based on the commission of the robbery

B. Larceny

C. Conspiracy to commit robbery

D. The prosecution may not charge the defendant with other crimes arising out of the same transaction.

QUESTION 83

Ten years ago, a landowner deeded land to a wildlife organization. The warranty deed stated that the land was transferred to the organization "provided that the land is maintained as a habitat for black-footed ferrets, an endangered species; if not, the organization's estate is subject to the grantor's right to re-enter." Five years ago, the landowner, by quitclaim deed, transferred any interest in the land to a speculator for $1,000. Two years ago, the landowner made a valid will that devised all real property interests to his friend. One year ago, the landowner died. By law, the landowner's daughter was his only heir.

The last surviving black-footed ferret recently died. Who holds the current possessory interest in the land?

A. The landowner's friend as the devisee of all of the landowner's real property interests.

B. The landowner's daughter as his only heir.

C. The speculator as the inter vivos purchaser of the landowner's interest in the land.

D. The wildlife organization.

QUESTION 84

A defendant was charged with assault. Upon learning that the defendant intended to testify in his own defense, the government gave the defense proper notice of its intent to introduce as impeachment evidence the defendant's conviction for embezzlement nine years prior. The defense filed a motion to exclude all evidence of the defendant's conviction, arguing that it would prejudice the defendant. In a pre-trial hearing, the judge noted that the conviction would likely have little prejudicial effect.

Is the judge likely to grant the defendant's motion?

A. No, because the conviction relates to a crime involving dishonesty and occurred within the last 10 years.

B. No, because the probative value of such a conviction outweighs its prejudicial effect.

C. Yes, because a prior conviction may not be used to impeach a defendant who testifies in his own defense.

D. Yes, because the conviction for embezzlement is not probative in determining whether the defendant committed an assault.

QUESTION 85

An honest dispute develops between a homeowner and an electrician over whether wiring and circuit breakers installed by the electrician satisfied contractual specifications. If the wiring and circuit breakers meet those specifications, the homeowner owes the electrician $10,000 under the terms of the contract. The homeowner offers to pay the electrician $8,000 in satisfaction of the homeowner's contractual obligations, if the electrician replaces the circuit breakers with a different brand. The electrician accepts the homeowner's offer. After the electrician replaces the circuit breakers, the homeowner refuses to pay the electrician. In a breach of contract action brought by the electrician, the fact-finder determines that the wiring and circuit breakers originally installed by the electrician did satisfy the contract specifications. The fact-finder also determines that the electrician and the homeowner entered into an accord for which the homeowner failed to prove the required satisfaction.

What is maximum amount that the electrician can seek in damages from the homeowner?

A. $18,000

B. $10,000

C. $8,000

D. Nothing

QUESTION 86

A builder constructed a residence and sold it to a buyer. The contract of sale stated that the residence was sold "as is." Before the buyer could move into the residence, he was killed in an accident, and his estate sold the residence to a new owner. The owner lived in the house for several years, during which the winters were uncharacteristically mild. One winter, by contrast, produced more typical, extremely cold temperatures. When attempting to heat her residence, the owner discovered that the size of the furnace was inadequate to properly do so. Due to an erroneous calculation, the builder had installed an incorrectly sized furnace. After unsuccessful attempts to convince the builder to install an adequately sized furnace, the owner brought suit against the builder for breach of the warranty of suitability, which has been recognized by the courts of the state in which the residence sits.

Which of the following is the builder's strongest defense to the owner's suit?

A. The builder was not aware that the size of the furnace was inadequate.

B. The builder disclaimed the warranty of suitability by selling the residence "as is."

C. The owner did not bring the suit within a reasonable time.

D. The owner did not purchase the residence from the builder.

QUESTION 87

On April 15, a librarian purchased a vacation home from a seller for $200,000 cash. She placed the deed in a safety deposit box but did not immediately record it. On April 20, the seller sold the vacation home to an engineer, who had no knowledge of the prior sale, for $250,000 cash. On April 22, the librarian recorded her deed. The engineer, who had placed the deed in a drawer and forgotten about it, did not record the deed until June 1. The recording statute in the jurisdiction states: "No conveyance or mortgage of real property shall be good against subsequent purchasers for value and without notice unless the same be recorded according to law."

In a subsequent action, who will prevail?

A. The librarian, because she was first to record the deed.

B. The librarian, because the engineer had constructive notice of her deed when he recorded his deed on June 1.

C. The engineer, because the librarian did not record her deed until after the engineer purchased the vacation home.

D. The engineer, because the paid value of his purchase was greater than that for the librarian.

QUESTION 88

In a civil trial for battery, the plaintiff's attorney called a witness to testify. When asked on the witness stand whether the defendant hit the plaintiff over the head with a flower pot, as plaintiff alleged, the witness responded that the previous week, she was speaking to her cousin on the phone when her cousin stated, "Oh my goodness! The guy next to me just hit a lady over the head with a flower pot!" The witness then testified that she responded with a question about what the man looked like, to which the cousin responded, "Who cares? Let's talk about it later. I won't forget; trust me." When then being questioned about the description of the man according her cousin, the witness testified that she did not know, as the day after the event, she and her cousin met for lunch, during which the cousin wrote on a napkin, "Flower Pot Guy is sitting at the next table! Let's get out of here before he smacks us with a plate!" The witness testified that she and her cousin immediately ran out without looking at the next table, so she neither saw the man nor received a description from her cousin. She also noted that they

brought the napkin with them and could produce it to the court. The defendant's attorney objected to the inclusion of the statement about a man hitting the woman on the head with a pot, as well as the written statement about the man at the next table.

How should the court rule on allowing the witness's testimony?

A. Allow the first statement only, as only it pertains to the actual incident in question.

B. Allow both statements.

C. Allow the second statement only, in light of the Best Evidence Rule.

D. Prohibit both statements as inadmissible hearsay not falling under any exception.

QUESTION 89

A niece provided live-in assistance to her uncle in his home, and the uncle promised to leave the home to her upon his death. While the uncle was hospitalized shortly before his death, the niece conveyed the home by a general warranty deed to a buyer who paid fair market value. The buyer was unaware that the niece did not own the home at the time of the conveyance. True to his word, the uncle devised the home to his niece in his will. Having second thoughts about moving out of her uncle's home, the niece then contested the buyer's right to home.

Which of the following would provide the least support to the buyer's contention that he is entitled to possession of the home?

A. After-acquired property doctrine.

B. The niece's breach of the covenant of the right to convey.

C. Estoppel by deed doctrine.

D. The niece's conveyance of the home by a general warranty deed.

QUESTION 90

A landowner owned property that was adjacent to a commercial bird hunting ranch. The property boasted a large bird population as well as an unwanted population of beavers, which were creating ponds that flooded the land. The landowner had installed several homemade beaver traps under leaves and brush around the property. While he was checking the traps one day, the landowner noticed numerous rifle shells. He surmised that hunters from the neighboring ranch were likely venturing onto his property. He decided not to notify the farm, instead posting a "no trespassers" sign and figuring that if he saw any hunters on his property, he would scare them off. One day, a hunter who had inadvertently wandered onto the property got his foot caught in one of the beaver traps and sustained serious injury to his foot. The hunter has sued the landowner for negligence.

Is the hunter likely to prevail?

A. No, because the landowner did not engage in any willful, wanton, or intentional misconduct toward the hunter.

B. No, because the landowner did not owe a duty of care to the hunter.

C. Yes, because the landowner had a duty to conduct reasonable inspections of the land.

D. Yes, because the landowner owed a duty to warn or protect the hunter from the beaver traps.

QUESTION 91

A golf instructor posted an advertisement for his services in a local newspaper. The advertisement read, "Do you want to improve your golf game? I want to help you. A lesson that normally would cost you $100 will be only $50. To get this fantastic rate, be the first at the driving range this Thursday at 8 AM with your clubs or be the first to give me a call to setup another time." A duffer, who had heard of the instructor through a friend but had not seen the ad, called the instructor. The duffer made an appointment to meet the instructor for a lesson at the driving range on Thursday at 9 AM. The price of the lesson was not discussed, but the duffer was the only person who called the instructor about a lesson prior to Thursday afternoon. Wednesday evening the duffer saw the instructor's ad for the first time. The duffer showed up at the driving range on Thursday at 8 AM with his clubs. No one else appeared for a lesson. The instructor gave the duffer a lesson. After the lesson, the duffer handed $50 to the instructor. The instructor stated that his fee was $100. The duffer refused to pay the additional $50.

In a breach of contract action by the instructor against the duffer, which of the following would NOT be an argument that the duffer could raise in his defense?

A. The instructor's advertisement constituted an offer rather than an invitation to make an offer.

B. The duffer accepted the instructor's offer by calling the instructor and making an appointment for a lesson.

C. The duffer accepted the instructor's offer by appearing at the driving range on Thursday at 8 AM.

D. The instructor could not revoke the offer once the duffer had accepted it.

QUESTION 92

A large manufacturer regularly purchased a rare earth metal from various sources in order to incorporate the metal into its products. The manufacturer entered into a contract to purchase a specific quantity of the processed metal from a supplier. The contract called for the metal to be delivered in 90 days, with payment due on delivery. Coincidentally, between the contract and the agreed-upon delivery date, the manufacturer purchased the metal from some of the sources that the supplier, itself, often turned to for the metal. As a consequence of these purchases, the supplier could only obtain half of the required quantity of the metal by the delivery date. If the supplier delivers half of the required quantity of the metal on the delivery date, will it have breached the contract?

A. No, because the supplier delivered the metal that it could in good faith obtain.

B. No, because the manufacturer's purchases of the metal were the cause of the supplier being unable to meet its contractual obligation.

C. Yes, because the supplier failed to deliver the required amount of the metal on the delivery date.

D. Yes, because merchants do not have the obligation to deal in good faith with one another.

QUESTION 93

A plaintiff initiated a libel action against her former boyfriend after he posted a written statement on his web site accusing the plaintiff of being able to afford a new car only because she worked as a prostitute. At trial, the defendant called a neighbor of the plaintiff to testify that he paid the plaintiff to have sex with him. The plaintiff objected to the testimony.

Should the court admit this testimony for the purpose of proving that the plaintiff is a prostitute?

A. No, because the introduction of evidence of sexual conduct in a civil action is prohibited.

B. No, because the testimony is inadmissible character evidence.

C. Yes, because the evidence is relevant to the defendant's defense.

D. Yes, because character evidence must be in the form of specific acts rather than reputation or opinion testimony.

QUESTION 94

A state enacted a statute imposing a tax on all negotiable notes issued by banks, including national banks, not incorporated within the state.

Would the statute be valid as applied to a national bank located in the state?

A. Yes, because the state has absolute authority to tax non-commercial activities in the state.

B. Yes, because the tax does not violate the dormant commerce clause.

C. No, because the national bank would be immune from state taxation.

D. No, because the tax is a means of regulation within the state's borders.

QUESTION 95

A plaintiff filed a claim against a defendant corporation in federal district court sitting in diversity jurisdiction, alleging negligence in the design of an automobile manufactured by the defendant. The plaintiff asserted that, when she was driving the automobile on a highway, the steering mechanism failed, causing her injuries. On April 1, the defendant served a request for admission on the plaintiff, asking the plaintiff to admit that at the time of the accident she was driving in excess of the posted speed limit. As of May 2, the plaintiff had not served any written answer to the defendant's request for admission.

How will the court treat the defendant's April 1 request for admission?

A. The matter in the defendant's request for admission is deemed denied.

B. The matter in the defendant's request for admission is deemed admitted.

C. The matter in the defendant's request for admission is neither deemed admitted nor denied, but the defendant may be able to recover any expenses incurred in proving the matter.

D. The court will require the defendant to make an application for an order to compel an answer to the request before the matter is admitted.

QUESTION 96

A mother told her neighbor that she planned to purchase a baby swing for her son's first birthday. The neighbor offered to sell the mother a swing that the neighbor had recently ordered from a large toy retailer. The neighbor explained that she had never used the swing because she did not like the color. The mother agreed, and they settled on a price. Later that month, the mother was pushing her son on the swing when the swing collapsed, injuring the son. The mother intends file a strict products liability action based on the theory that a defective component in the swing caused the swing to collapse.

Which parties should the mother include as defendants in her suit?

A. The manufacturer of the swing.

B. The manufacturer of the swing and the manufacturer of the defective component.

C. The manufacturer of the swing, the manufacturer of the defective component, and the retailer.

D. The manufacturer of the swing, the manufacturer of the defective component, the retailer, and the neighbor.

QUESTION 97

A man and a woman planned to rob a liquor store. The man entered the store while the woman stayed in the car to act as a lookout and getaway driver. As a police officer walked by the store, the woman turned on the car lights, which was the signal she had arranged to warn the man in the store if anyone was coming. Seeing the signal, the man ran out the door right into the police officer. Realizing that an armed robbery was in progress, the police officer shot and killed the man, after appropriate warnings.

Should the woman be found guilty of felony murder of the man?

A. No, because the killing by the policeman was justifiable.

B. No, because the death of the man was not foreseeable.

C. Yes, because she was a co-conspirator in the robbery.

D. Yes, under the proximate cause theory.

QUESTION 98

In a will contest, the contestant's attorney sought to show that the decedent lacked the requisite mental capacity to execute a valid will. The contestant's attorney called a witness who was present at the will signing. When asked by the contestant's attorney to describe the signing of the will, the witness said, "Right before the decedent signed the will, she stood up and said 'I should not have stopped taking my pills. I have clearly lost my mind if I am giving anything to my ungrateful, snotty children.'" The decedent's attorney objected to the testimony.

Should the court allow the witness's testimony?

A. No, because the testimony is hearsay not within any exception.

B. No, because the testimony violates the Dead Man's Statute.

C. Yes, because the testimony is hearsay, but it falls within an exception to the hearsay rule.

D. Yes, because the testimony is not hearsay.

QUESTION 99

A mother was in the hospital with a terminal illness. One of her daughters went to visit her, and they became engaged in a conversation about the mother's engagement ring, which the daughter and her sisters had long admired. The mother told her daughter that she planned to leave the ring to the daughter's sister. Angered by her mother's decision, the daughter took the ring from her mother's bedside table that night after her mother fell asleep. As soon as she got to her car, however, the daughter had a change of heart and returned the ring to her mother's table. Later that day, the mother died. Contrary to her statement, she left the ring to the daughter in her will.

Could the daughter be convicted of any of the following crimes?

A. Attempted larceny only.

B. Larceny only.

C. Larceny and attempted larceny.

D. The daughter may not be convicted of any theft crime.

QUESTION 100

The holder of a joint tenancy interest in land entered into a valid written contract with a buyer to sell her interest for $25,000, to be paid at closing. The next day, before either party had taken any action with regard to the contract, the seller phoned the buyer and sought to withdraw from the contract. The buyer consented, without demanding any monetary compensation. Later that day, however, the buyer had a change of heart and called the seller to withdraw her consent. The seller has refused to honor the contract.

May the buyer enforce the contract?

A. No, because the parties to the contract rescinded it.

B. No, because a joint tenancy interest cannot be transferred inter vivos.

C. Yes, because the rescission of the contract was not in writing.

D. Yes, because the seller did not provide the buyer with consideration for rescinding the contract.

Item	Answer	Subject	Item	Answer	Subject	Item	Answer	Subject
1	C	EVIDENCE	35	C	TORTS	69	A	CONST. LAW
2	B	CRIMINAL LAW	36	B	CONST. LAW	70	C	TORTS
3	C	CONST. LAW	37	C	REAL PROP.	71	D	REAL PROP.
4	D	TORTS	38	D	CONST. LAW	72	D	CRIM. PROC.
5	C	REAL PROP.	39	B	REAL PROP.	73	D	CRIM. PROC.
6	C	CIVIL PROC.	40	B	REAL PROP.	74	A	TORTS
7	D	CRIM. PROC.	41	C	TORTS	75	B	CIVIL PROC.
8	B	EVIDENCE	42	D	CRIM. LAW	76	D	CONST. LAW
9	A	CIVIL PROC.	43	D	CRIM. PROC.	77	B	CIVIL PROC.
10	C	EVIDENCE	44	D	CIVIL PROC.	78	A	CONST. LAW
11	B	EVIDENCE	45	B	CONTRACTS	79	C	CONTRACTS
12	B	CONTRACTS	46	D	EVIDENCE	80	D	TORTS
13	A	TORTS	47	D	CONST. LAW	81	A	TORTS
14	D	CONTRACTS	48	D	CONTRACTS	82	C	CRIM. PROC.
15	A	CONST. LAW	49	D	CIVIL PROC.	83	D	REAL PROP.
16	B	CONST. LAW	50	C	CONTRACTS	84	A	EVIDENCE
17	A	EVIDENCE	51	B	REAL PROP.	85	B	CONTRACTS
18	A	CONTRACTS	52	C	CONTRACTS	86	C	REAL PROP.
19	B	CONTRACTS	53	C	REAL PROP.	87	C	REAL PROP.
20	B	CIVIL PROC.	54	D	CRIM. PROC.	88	B	EVIDENCE
21	C	CONST. LAW	55	A	TORTS	89	B	REAL PROP.
22	B	CONTRACTS	56	C	CRIM. LAW	90	D	TORTS
23	A	TORTS	57	A	EVIDENCE	91	B	CONTRACTS
24	D	TORTS	58	D	CIVIL PROC.	92	C	CONTRACTS
25	A	CONST. LAW	59	D	CONTRACTS	93	C	EVIDENCE
26	B	CRIM. PROC.	60	D	CONTRACTS	94	C	CONST. LAW
27	A	CONTRACTS	61	D	REAL PROP.	95	B	CIVIL PROC.
28	B	EVIDENCE	62	A	EVIDENCE	96	C	TORTS
29	B	CIVIL PROC.	63	B	TORTS	97	A	CRIM. LAW
30	D	CONST. LAW	64	C	TORTS	98	A	EVIDENCE
31	A	CRIM. PROC.	65	A	CIVIL PROC.	99	B	CRIM. LAW
32	C	CONTRACTS	66	B	REAL PROP.	100	A	REAL PROP.
33	C	CIVIL PROC.	67	A	EVIDENCE			
34	C	TORTS	68	B	CONST. LAW			